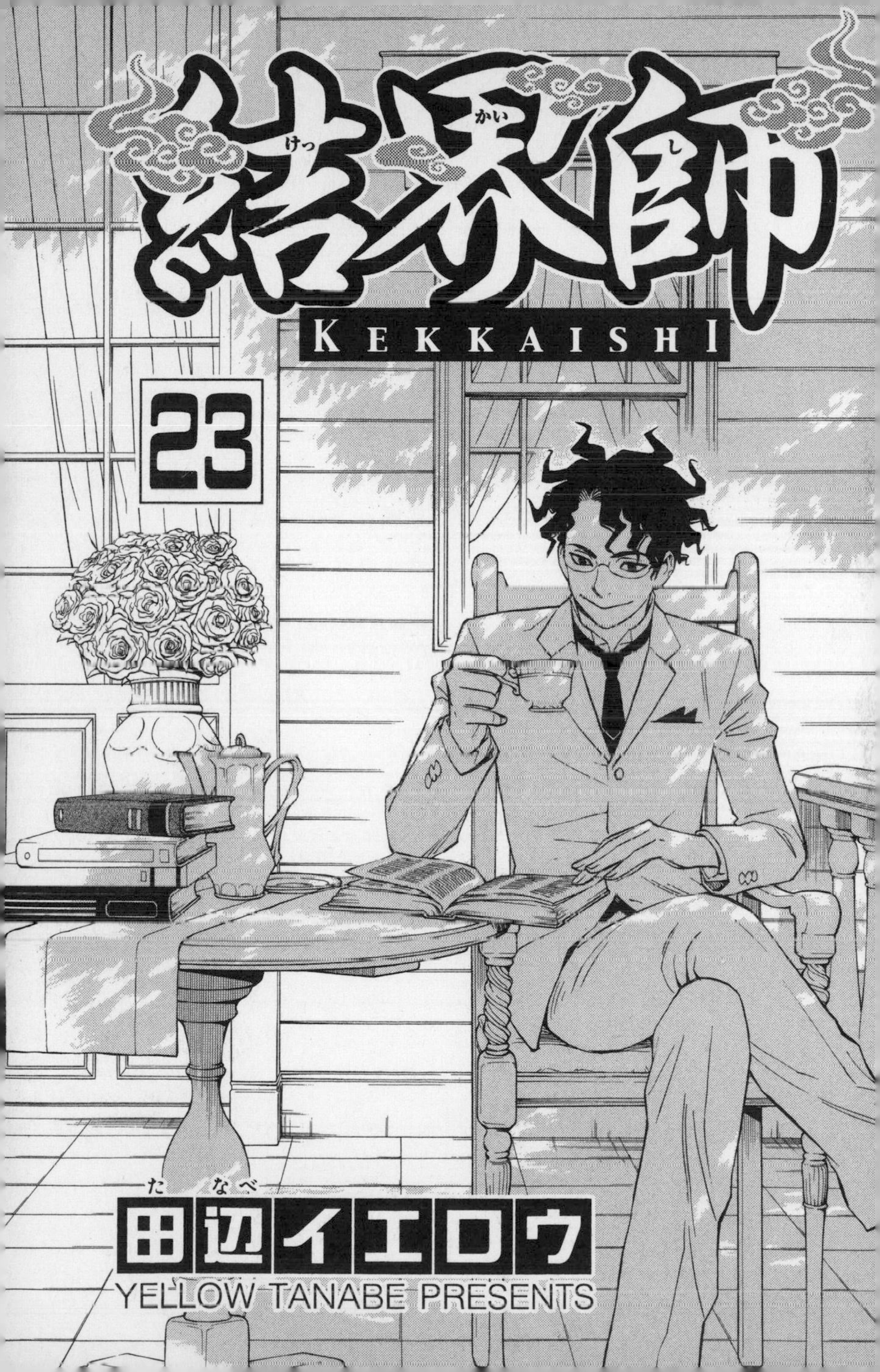
結界師
けっかいし
KEKKAISHI
23
田辺イエロウ
たなべ
YELLOW TANABE PRESENTS

THE STORY THUS FAR

Yoshimori Sumimura and Tokine Yukimura have an ancestral duty to protect the Karasumori Forest from supernatural beings called ayakashi. People with their gift for terminating *ayakashi* are called *kekkaishi*, or "barrier masters."

To protect the Karasumori Site, Tokine slays a guardian deity—a serious crime. Special Investigations Unit agents haul her to their headquarters for questioning. Mistrusting the agents' motives, Yoshimori and his Night Troops allies set out to bring her back.

Tokine escapes with the help of Yugami, one of the investigators. A vicious operative named Saiko pursues Tokine, but Yoshimori saves her. The two kekkaishi barely manage to catch their breaths before they are faced with a new challenge...

KEKKAISHI VOL. 23
TABLE OF CONTENTS

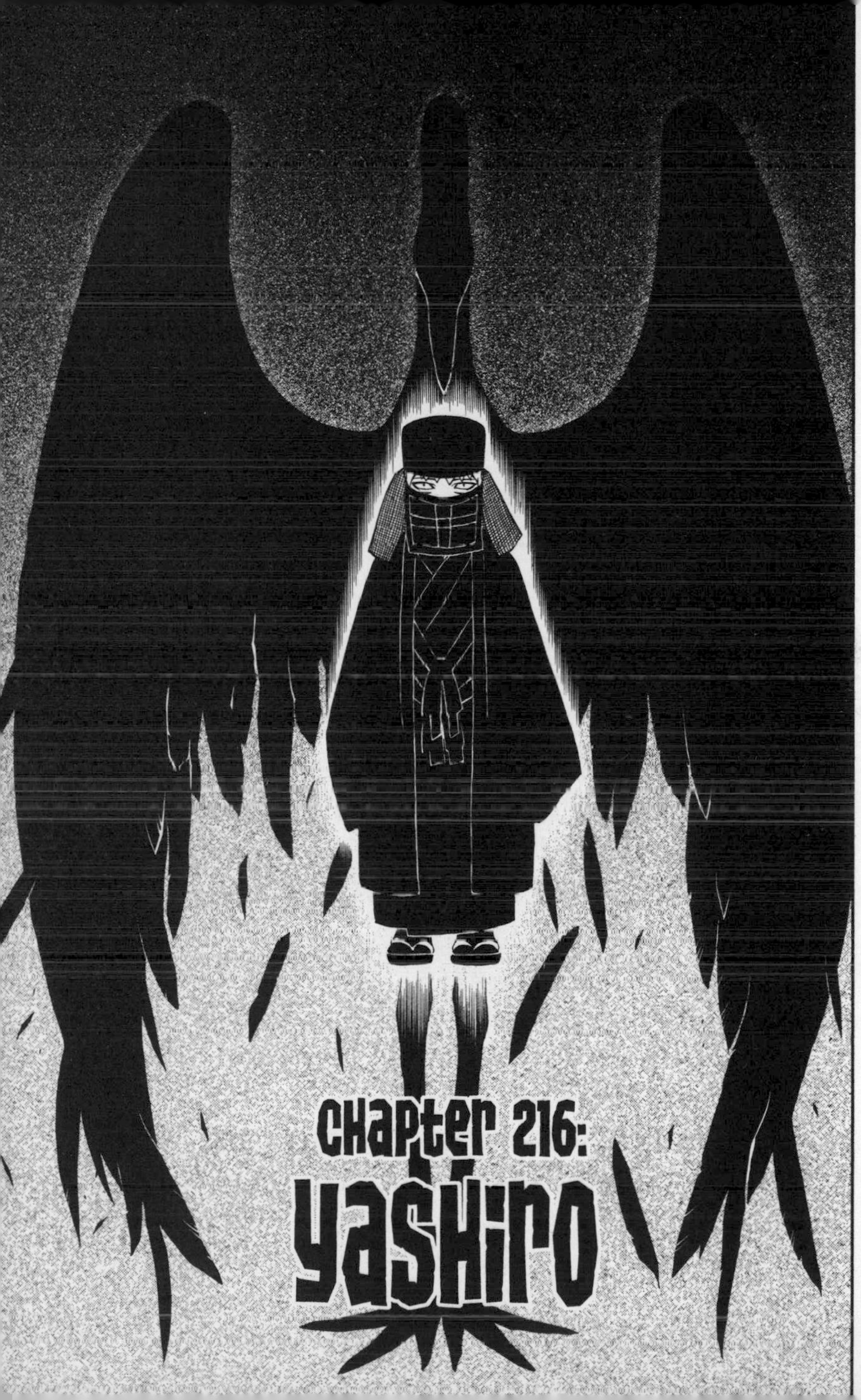
Chapter 216:
Yashiro

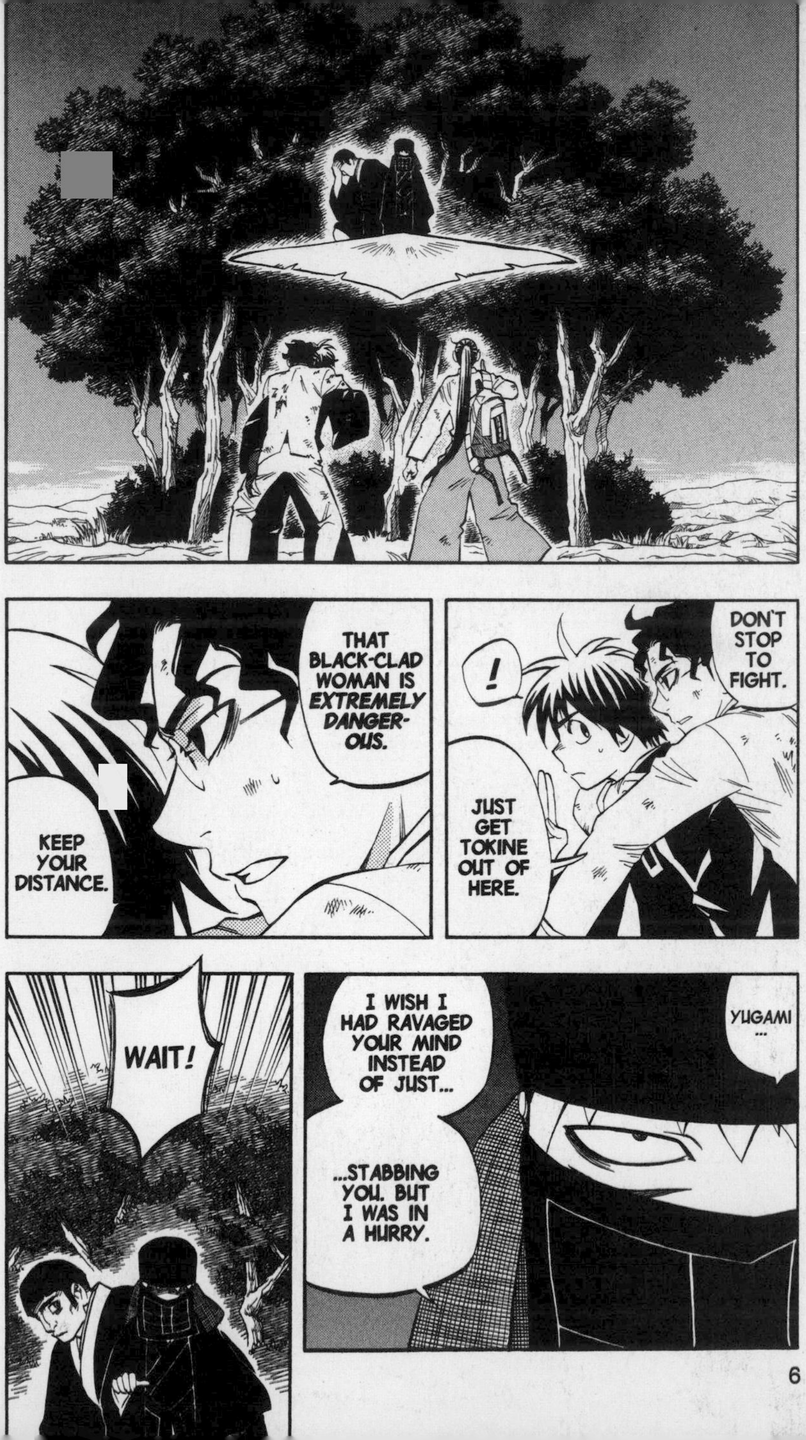
DON'T STOP TO FIGHT.
!
JUST GET TOKINE OUT OF HERE.
THAT BLACK-CLAD WOMAN IS EXTREMELY DANGEROUS.
KEEP YOUR DISTANCE.
YUGAMI...
I WISH I HAD RAVAGED YOUR MIND INSTEAD OF JUST...
...STABBING YOU. BUT I WAS IN A HURRY.
WAIT!

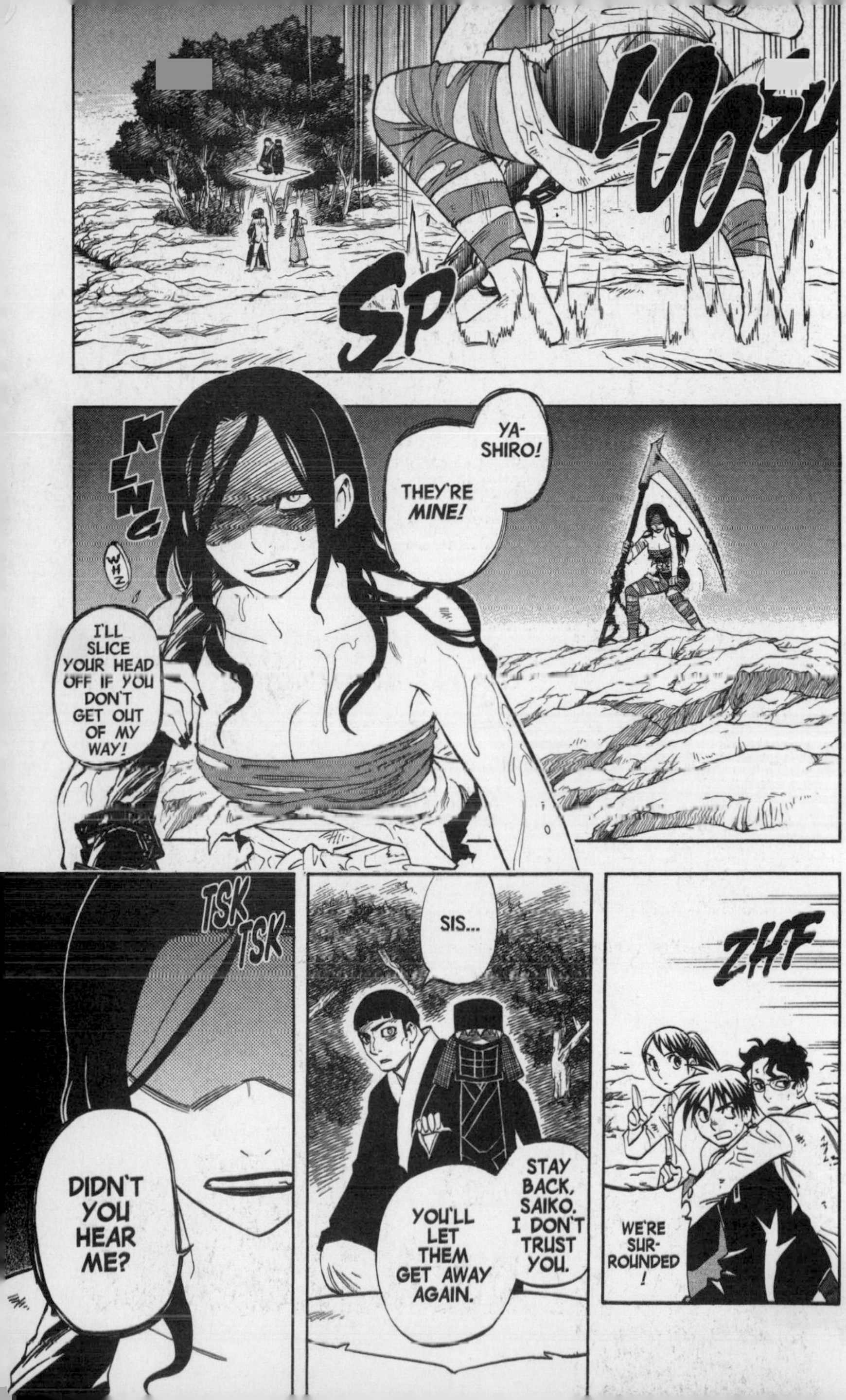
SP
YA-SHIRO!
THEY'RE MINE!
KLNG
WHZ
I'LL SLICE YOUR HEAD OFF IF YOU DON'T GET OUT OF MY WAY!
ZHF
WE'RE SUR-ROUNDED!
SIS...
STAY BACK, SAIKO. I DON'T TRUST YOU.
YOU'LL LET THEM GET AWAY AGAIN.
TSK TSK
DIDN'T YOU HEAR ME?

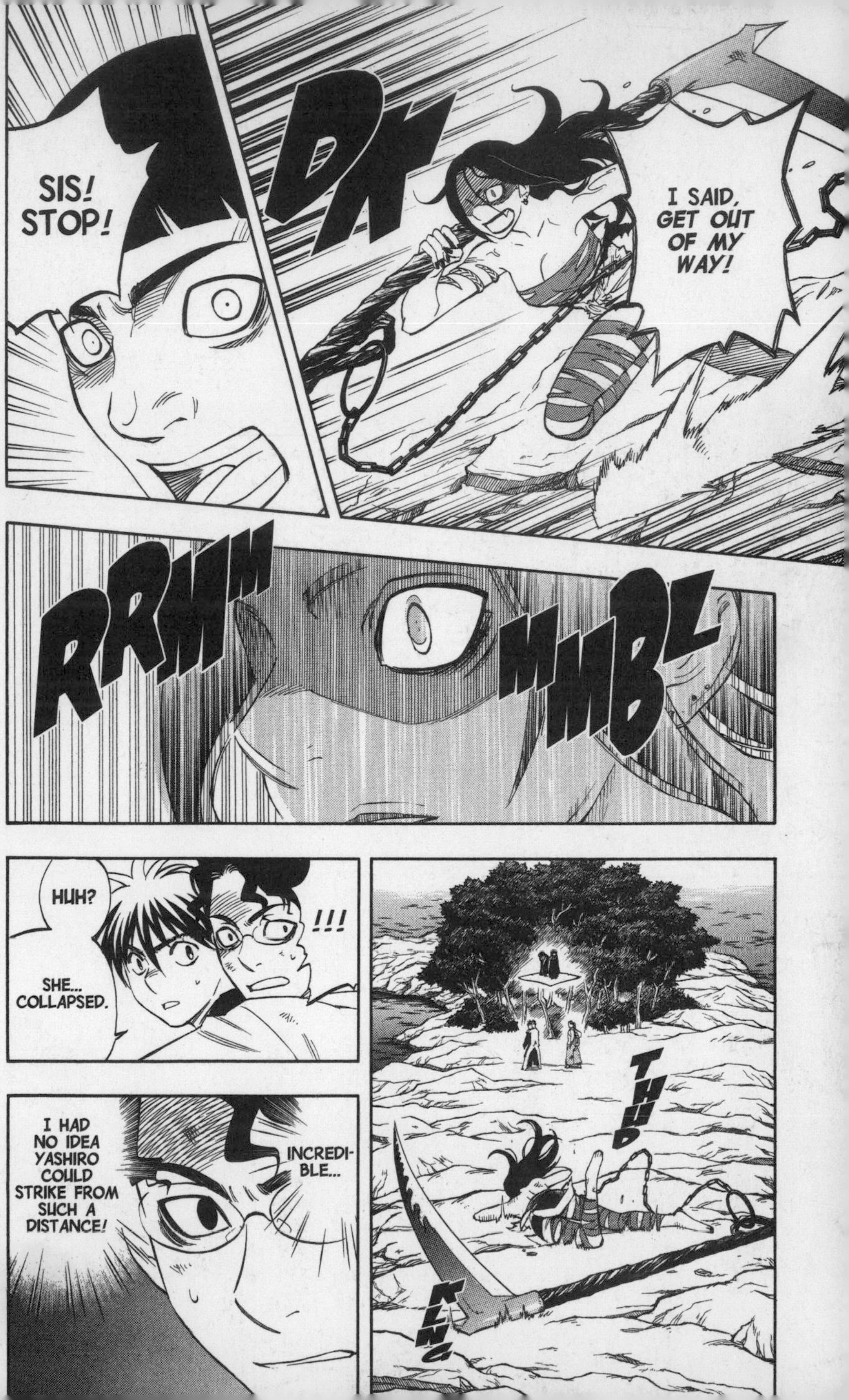

I SAID, GET OUT OF MY WAY!
DA
SIS! STOP!
RRMM
MMBL
THUD
KLNG
!!!
HUH?
SHE... COLLAPSED.
INCREDIBLE...
I HAD NO IDEA YASHIRO COULD STRIKE FROM SUCH A DISTANCE!

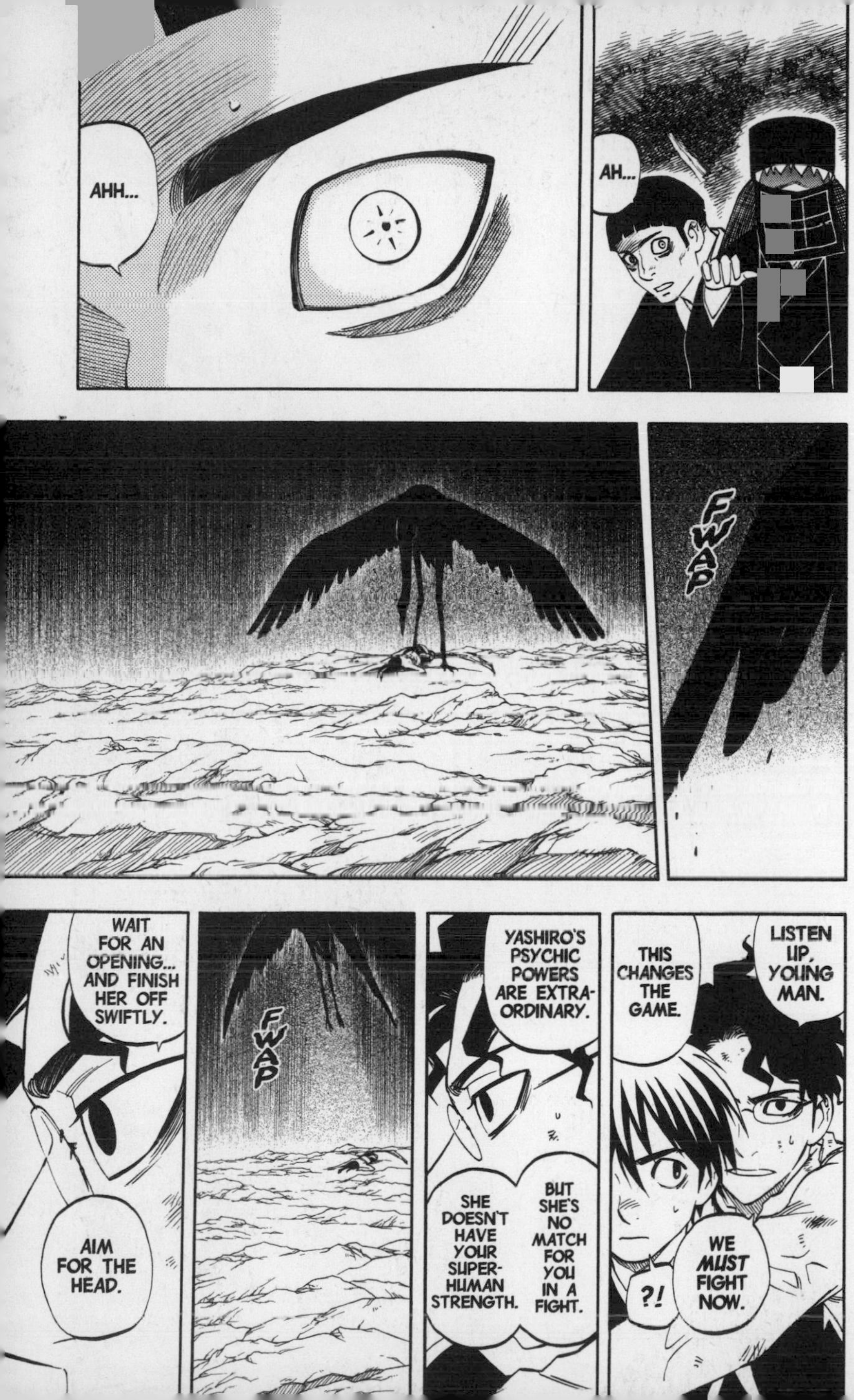
AH...
AHH...
FWAP
LISTEN UP, YOUNG MAN.
THIS CHANGES THE GAME.
WE MUST FIGHT NOW.
?!
YASHIRO'S PSYCHIC POWERS ARE EXTRA-ORDINARY.
BUT SHE'S NO MATCH FOR YOU IN A FIGHT.
SHE DOESN'T HAVE YOUR SUPER-HUMAN STRENGTH.
FWAP
WAIT FOR AN OPENING... AND FINISH HER OFF SWIFTLY.
AIM FOR THE HEAD.

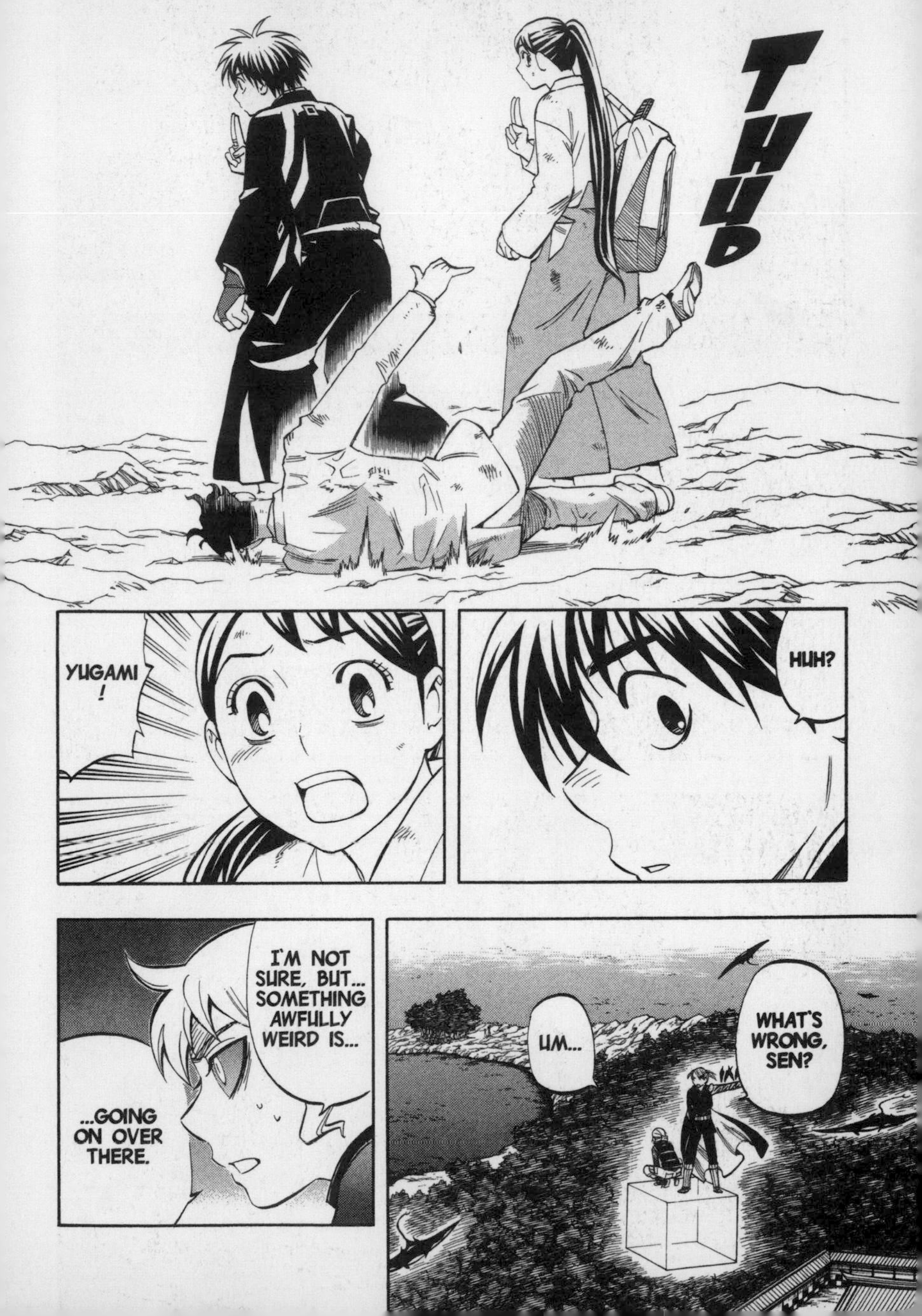
THUD
HUH?
YUGAMI!
WHAT'S WRONG, SEN?
UM...
I'M NOT SURE, BUT... SOMETHING AWFULLY WEIRD IS...
...GOING ON OVER THERE.

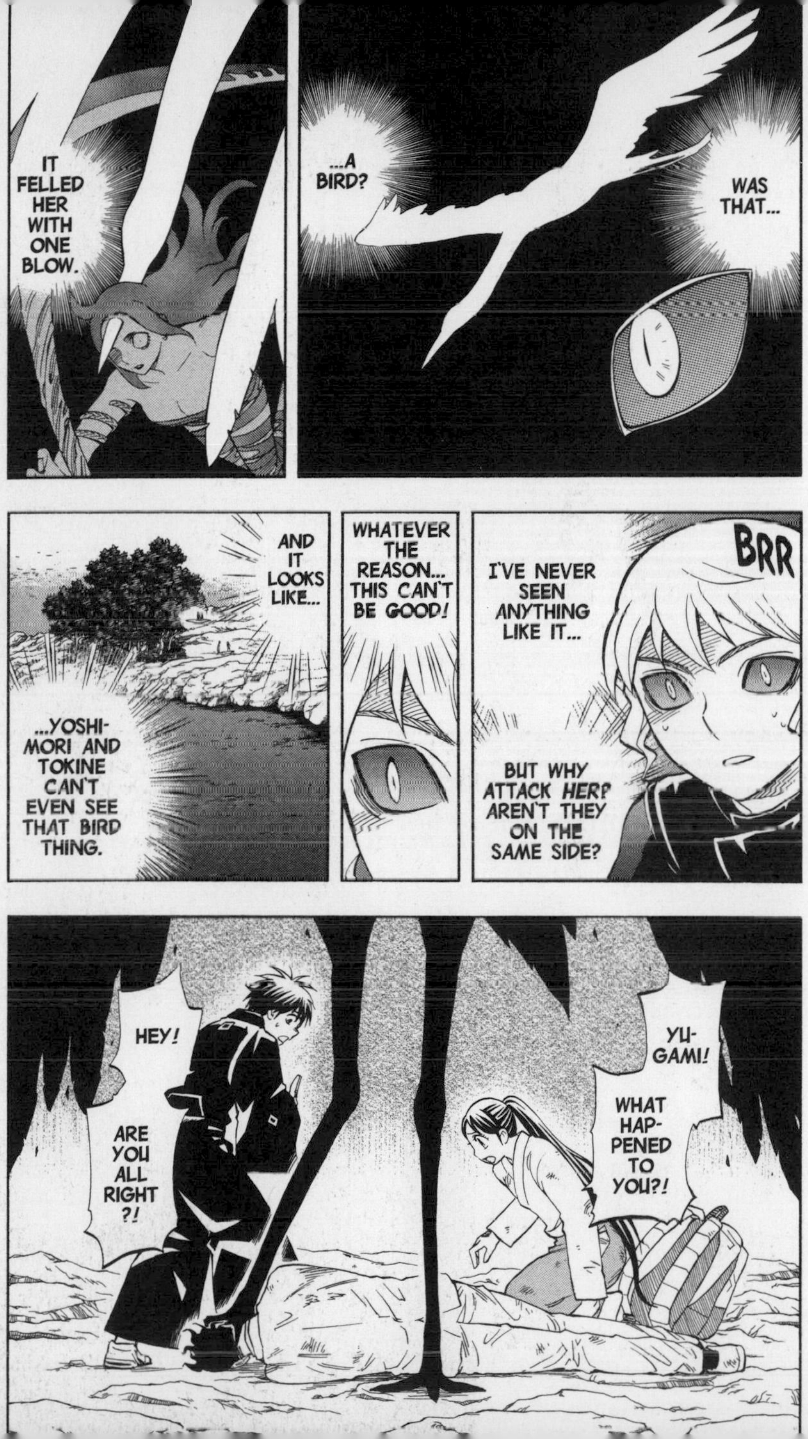
WAS THAT...
...A BIRD?
IT FELLED HER WITH ONE BLOW.
BRR
I'VE NEVER SEEN ANYTHING LIKE IT...
BUT WHY ATTACK HER? AREN'T THEY ON THE SAME SIDE?
WHATEVER THE REASON... THIS CAN'T BE GOOD!
AND IT LOOKS LIKE...
...YOSHIMORI AND TOKINE CAN'T EVEN SEE THAT BIRD THING.
YU-GAMI!
WHAT HAPPENED TO YOU?!
HEY!
ARE YOU ALL RIGHT?!

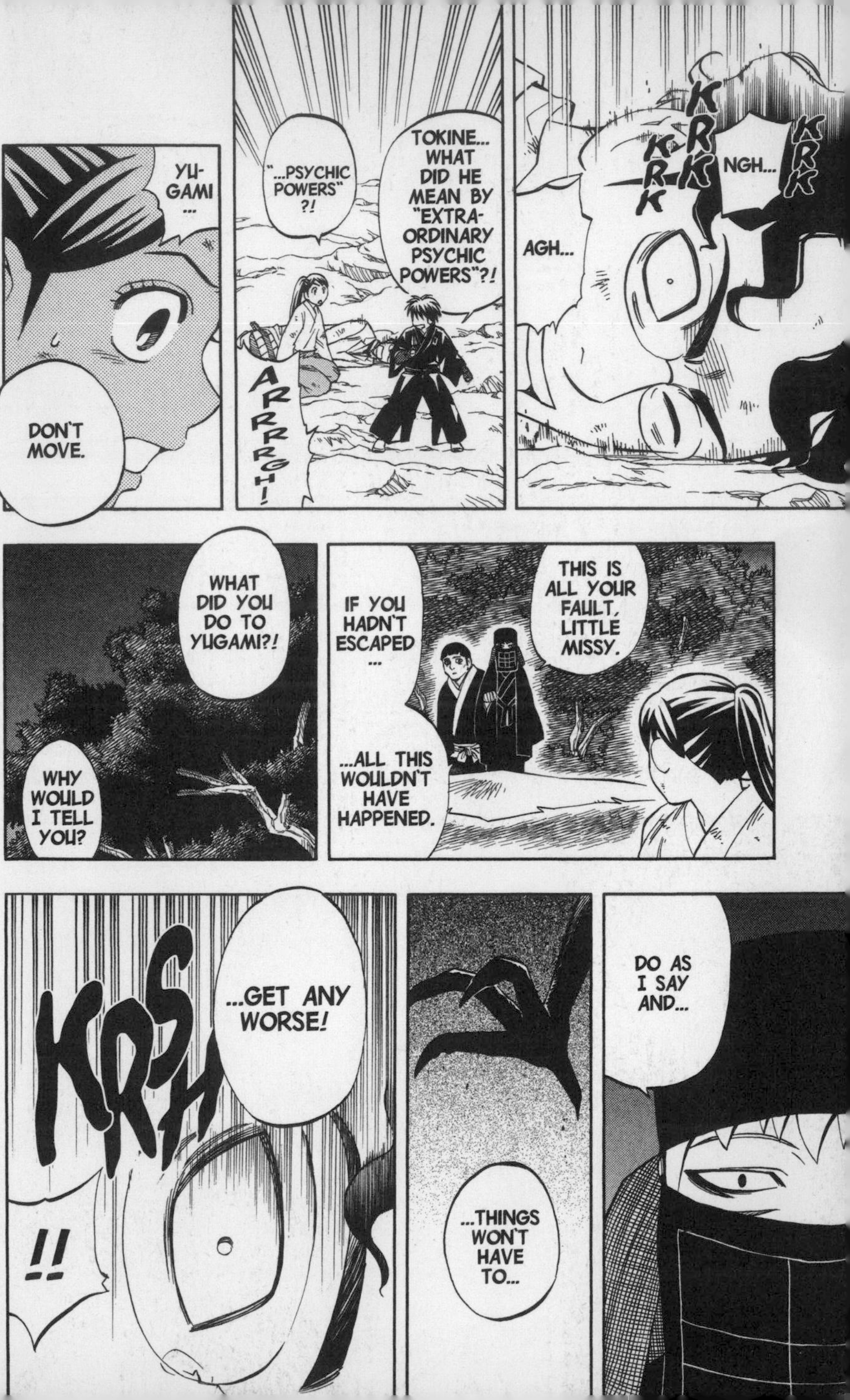
KRK
NGH...
KRK
K-R-K
AGH...
TOKINE... WHAT DID HE MEAN BY "EXTRA-ORDINARY PSYCHIC POWERS"?!
"...PSYCHIC POWERS" ?!
ARRRRGH!
YU-GAMI ...
DON'T MOVE.
THIS IS ALL YOUR FAULT, LITTLE MISSY.
IF YOU HADN'T ESCAPED ...
...ALL THIS WOULDN'T HAVE HAPPENED.
WHAT DID YOU DO TO YUGAMI?!
WHY WOULD I TELL YOU?
DO AS I SAY AND...
...THINGS WON'T HAVE TO...
...GET ANY WORSE!
KRSH
!!

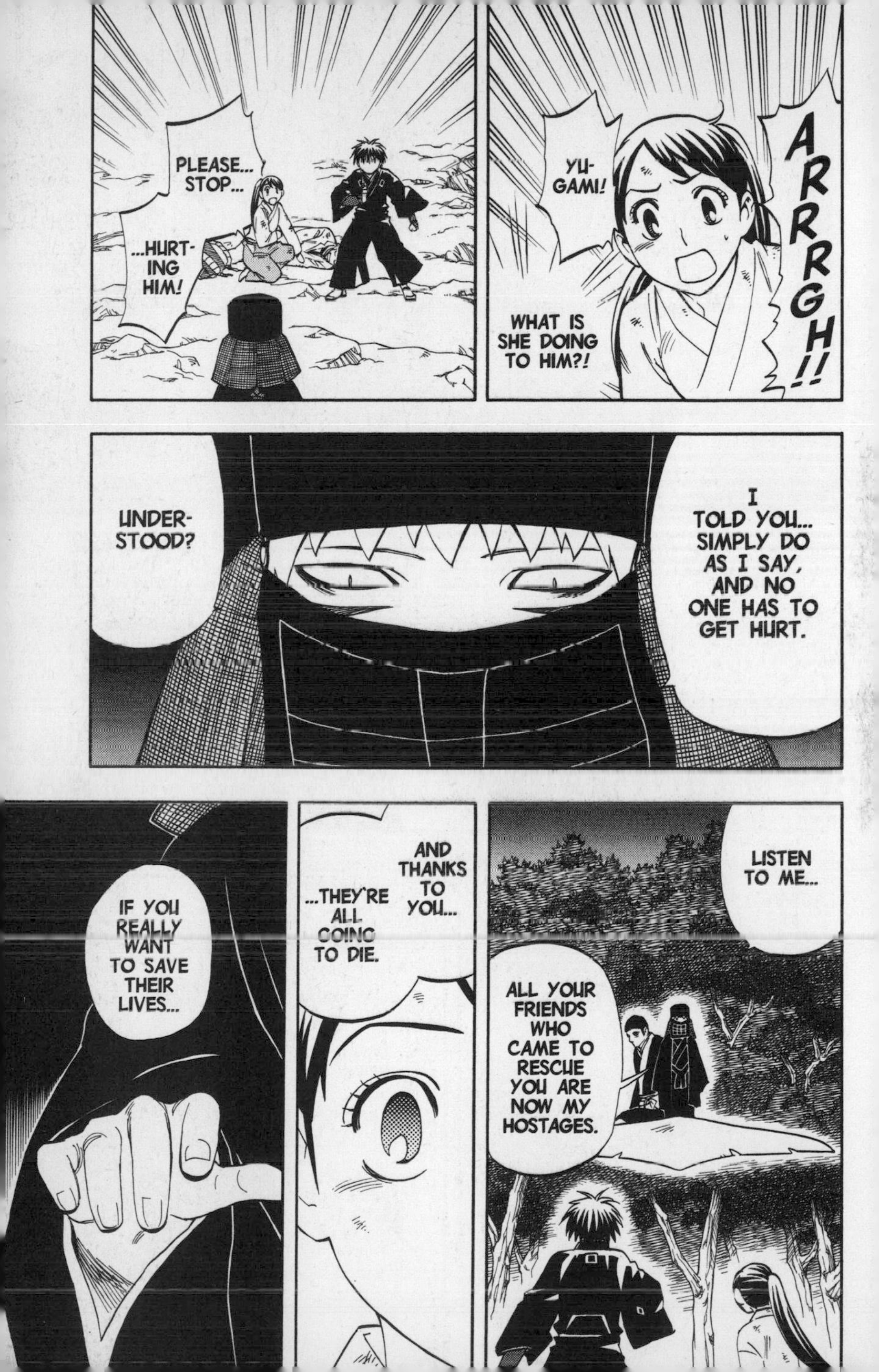
ARRRGH!!
YUGAMI!
WHAT IS SHE DOING TO HIM?!
PLEASE... STOP...
...HURTING HIM!
I TOLD YOU... SIMPLY DO AS I SAY, AND NO ONE HAS TO GET HURT.
UNDERSTOOD?
LISTEN TO ME...
ALL YOUR FRIENDS WHO CAME TO RESCUE YOU ARE NOW MY HOSTAGES.
AND THANKS TO YOU...
...THEY'RE ALL GOING TO DIE.
IF YOU REALLY WANT TO SAVE THEIR LIVES...

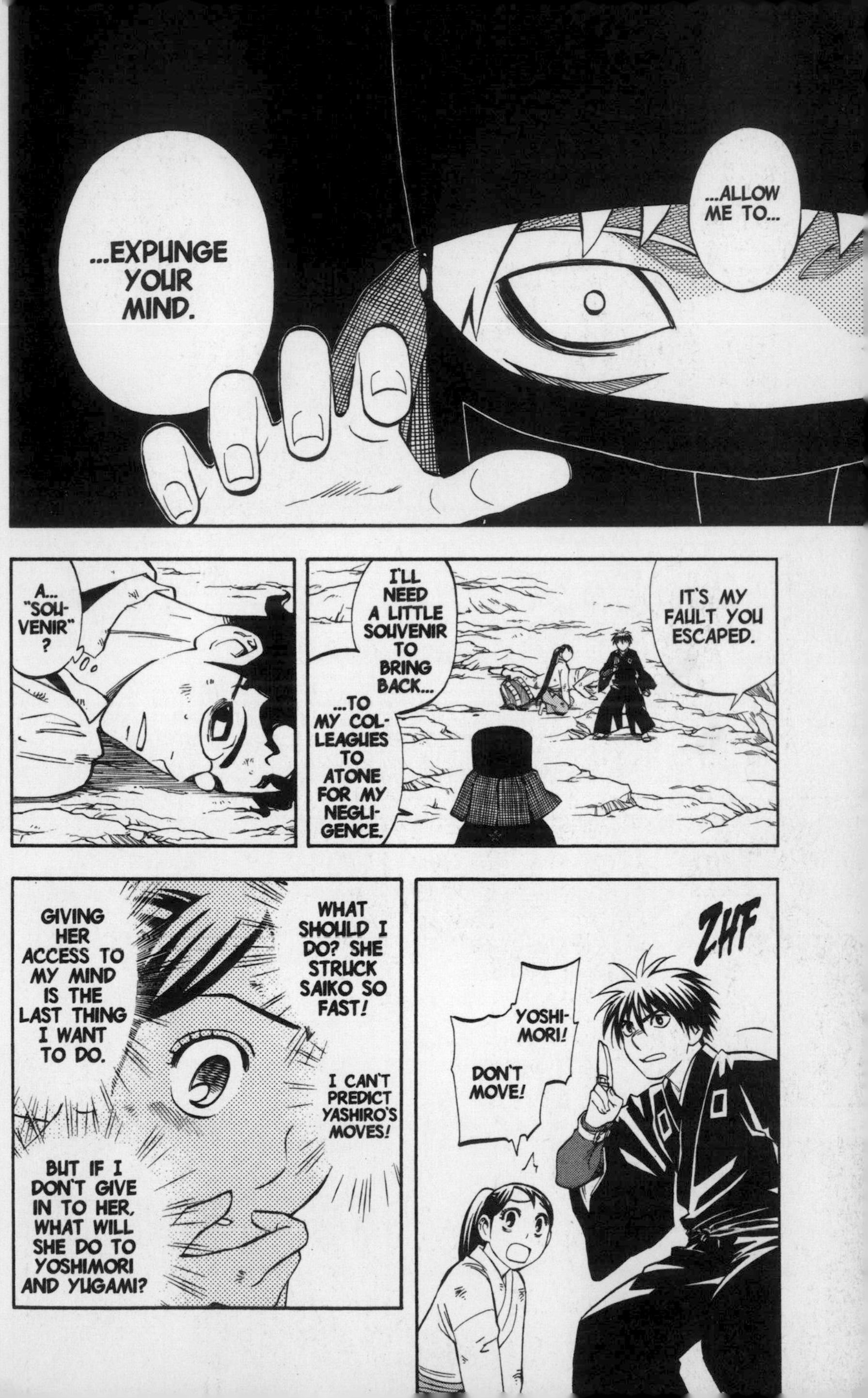
...ALLOW ME TO...
...EXPUNGE YOUR MIND.
IT'S MY FAULT YOU ESCAPED.
I'LL NEED A LITTLE SOUVENIR TO BRING BACK...
...TO MY COL-LEAGUES TO ATONE FOR MY NEGLI-GENCE.
A... "SOU-VENIR"?
ZHF
YOSHI-MORI!
DON'T MOVE!
WHAT SHOULD I DO? SHE STRUCK SAIKO SO FAST!
GIVING HER ACCESS TO MY MIND IS THE LAST THING I WANT TO DO.
I CAN'T PREDICT YASHIRO'S MOVES!
BUT IF I DON'T GIVE IN TO HER, WHAT WILL SHE DO TO YOSHIMORI AND YUGAMI?

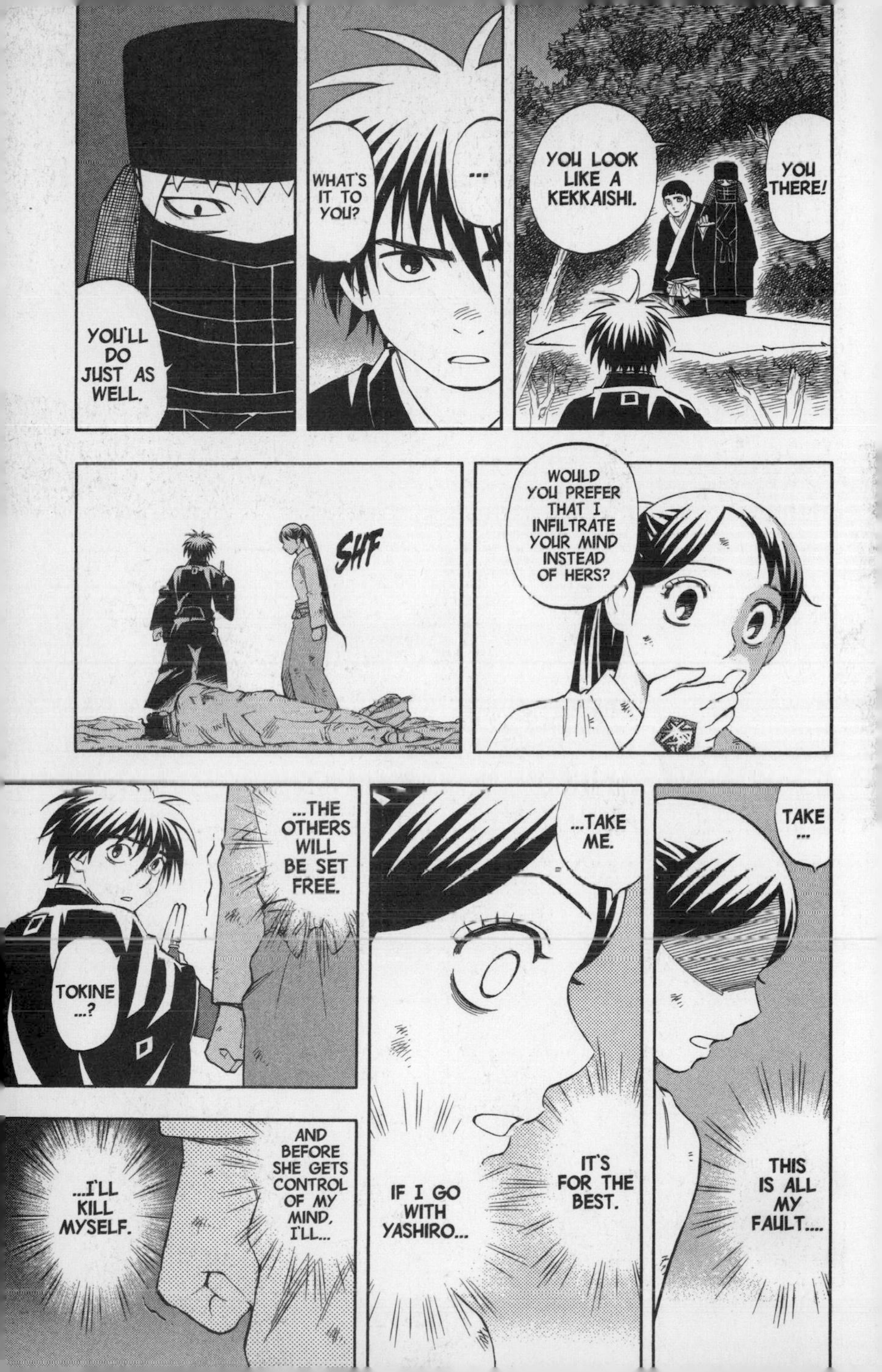
YOU THERE!
YOU LOOK LIKE A KEKKAISHI.
...
WHAT'S IT TO YOU?
YOU'LL DO JUST AS WELL.
WOULD YOU PREFER THAT I INFILTRATE YOUR MIND INSTEAD OF HERS?
SHF
TAKE ...
THIS IS ALL MY FAULT....
...TAKE ME.
IT'S FOR THE BEST.
IF I GO WITH YASHIRO...
...THE OTHERS WILL BE SET FREE.
TOKINE ...?
AND BEFORE SHE GETS CONTROL OF MY MIND, I'LL...
...I'LL KILL MYSELF.

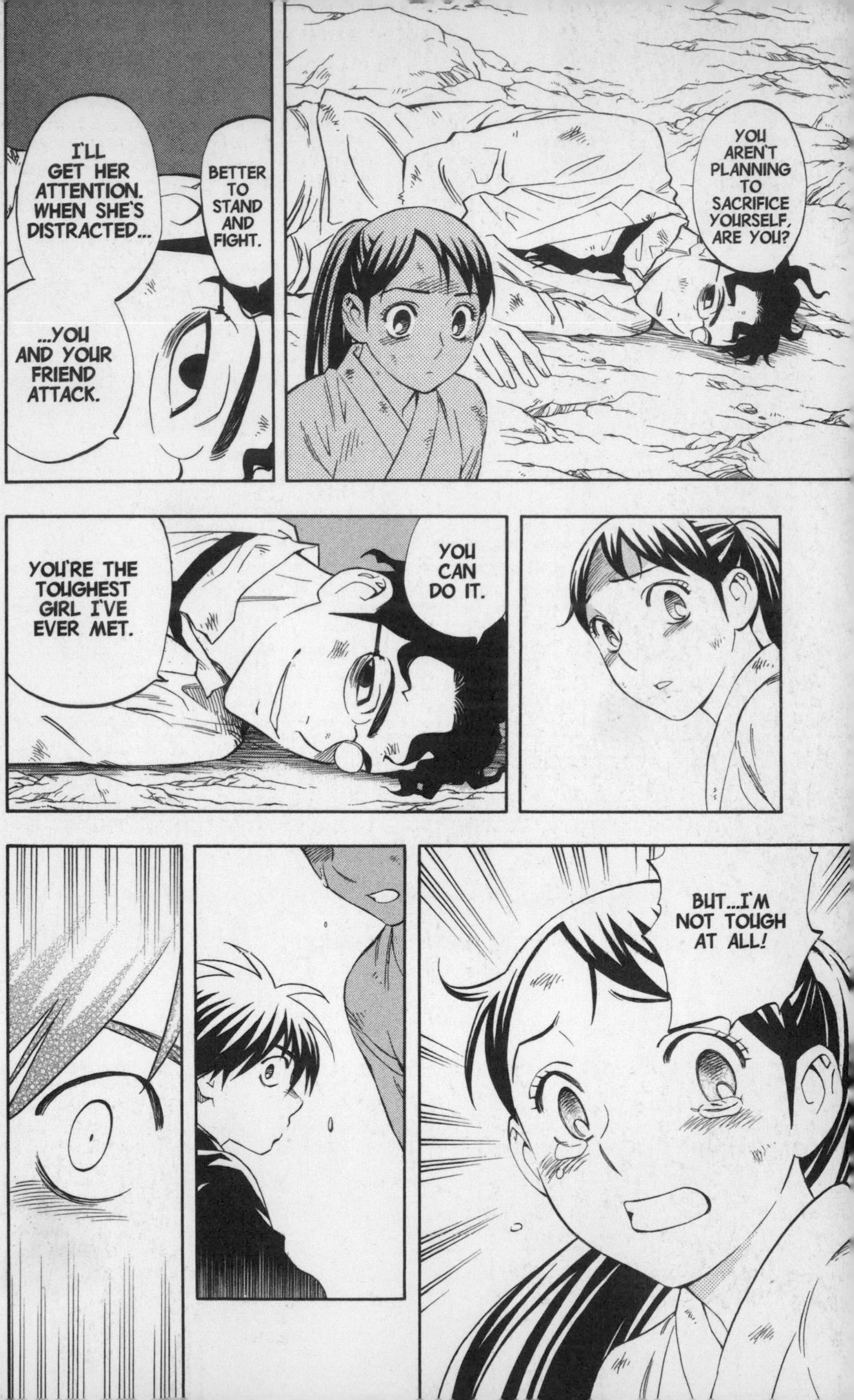
YOU AREN'T PLANNING TO SACRIFICE YOURSELF, ARE YOU?
BETTER TO STAND AND FIGHT.
I'LL GET HER ATTENTION. WHEN SHE'S DISTRACTED...
...YOU AND YOUR FRIEND ATTACK.
YOU CAN DO IT.
YOU'RE THE TOUGHEST GIRL I'VE EVER MET.
BUT...I'M NOT TOUGH AT ALL!

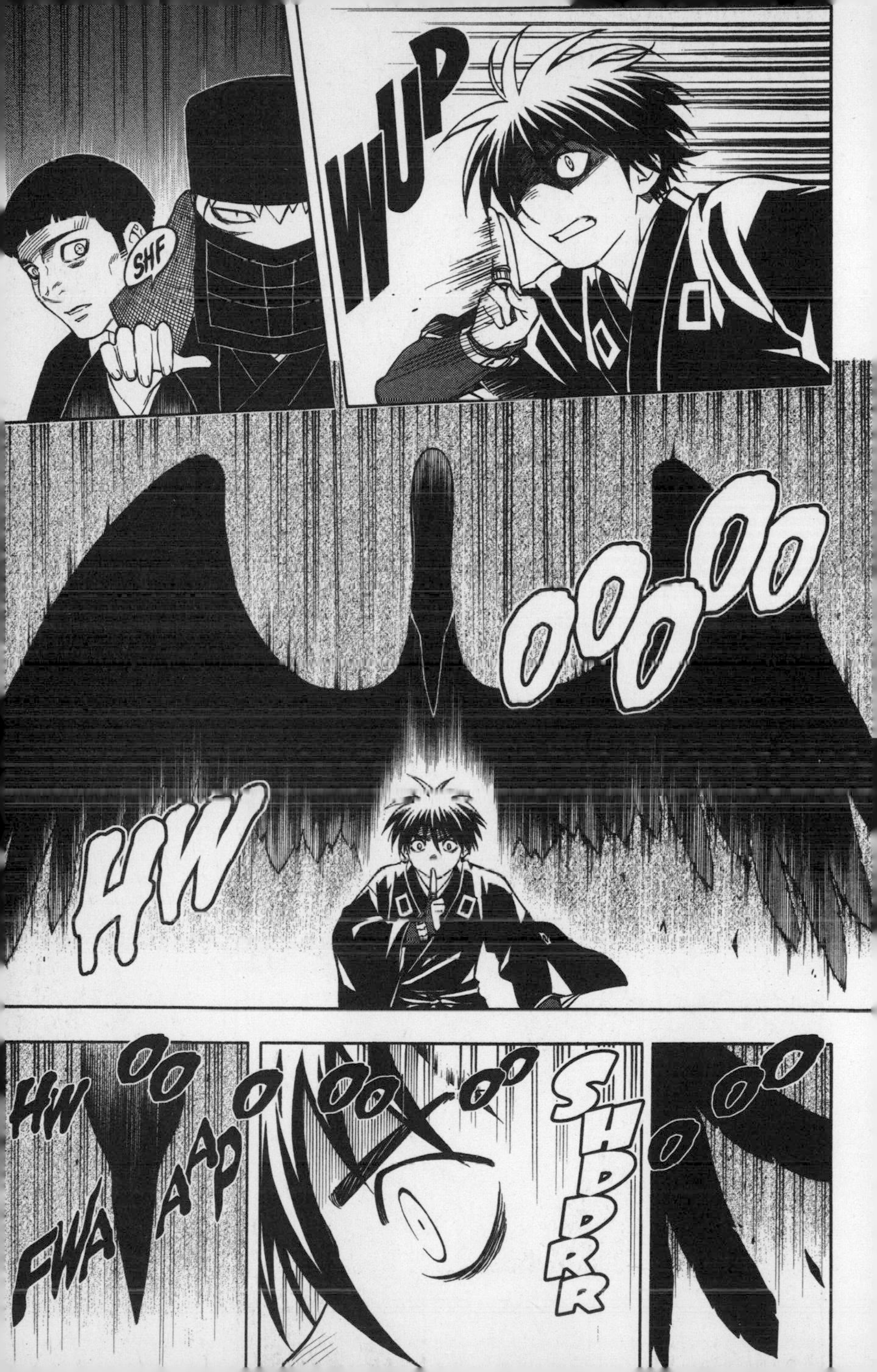
WUP
SHF
OOOOOOO
HW
OOO
SHDRR
OOOOO
HW
OO
FWAAAP

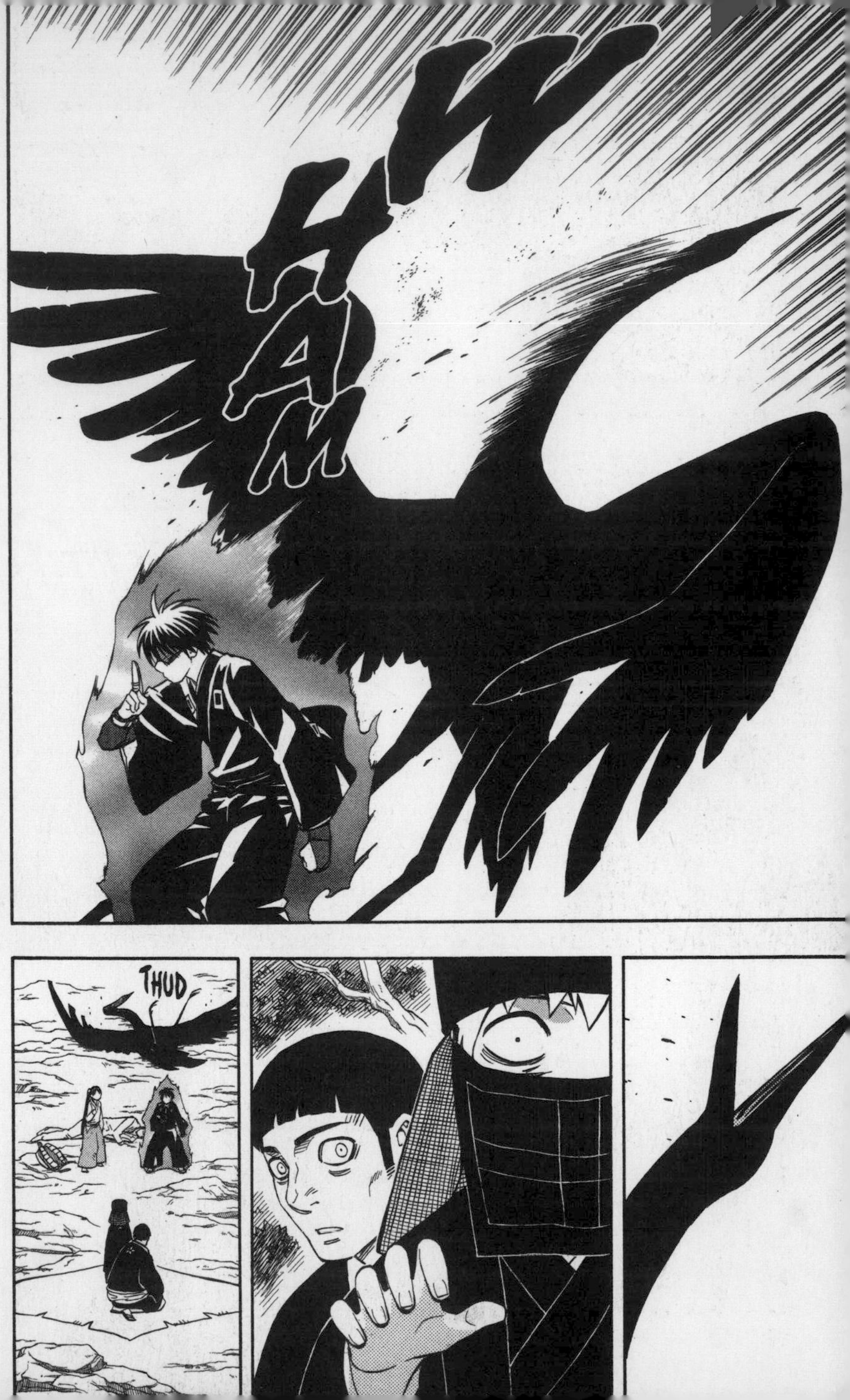
WHAM
THUD

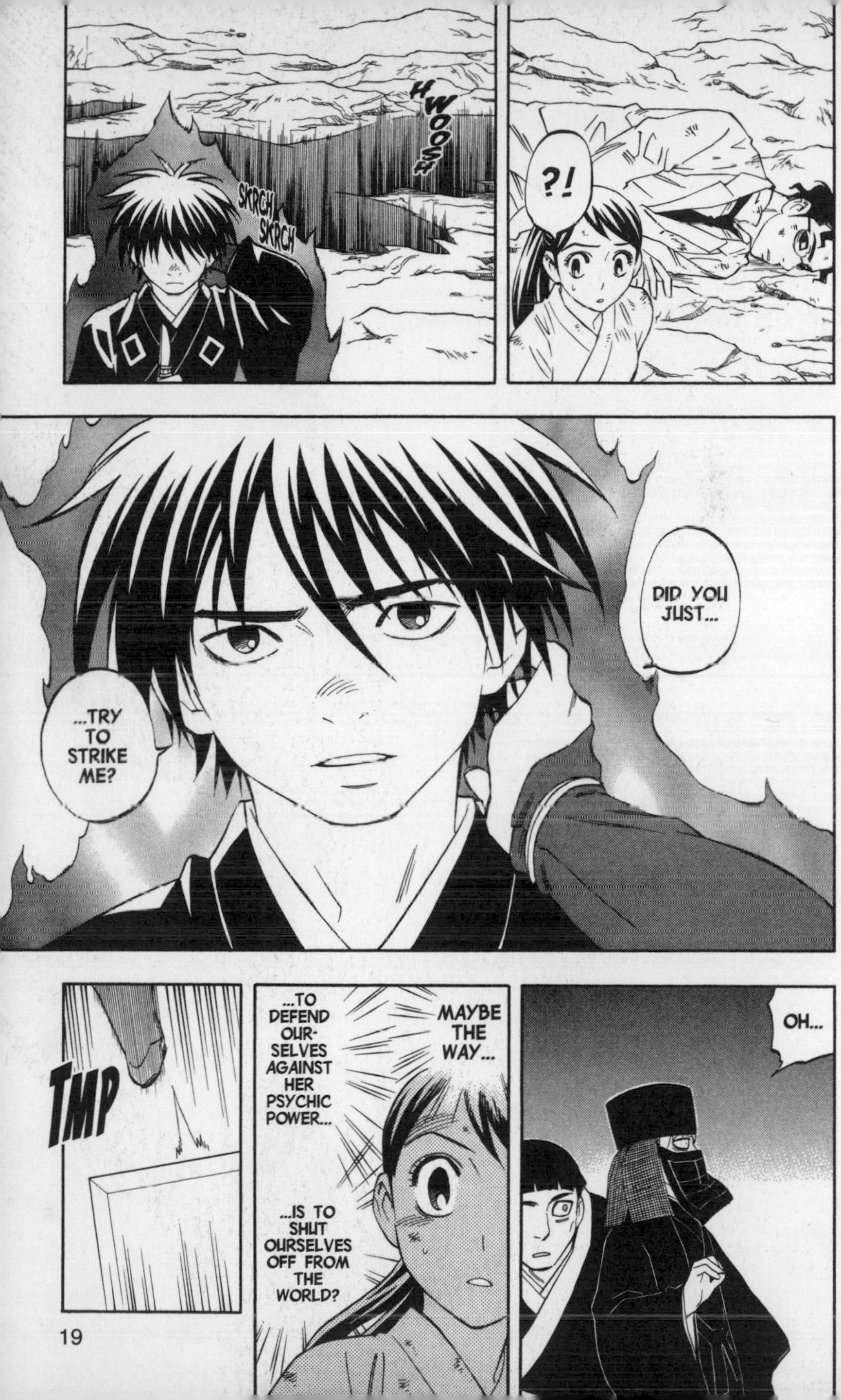
?!
HWOOSH
SKRCH SKRCH
DID YOU JUST...
...TRY TO STRIKE ME?
OH...
MAYBE THE WAY...
...TO DEFEND OUR-SELVES AGAINST HER PSYCHIC POWER...
...IS TO SHUT OURSELVES OFF FROM THE WORLD?
TMP

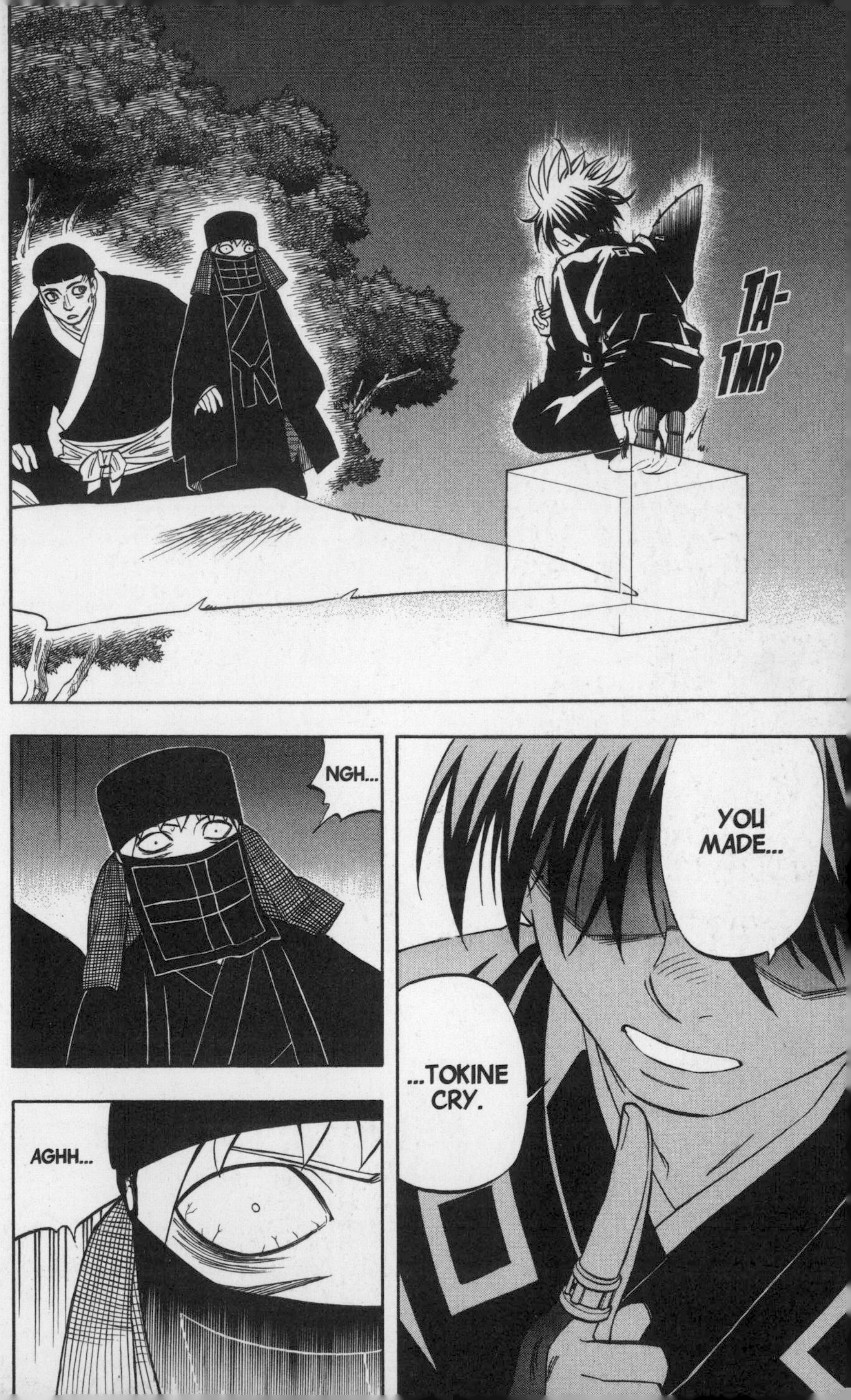
TA-TMP
YOU MADE...
...TOKINE CRY.
NGH...
AGHH...

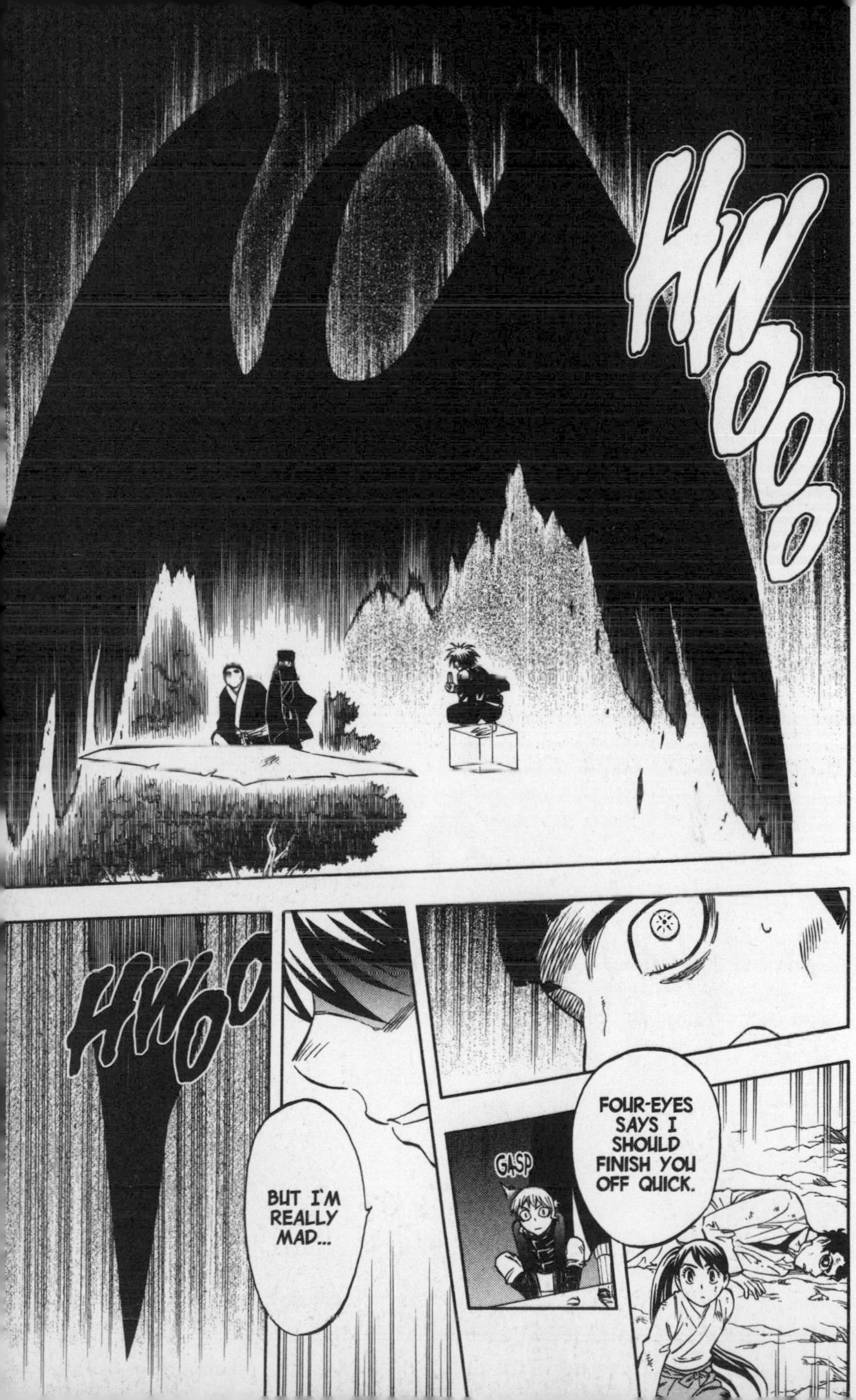
HWOOO
FOUR-EYES SAYS I SHOULD FINISH YOU OFF QUICK.
GASP
BUT I'M REALLY MAD...
HWOO

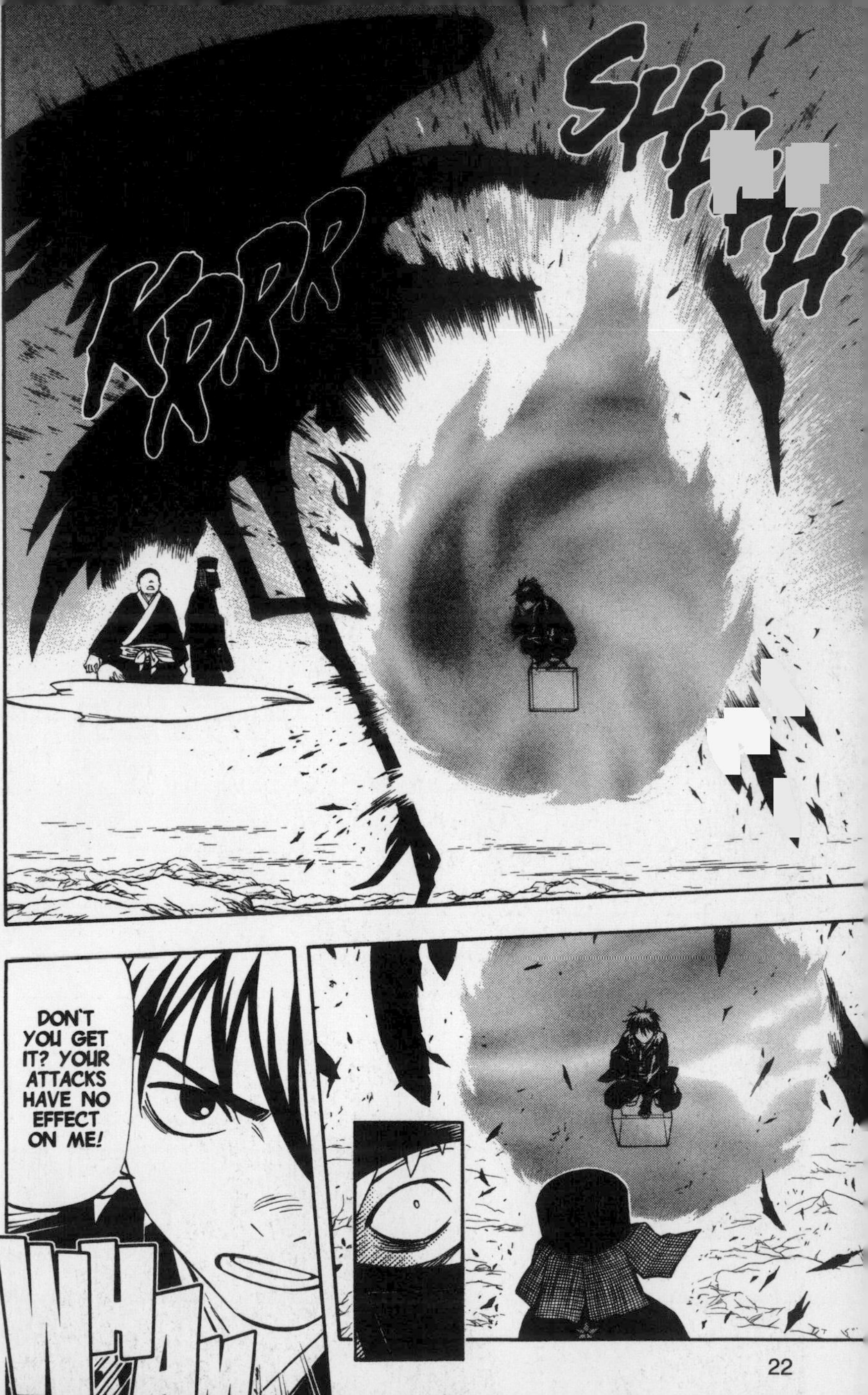
SHHH
KPPR
DON'T YOU GET IT? YOUR ATTACKS HAVE NO EFFECT ON ME!
WHAM

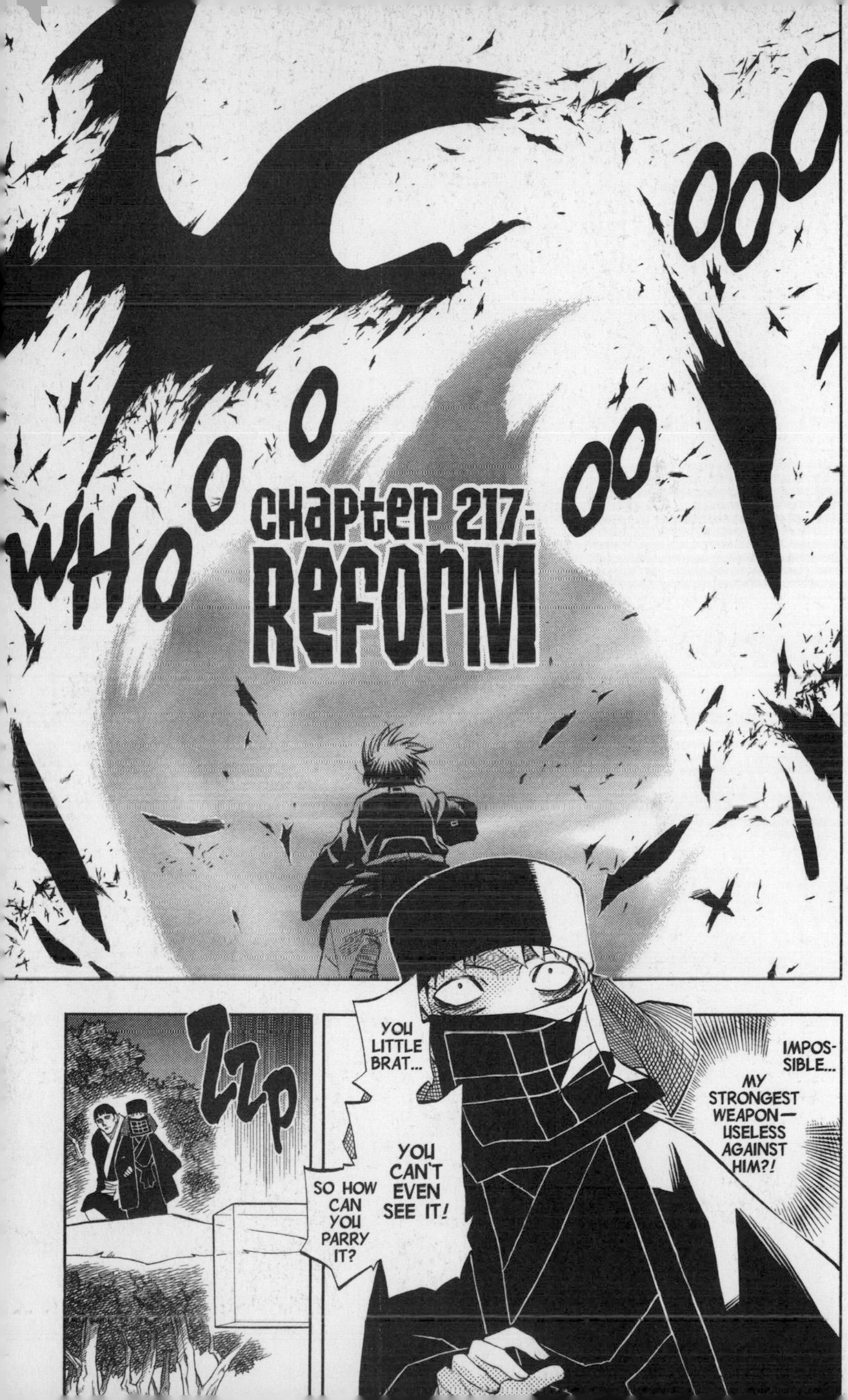
WHOOOOOOOOO
CHAPTER 217:
REFORM
IMPOSSIBLE... MY STRONGEST WEAPON—USELESS AGAINST HIM?!
YOU LITTLE BRAT...
YOU CAN'T EVEN SEE IT!
SO HOW CAN YOU PARRY IT?
ZZP

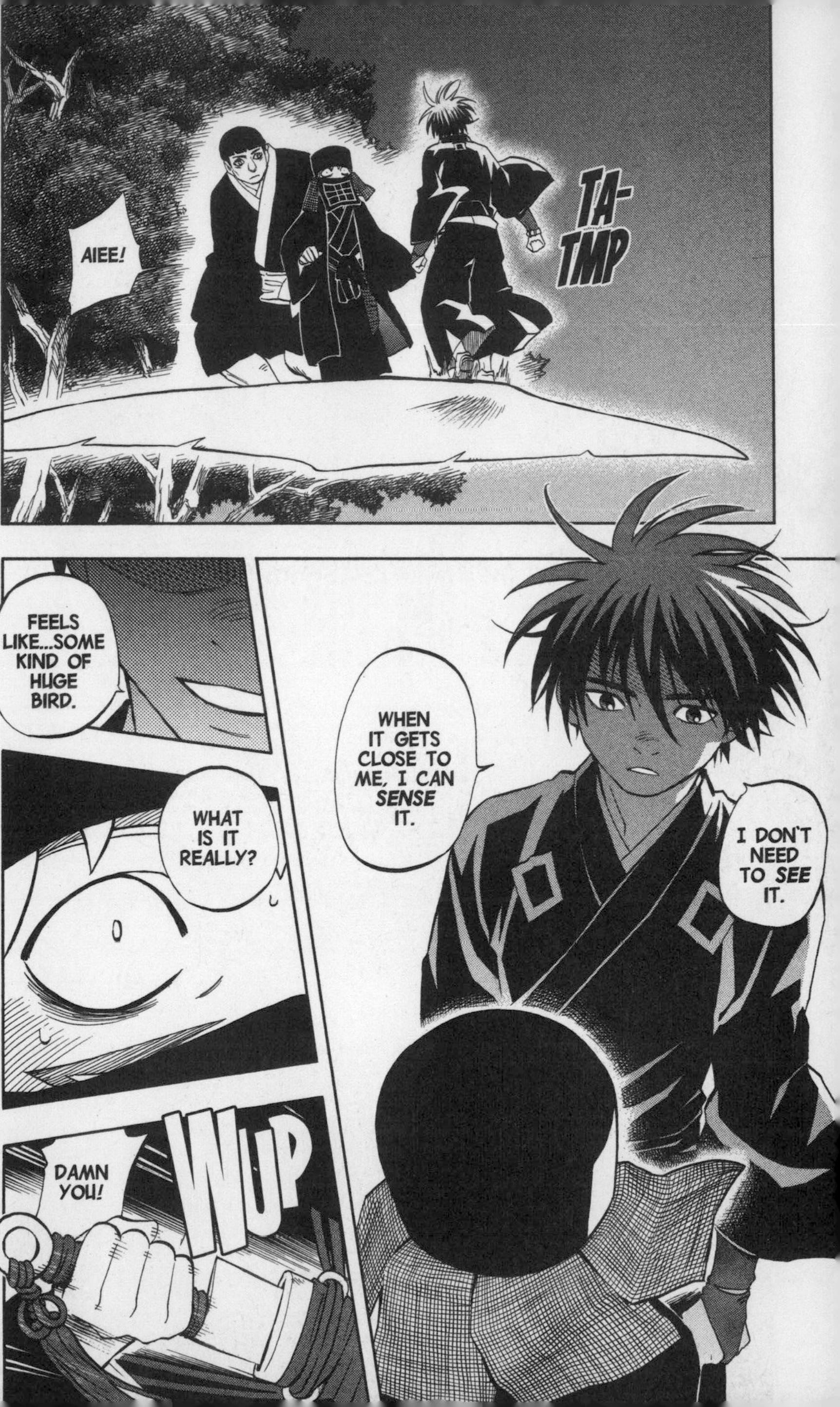
TA-TMP
AIEE!
I DON'T NEED TO SEE IT.
WHEN IT GETS CLOSE TO ME, I CAN SENSE IT.
FEELS LIKE...SOME KIND OF HUGE BIRD.
WHAT IS IT REALLY?
WUP
DAMN YOU!

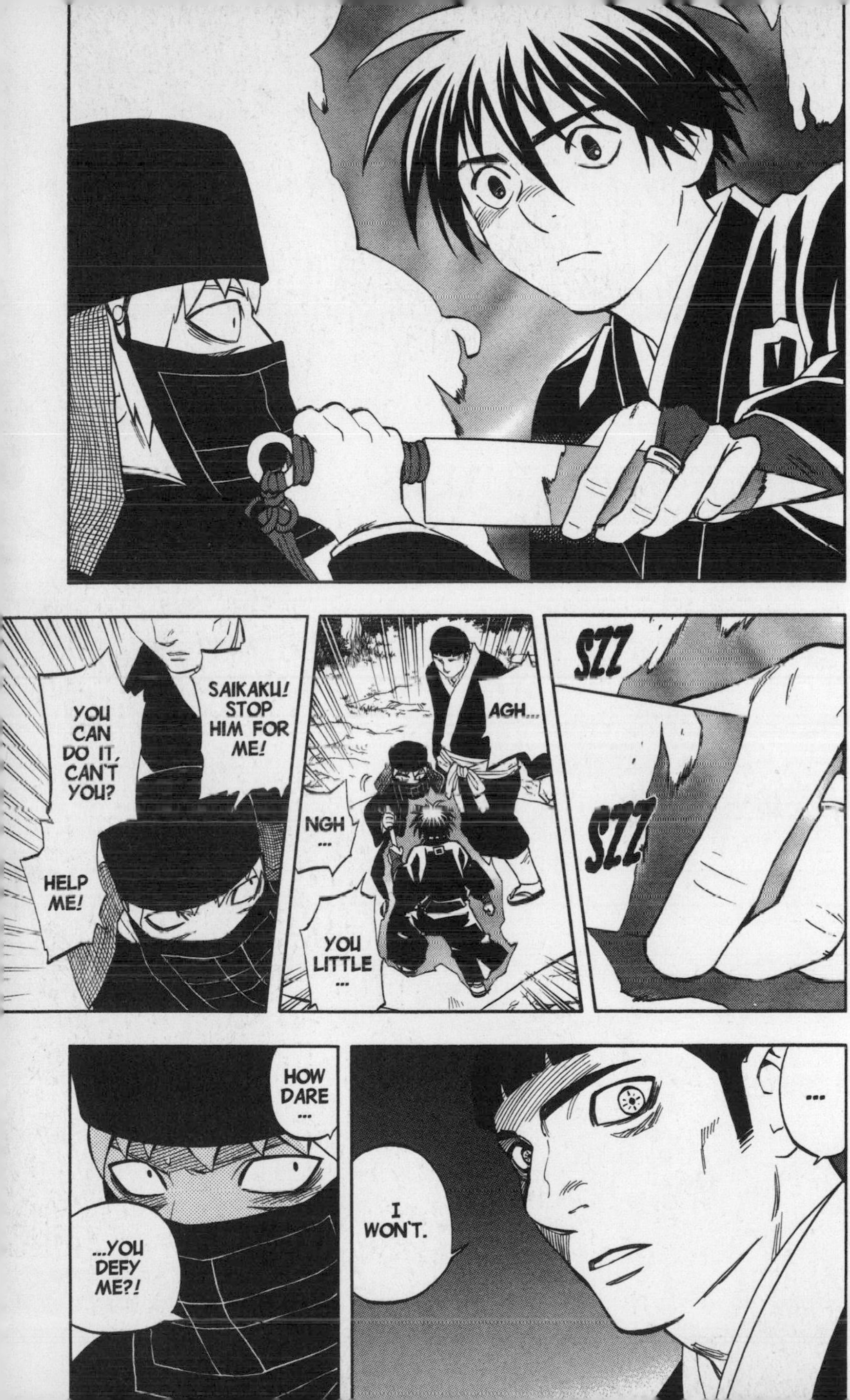
SZZ
SZZ
AGH...
NGH...
YOU LITTLE...
SAIKAKU! STOP HIM FOR ME!
YOU CAN DO IT, CAN'T YOU?
HELP ME!
...
I WON'T.
HOW DARE...
...YOU DEFY ME?!

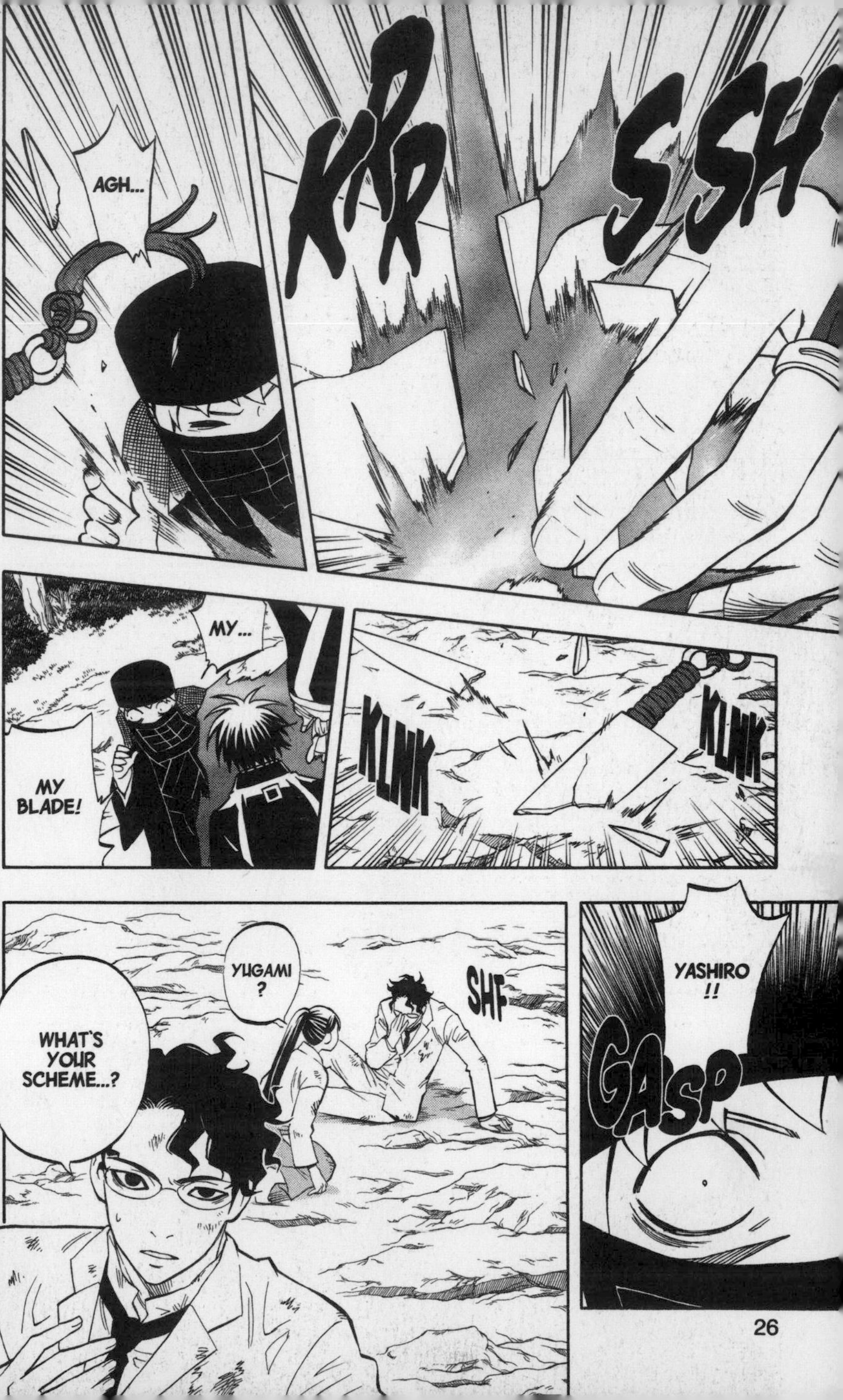
KRR
SSH
AGH...
KLNK
KLNK
MY...
MY BLADE!
YASHIRO !!
GASP
SHF
YUGAMI ?
WHAT'S YOUR SCHEME...?

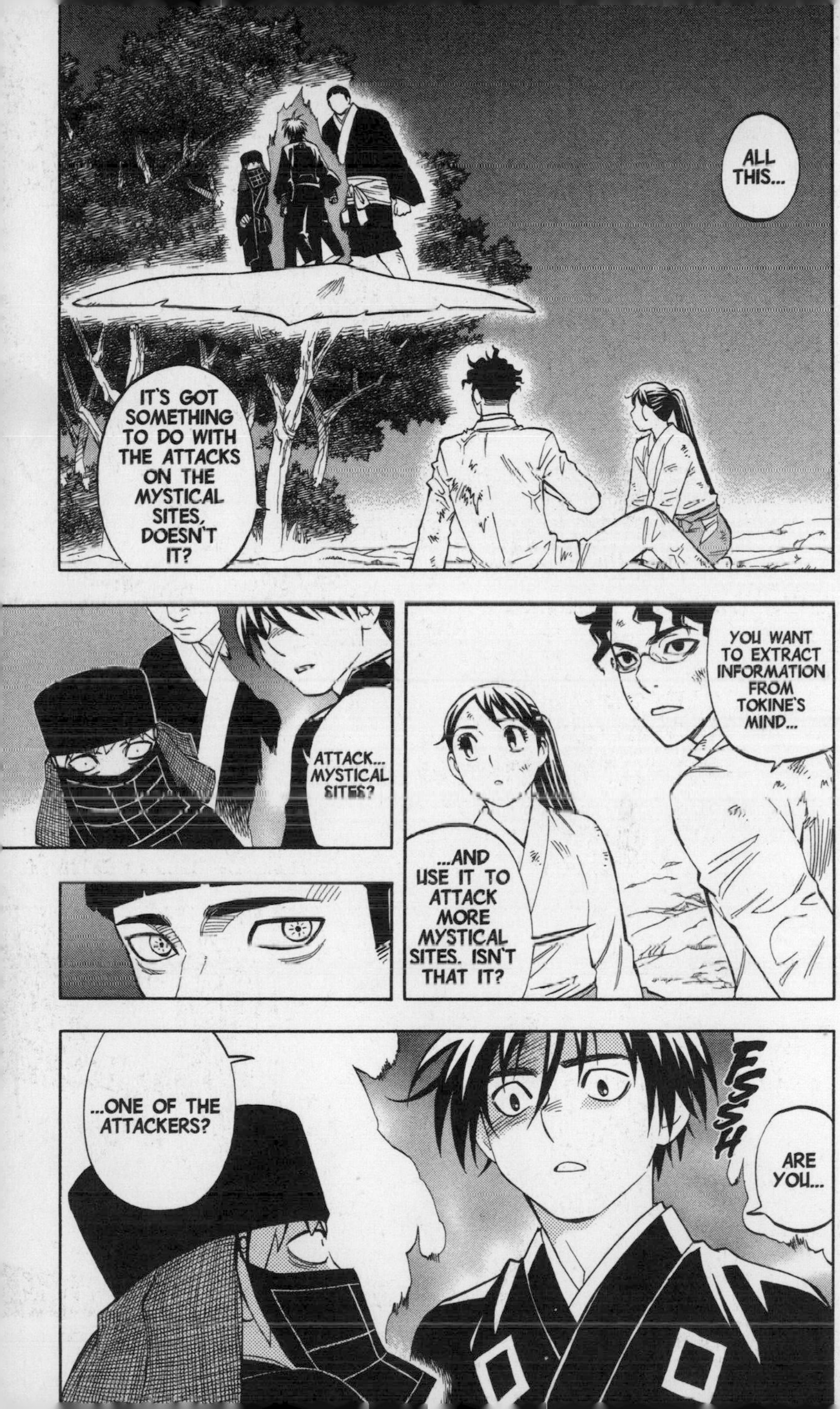
ALL THIS...
IT'S GOT SOMETHING TO DO WITH THE ATTACKS ON THE MYSTICAL SITES, DOESN'T IT?
YOU WANT TO EXTRACT INFORMATION FROM TOKINE'S MIND...
...AND USE IT TO ATTACK MORE MYSTICAL SITES. ISN'T THAT IT?
ATTACK... MYSTICAL SITES?
FSSH
ARE YOU...
...ONE OF THE ATTACKERS?

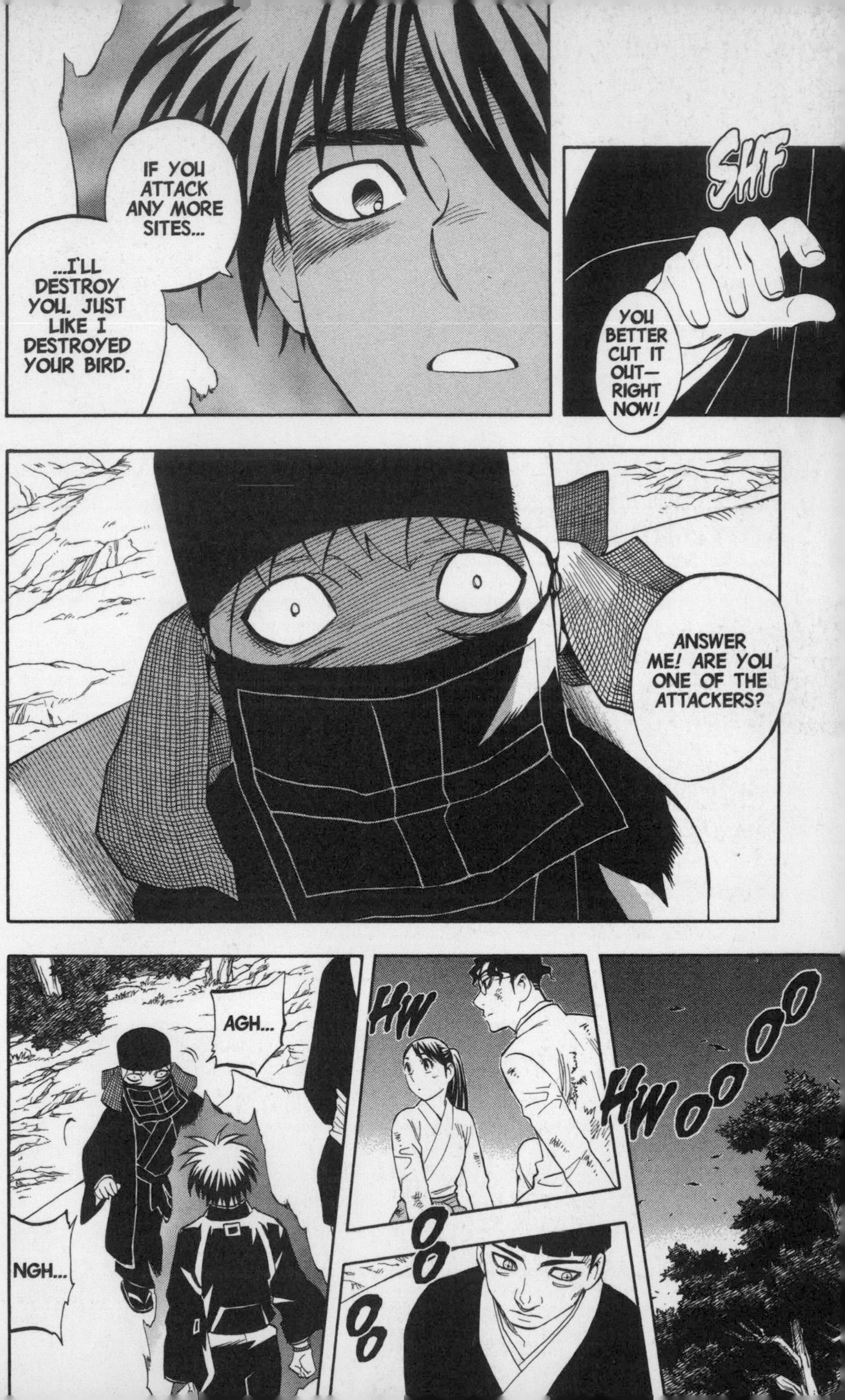
SHF
YOU BETTER CUT IT OUT—RIGHT NOW!
IF YOU ATTACK ANY MORE SITES...
...I'LL DESTROY YOU. JUST LIKE I DESTROYED YOUR BIRD.
ANSWER ME! ARE YOU ONE OF THE ATTACKERS?
HWOOOOOO
HW
OOO
AGH...
NGH...

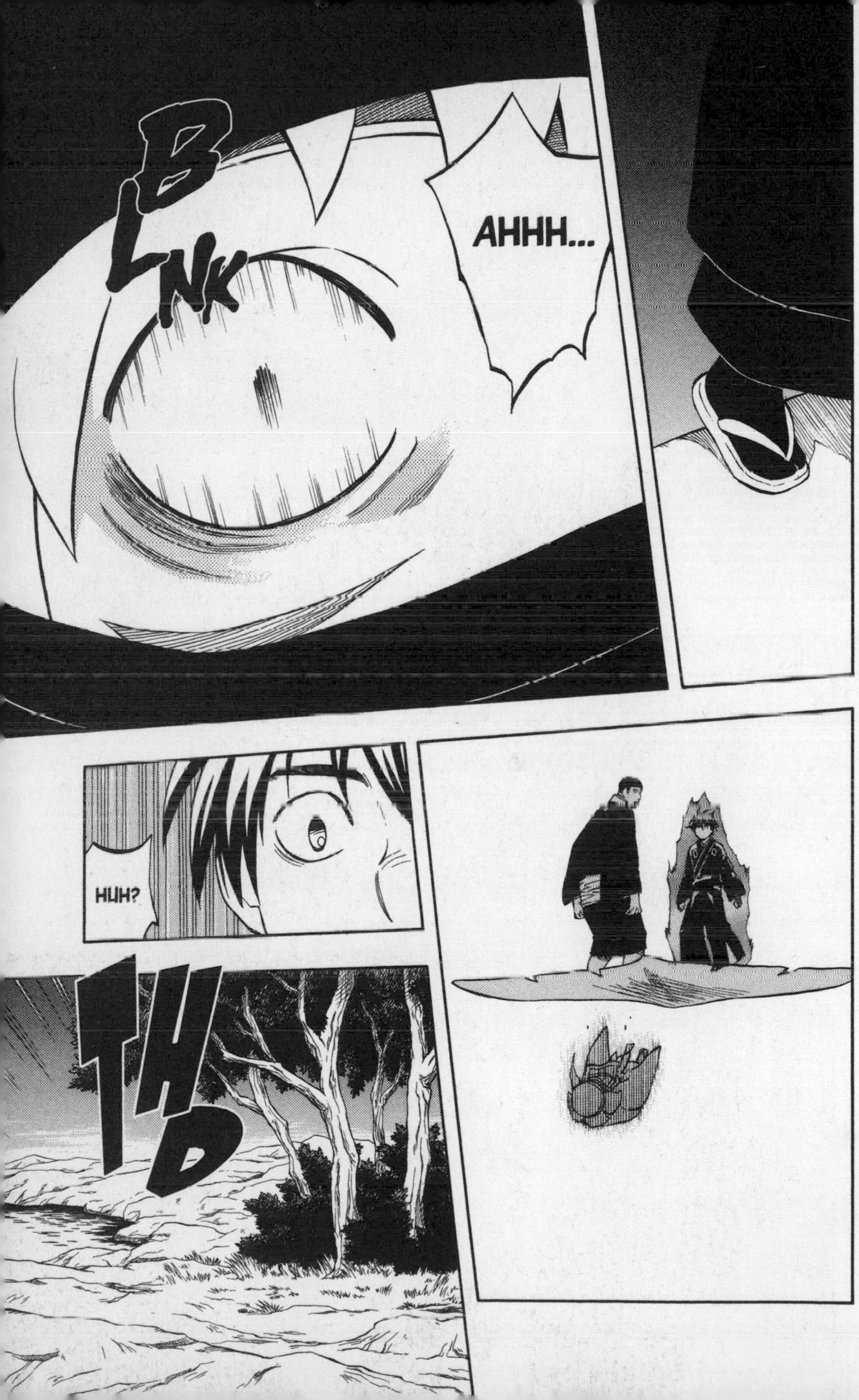
AHHH...
BLNK
HUH?
THD

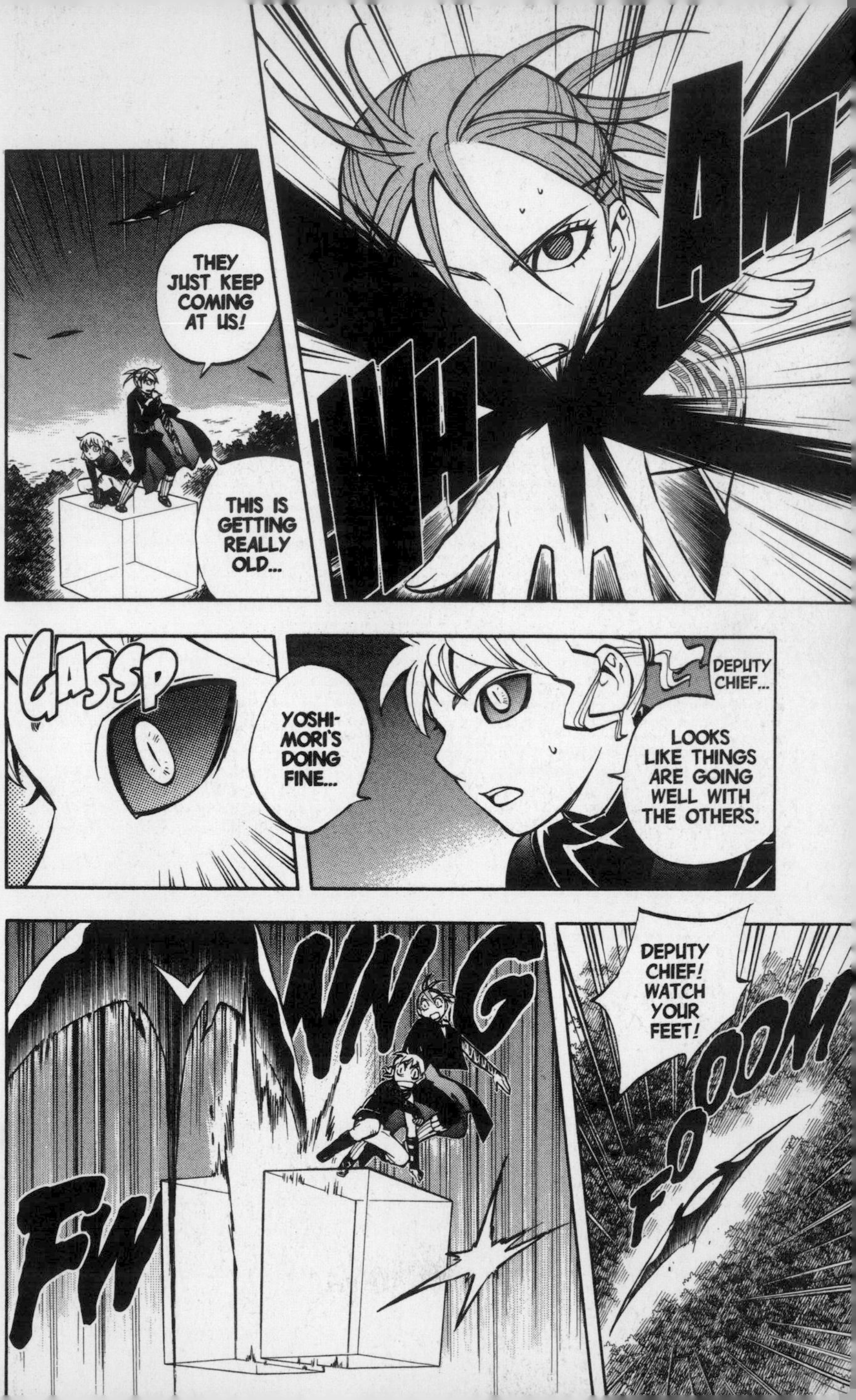
WH
AM
THEY JUST KEEP COMING AT US!
THIS IS GETTING REALLY OLD...
DEPUTY CHIEF...
LOOKS LIKE THINGS ARE GOING WELL WITH THE OTHERS.
YOSHI-MORI'S DOING FINE...
GASSP
DEPUTY CHIEF! WATCH YOUR FEET!
FOOOOM
WNG
FW

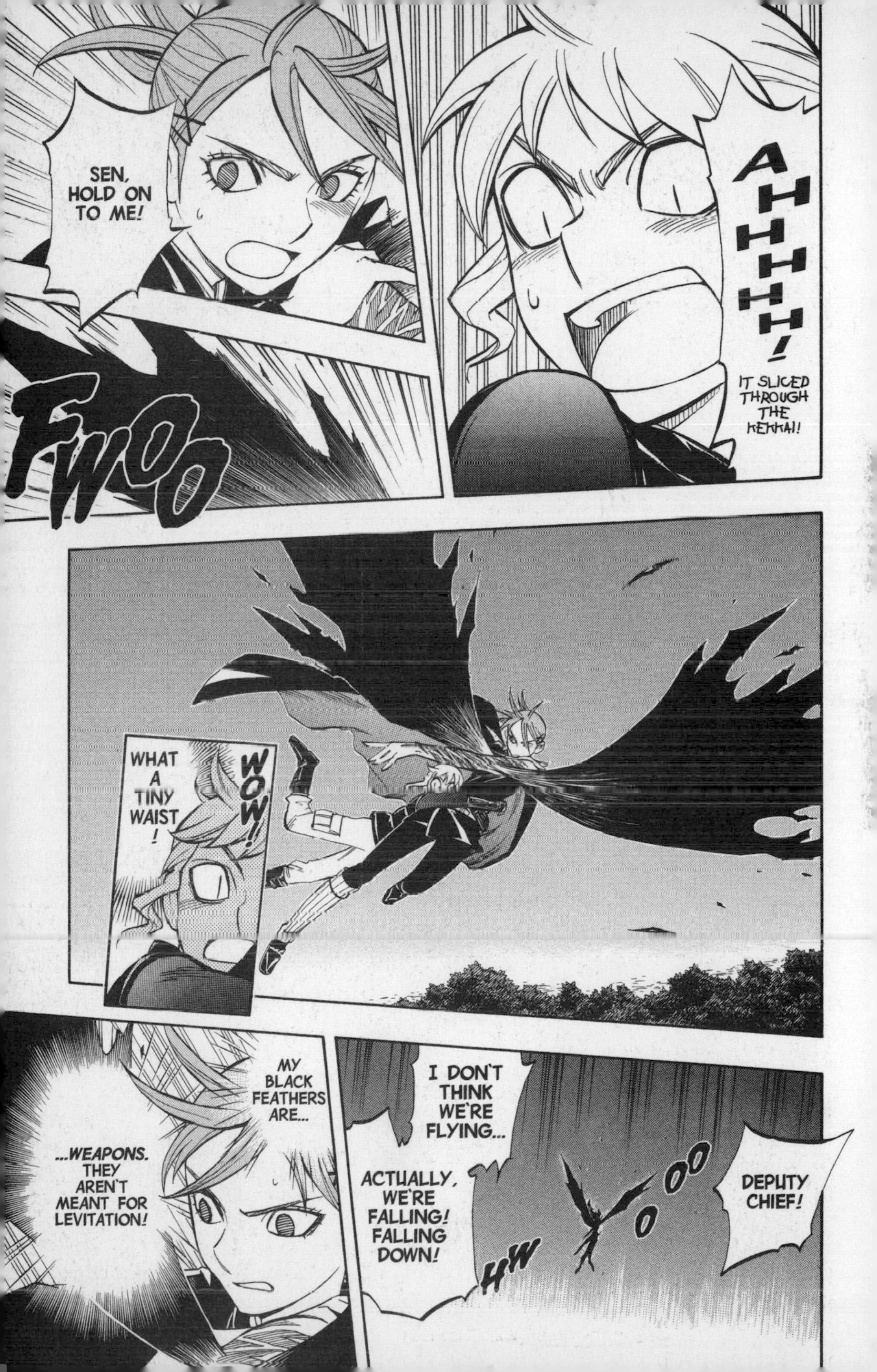
AHHHHH!
IT SLICED THROUGH THE KEKKAI!
SEN, HOLD ON TO ME!
FWOO
WOW!!
WHAT A TINY WAIST!
I DON'T THINK WE'RE FLYING...
DEPUTY CHIEF!
ACTUALLY, WE'RE FALLING! FALLING DOWN!
HWOOO
MY BLACK FEATHERS ARE...
...WEAPONS. THEY AREN'T MEANT FOR LEVITATION!

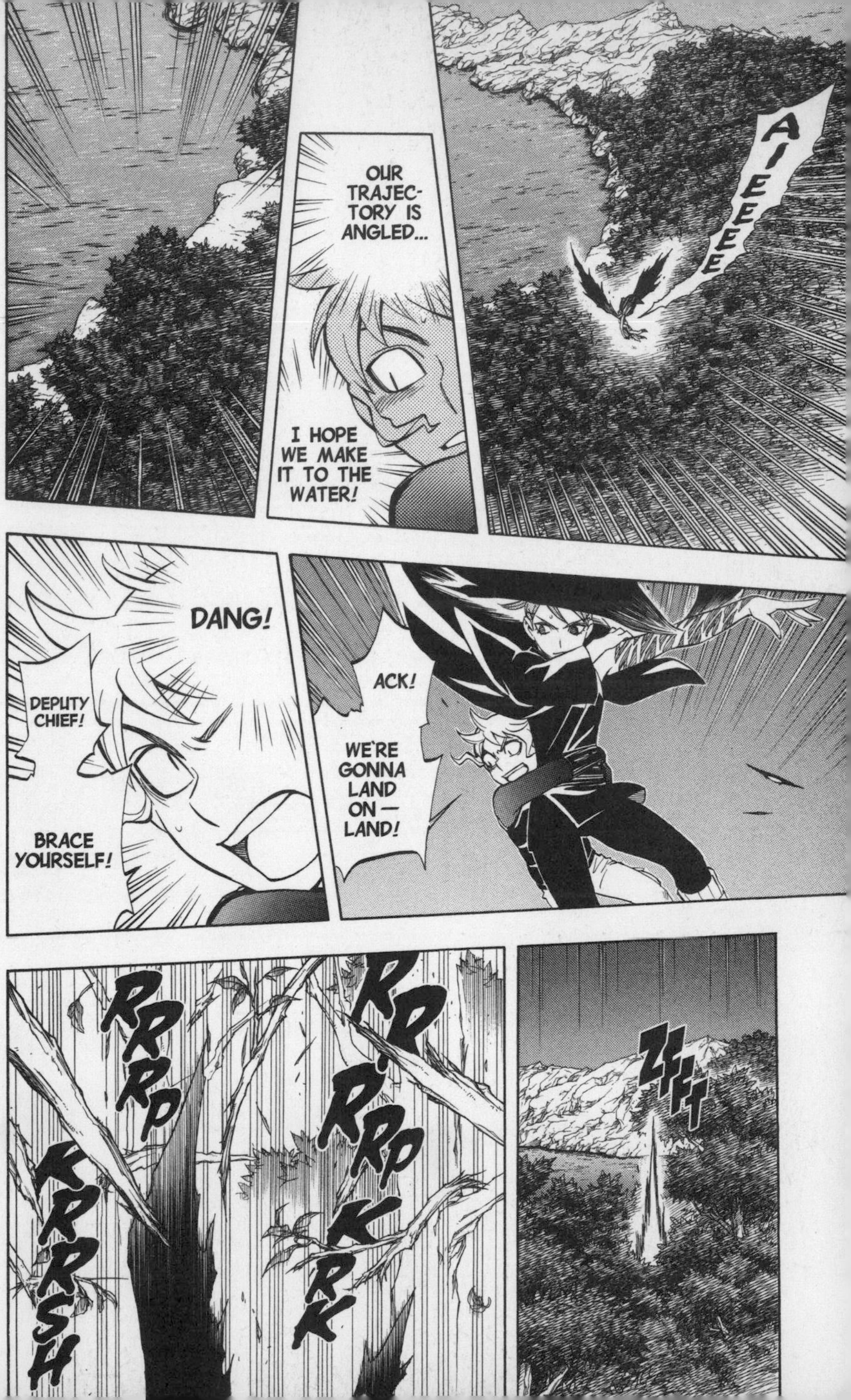
AIEEEEE
OUR TRAJEC-TORY IS ANGLED...
I HOPE WE MAKE IT TO THE WATER!
ACK!
WE'RE GONNA LAND ON—LAND!
DANG!
DEPUTY CHIEF!
BRACE YOURSELF!
ZFFT
RRRRRP
KRKRK
RRRRP
KRRRSH

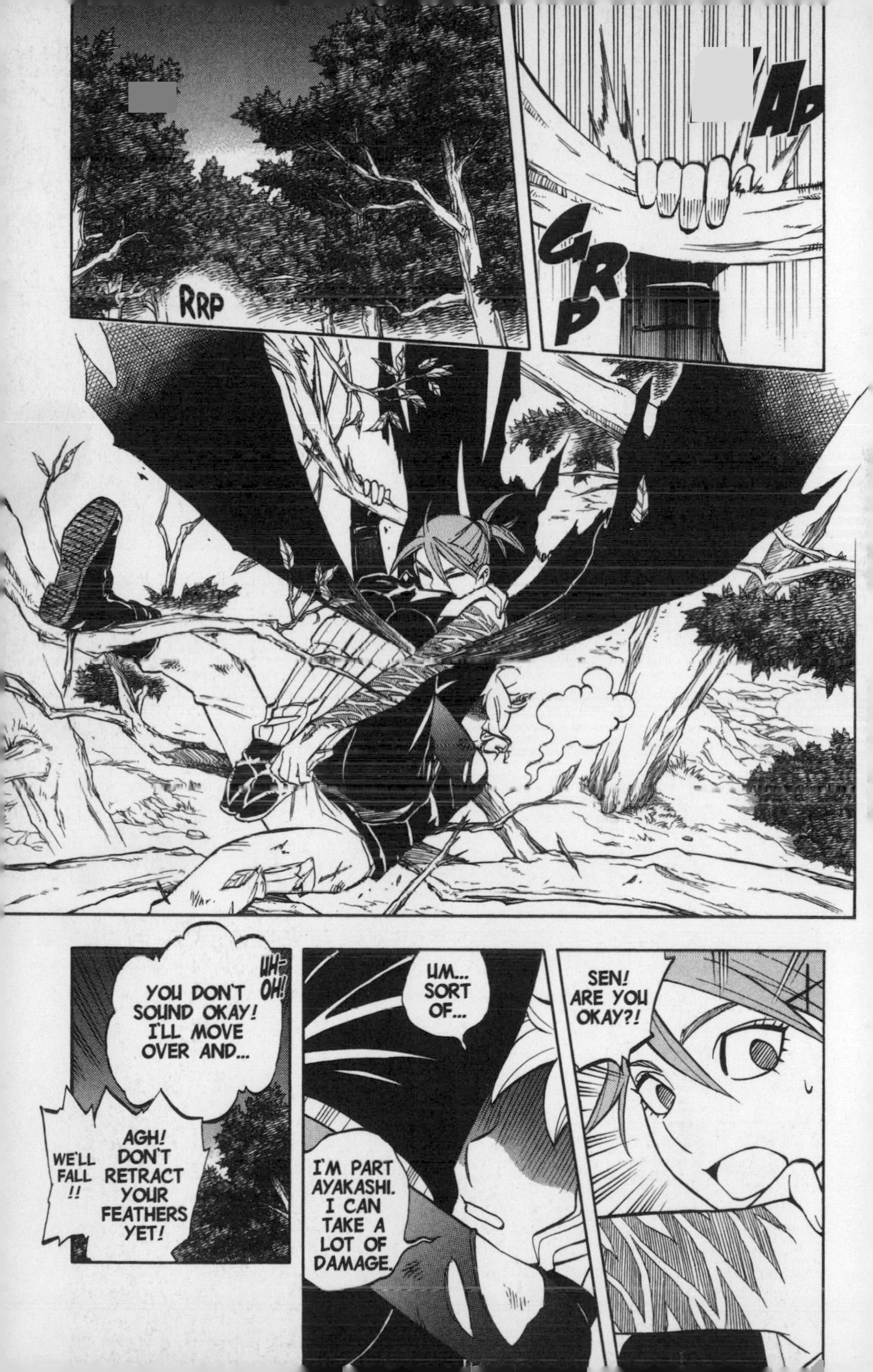
AP
GRP
RRP
SEN! ARE YOU OKAY?!
UM... SORT OF...
I'M PART AYAKASHI. I CAN TAKE A LOT OF DAMAGE.
YOU DON'T SOUND OKAY! I'LL MOVE OVER AND...
UH-OH!
AGH! DON'T RETRACT YOUR FEATHERS YET!
WE'LL FALL !!

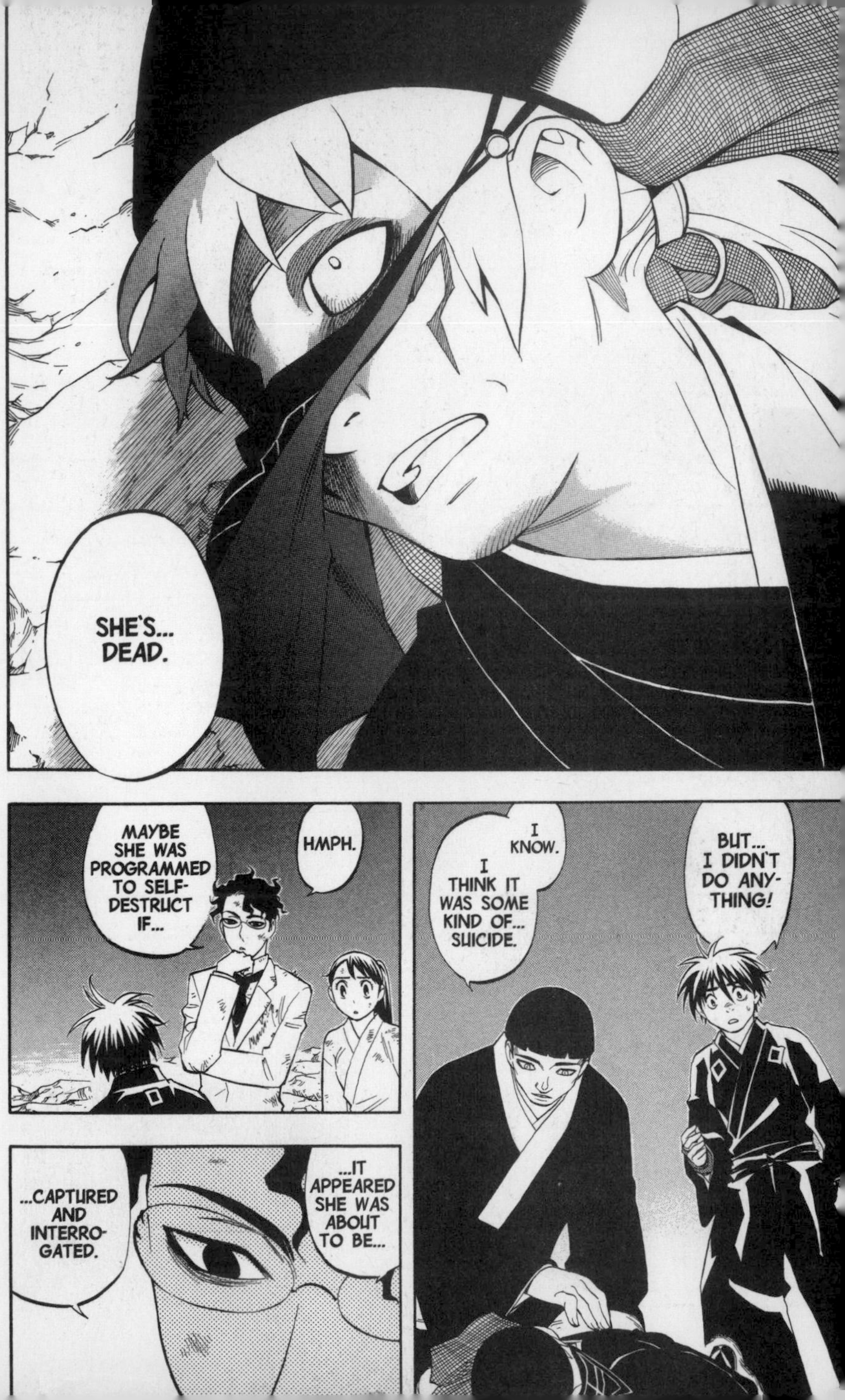
SHE'S... DEAD.
BUT... I DIDN'T DO ANYTHING!
I KNOW.
I THINK IT WAS SOME KIND OF... SUICIDE.
HMPH.
MAYBE SHE WAS PROGRAMMED TO SELF-DESTRUCT IF...
...IT APPEARED SHE WAS ABOUT TO BE...
...CAPTURED AND INTERROGATED.

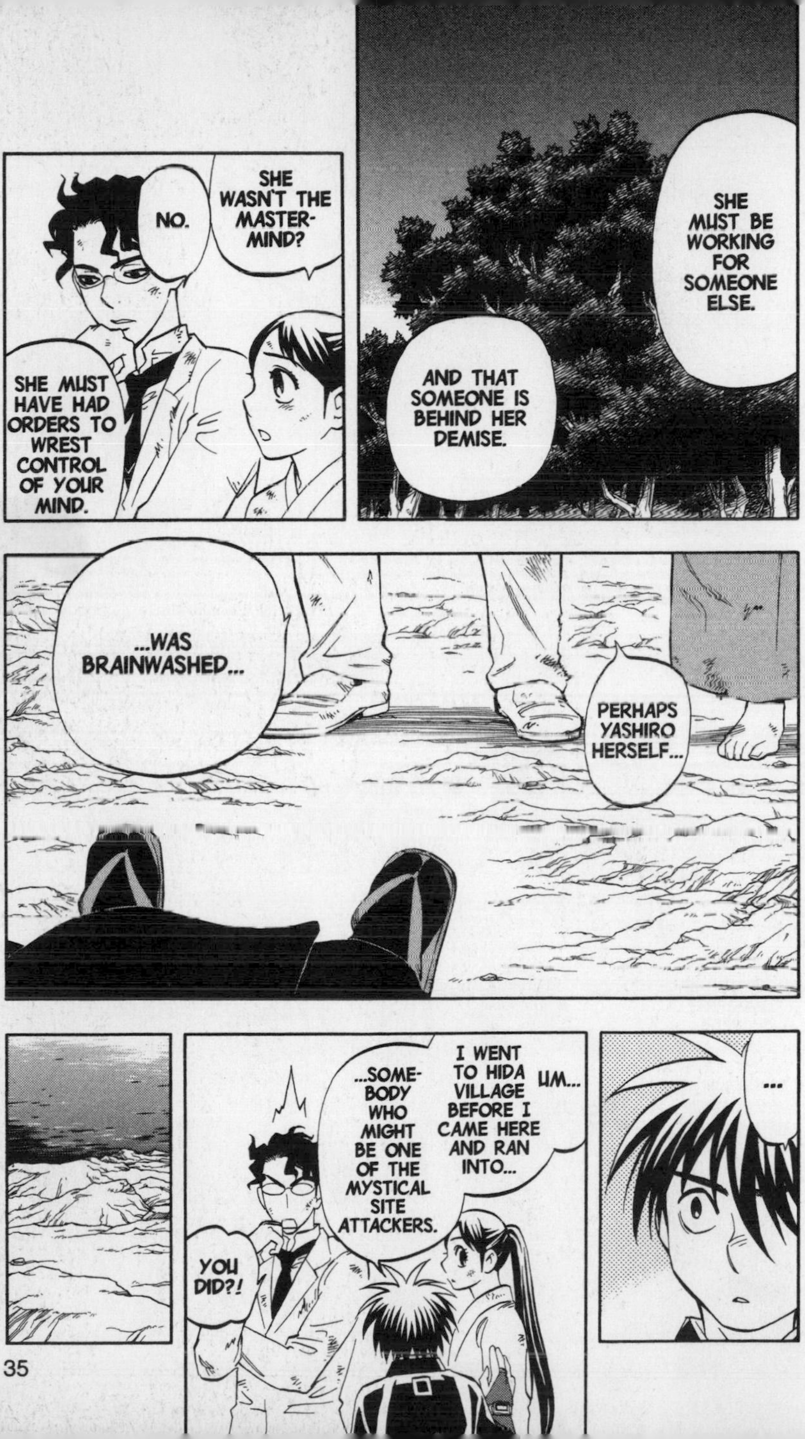
SHE MUST BE WORKING FOR SOMEONE ELSE.
AND THAT SOMEONE IS BEHIND HER DEMISE.
SHE WASN'T THE MASTER-MIND?
NO.
SHE MUST HAVE HAD ORDERS TO WREST CONTROL OF YOUR MIND.
PERHAPS YASHIRO HERSELF...
...WAS BRAINWASHED...
...
UM...
I WENT TO HIDA VILLAGE BEFORE I CAME HERE AND RAN INTO...
...SOME-BODY WHO MIGHT BE ONE OF THE MYSTICAL SITE ATTACKERS.
YOU DID?!

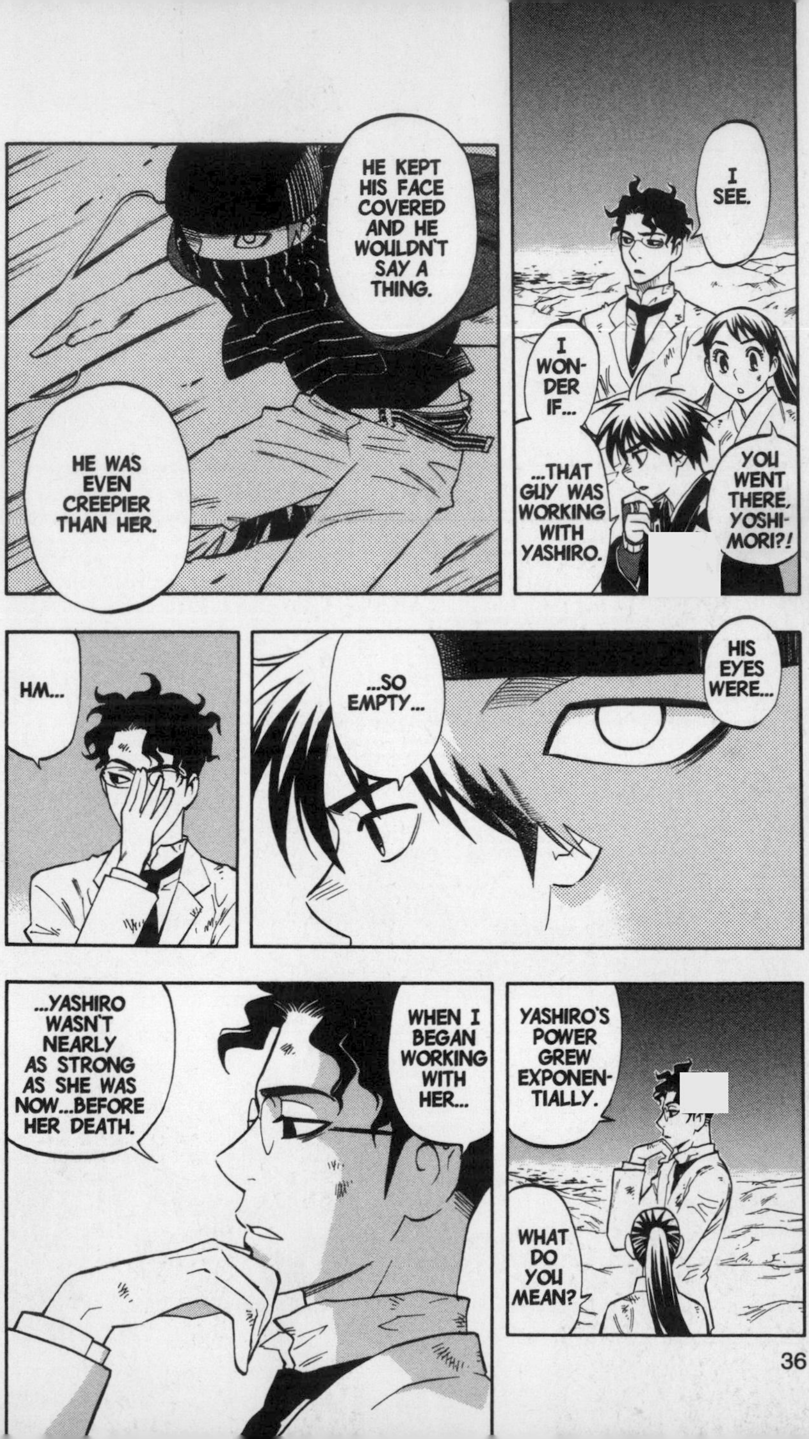
I SEE.
YOU WENT THERE, YOSHIMORI?!
I WONDER IF...
...THAT GUY WAS WORKING WITH YASHIRO.
HE KEPT HIS FACE COVERED AND HE WOULDN'T SAY A THING.
HE WAS EVEN CREEPIER THAN HER.
HIS EYES WERE...
...SO EMPTY...
HM...
YASHIRO'S POWER GREW EXPONENTIALLY.
WHAT DO YOU MEAN?
WHEN I BEGAN WORKING WITH HER...
...YASHIRO WASN'T NEARLY AS STRONG AS SHE WAS NOW...BEFORE HER DEATH.

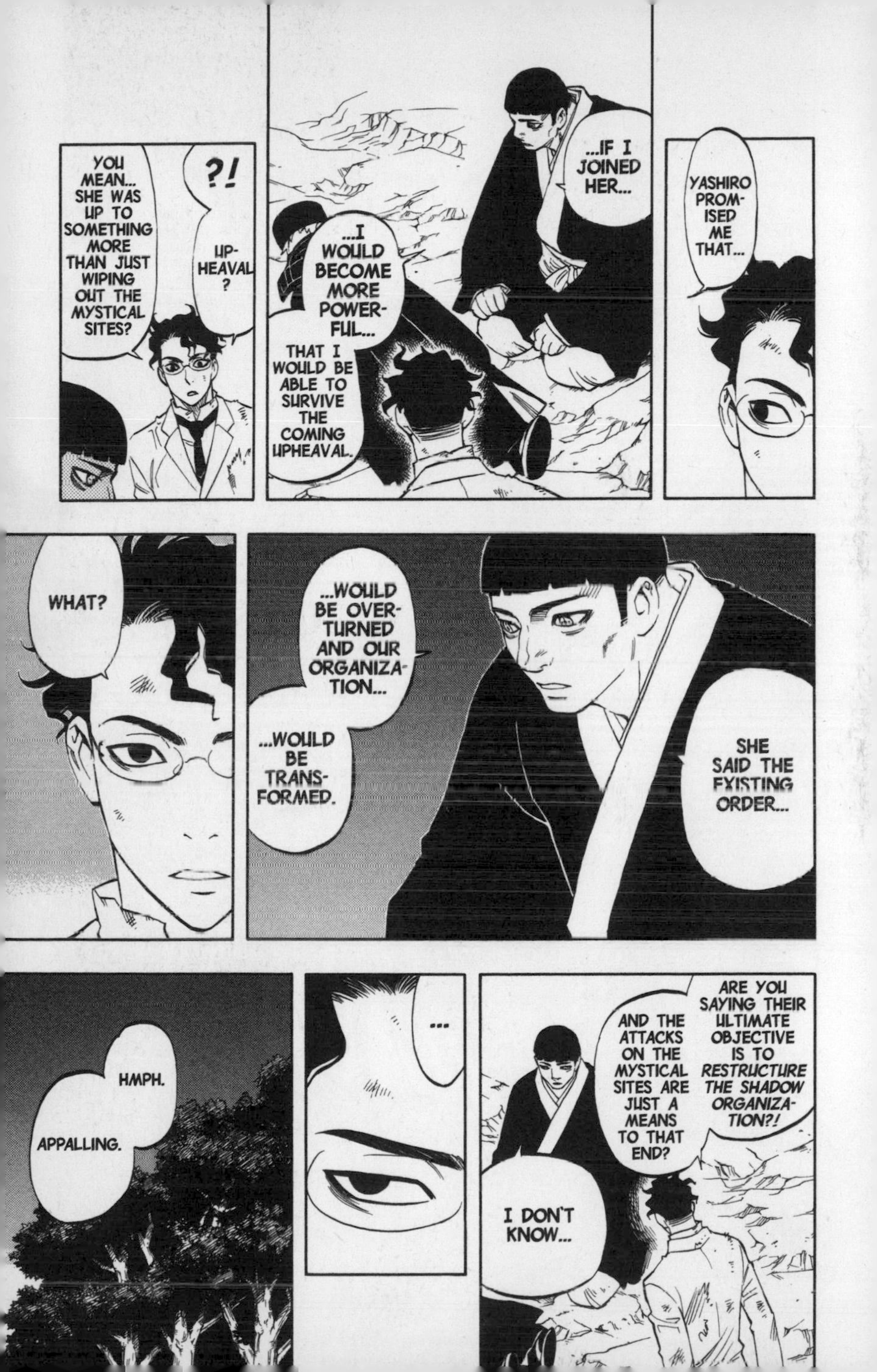
YASHIRO PROMISED ME THAT...
...IF I JOINED HER...
...I WOULD BECOME MORE POWERFUL...
THAT I WOULD BE ABLE TO SURVIVE THE COMING UPHEAVAL.
?!
UPHEAVAL?
YOU MEAN... SHE WAS UP TO SOMETHING MORE THAN JUST WIPING OUT THE MYSTICAL SITES?
SHE SAID THE EXISTING ORDER...
...WOULD BE OVERTURNED AND OUR ORGANIZATION...
...WOULD BE TRANSFORMED.
WHAT?
ARE YOU SAYING THEIR ULTIMATE OBJECTIVE IS TO *RESTRUCTURE THE SHADOW ORGANIZATION?!*
AND THE ATTACKS ON THE MYSTICAL SITES ARE JUST A MEANS TO THAT END?
I DON'T KNOW...
...
HMPH.
APPALLING.

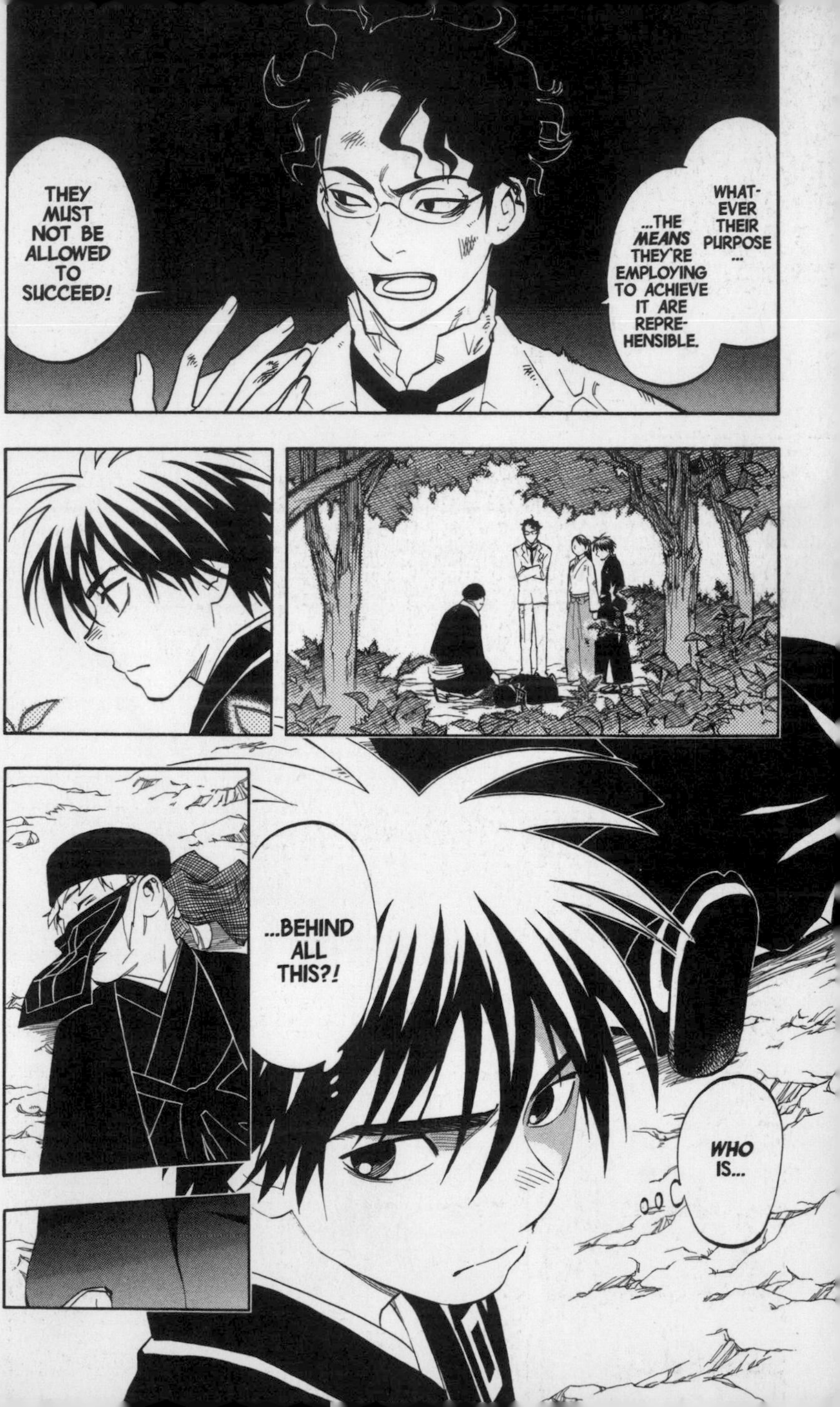
WHAT-EVER THEIR PURPOSE...
...THE *MEANS* THEY'RE EMPLOYING TO ACHIEVE IT ARE REPRE-HENSIBLE.
THEY MUST NOT BE ALLOWED TO SUCCEED!
WHO IS...
...BEHIND ALL THIS?!

RGGL
RGGL
RGGL
TUP

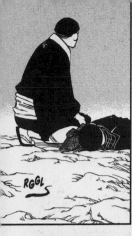

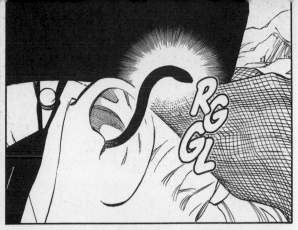

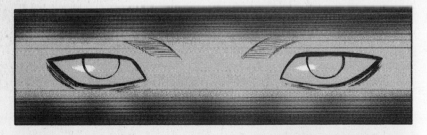

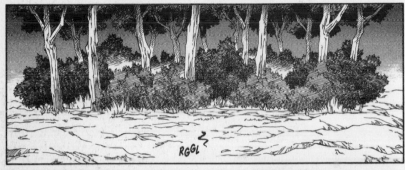

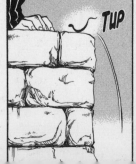

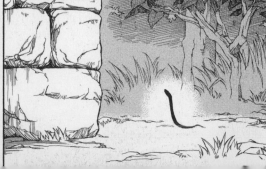

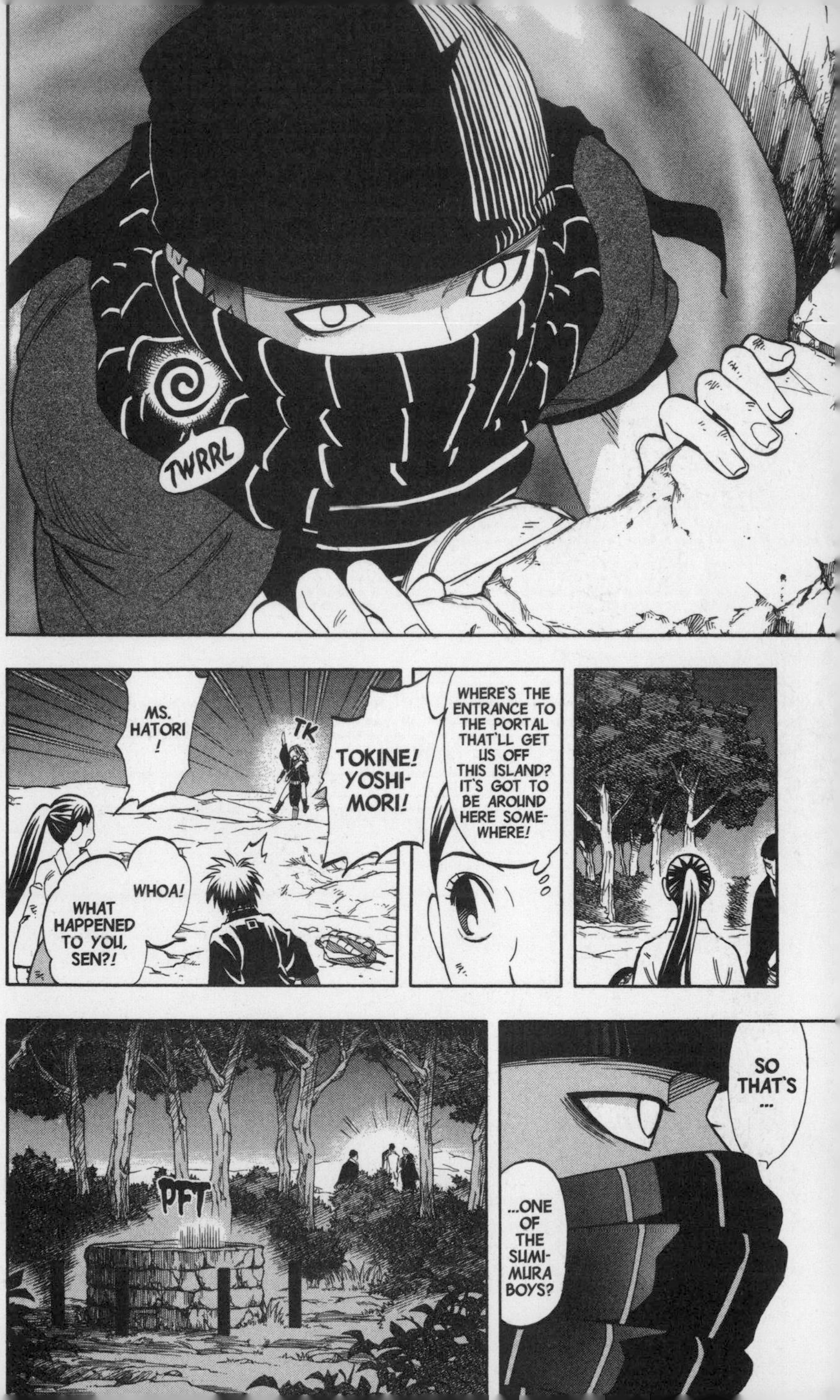
TWRRL
WHERE'S THE ENTRANCE TO THE PORTAL THAT'LL GET US OFF THIS ISLAND? IT'S GOT TO BE AROUND HERE SOMEWHERE!
TK
TOKINE! YOSHIMORI!
MS. HATORI!
WHOA!
WHAT HAPPENED TO YOU, SEN?!
SO THAT'S...
...ONE OF THE SUMIMURA BOYS?
PFT

Chapter 218:

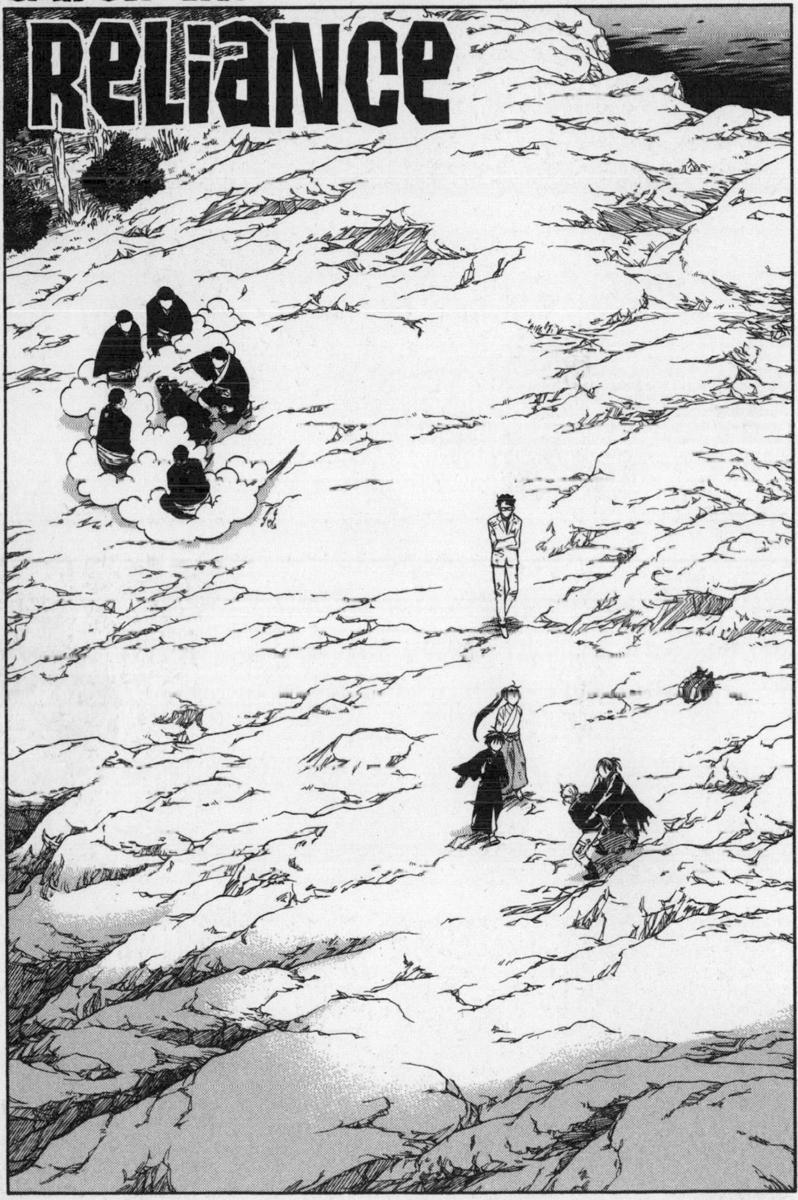
Reliance

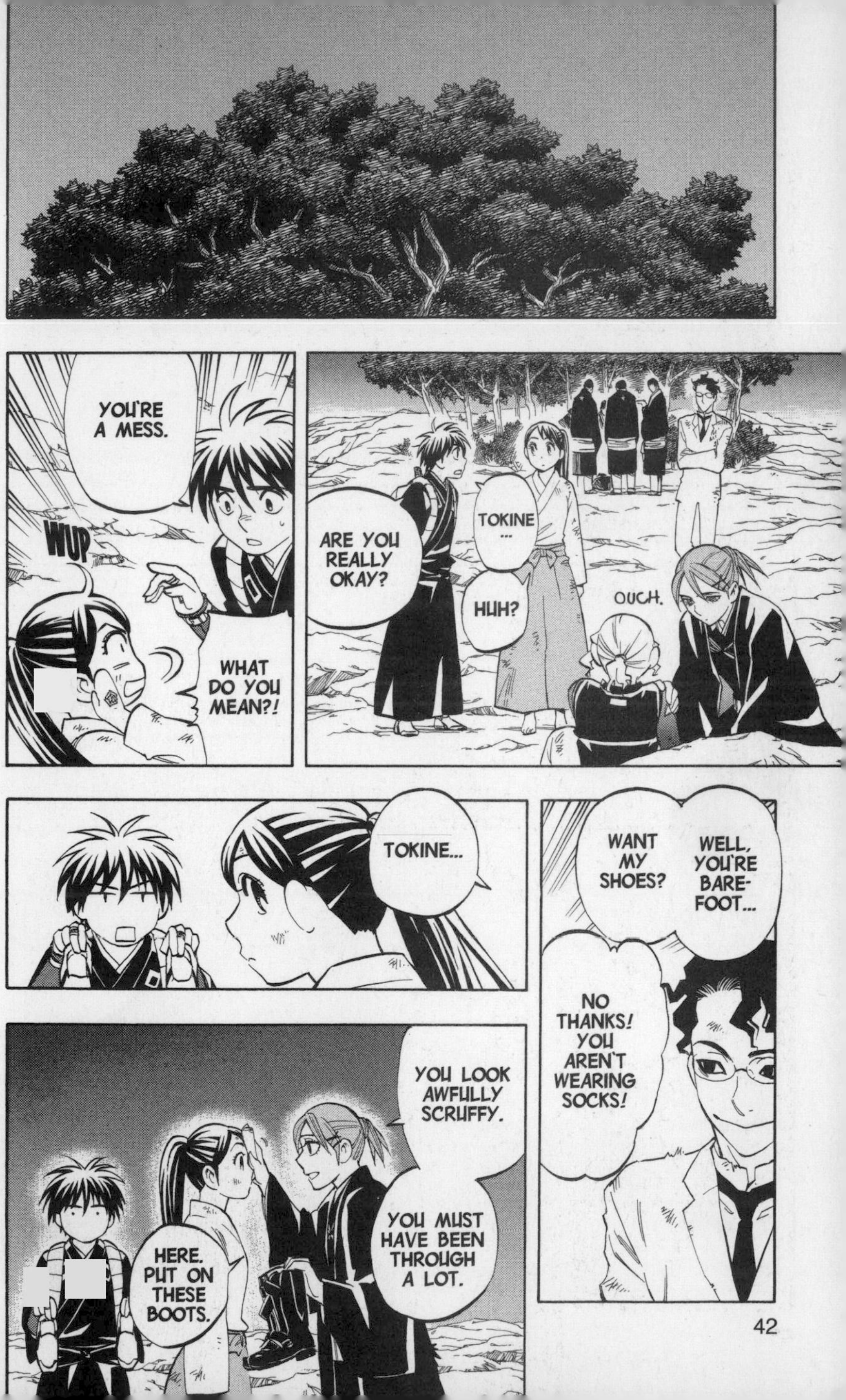
TOKINE...
ARE YOU REALLY OKAY?
HUH?
OUCH.
YOU'RE A MESS.
WUP
WHAT DO YOU MEAN?!
WELL, YOU'RE BARE-FOOT...
WANT MY SHOES?
NO THANKS! YOU AREN'T WEARING SOCKS!
TOKINE...
YOU LOOK AWFULLY SCRUFFY.
YOU MUST HAVE BEEN THROUGH A LOT.
HERE. PUT ON THESE BOOTS.

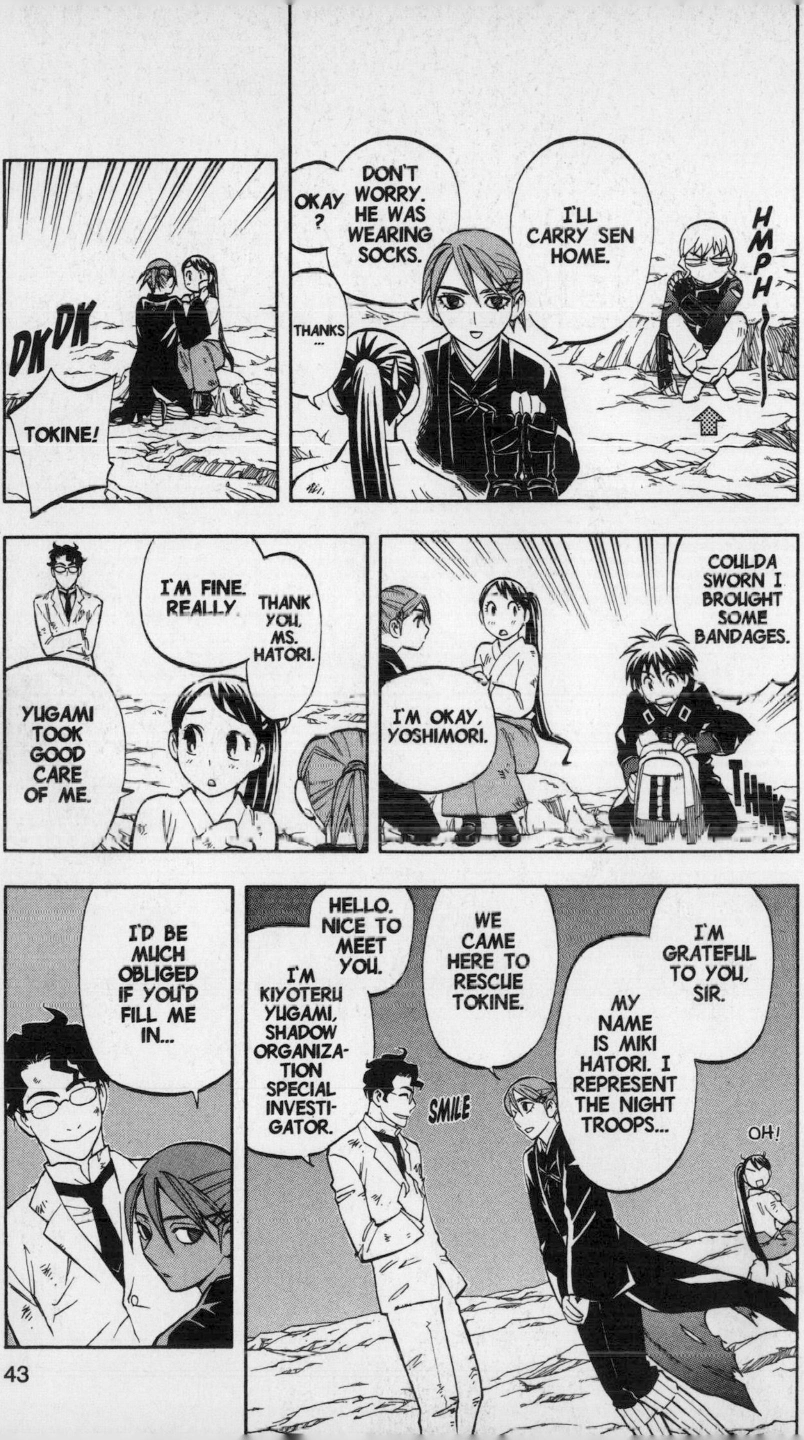
HMPH
I'LL CARRY SEN HOME.
DON'T WORRY. HE WAS WEARING SOCKS.
OKAY?
THANKS...
DK DK
TOKINE!
COULDA SWORN I BROUGHT SOME BANDAGES.
THUNK
I'M OKAY, YOSHIMORI.
THANK YOU, MS. HATORI.
I'M FINE. REALLY.
YUGAMI TOOK GOOD CARE OF ME.
I'M GRATEFUL TO YOU, SIR.
MY NAME IS MIKI HATORI. I REPRESENT THE NIGHT TROOPS...
OH!
WE CAME HERE TO RESCUE TOKINE.
HELLO. NICE TO MEET YOU.
I'M KIYOTERU YUGAMI, SHADOW ORGANIZATION SPECIAL INVESTIGATOR.
SMILE
I'D BE MUCH OBLIGED IF YOU'D FILL ME IN...

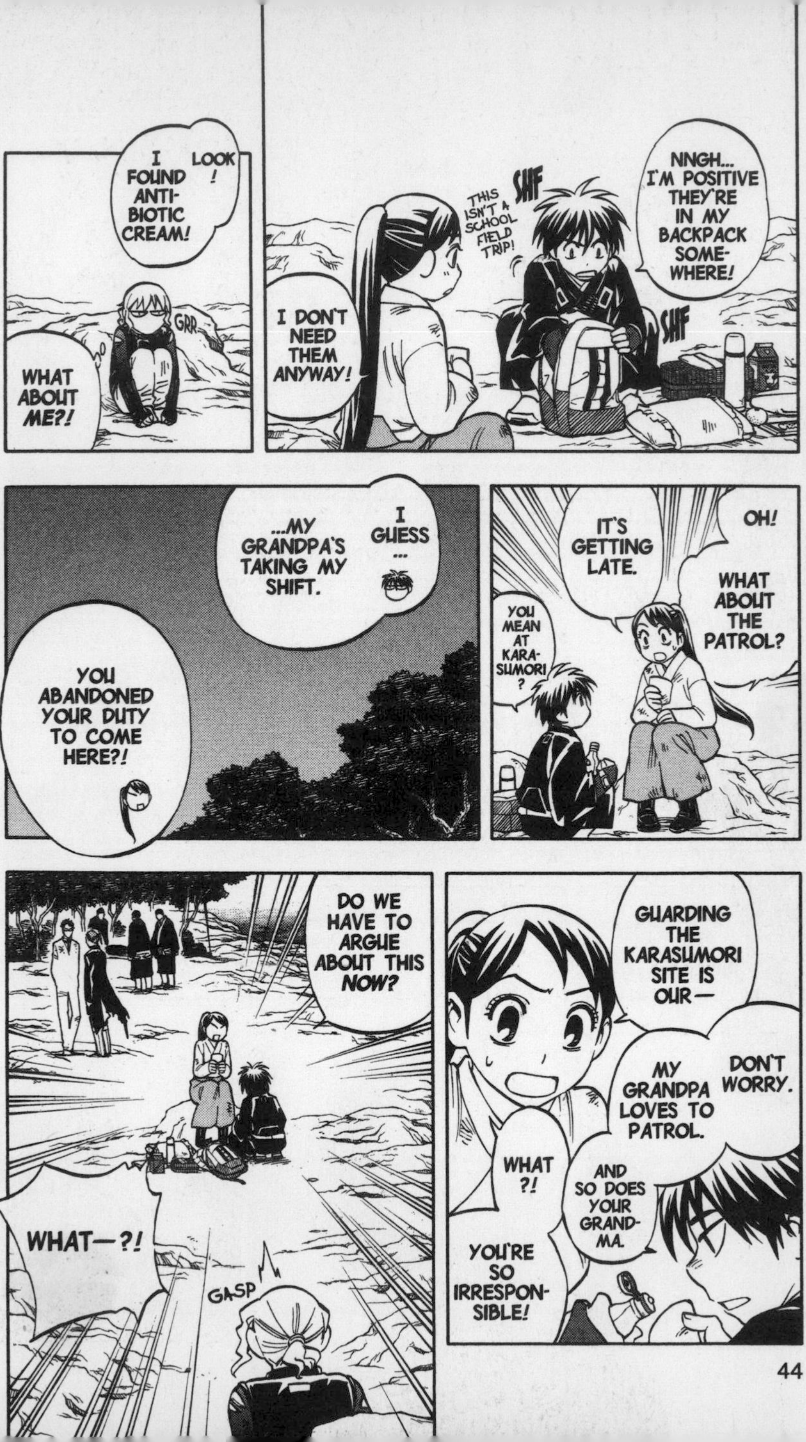
NNGH... I'M POSITIVE THEY'RE IN MY BACKPACK SOMEWHERE!
SHF
THIS ISN'T A SCHOOL FIELD TRIP!
SHF
I DON'T NEED THEM ANYWAY!
LOOK! I FOUND ANTI-BIOTIC CREAM!
GRR
WHAT ABOUT ME?!
OH! WHAT ABOUT THE PATROL?
IT'S GETTING LATE.
YOU MEAN AT KARASUMORI?
I GUESS... ...MY GRANDPA'S TAKING MY SHIFT.
YOU ABANDONED YOUR DUTY TO COME HERE?!
GUARDING THE KARASUMORI SITE IS OUR—
DON'T WORRY. MY GRANDPA LOVES TO PATROL.
AND SO DOES YOUR GRANDMA.
WHAT?!
YOU'RE SO IRRESPONSIBLE!
DO WE HAVE TO ARGUE ABOUT THIS NOW?
WHAT—?!
GASP

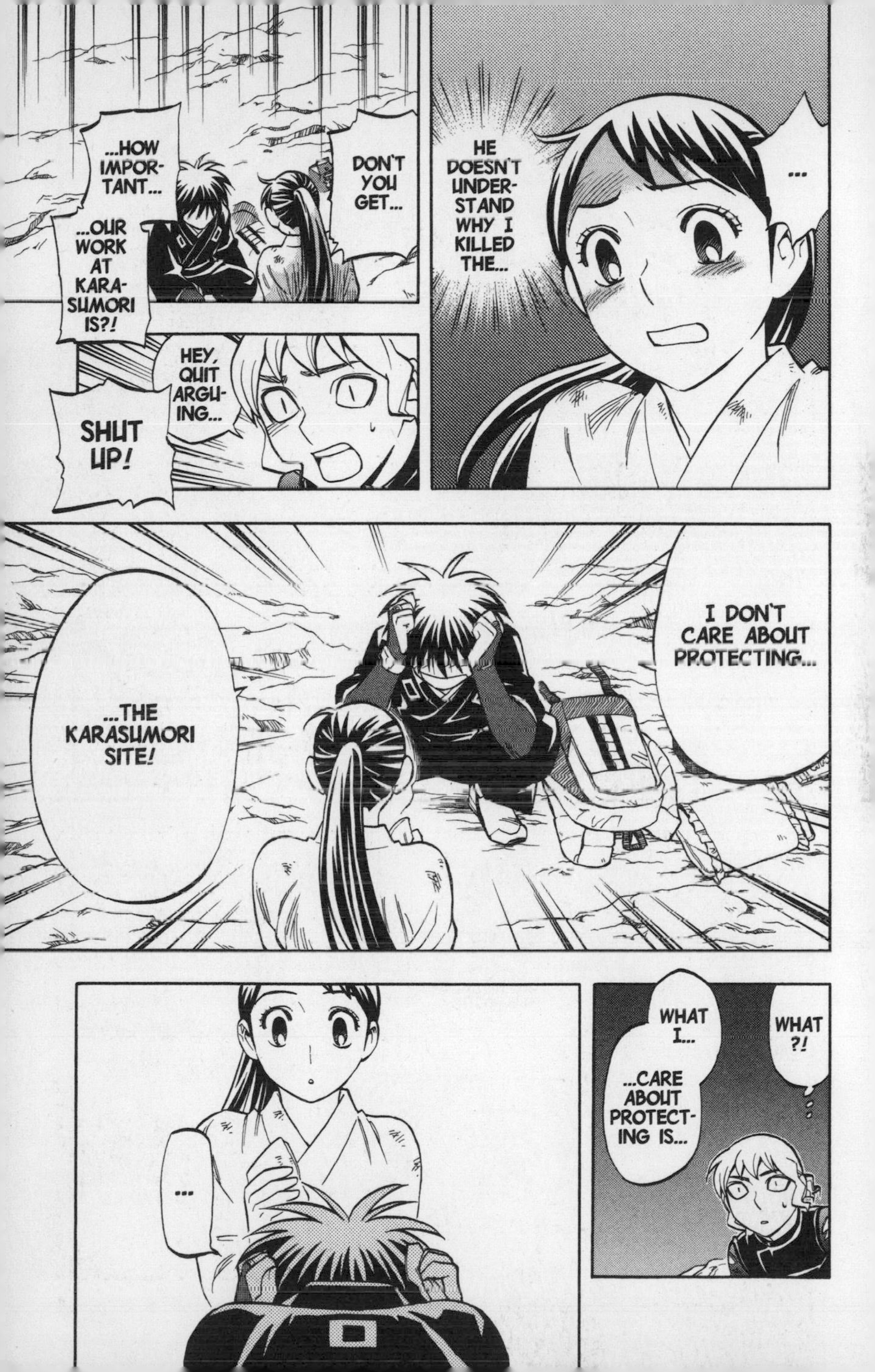
...
HE DOESN'T UNDERSTAND WHY I KILLED THE...
DON'T YOU GET...
...HOW IMPORTANT...
...OUR WORK AT KARASUMORI IS?!
HEY, QUIT ARGUING...
SHUT UP!
I DON'T CARE ABOUT PROTECTING...
...THE KARASUMORI SITE!
WHAT?!
WHAT I...
...CARE ABOUT PROTECTING IS...
...

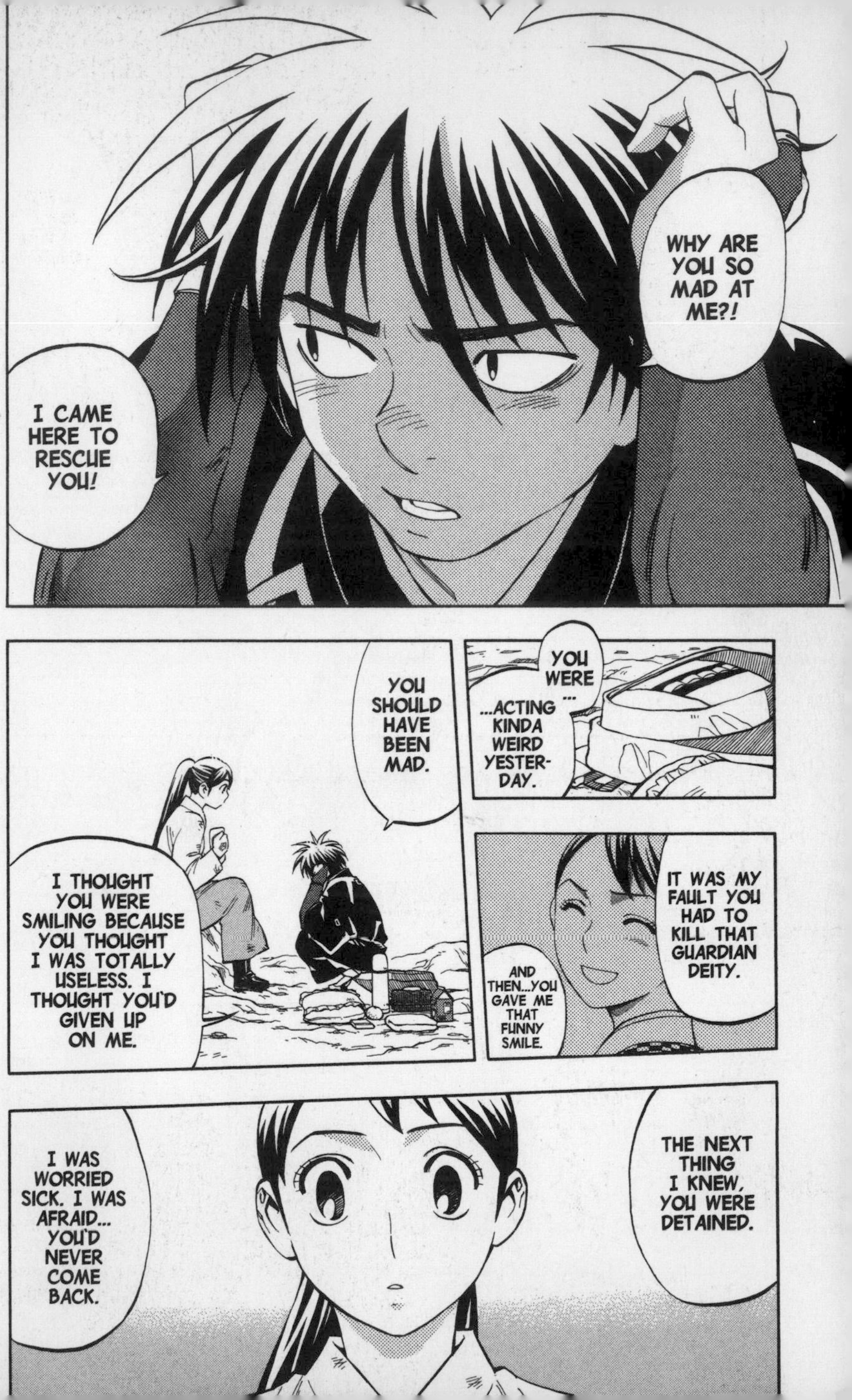
WHY ARE YOU SO MAD AT ME?!
I CAME HERE TO RESCUE YOU!
YOU WERE...
...ACTING KINDA WEIRD YESTERDAY.
IT WAS MY FAULT YOU HAD TO KILL THAT GUARDIAN DEITY.
AND THEN...YOU GAVE ME THAT FUNNY SMILE.
YOU SHOULD HAVE BEEN MAD.
I THOUGHT YOU WERE SMILING BECAUSE YOU THOUGHT I WAS TOTALLY USELESS. I THOUGHT YOU'D GIVEN UP ON ME.
THE NEXT THING I KNEW, YOU WERE DETAINED.
I WAS WORRIED SICK. I WAS AFRAID... YOU'D NEVER COME BACK.

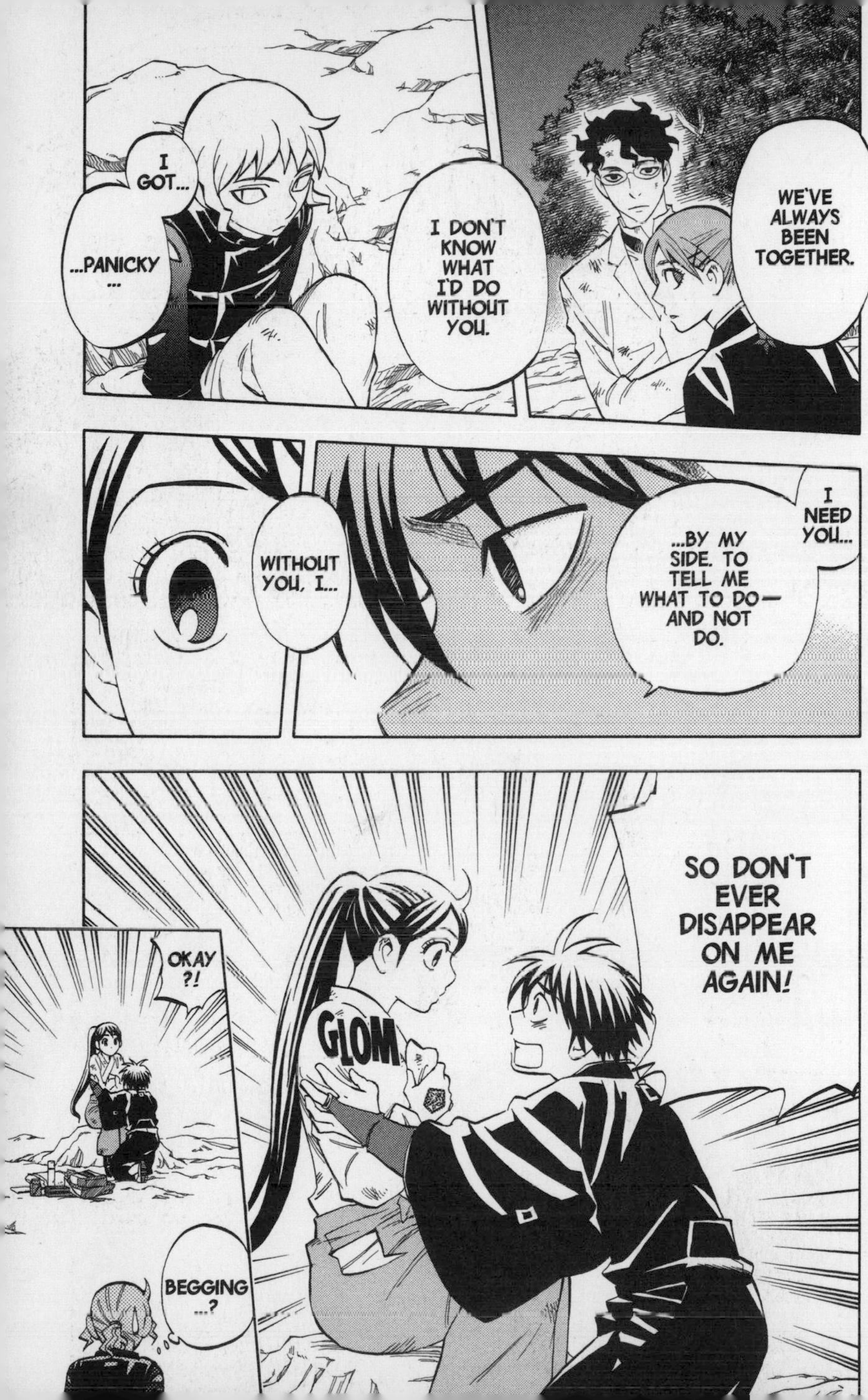
WE'VE ALWAYS BEEN TOGETHER.
I DON'T KNOW WHAT I'D DO WITHOUT YOU.
I GOT...
...PANICKY...
I NEED YOU...
...BY MY SIDE. TO TELL ME WHAT TO DO— AND NOT DO.
WITHOUT YOU, I...
SO DON'T EVER DISAPPEAR ON ME AGAIN!
GLOM
OKAY?!
BEGGING...?

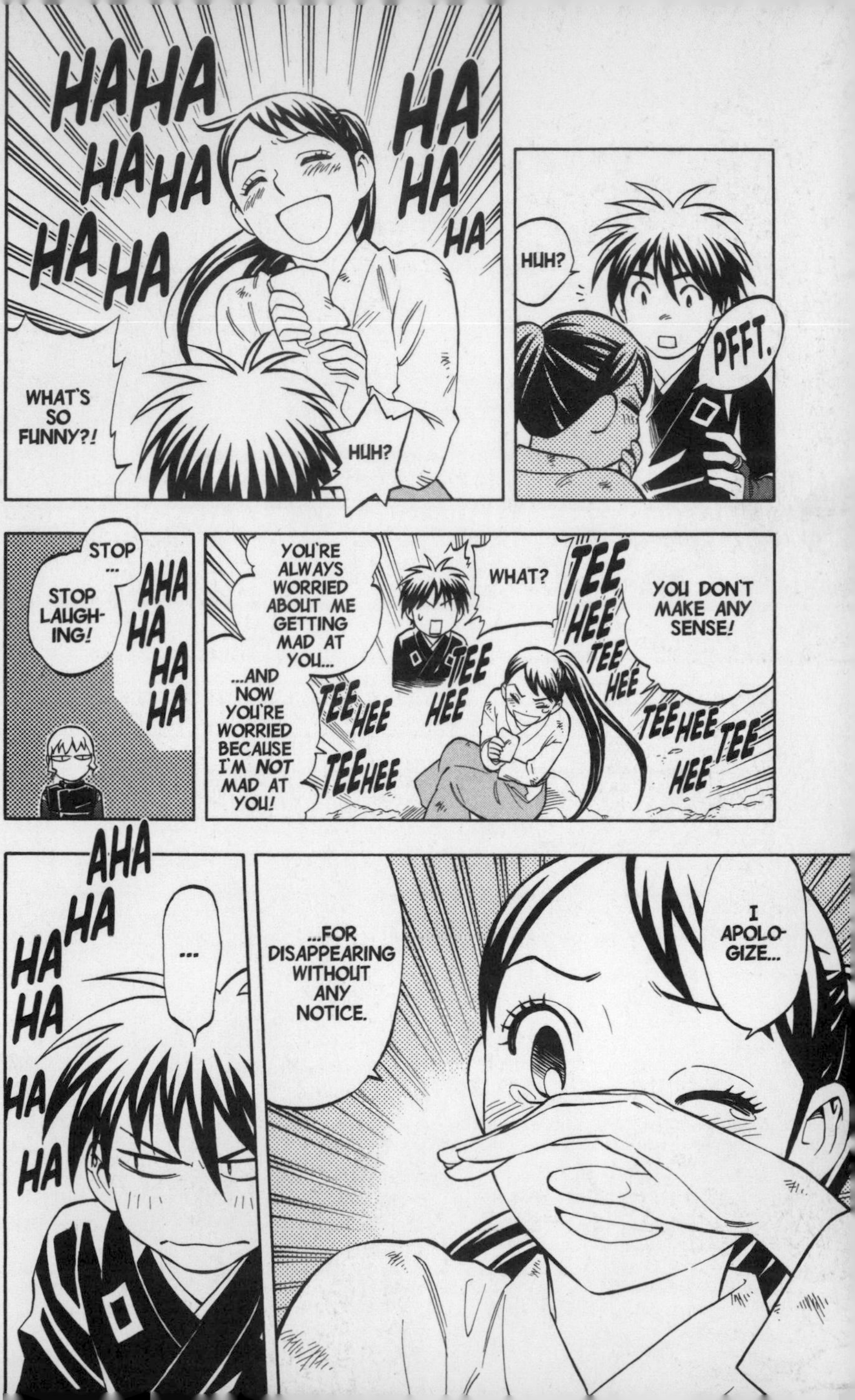
HUH?
PFFT.
HAHA HA HA HA HA
HA HA HA
WHAT'S SO FUNNY?!
HUH?
YOU DON'T MAKE ANY SENSE!
TEE HEE TEE HEE
TEE HEE TEE HEE
WHAT?
YOU'RE ALWAYS WORRIED ABOUT ME GETTING MAD AT YOU...
TEE HEE
...AND NOW YOU'RE WORRIED BECAUSE I'M NOT MAD AT YOU!
TEE HEE TEE HEE
STOP... STOP LAUGHING!
AHA HA HA HA HA
I APOLOGIZE...
...FOR DISAPPEARING WITHOUT ANY NOTICE.
...
AHA HA HA HA HA HA

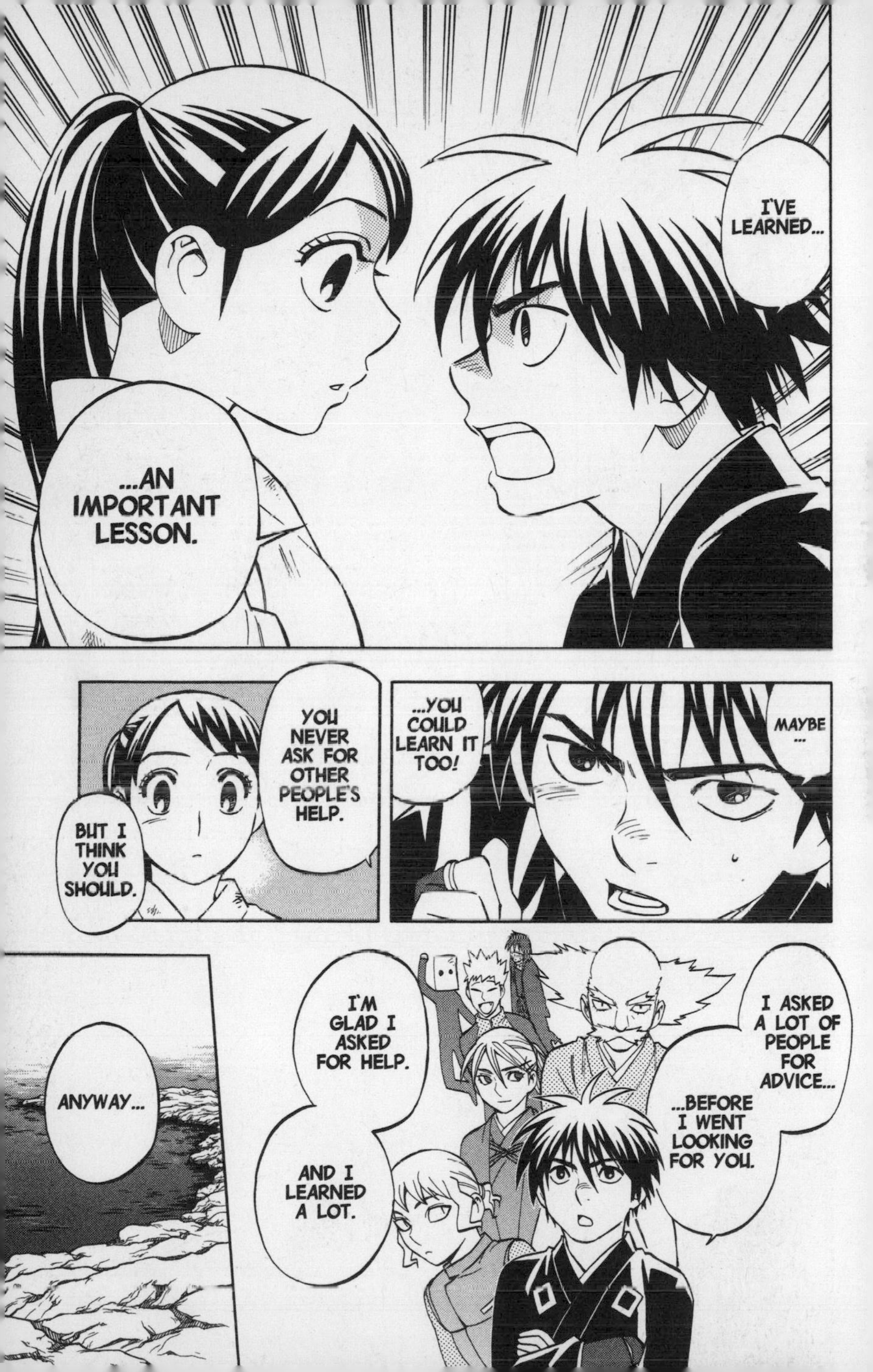
I'VE LEARNED...
...AN IMPORTANT LESSON.
MAYBE ...
...YOU COULD LEARN IT TOO!
YOU NEVER ASK FOR OTHER PEOPLE'S HELP.
BUT I THINK YOU SHOULD.
I ASKED A LOT OF PEOPLE FOR ADVICE...
...BEFORE I WENT LOOKING FOR YOU.
I'M GLAD I ASKED FOR HELP.
AND I LEARNED A LOT.
ANYWAY...

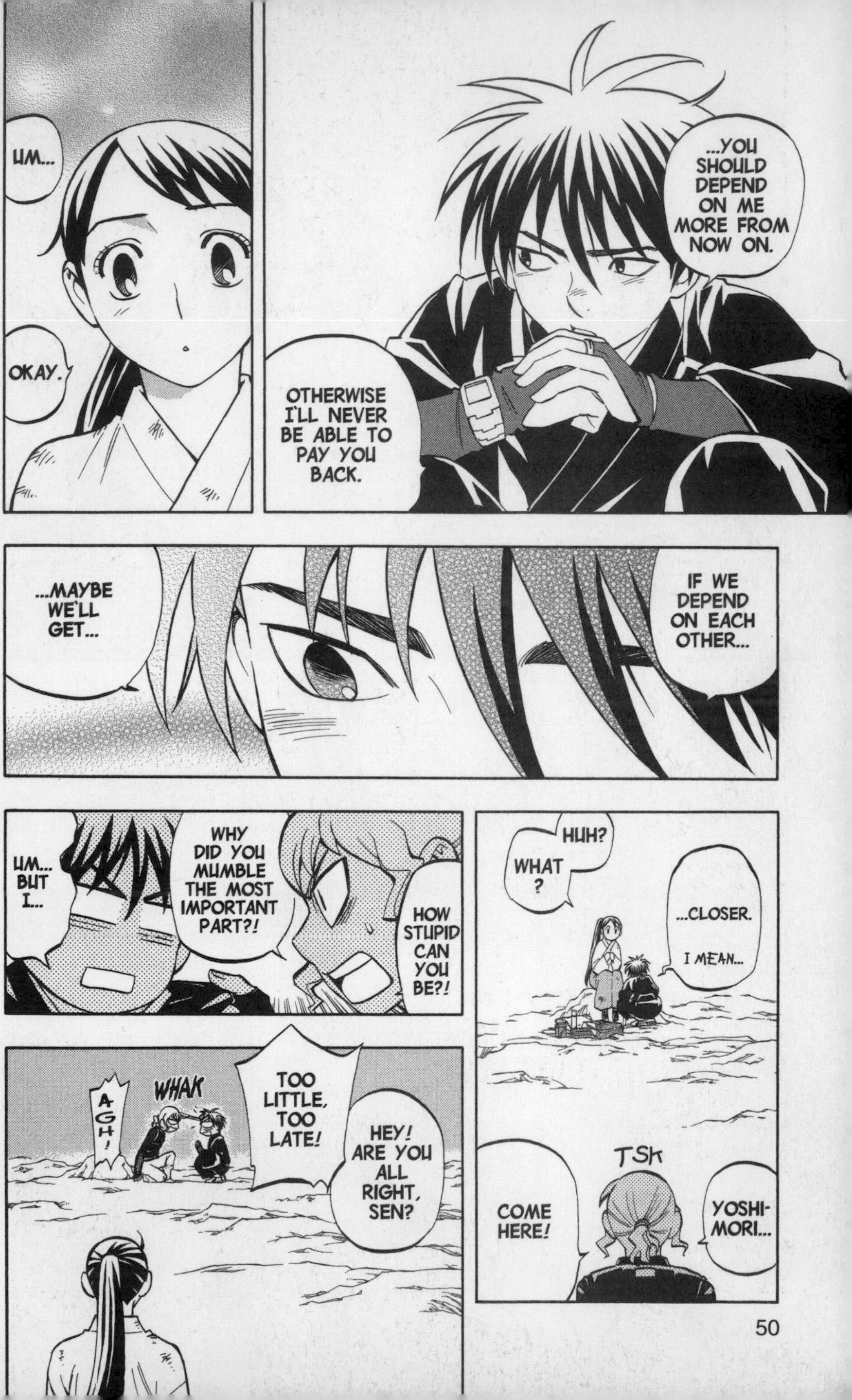
...YOU SHOULD DEPEND ON ME MORE FROM NOW ON.
OTHERWISE I'LL NEVER BE ABLE TO PAY YOU BACK.
UM...
OKAY.
IF WE DEPEND ON EACH OTHER...
...MAYBE WE'LL GET...
HUH?
WHAT?
...CLOSER.
I MEAN...
YOSHIMORI...
TSK
COME HERE!
HOW STUPID CAN YOU BE?!
WHY DID YOU MUMBLE THE MOST IMPORTANT PART?!
UM... BUT I...
TOO LITTLE, TOO LATE!
WHAK
AGH!
HEY! ARE YOU ALL RIGHT, SEN?

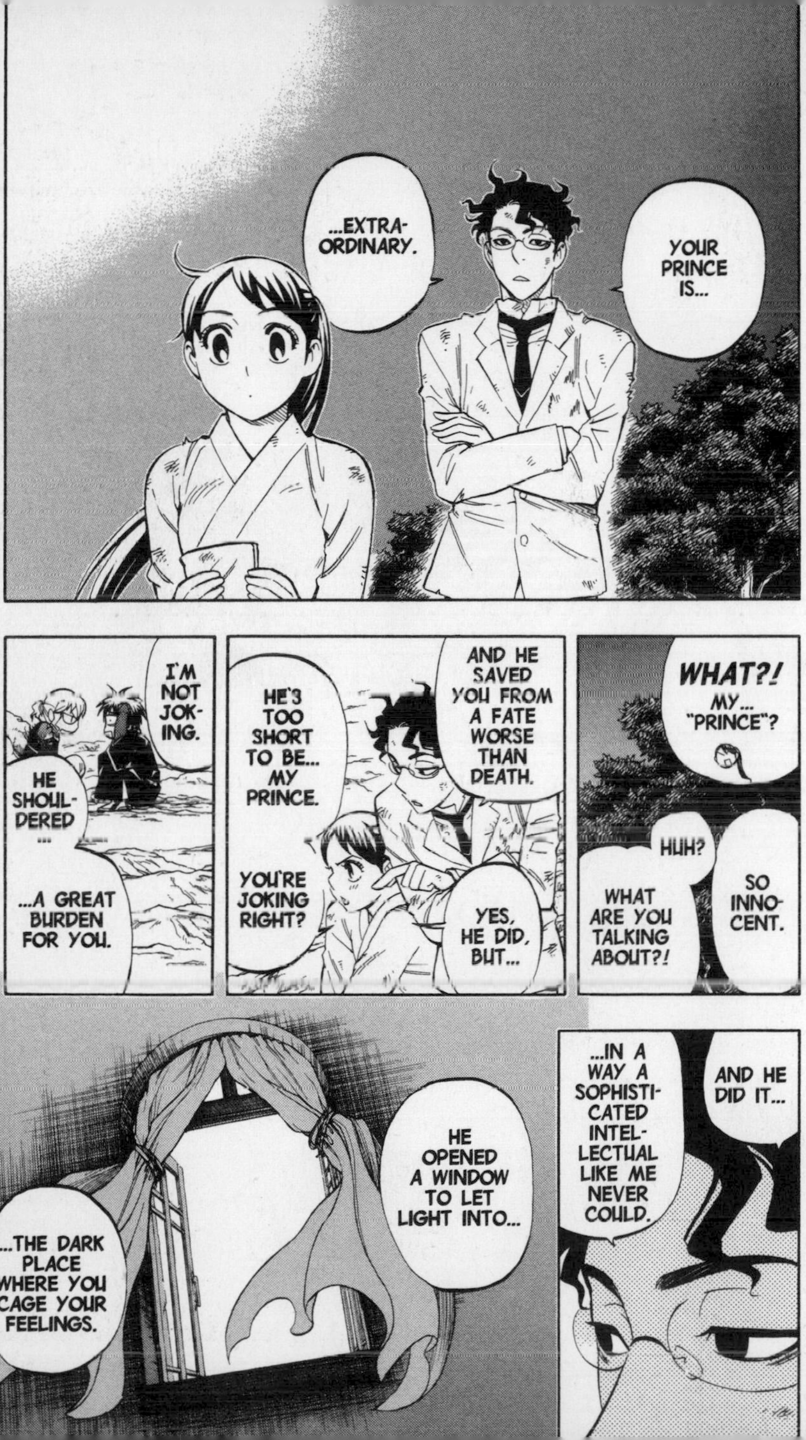
YOUR PRINCE IS...
...EXTRA-ORDINARY.
WHAT?! MY... "PRINCE"?
SO INNOCENT.
HUH?
WHAT ARE YOU TALKING ABOUT?!
AND HE SAVED YOU FROM A FATE WORSE THAN DEATH.
YES, HE DID, BUT...
HE'S TOO SHORT TO BE... MY PRINCE.
YOU'RE JOKING RIGHT?
I'M NOT JOKING.
HE SHOULDERED...
...A GREAT BURDEN FOR YOU.
AND HE DID IT...
...IN A WAY A SOPHISTICATED INTELLECTUAL LIKE ME NEVER COULD.
HE OPENED A WINDOW TO LET LIGHT INTO...
...THE DARK PLACE WHERE YOU CAGE YOUR FEELINGS.

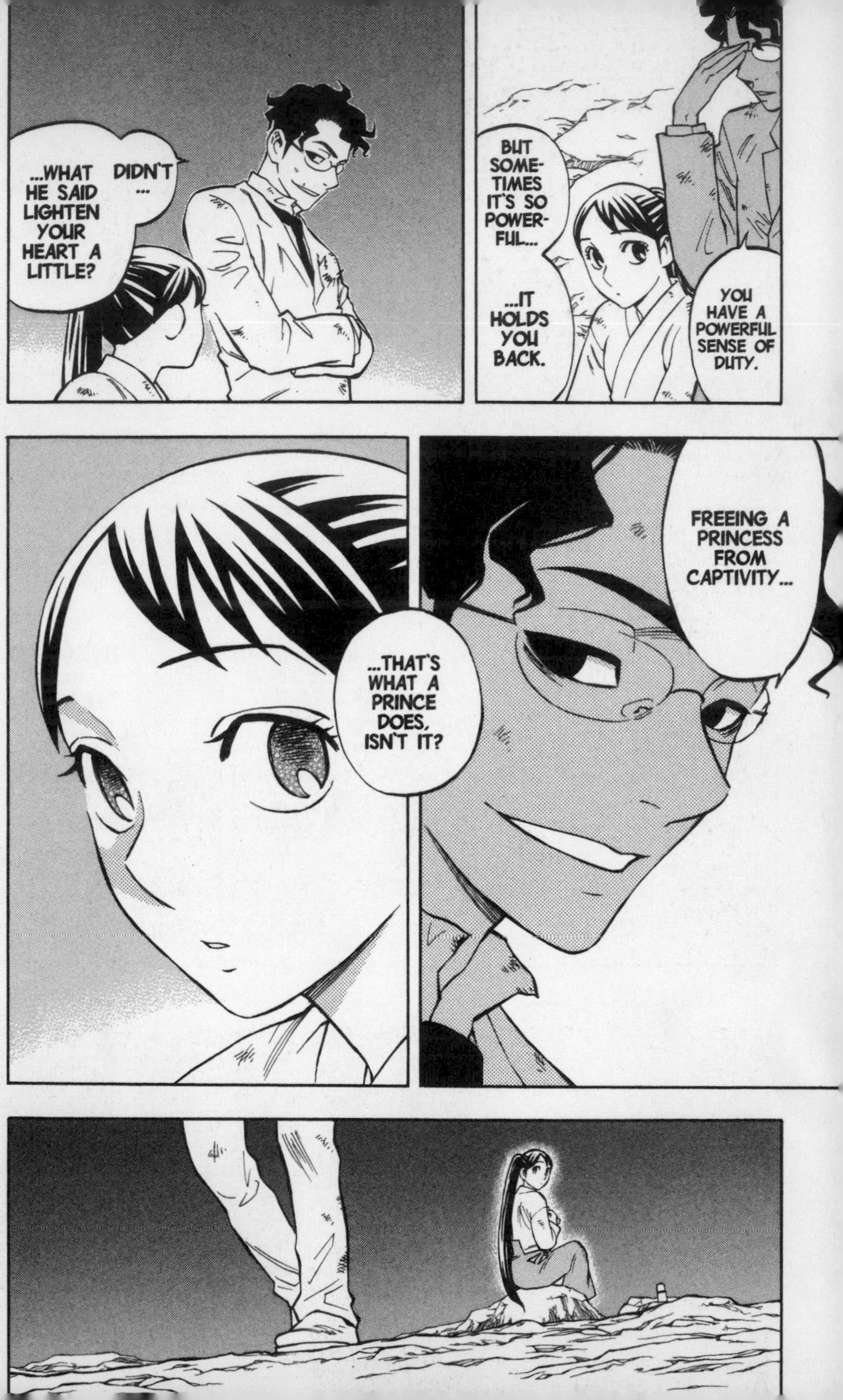
YOU HAVE A POWERFUL SENSE OF DUTY.
BUT SOMETIMES IT'S SO POWERFUL...
...IT HOLDS YOU BACK.
DIDN'T ... ...WHAT HE SAID LIGHTEN YOUR HEART A LITTLE?
FREEING A PRINCESS FROM CAPTIVITY...
...THAT'S WHAT A PRINCE DOES, ISN'T IT?

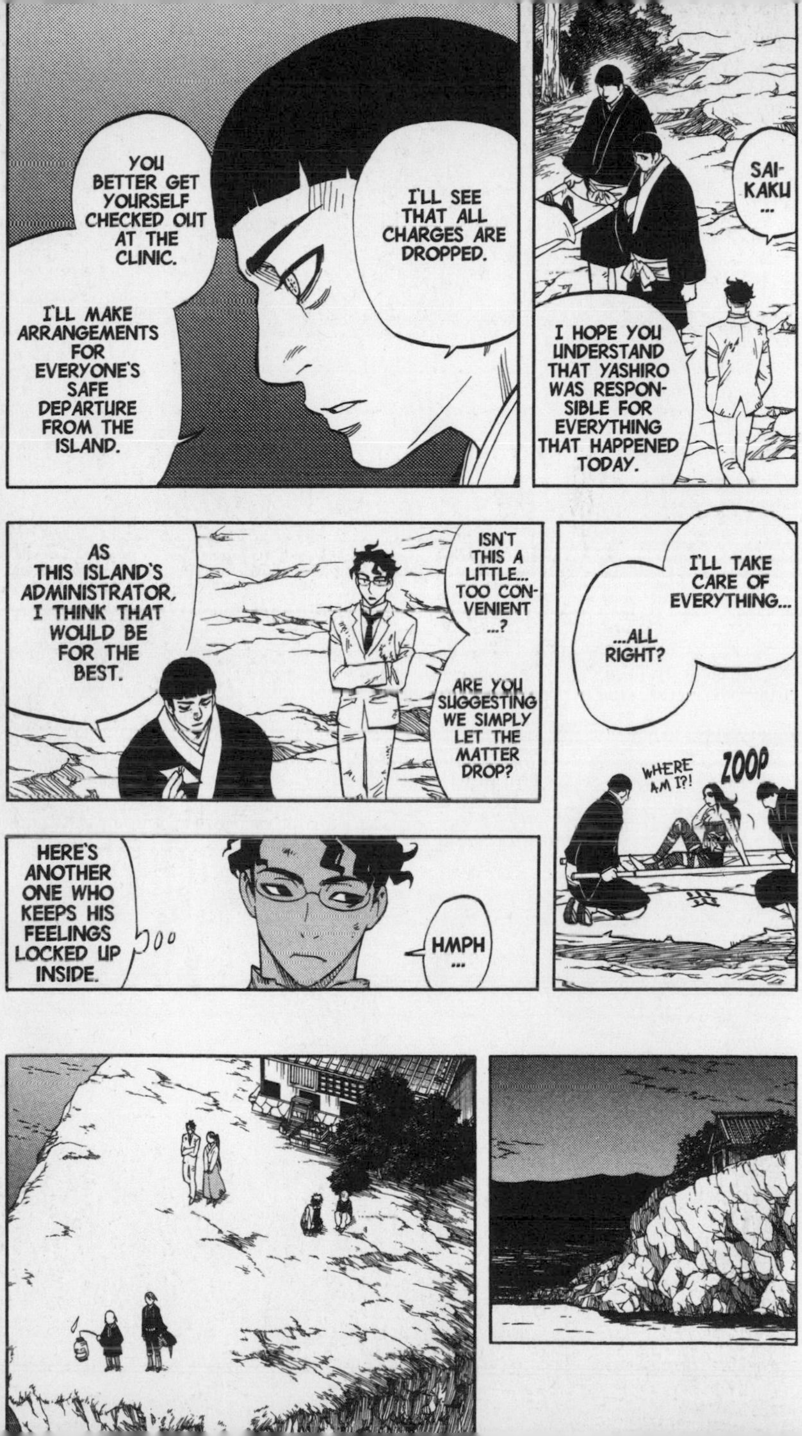
SAI-KAKU...
I HOPE YOU UNDERSTAND THAT YASHIRO WAS RESPONSIBLE FOR EVERYTHING THAT HAPPENED TODAY.
I'LL SEE THAT ALL CHARGES ARE DROPPED.
YOU BETTER GET YOURSELF CHECKED OUT AT THE CLINIC.
I'LL MAKE ARRANGEMENTS FOR EVERYONE'S SAFE DEPARTURE FROM THE ISLAND.
I'LL TAKE CARE OF EVERYTHING...
...ALL RIGHT?
ZOOP
WHERE AM I?!
ISN'T THIS A LITTLE... TOO CONVENIENT...?
ARE YOU SUGGESTING WE SIMPLY LET THE MATTER DROP?
AS THIS ISLAND'S ADMINISTRATOR, I THINK THAT WOULD BE FOR THE BEST.
HMPH...
HERE'S ANOTHER ONE WHO KEEPS HIS FEELINGS LOCKED UP INSIDE.

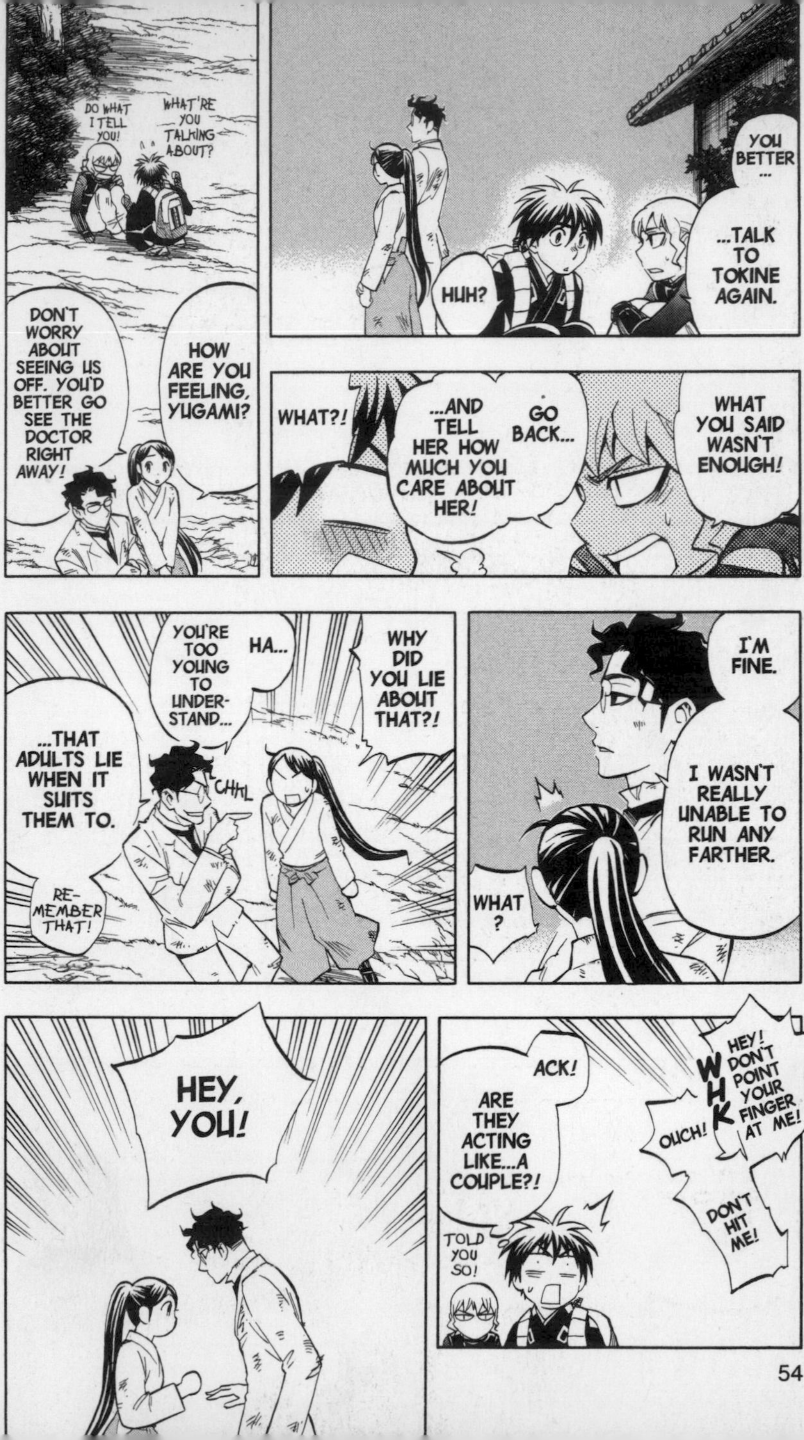
YOU BETTER ...
...TALK TO TOKINE AGAIN.
HUH?
WHAT YOU SAID WASN'T ENOUGH!
GO BACK...
...AND TELL HER HOW MUCH YOU CARE ABOUT HER!
WHAT?!
WHAT'RE YOU TALKING ABOUT?
DO WHAT I TELL YOU!
HOW ARE YOU FEELING, YUGAMI?
DON'T WORRY ABOUT SEEING US OFF. YOU'D BETTER GO SEE THE DOCTOR RIGHT AWAY!
I'M FINE.
I WASN'T REALLY UNABLE TO RUN ANY FARTHER.
WHAT?
WHY DID YOU LIE ABOUT THAT?!
HA...
YOU'RE TOO YOUNG TO UNDER-STAND...
...THAT ADULTS LIE WHEN IT SUITS THEM TO.
CHKL
RE-MEMBER THAT!
HEY! DON'T POINT YOUR FINGER AT ME!
WHK
OUCH!
DON'T HIT ME!
ACK!
ARE THEY ACTING LIKE...A COUPLE?!
TOLD YOU SO!
HEY, YOU!

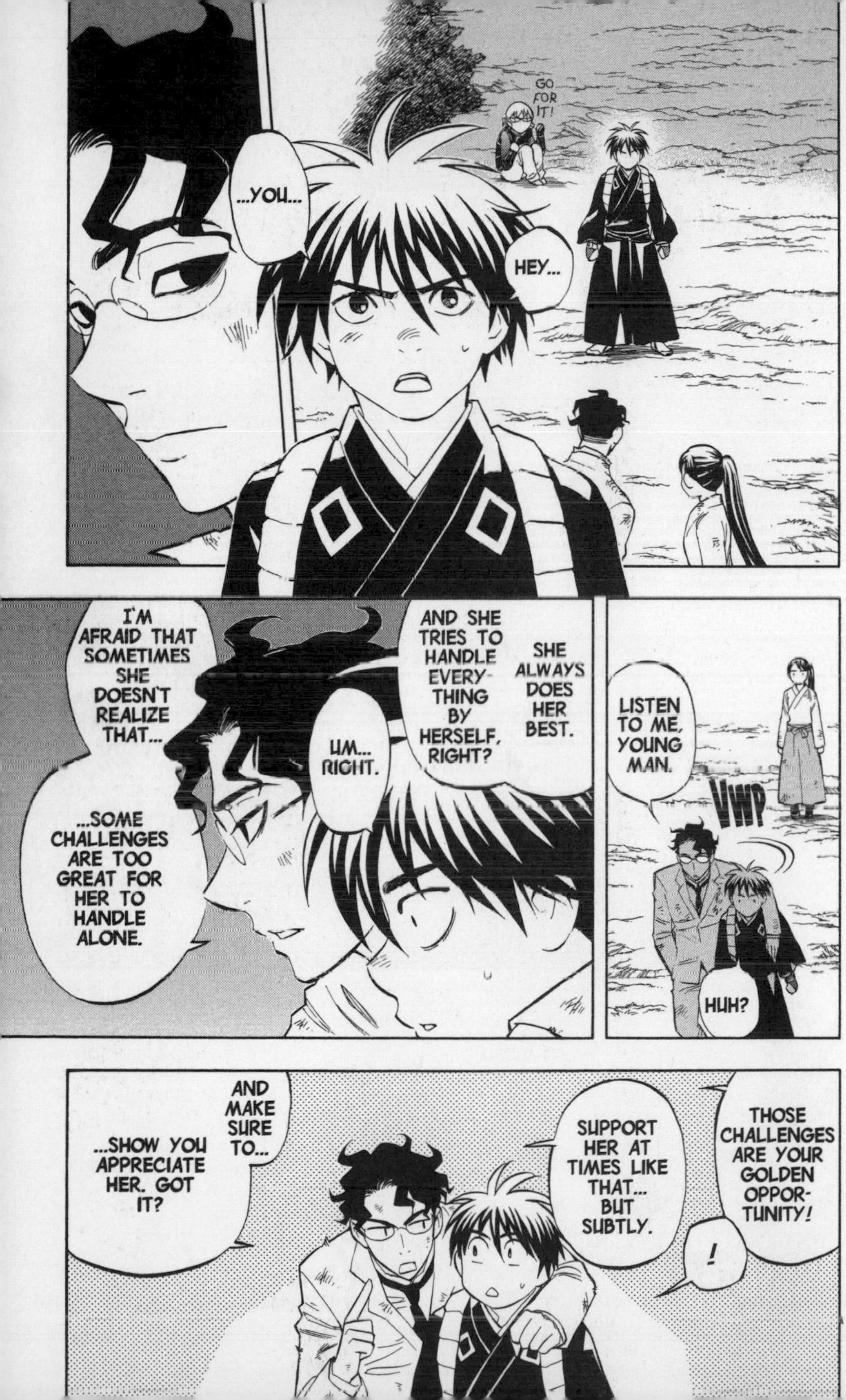
GO FOR IT!
HEY...
...YOU...
LISTEN TO ME, YOUNG MAN.
VWP
HUH?
SHE ALWAYS DOES HER BEST.
AND SHE TRIES TO HANDLE EVERY-THING BY HERSELF, RIGHT?
UM... RIGHT.
I'M AFRAID THAT SOMETIMES SHE DOESN'T REALIZE THAT...
...SOME CHALLENGES ARE TOO GREAT FOR HER TO HANDLE ALONE.
THOSE CHALLENGES ARE YOUR GOLDEN OPPOR-TUNITY!
!
SUPPORT HER AT TIMES LIKE THAT... BUT SUBTLY.
AND MAKE SURE TO...
...SHOW YOU APPRECIATE HER. GOT IT?

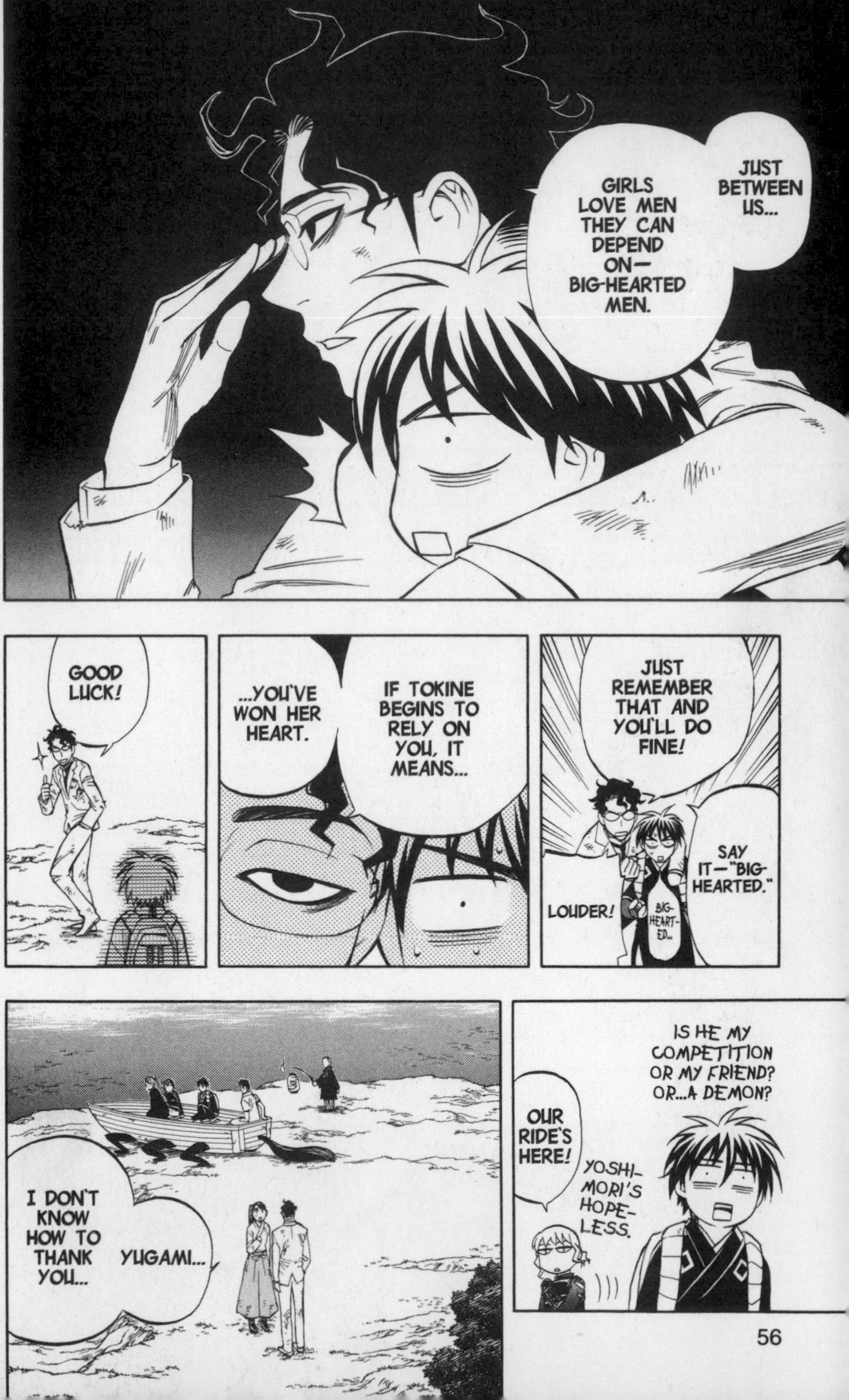
JUST BETWEEN US...
GIRLS LOVE MEN THEY CAN DEPEND ON—BIG-HEARTED MEN.
JUST REMEMBER THAT AND YOU'LL DO FINE!
SAY IT—"BIG-HEARTED."
BIG-HEART-ED...
LOUDER!
IF TOKINE BEGINS TO RELY ON YOU, IT MEANS...
...YOU'VE WON HER HEART.
GOOD LUCK!
IS HE MY COMPETITION OR MY FRIEND? OR...A DEMON?
OUR RIDE'S HERE!
YOSHIMORI'S HOPELESS.
YUGAMI...
I DON'T KNOW HOW TO THANK YOU...

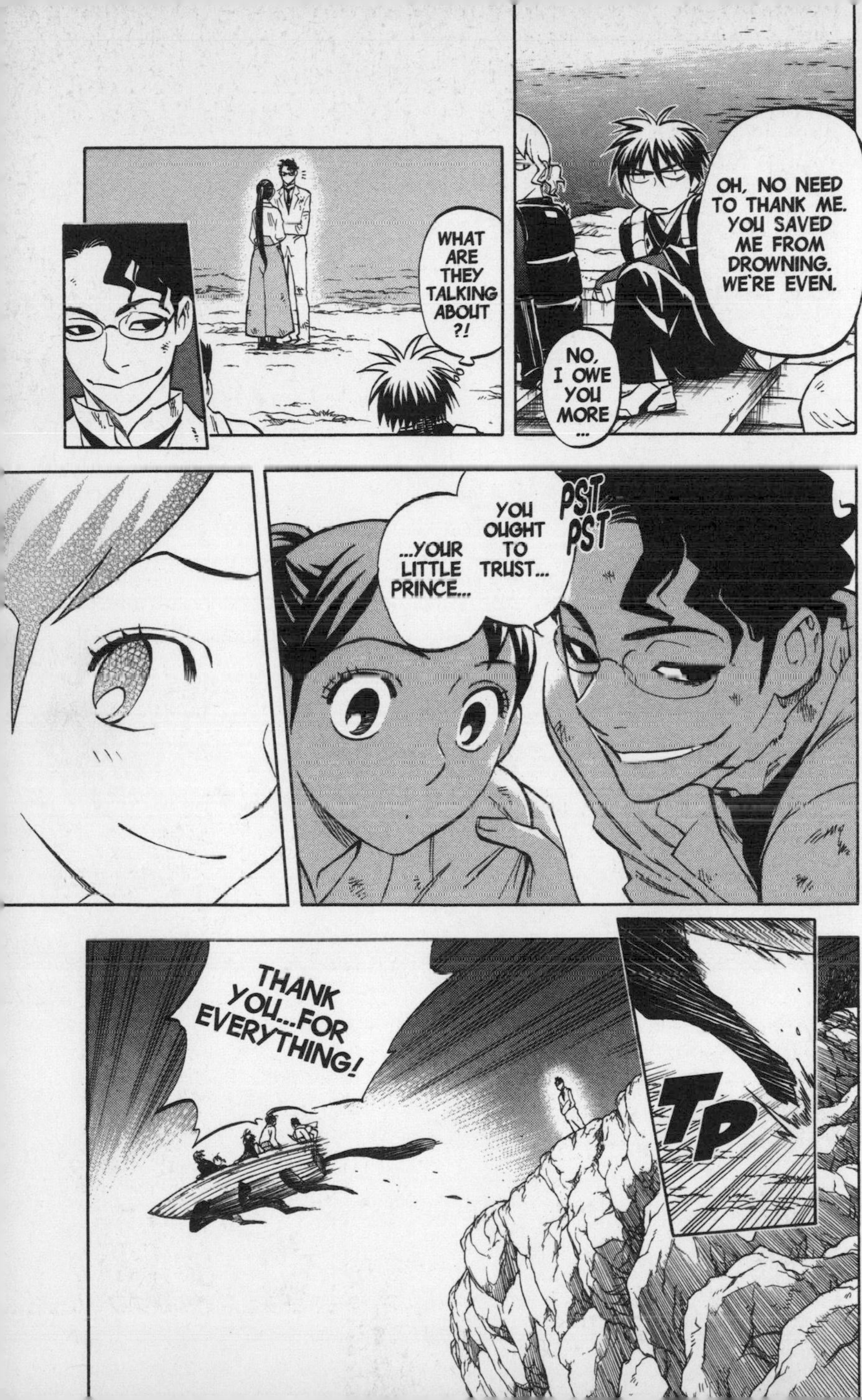

OH, NO NEED TO THANK ME. YOU SAVED ME FROM DROWNING. WE'RE EVEN.
NO, I OWE YOU MORE ...
WHAT ARE THEY TALKING ABOUT ?!
PST PST
YOU OUGHT TO TRUST...
...YOUR LITTLE PRINCE...
TP
THANK YOU...FOR EVERYTHING!

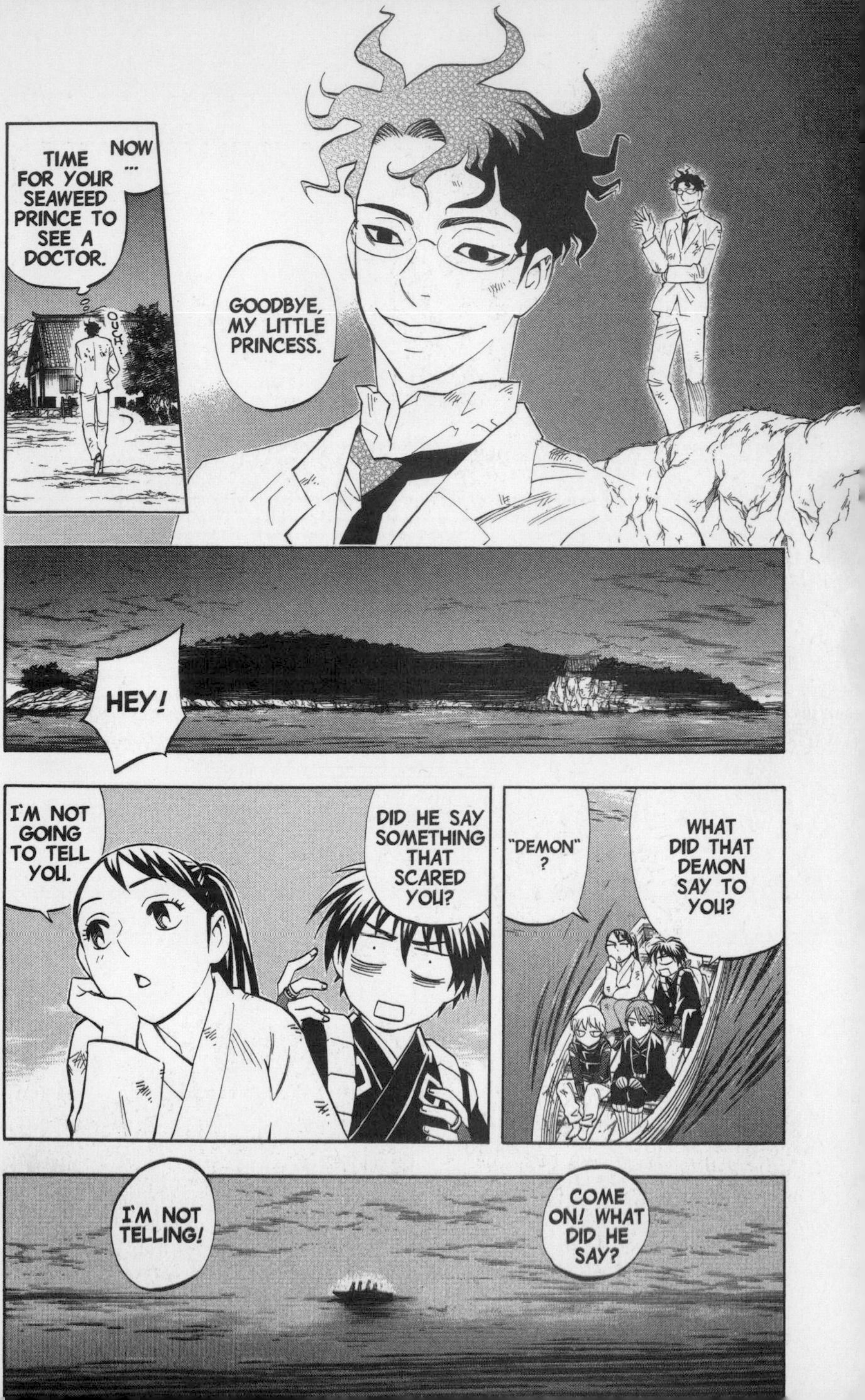
GOODBYE, MY LITTLE PRINCESS.
NOW ... TIME FOR YOUR SEAWEED PRINCE TO SEE A DOCTOR.
OUCH...
HEY!
WHAT DID THAT DEMON SAY TO YOU?
"DEMON"?
DID HE SAY SOMETHING THAT SCARED YOU?
I'M NOT GOING TO TELL YOU.
COME ON! WHAT DID HE SAY?
I'M NOT TELLING!

Chapter 219: Big-Hearted

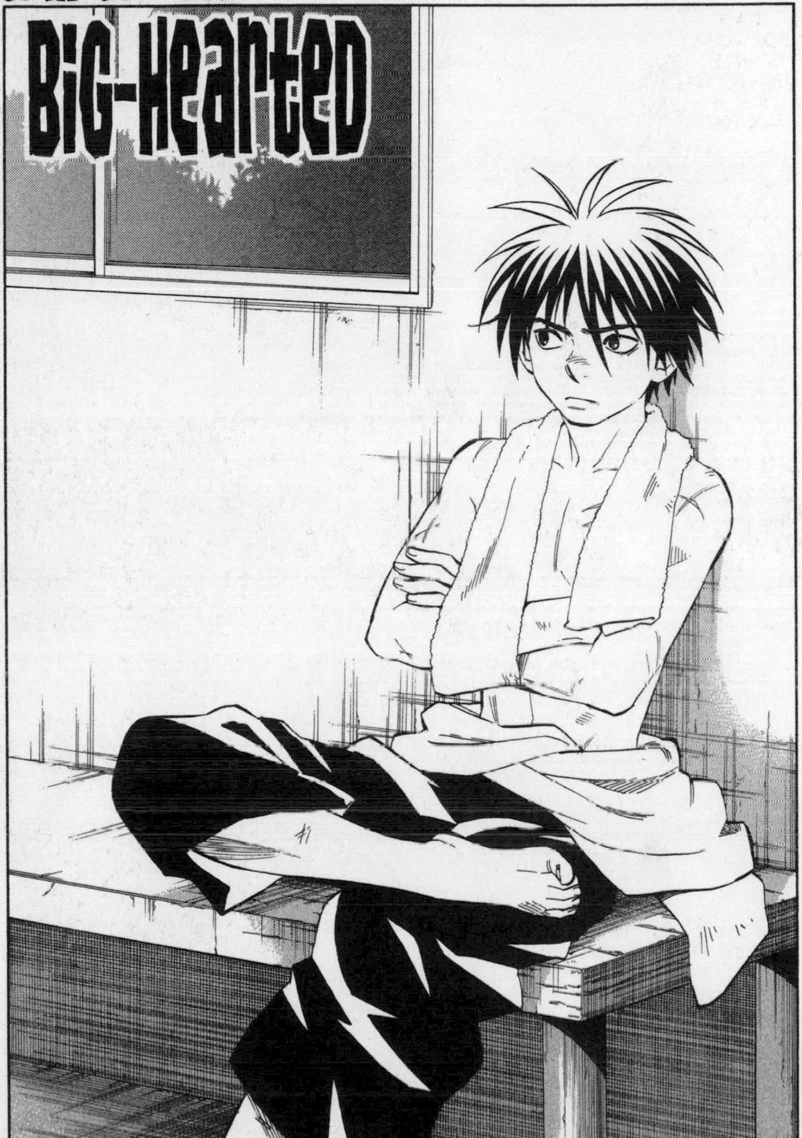

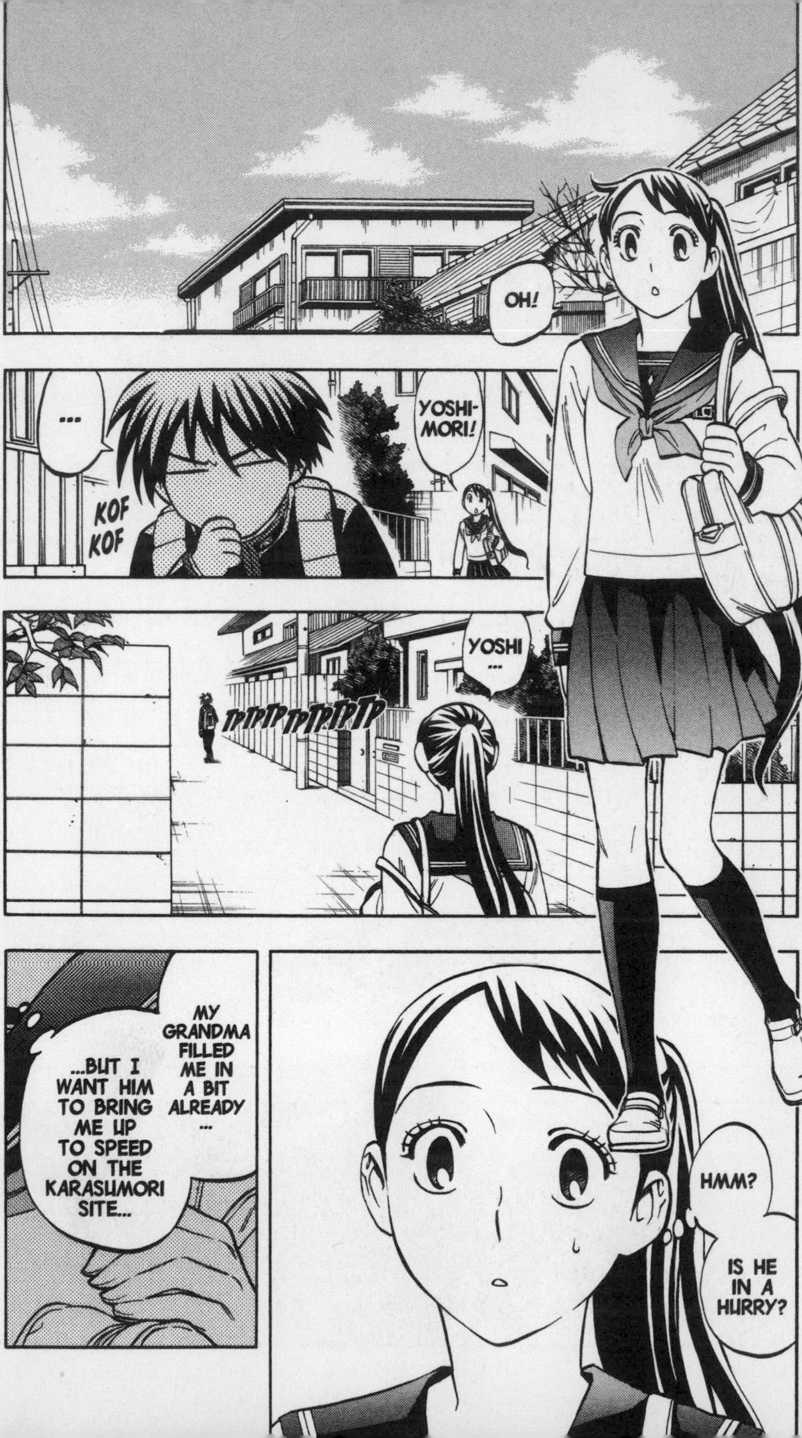
OH!
YOSHI-MORI!
...
KOF KOF
YOSHI ...
TPTPTP TPTPTPTP
HMM?
IS HE IN A HURRY?
MY GRANDMA FILLED ME IN A BIT ALREADY ...
...BUT I WANT HIM TO BRING ME UP TO SPEED ON THE KARASUMORI SITE...

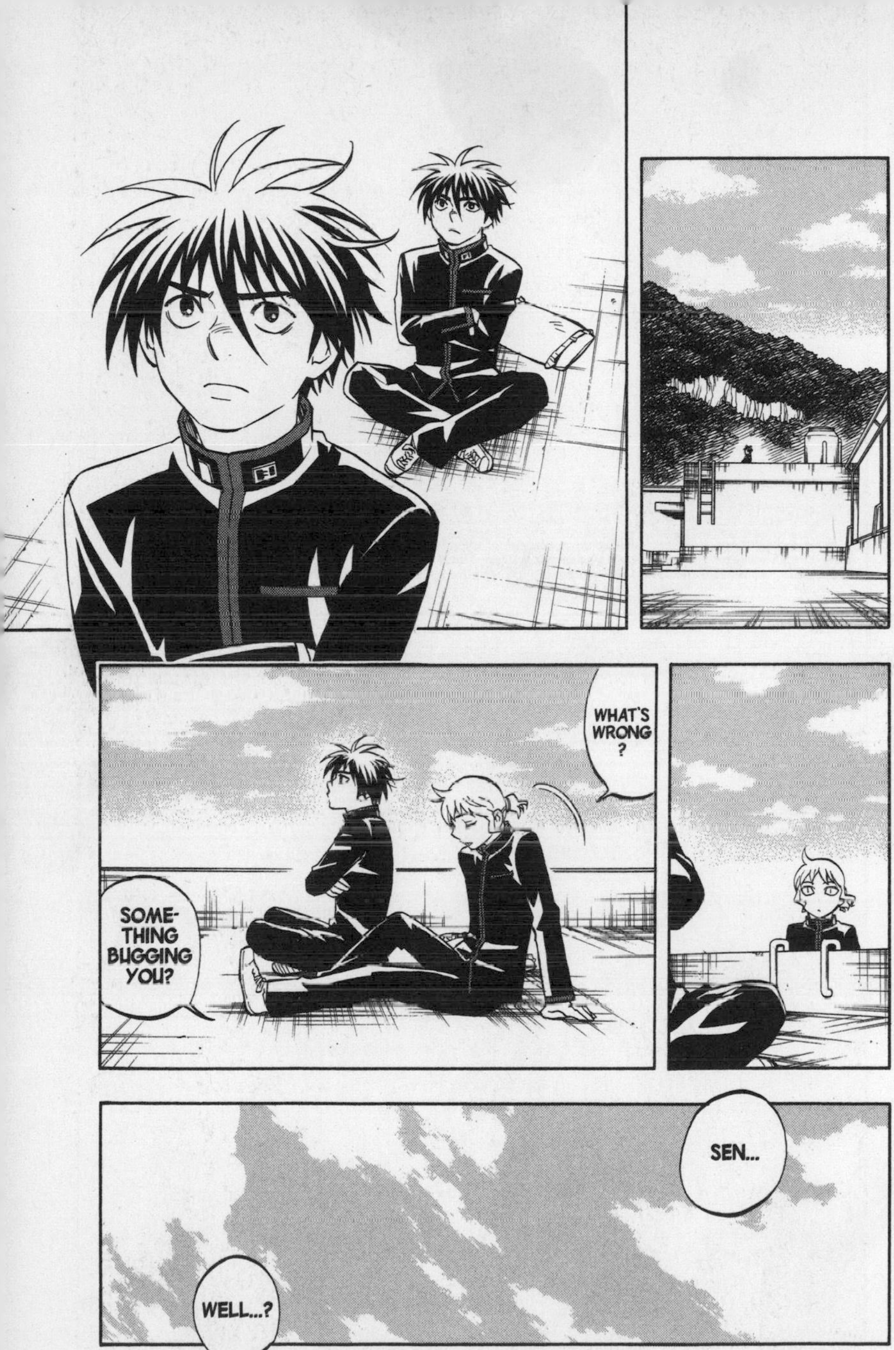
WHAT'S WRONG?
SOME-THING BUGGING YOU?
SEN...
WELL...?

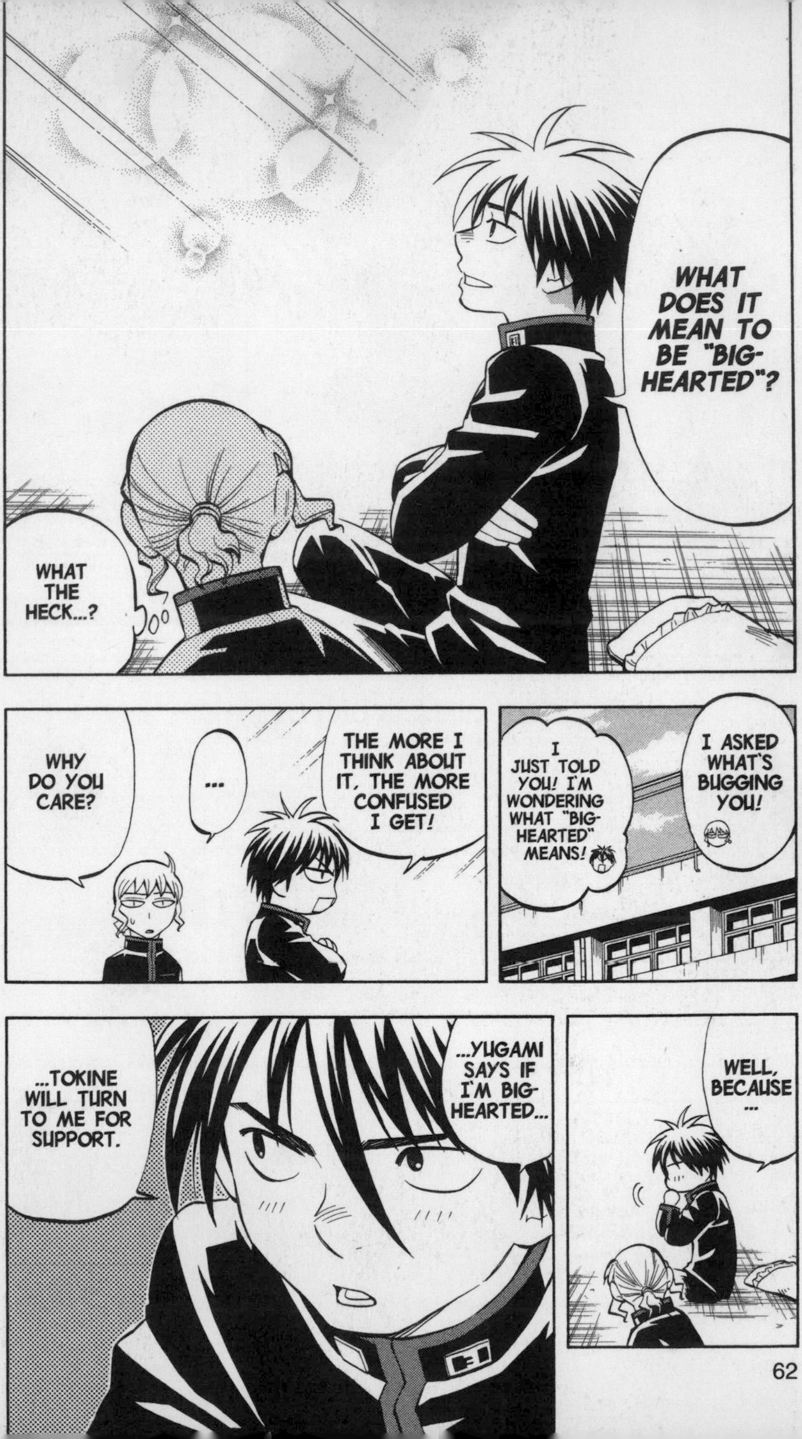
WHAT DOES IT MEAN TO BE "BIG-HEARTED"?
WHAT THE HECK...?
I ASKED WHAT'S BUGGING YOU!
I JUST TOLD YOU! I'M WONDERING WHAT "BIG-HEARTED" MEANS!
THE MORE I THINK ABOUT IT, THE MORE CONFUSED I GET!
...
WHY DO YOU CARE?
WELL, BECAUSE ...
...YUGAMI SAYS IF I'M BIG-HEARTED...
...TOKINE WILL TURN TO ME FOR SUPPORT.

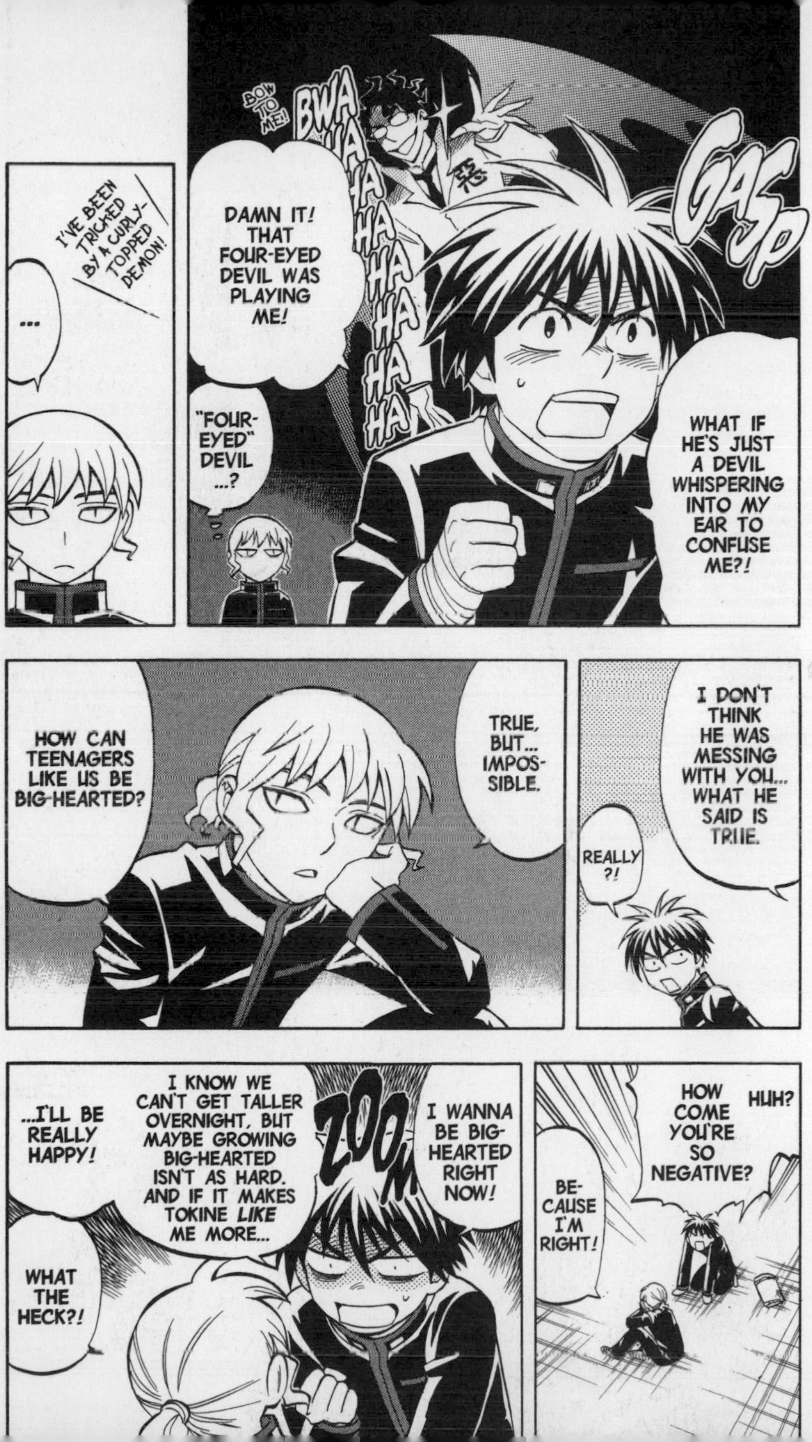
GASP
WHAT IF HE'S JUST A DEVIL WHISPERING INTO MY EAR TO CONFUSE ME?!
BOW TO ME!
BWAHAHAHAHAHAHA
DAMN IT! THAT FOUR-EYED DEVIL WAS PLAYING ME!
"FOUR-EYED" DEVIL ...?
I'VE BEEN TRICKED BY A CURLY-TOPPED DEMON!
...
I DON'T THINK HE WAS MESSING WITH YOU... WHAT HE SAID IS TRUE.
REALLY?!
TRUE, BUT... IMPOSSIBLE.
HOW CAN TEENAGERS LIKE US BE BIG-HEARTED?
HUH?
HOW COME YOU'RE SO NEGATIVE?
BE-CAUSE I'M RIGHT!
I WANNA BE BIG-HEARTED RIGHT NOW!
ZOOM
I KNOW WE CAN'T GET TALLER OVERNIGHT, BUT MAYBE GROWING BIG-HEARTED ISN'T AS HARD. AND IF IT MAKES TOKINE *LIKE* ME MORE...
...I'LL BE REALLY HAPPY!
WHAT THE HECK?!

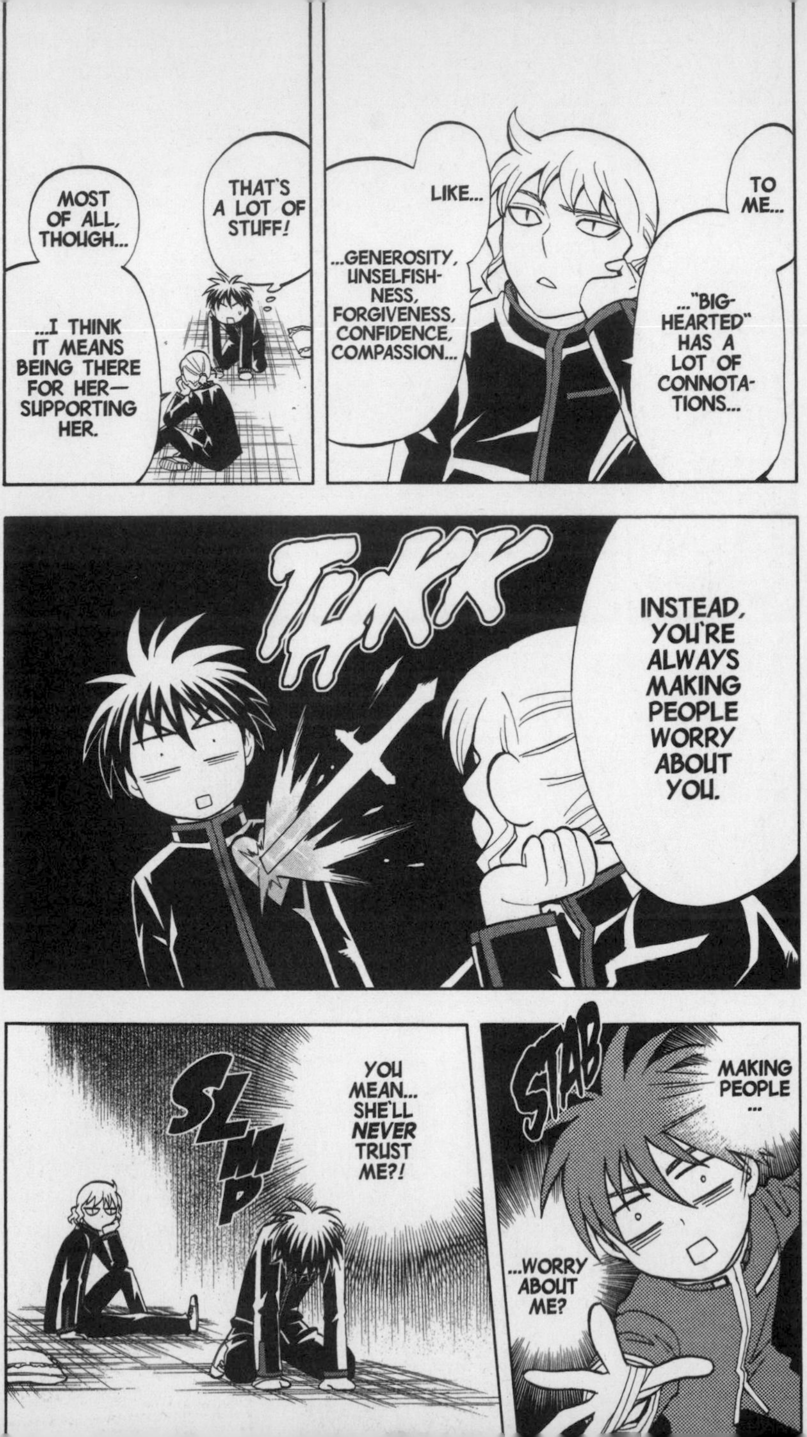
TO ME...
..."BIG-HEARTED" HAS A LOT OF CONNOTATIONS...
LIKE...
...GENEROSITY, UNSELFISHNESS, FORGIVENESS, CONFIDENCE, COMPASSION...
THAT'S A LOT OF STUFF!
MOST OF ALL, THOUGH...
...I THINK IT MEANS BEING THERE FOR HER—SUPPORTING HER.
INSTEAD, YOU'RE ALWAYS MAKING PEOPLE WORRY ABOUT YOU.
TINK
STAB
MAKING PEOPLE ...
...WORRY ABOUT ME?
YOU MEAN... SHE'LL *NEVER* TRUST ME?!
SLUMP

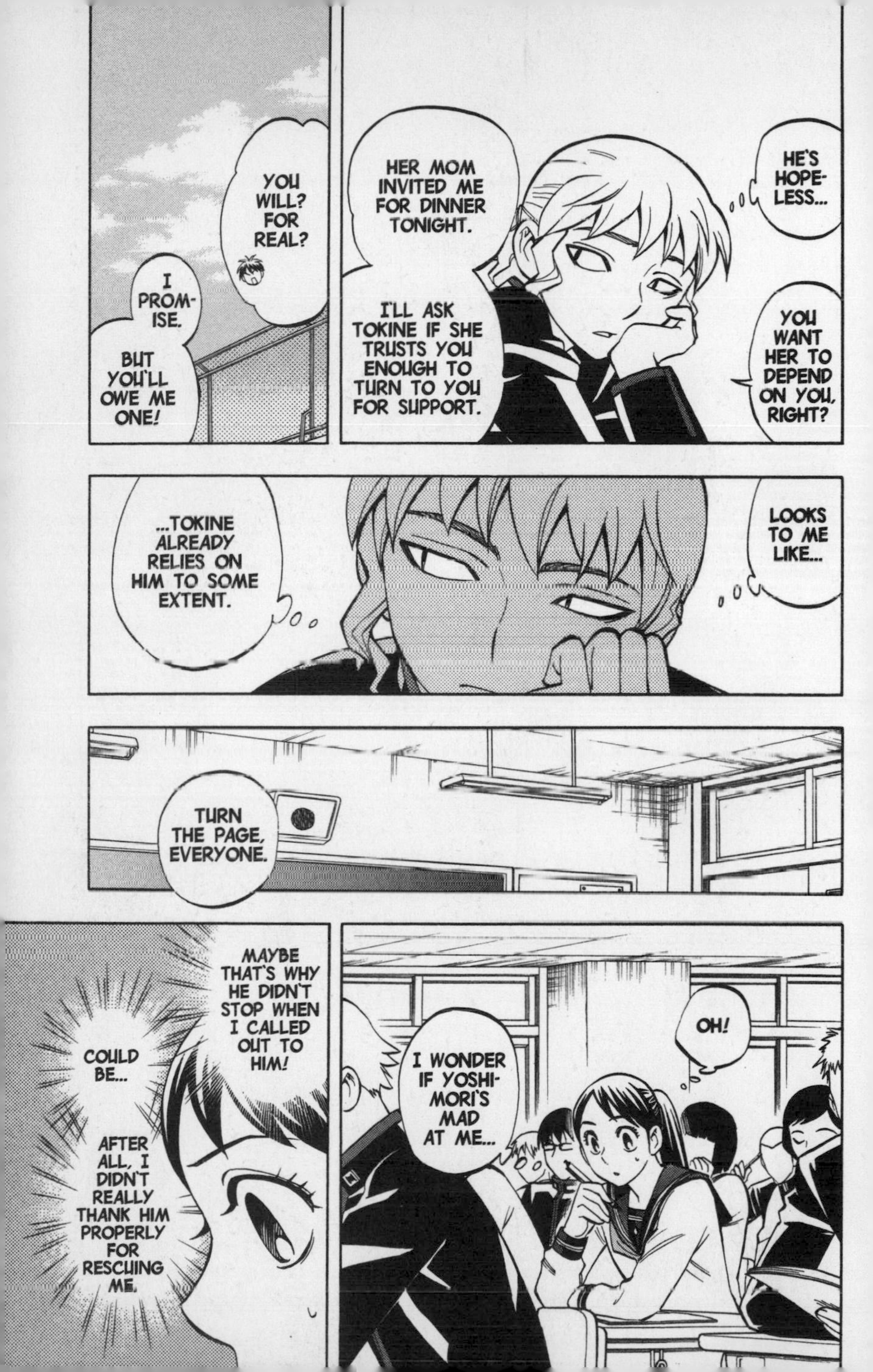
HE'S HOPE-LESS...
YOU WANT HER TO DEPEND ON YOU, RIGHT?
HER MOM INVITED ME FOR DINNER TONIGHT.
I'LL ASK TOKINE IF SHE TRUSTS YOU ENOUGH TO TURN TO YOU FOR SUPPORT.
YOU WILL? FOR REAL?
I PROMISE.
BUT YOU'LL OWE ME ONE!
LOOKS TO ME LIKE...
...TOKINE ALREADY RELIES ON HIM TO SOME EXTENT.
TURN THE PAGE, EVERYONE.
OH!
I WONDER IF YOSHIMORI'S MAD AT ME...
MAYBE THAT'S WHY HE DIDN'T STOP WHEN I CALLED OUT TO HIM!
COULD BE...
AFTER ALL, I DIDN'T REALLY THANK HIM PROPERLY FOR RESCUING ME.

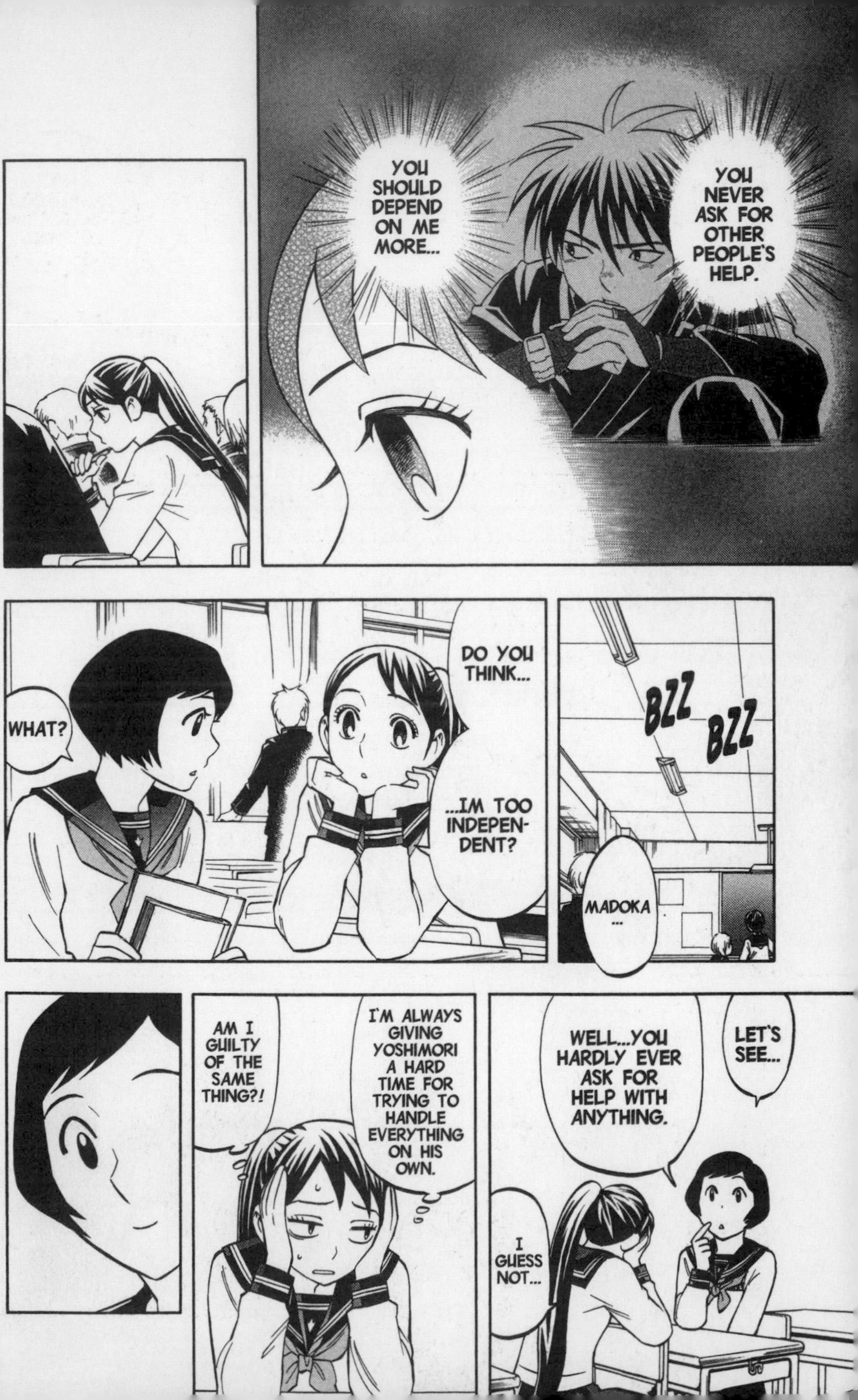
YOU NEVER ASK FOR OTHER PEOPLE'S HELP.
YOU SHOULD DEPEND ON ME MORE...
BZZ
BZZ
MADOKA...
DO YOU THINK...
...IM TOO INDEPENDENT?
WHAT?
LET'S SEE...
WELL...YOU HARDLY EVER ASK FOR HELP WITH ANYTHING.
I GUESS NOT...
I'M ALWAYS GIVING YOSHIMORI A HARD TIME FOR TRYING TO HANDLE EVERYTHING ON HIS OWN.
AM I GUILTY OF THE SAME THING?!

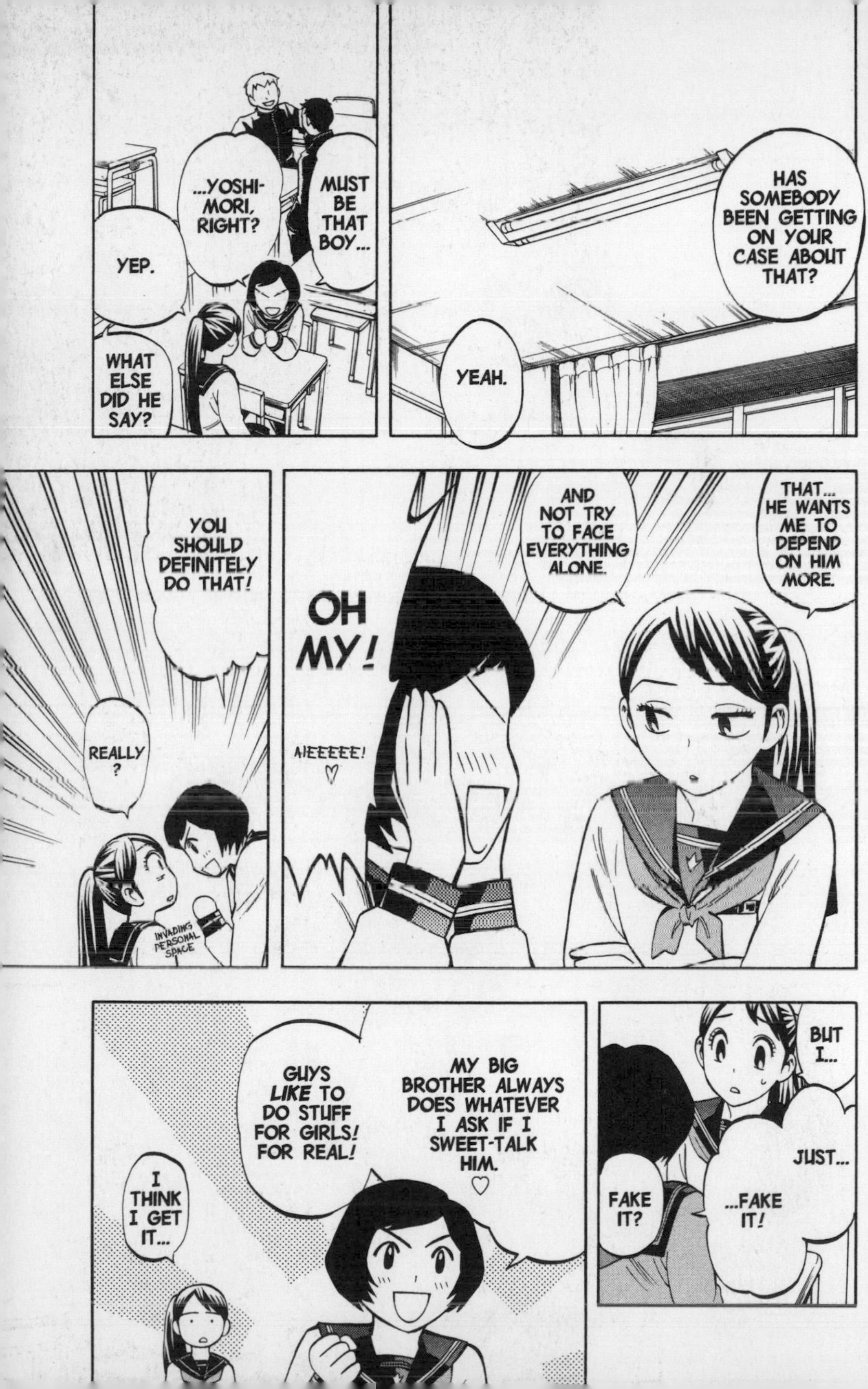
HAS SOMEBODY BEEN GETTING ON YOUR CASE ABOUT THAT?
YEAH.
MUST BE THAT BOY...
...YOSHI-MORI, RIGHT?
YEP.
WHAT ELSE DID HE SAY?
THAT... HE WANTS ME TO DEPEND ON HIM MORE.
AND NOT TRY TO FACE EVERYTHING ALONE.
OH MY!
AIEEEEE! ♡
YOU SHOULD DEFINITELY DO THAT!
REALLY?
INVADING PERSONAL SPACE
BUT I...
JUST...
...FAKE IT!
FAKE IT?
MY BIG BROTHER ALWAYS DOES WHATEVER I ASK IF I SWEET-TALK HIM. ♡
GUYS *LIKE* TO DO STUFF FOR GIRLS! FOR REAL!
I THINK I GET IT...

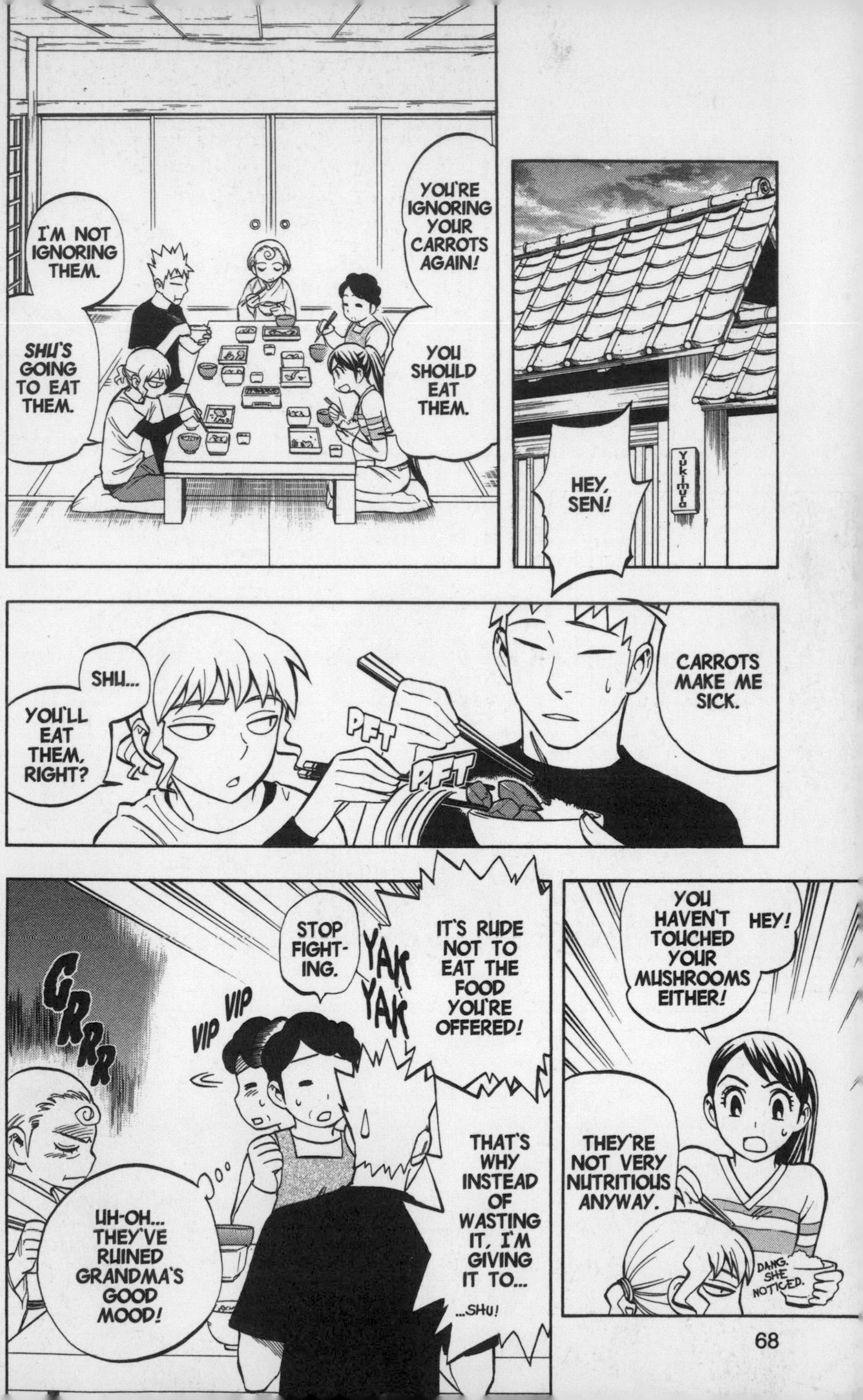
HEY, SEN!
Yukimura
YOU'RE IGNORING YOUR CARROTS AGAIN!
YOU SHOULD EAT THEM.
I'M NOT IGNORING THEM.
SHU'S GOING TO EAT THEM.
CARROTS MAKE ME SICK.
PFT
PFT
SHU...
YOU'LL EAT THEM, RIGHT?
HEY!
YOU HAVEN'T TOUCHED YOUR MUSHROOMS EITHER!
THEY'RE NOT VERY NUTRITIOUS ANYWAY.
DANG. SHE NOTICED.
IT'S RUDE NOT TO EAT THE FOOD YOU'RE OFFERED!
YAK YAK
STOP FIGHT-ING.
THAT'S WHY INSTEAD OF WASTING IT, I'M GIVING IT TO...
...SHU!
VIP VIP
GRRR
UH-OH... THEY'VE RUINED GRANDMA'S GOOD MOOD!

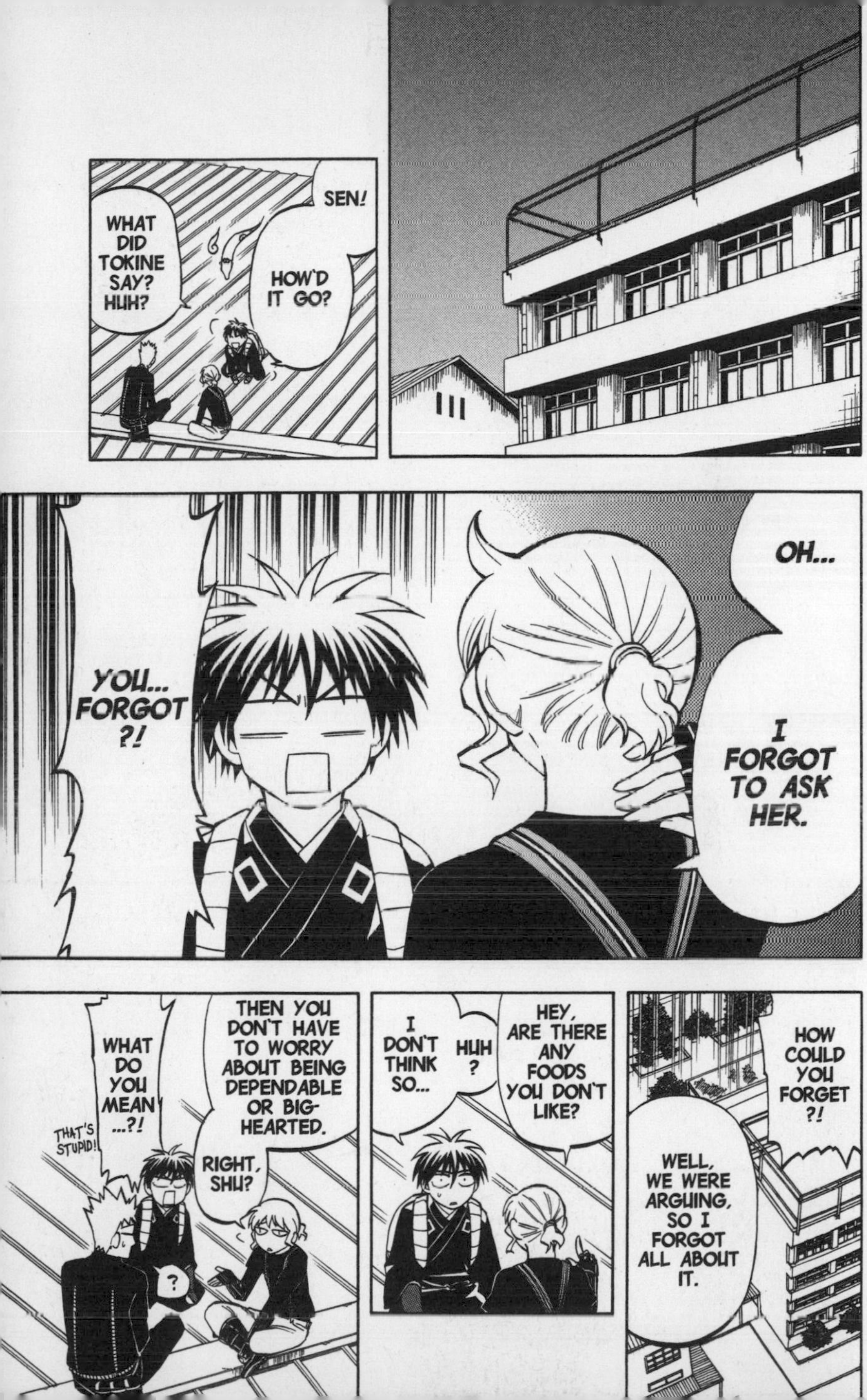
SEN!
HOW'D IT GO?
WHAT DID TOKINE SAY? HUH?
OH...
I FORGOT TO ASK HER.
YOU... FORGOT ?!
HOW COULD YOU FORGET ?!
WELL, WE WERE ARGUING, SO I FORGOT ALL ABOUT IT.
HEY, ARE THERE ANY FOODS YOU DON'T LIKE?
HUH ?
I DON'T THINK SO...
THEN YOU DON'T HAVE TO WORRY ABOUT BEING DEPENDABLE OR BIG-HEARTED.
RIGHT, SHU?
WHAT DO YOU MEAN ...?!
THAT'S STUPID!

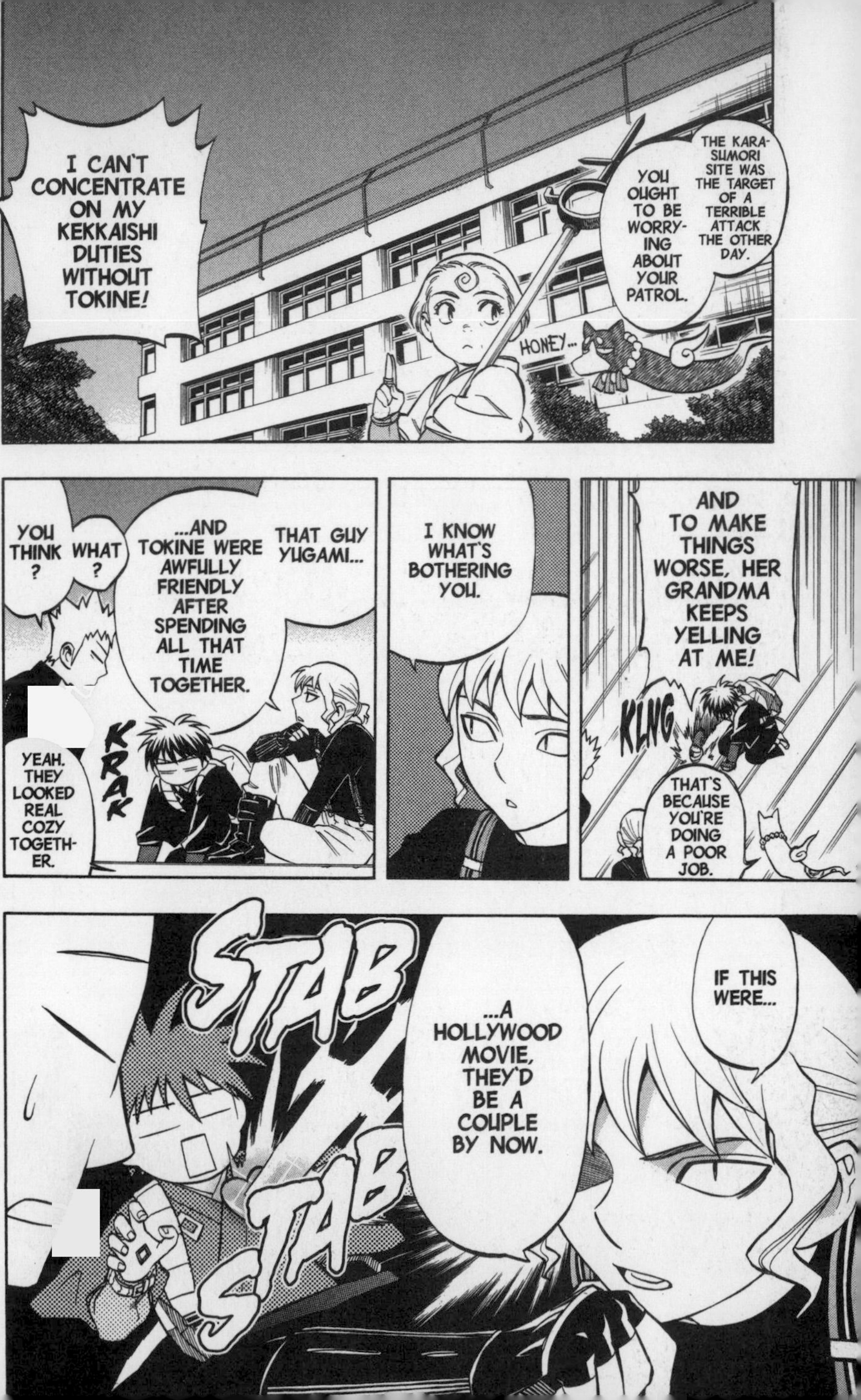
I CAN'T CONCENTRATE ON MY KEKKAISHI DUTIES WITHOUT TOKINE!
HONEY...
THE KARA-SUMORI SITE WAS THE TARGET OF A TERRIBLE ATTACK THE OTHER DAY.
YOU OUGHT TO BE WORRY-ING ABOUT YOUR PATROL.
AND TO MAKE THINGS WORSE, HER GRANDMA KEEPS YELLING AT ME!
KLNG
THAT'S BECAUSE YOU'RE DOING A POOR JOB.
I KNOW WHAT'S BOTHERING YOU.
THAT GUY YUGAMI...
...AND TOKINE WERE AWFULLY FRIENDLY AFTER SPENDING ALL THAT TIME TOGETHER.
WHAT?
YOU THINK?
KRAK
YEAH. THEY LOOKED REAL COZY TOGETH-ER.
IF THIS WERE...
...A HOLLYWOOD MOVIE, THEY'D BE A COUPLE BY NOW.
STAB
STAB

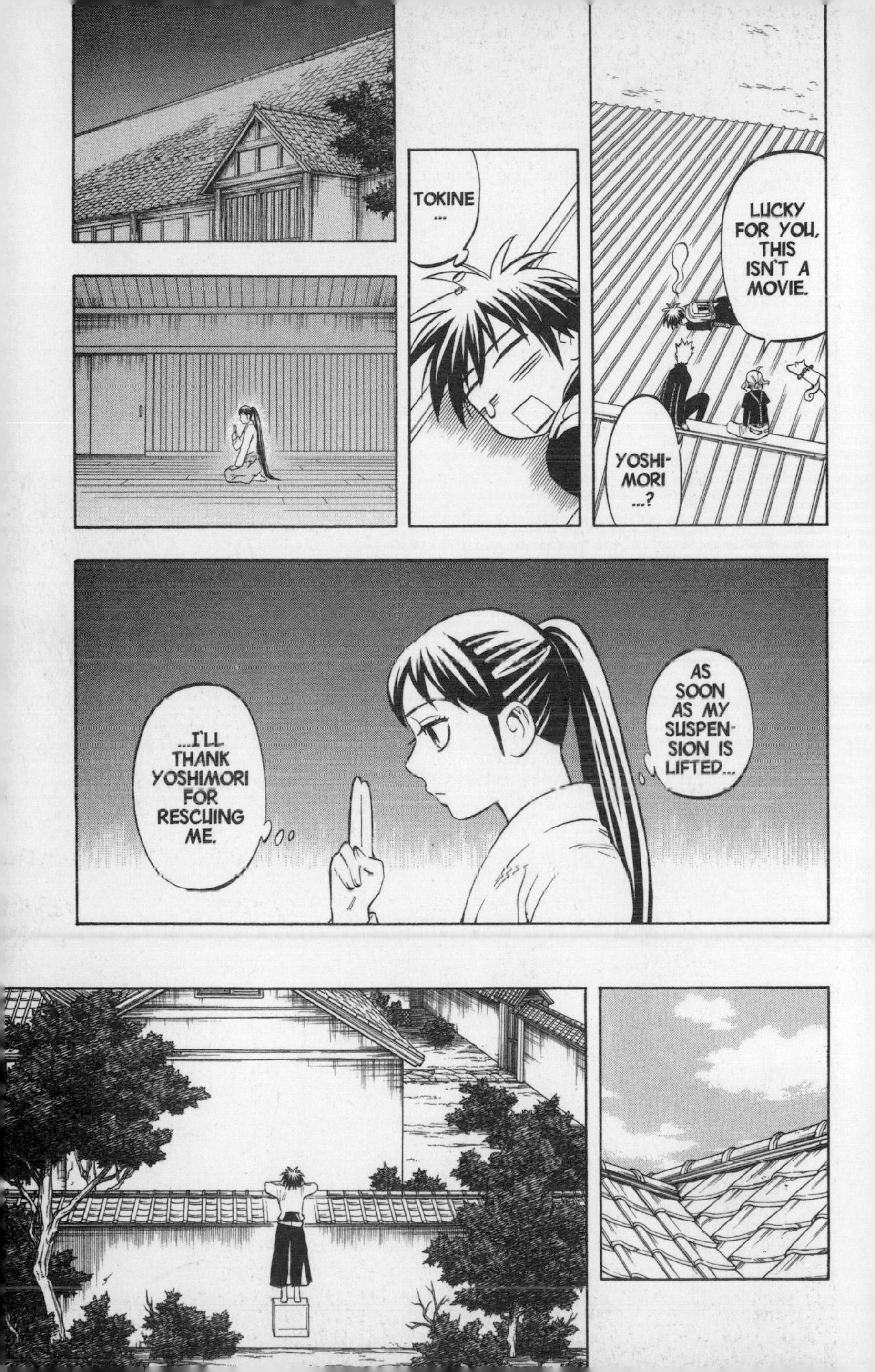
LUCKY FOR YOU, THIS ISN'T A MOVIE.
YOSHI-MORI ...?
TOKINE ...
AS SOON AS MY SUSPEN-SION IS LIFTED...
...I'LL THANK YOSHIMORI FOR RESCUING ME.

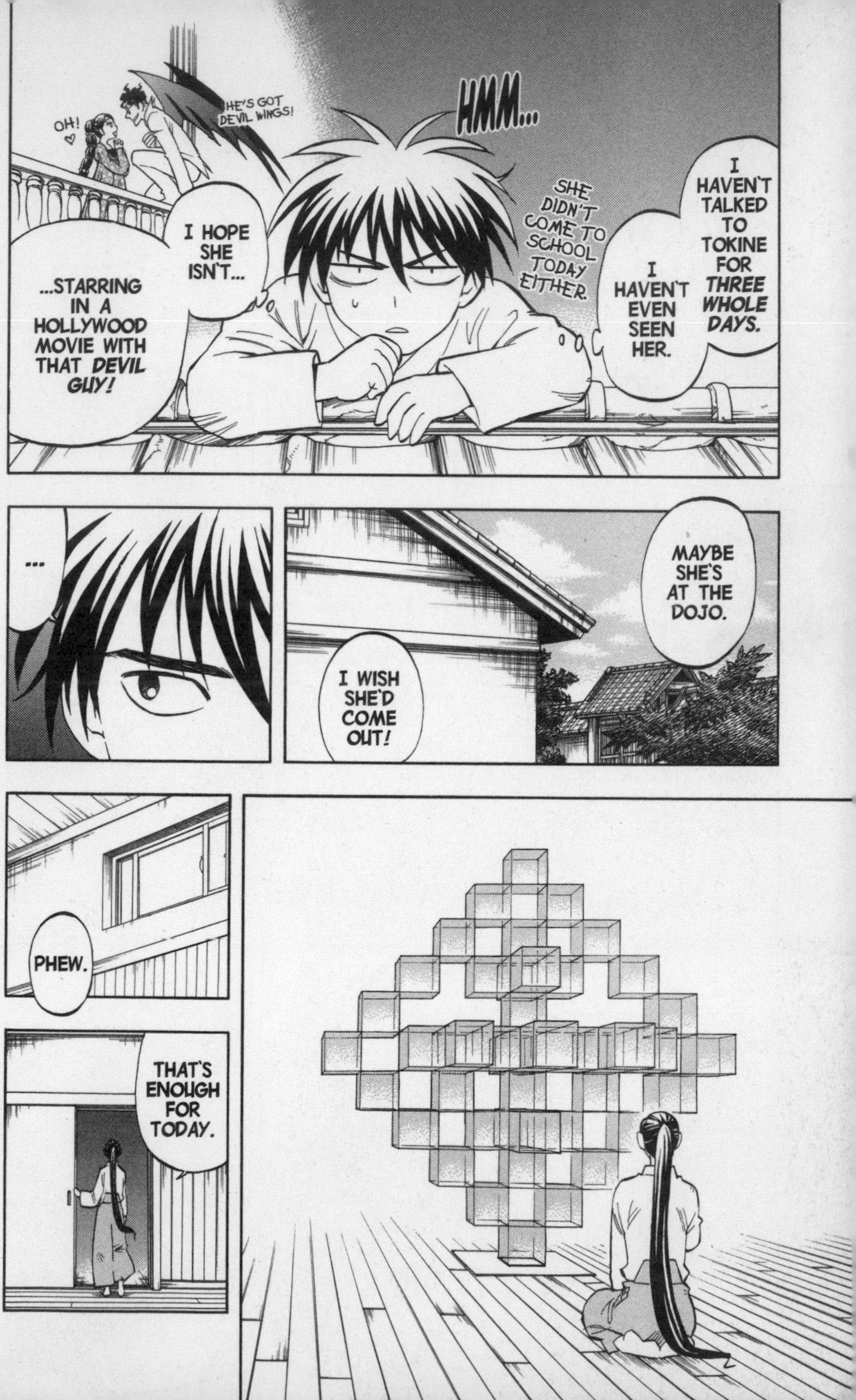
I HAVEN'T TALKED TO TOKINE FOR THREE WHOLE DAYS.
I HAVEN'T EVEN SEEN HER.
SHE DIDN'T COME TO SCHOOL TODAY EITHER.
HMM...
I HOPE SHE ISN'T...
...STARRING IN A HOLLYWOOD MOVIE WITH THAT DEVIL GUY!
HE'S GOT DEVIL WINGS!
OH! ♡
MAYBE SHE'S AT THE DOJO.
I WISH SHE'D COME OUT!
...
PHEW.
THAT'S ENOUGH FOR TODAY.

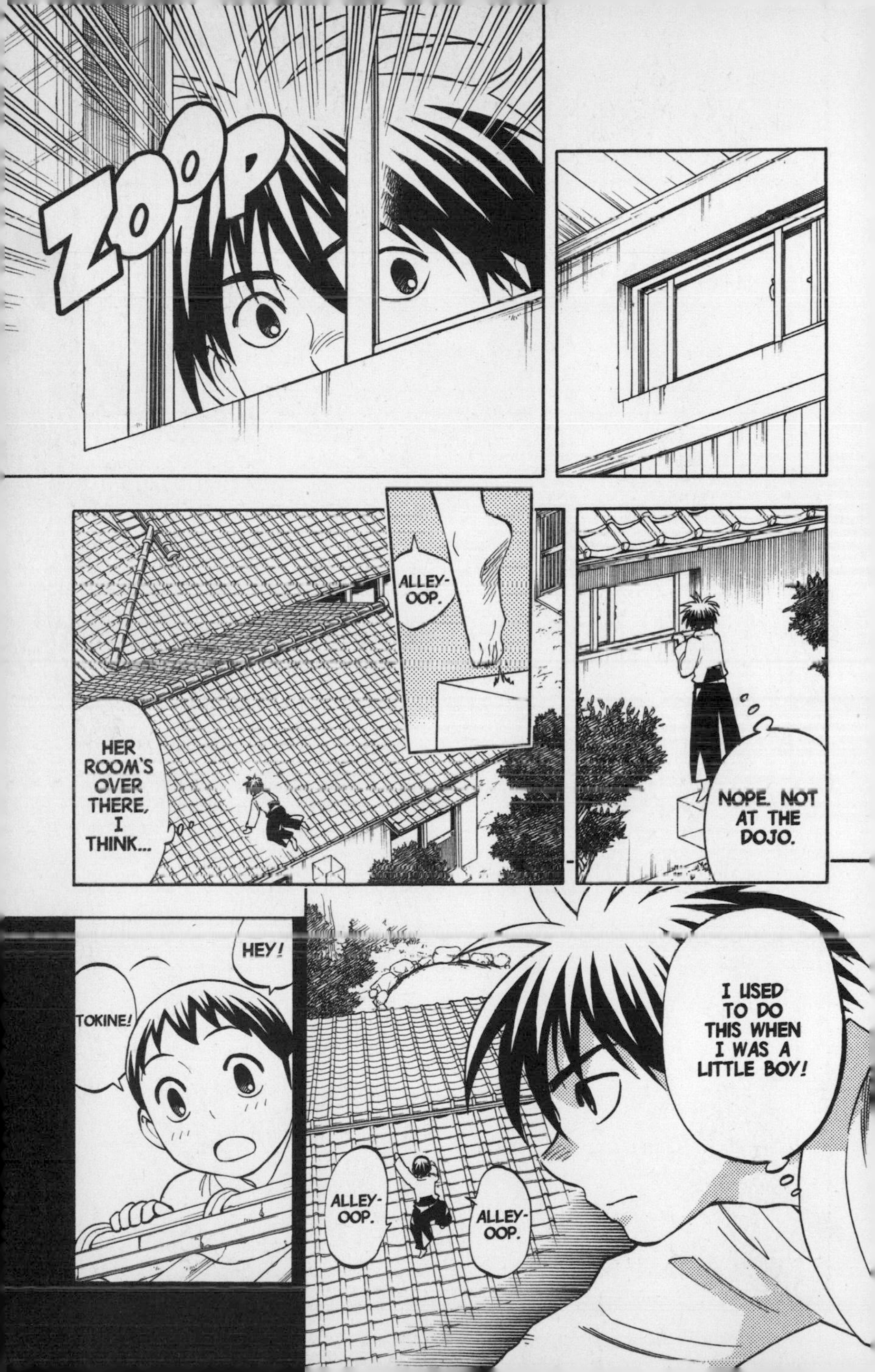
ZOOP
NOPE. NOT AT THE DOJO.
ALLEY-OOP.
HER ROOM'S OVER THERE, I THINK...
I USED TO DO THIS WHEN I WAS A LITTLE BOY!
ALLEY-OOP.
ALLEY-OOP.
HEY!
TOKINE!

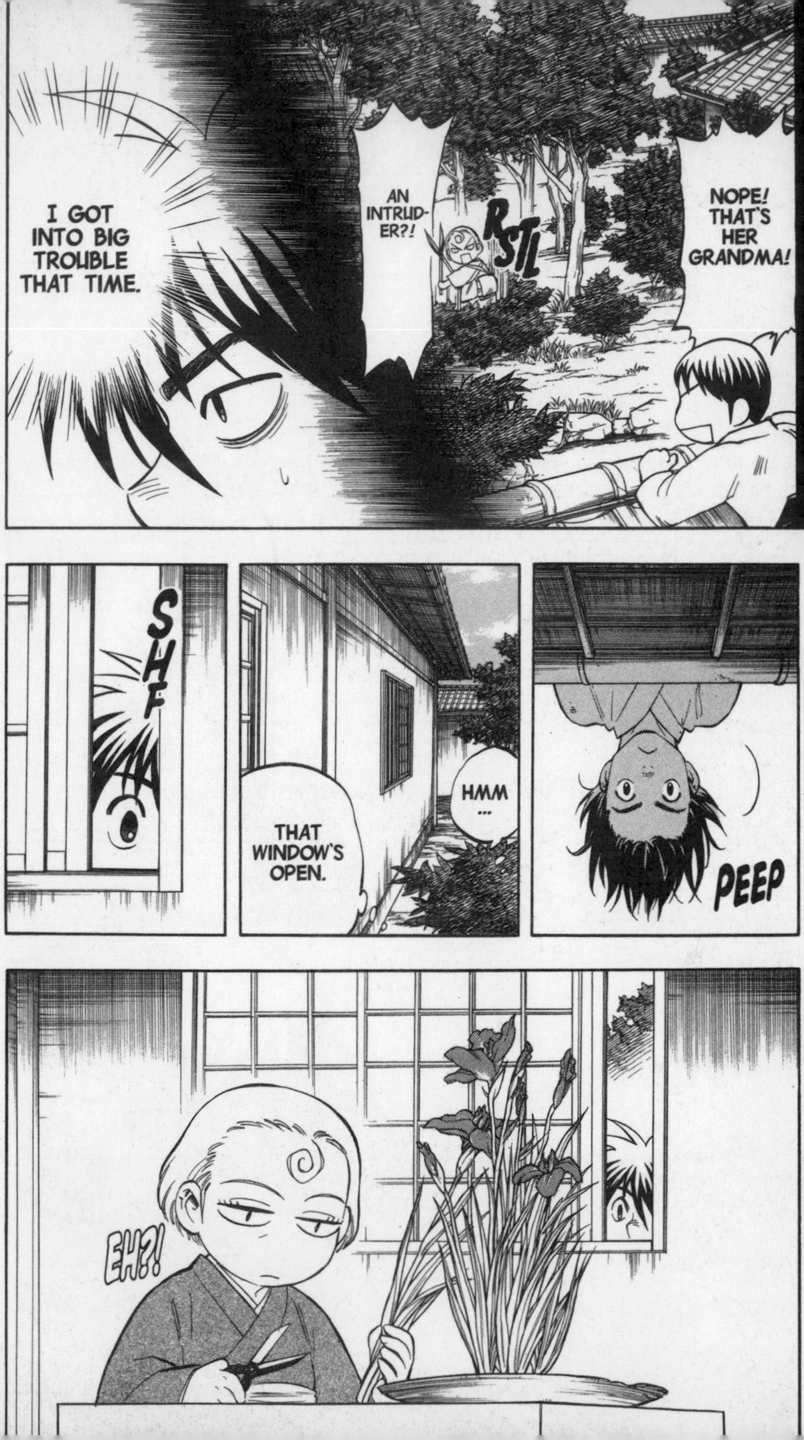
NOPE! THAT'S HER GRANDMA!
RSTL
AN INTRUDER?!
I GOT INTO BIG TROUBLE THAT TIME.
PEEP
HMM ...
THAT WINDOW'S OPEN.
SHF
EH?!

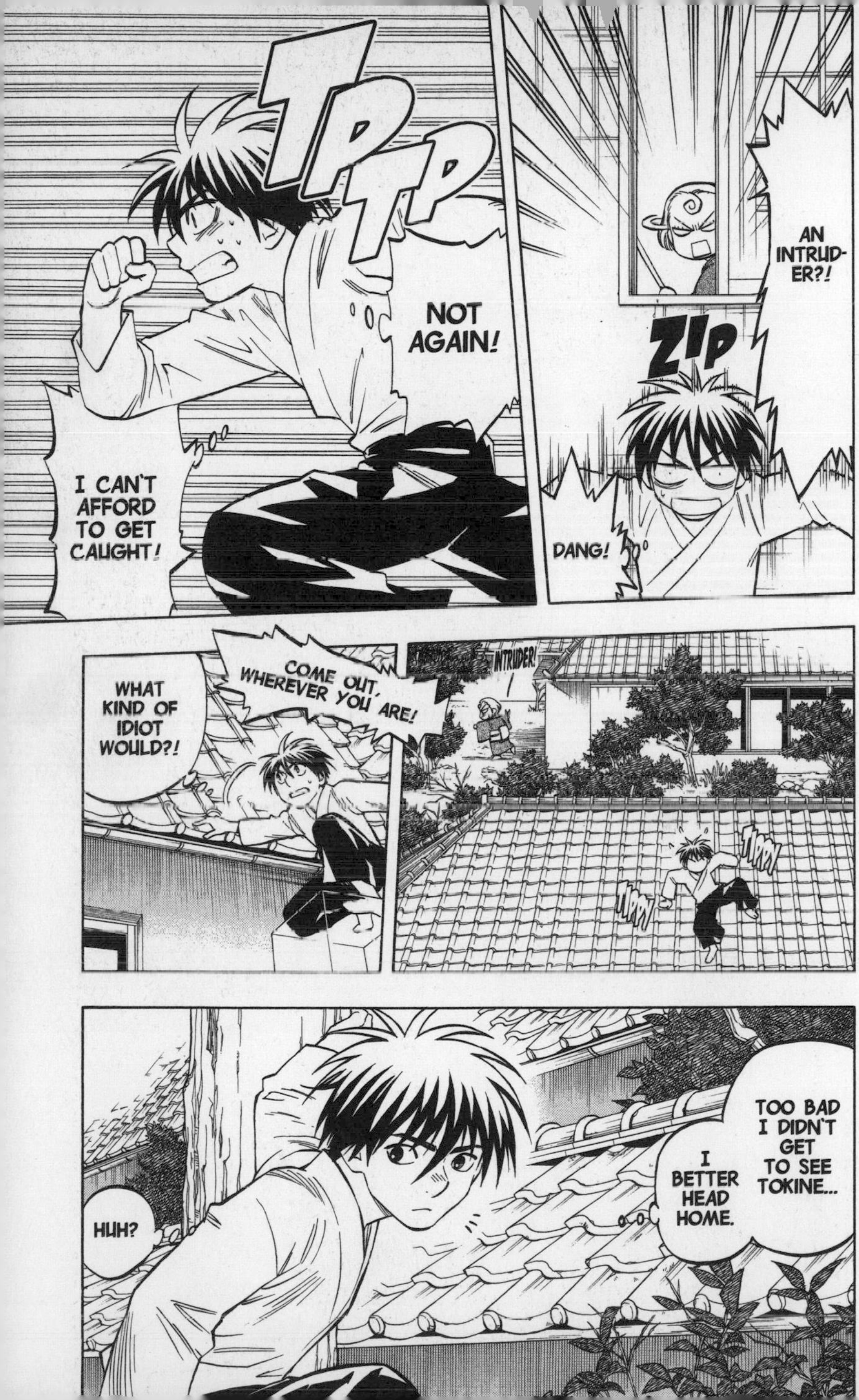
AN INTRUDER?!
ZIP
DANG!
TPTP
NOT AGAIN!
I CAN'T AFFORD TO GET CAUGHT!
INTRUDER!
COME OUT, WHEREVER YOU ARE!
WHAT KIND OF IDIOT WOULD?!
TOO BAD I DIDN'T GET TO SEE TOKINE...
I BETTER HEAD HOME.
HUH?

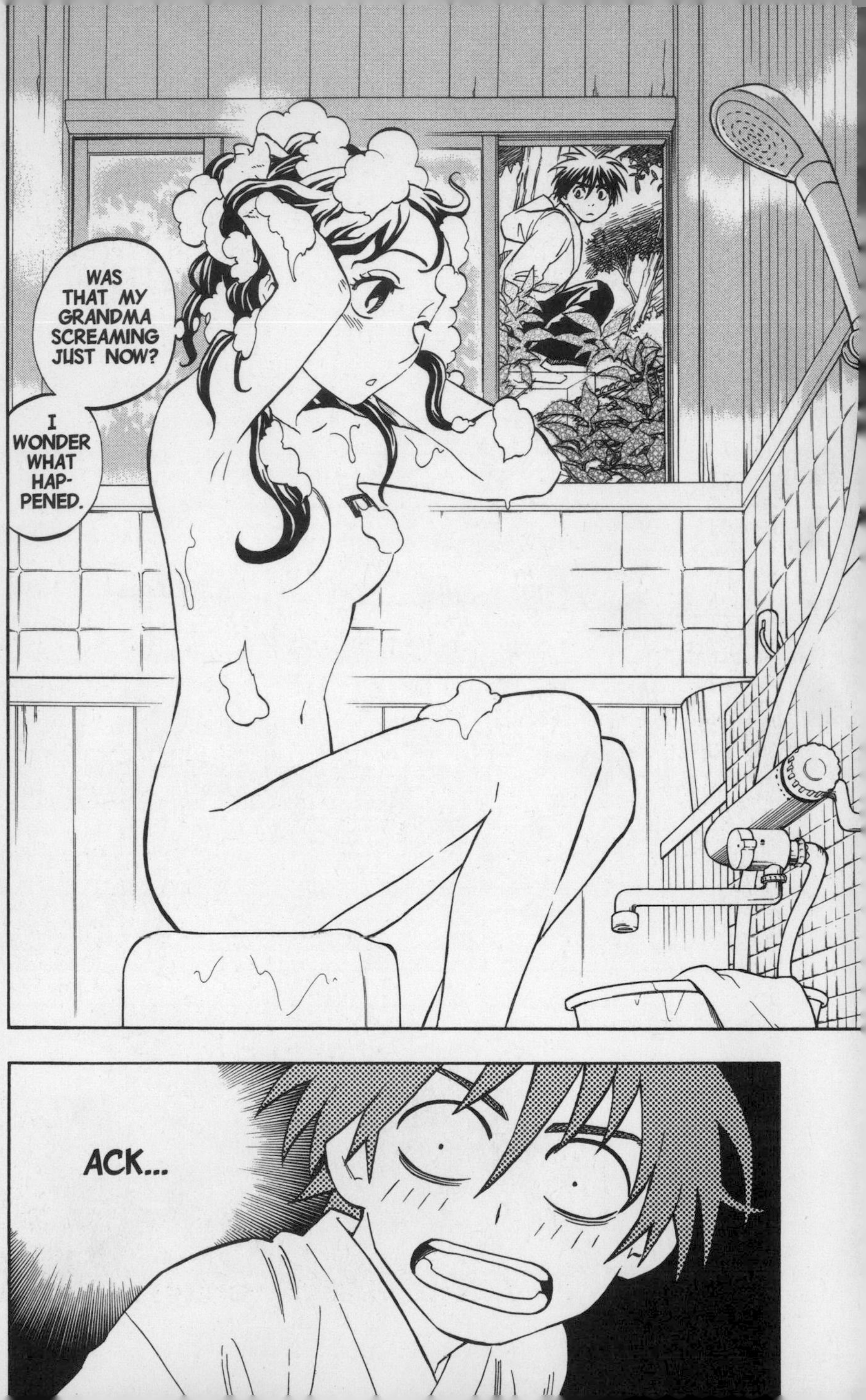
WAS THAT MY GRANDMA SCREAMING JUST NOW?
I WONDER WHAT HAP-PENED.
ACK...

Chapter 220: Distraction

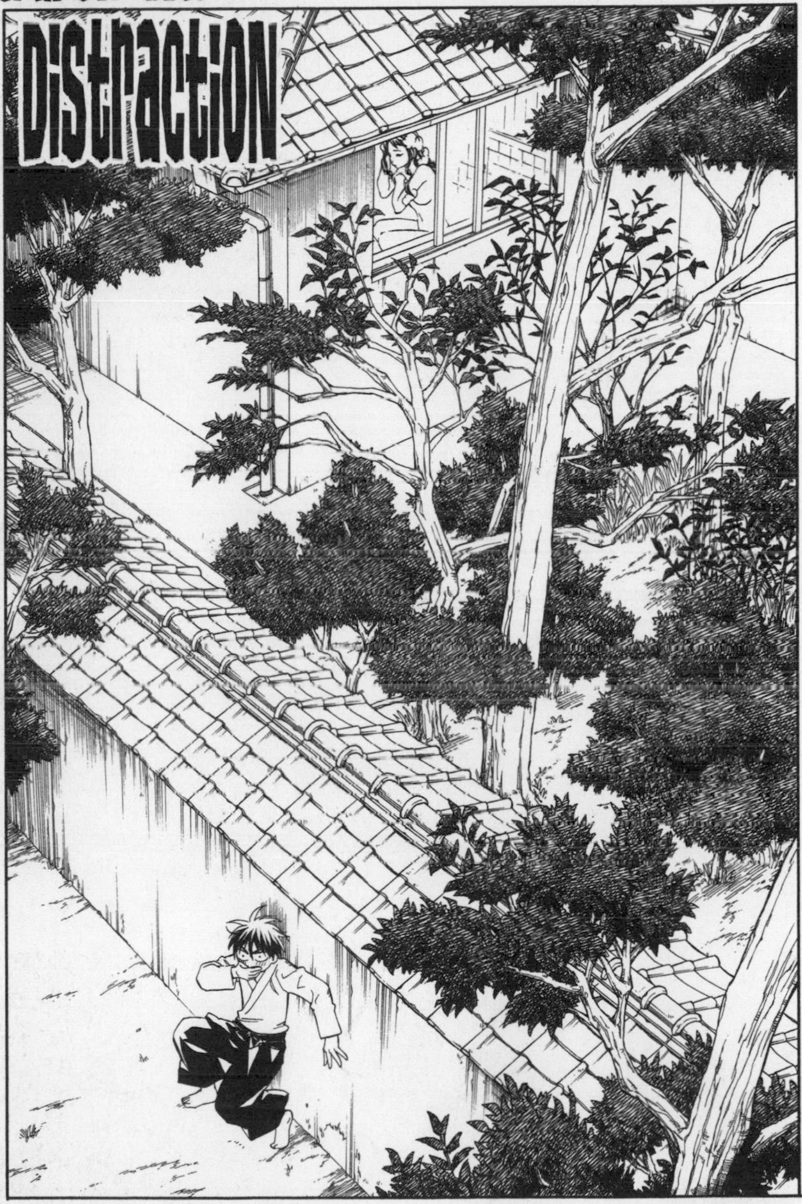

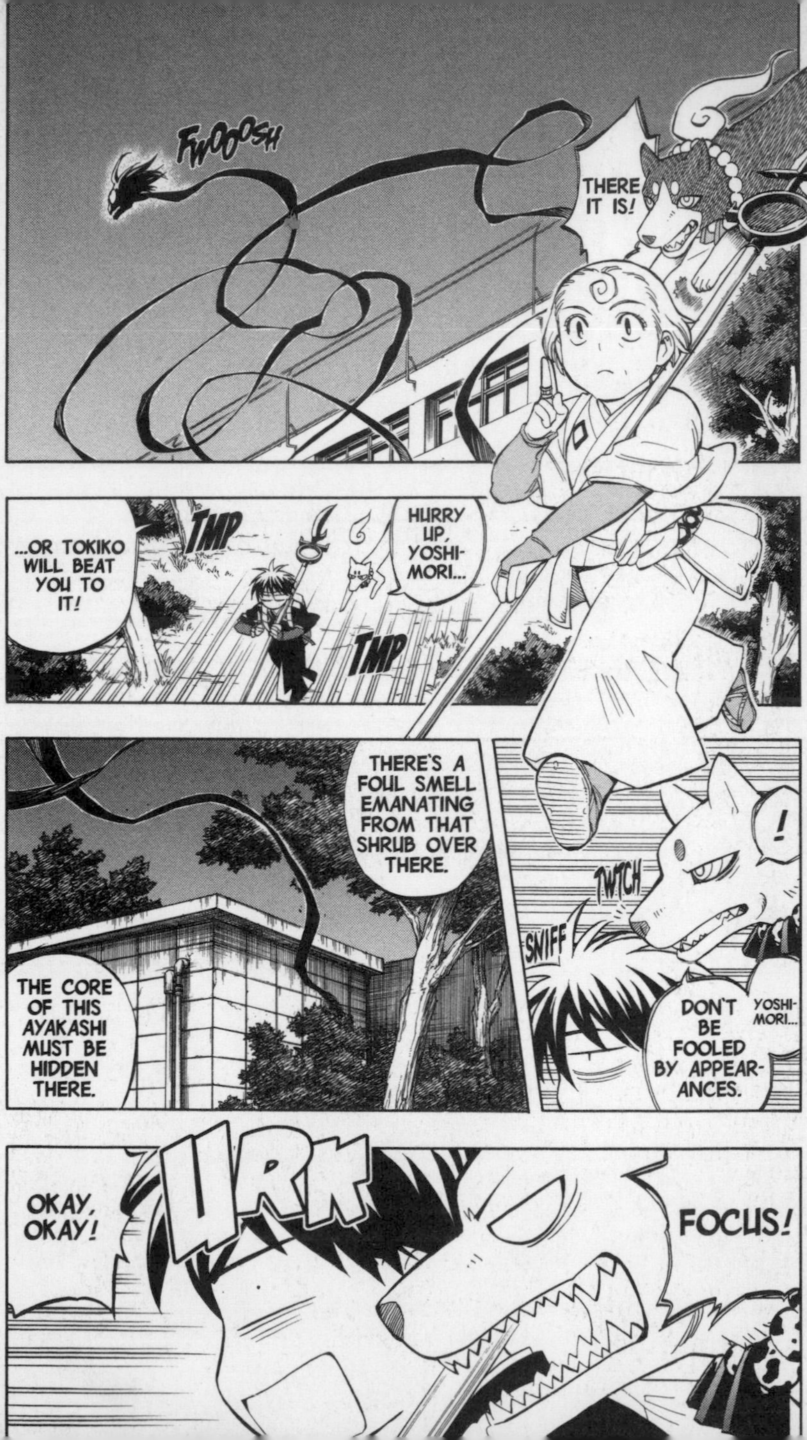
THERE IT IS!
FWOOOSH
HURRY UP, YOSHIMORI...
TMP
...OR TOKIKO WILL BEAT YOU TO IT!
TMP
!
TWITCH
SNIFF
YOSHIMORI...
DON'T BE FOOLED BY APPEARANCES.
THERE'S A FOUL SMELL EMANATING FROM THAT SHRUB OVER THERE.
THE CORE OF THIS AYAKASHI MUST BE HIDDEN THERE.
FOCUS!
URK
OKAY, OKAY!

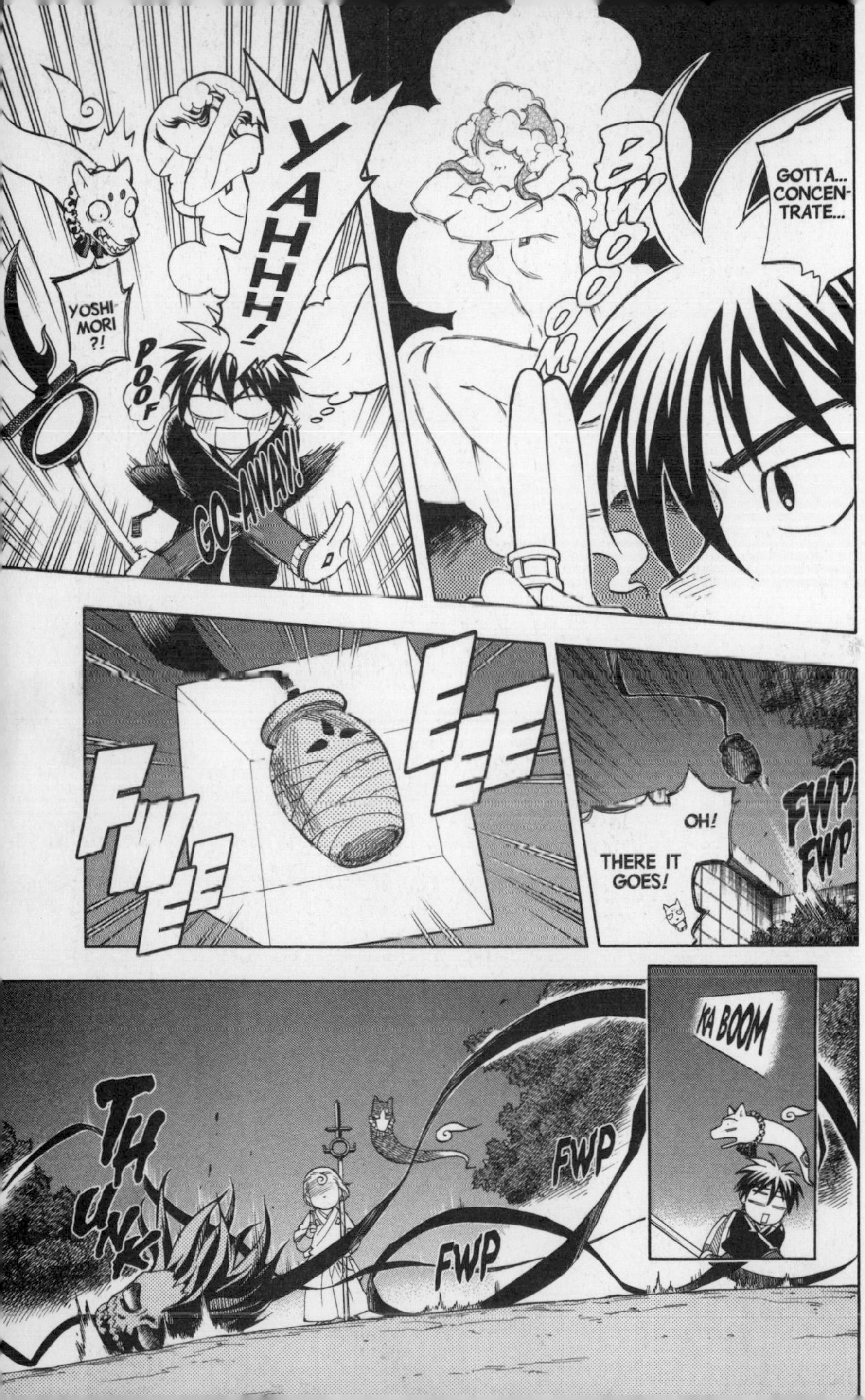
GOTTA... CONCENTRATE...
BWOOOOM
YAHHH!
YOSHIMORI?!
POOF
GO AWAY!
OH!
THERE IT GOES!
FWP FWP
EEEE
FWEEE
KA BOOM
FWP
FWP
THUNK

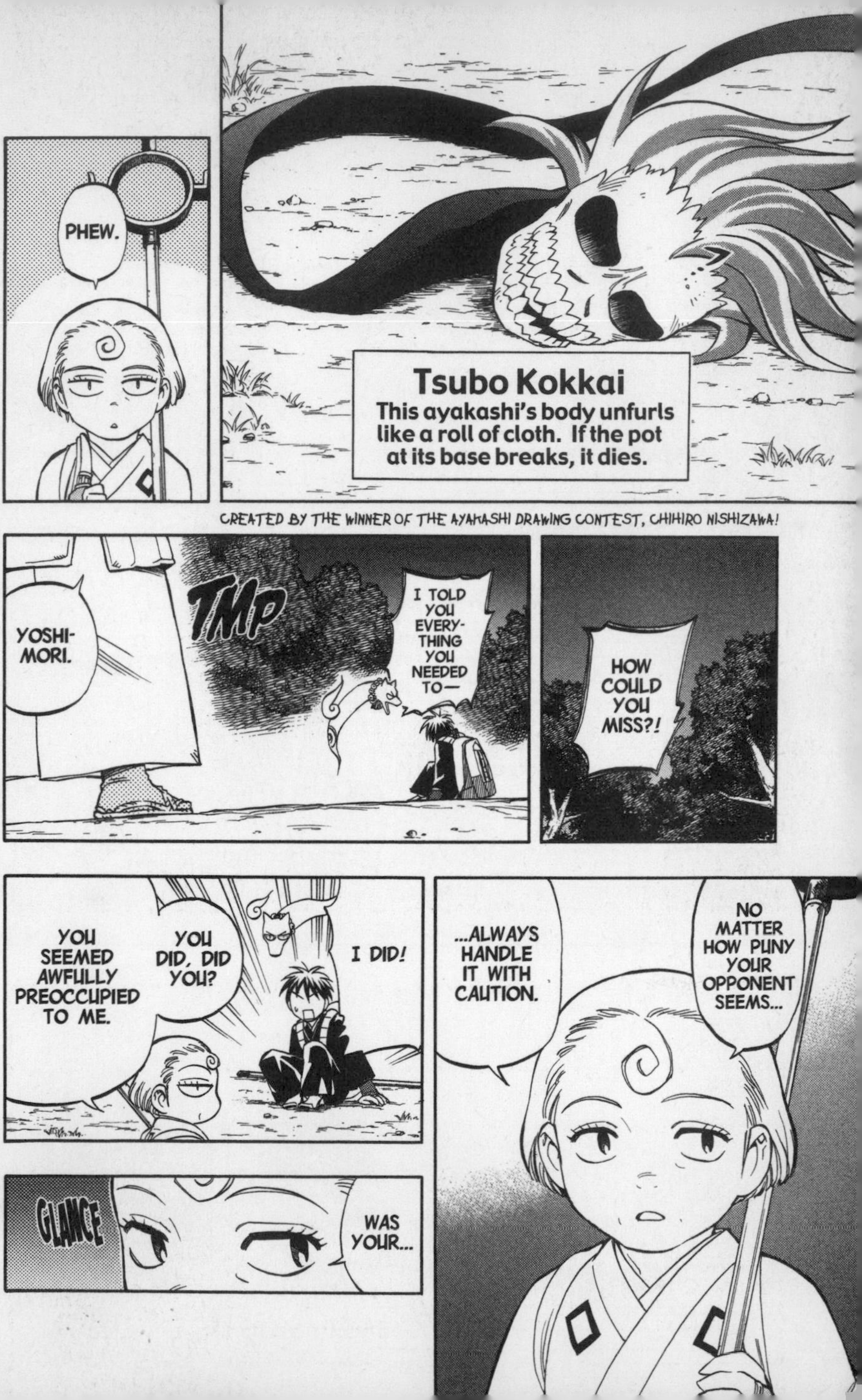
Tsubo Kokkai
This ayakashi's body unfurls like a roll of cloth. If the pot at its base breaks, it dies.
PHEW.
CREATED BY THE WINNER OF THE AYAKASHI DRAWING CONTEST, CHIHIRO NISHIZAWA!
HOW COULD YOU MISS?!
I TOLD YOU EVERYTHING YOU NEEDED TO—
TMP
YOSHIMORI.
NO MATTER HOW PUNY YOUR OPPONENT SEEMS...
...ALWAYS HANDLE IT WITH CAUTION.
I DID!
YOU DID, DID YOU?
YOU SEEMED AWFULLY PREOCCUPIED TO ME.
WAS YOUR...
GLANCE

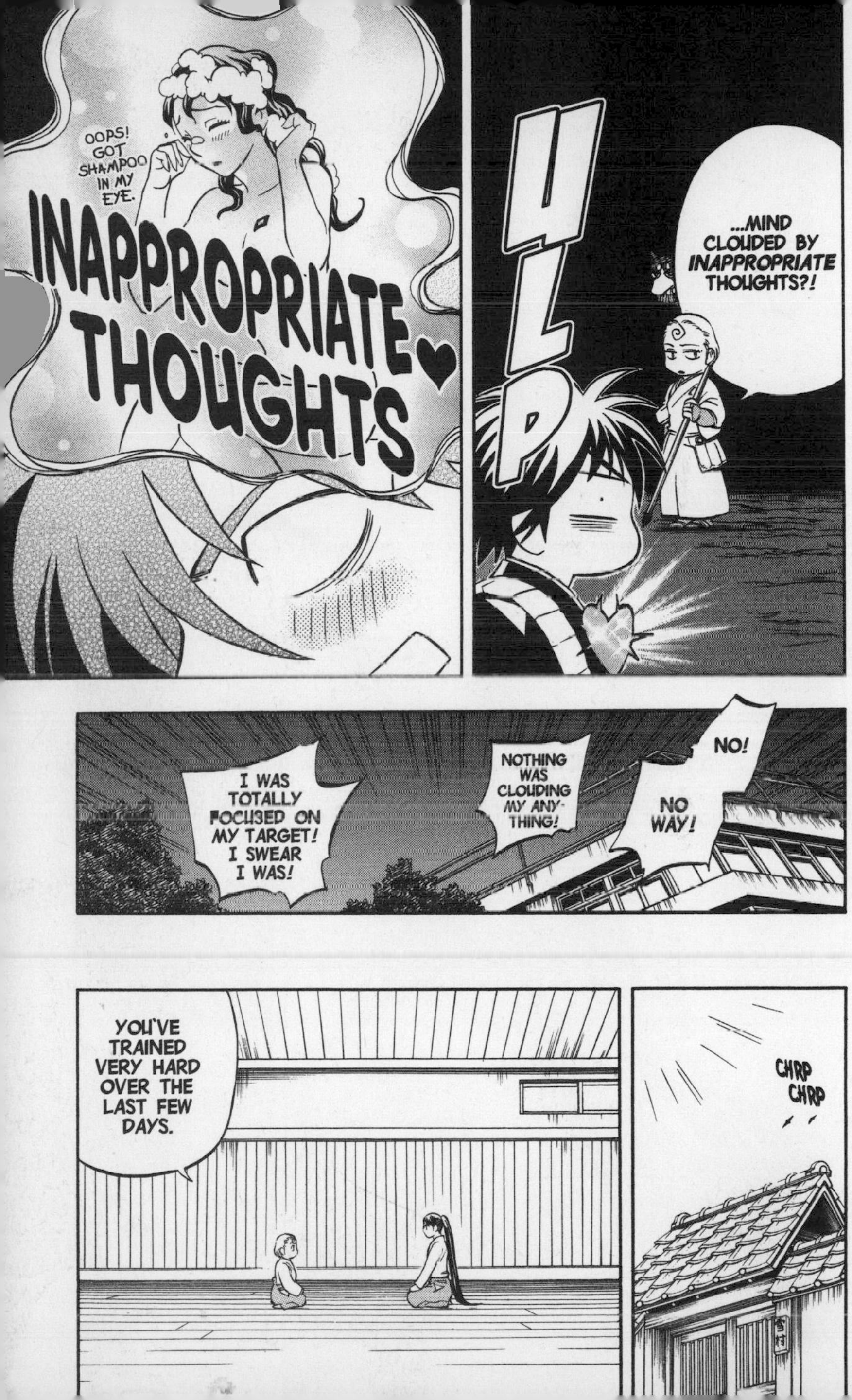
ULP
...MIND CLOUDED BY INAPPROPRIATE THOUGHTS?!
OOPS! GOT SHAMPOO IN MY EYE.
INAPPROPRIATE THOUGHTS
NO!
NO WAY!
NOTHING WAS CLOUDING MY ANYTHING!
I WAS TOTALLY FOCUSED ON MY TARGET! I SWEAR I WAS!
CHRP CHRP
YOU'VE TRAINED VERY HARD OVER THE LAST FEW DAYS.

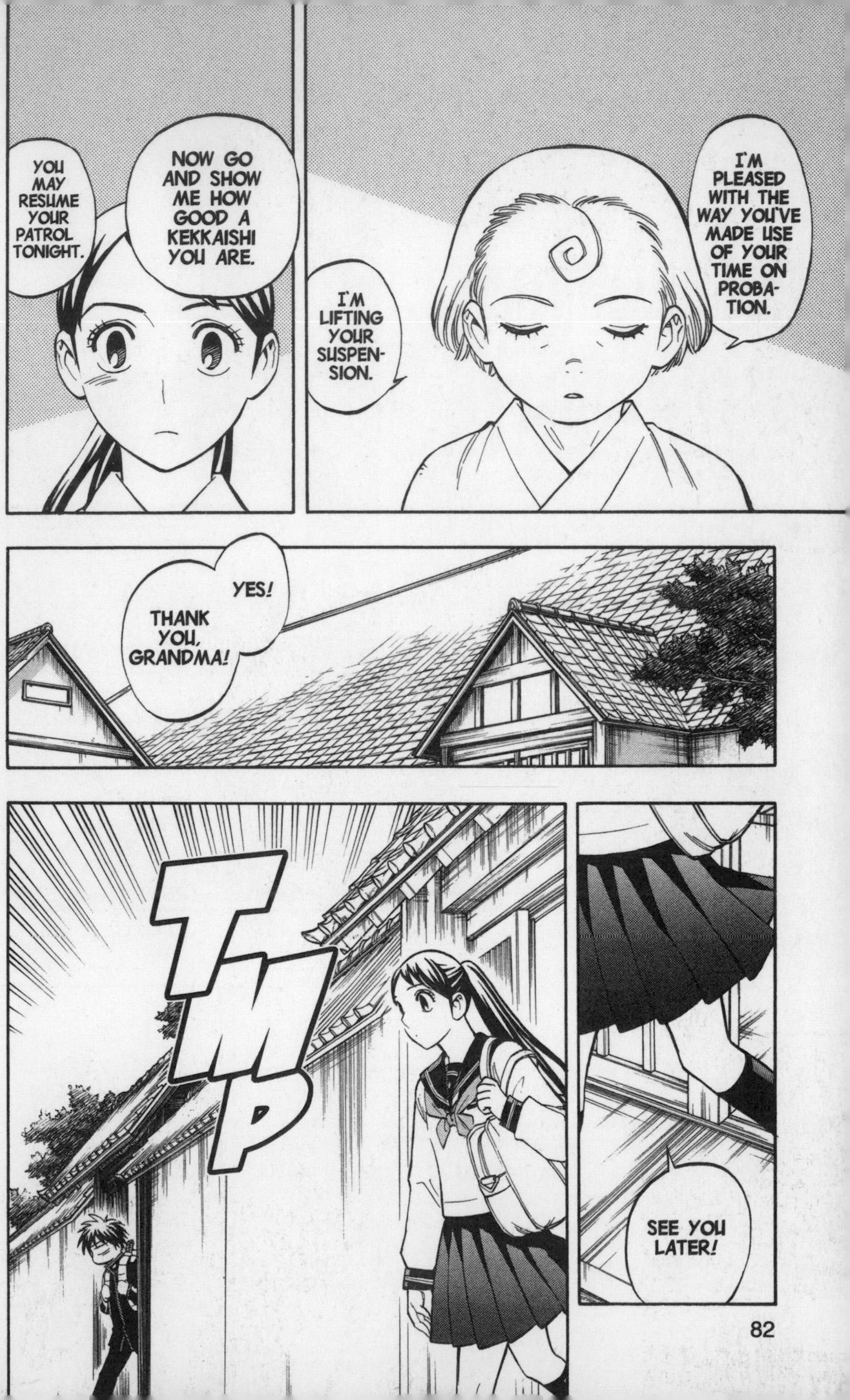
I'M PLEASED WITH THE WAY YOU'VE MADE USE OF YOUR TIME ON PROBATION.
I'M LIFTING YOUR SUSPENSION.
NOW GO AND SHOW ME HOW GOOD A KEKKAISHI YOU ARE.
YOU MAY RESUME YOUR PATROL TONIGHT.
YES!
THANK YOU, GRANDMA!
SEE YOU LATER!
TMP

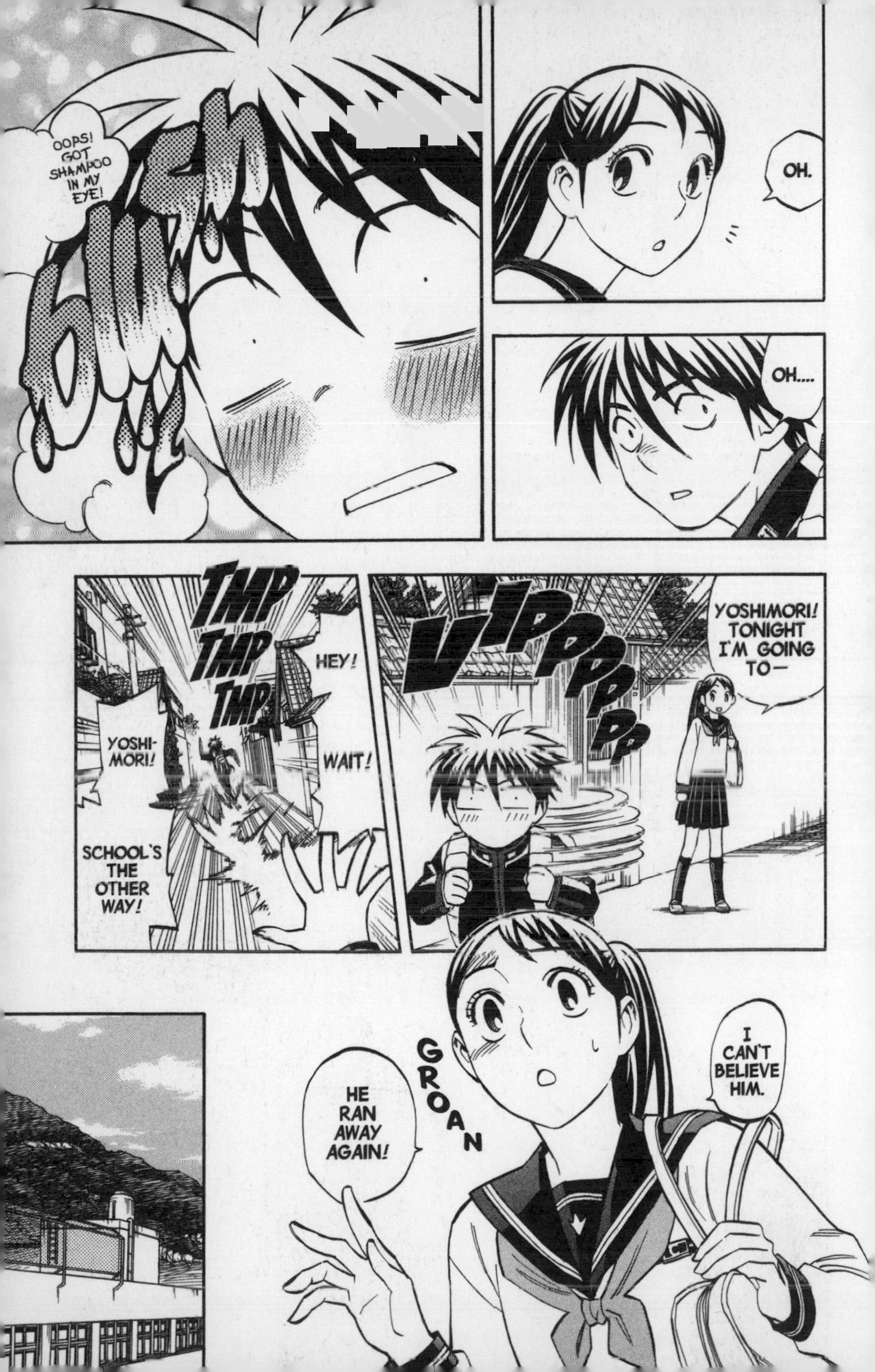
OH.
OH....
OOPS! GOT SHAMPOO IN MY EYE!
YOSHIMORI! TONIGHT I'M GOING TO—
VIPPPPPP
TMP TMP TMP
HEY!
WAIT!
YOSHI-MORI!
SCHOOL'S THE OTHER WAY!
I CAN'T BELIEVE HIM.
GROAN
HE RAN AWAY AGAIN!

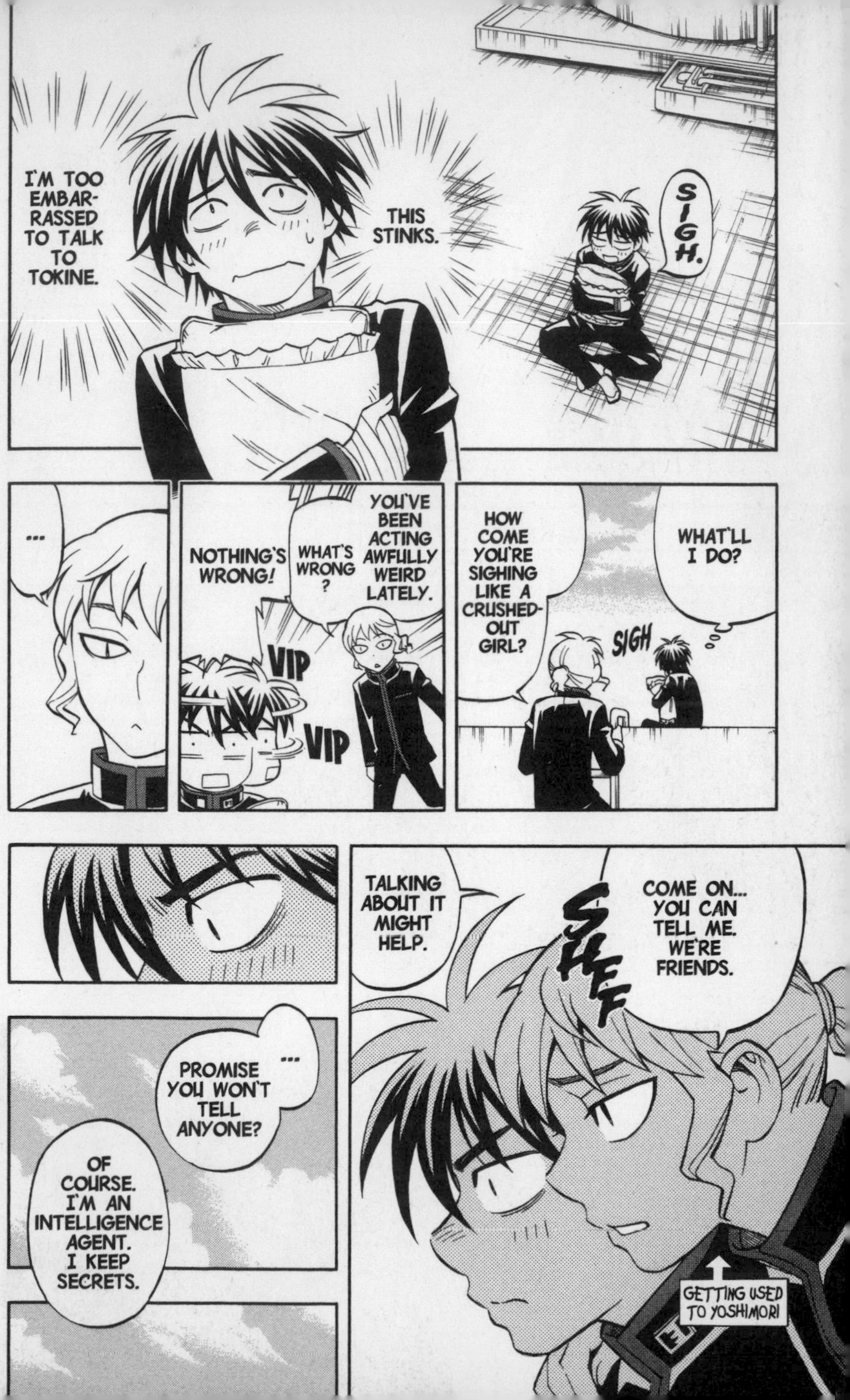
SIGH.
THIS STINKS.
I'M TOO EMBAR-RASSED TO TALK TO TOKINE.
WHAT'LL I DO?
HOW COME YOU'RE SIGHING LIKE A CRUSHED-OUT GIRL?
SIGH
YOU'VE BEEN ACTING AWFULLY WEIRD LATELY.
WHAT'S WRONG?
NOTHING'S WRONG!
VIP
VIP
...
COME ON... YOU CAN TELL ME. WE'RE FRIENDS.
SHEF
TALKING ABOUT IT MIGHT HELP.
GETTING USED TO YOSHIMORI
...
PROMISE YOU WON'T TELL ANYONE?
OF COURSE. I'M AN INTELLIGENCE AGENT. I KEEP SECRETS.

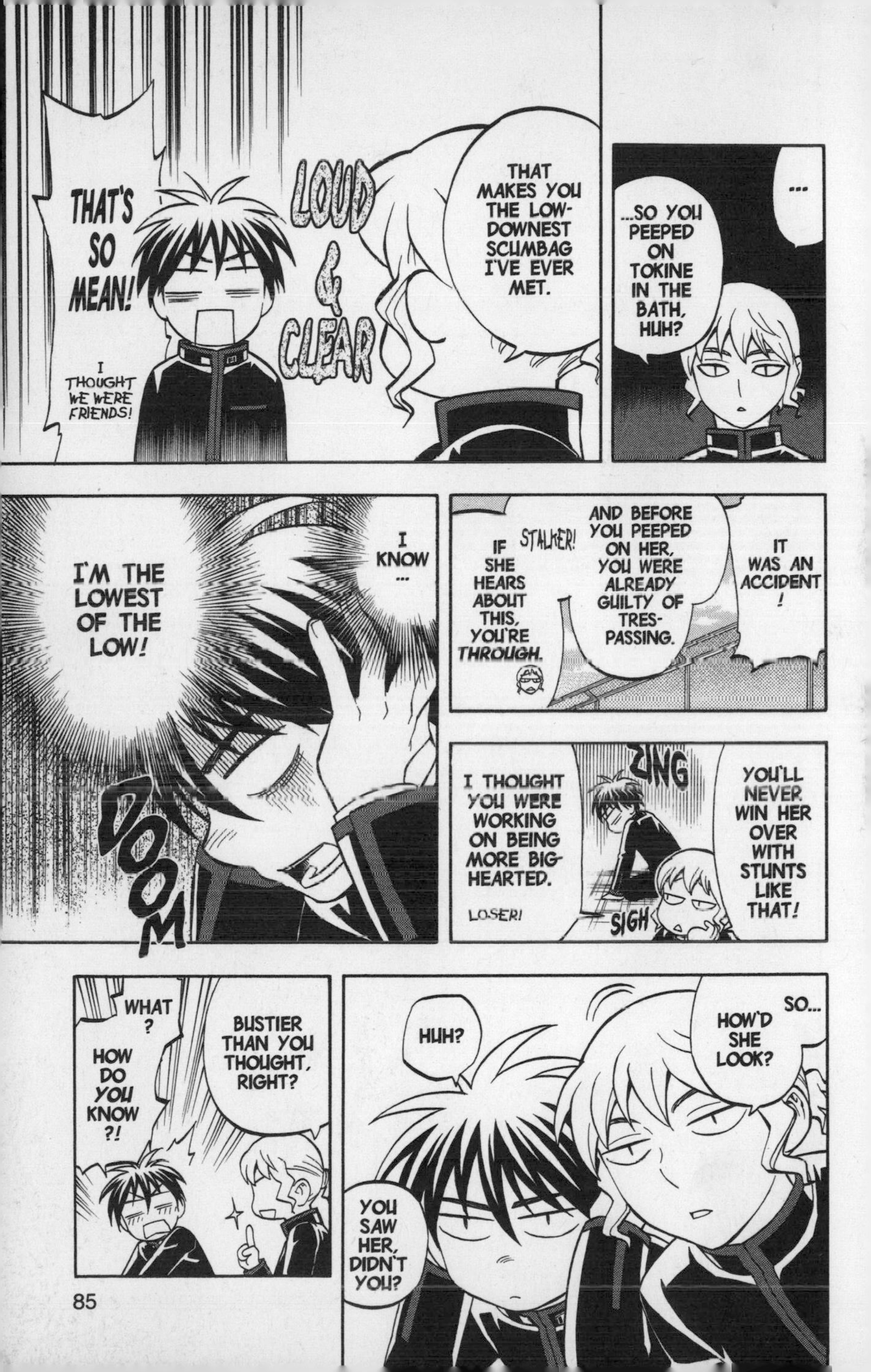
...
...SO YOU PEEPED ON TOKINE IN THE BATH, HUH?
THAT MAKES YOU THE LOW-DOWNEST SCUMBAG I'VE EVER MET.
LOUD & CLEAR
THAT'S SO MEAN!
I THOUGHT WE WERE FRIENDS!
IT WAS AN ACCIDENT!
AND BEFORE YOU PEEPED ON HER, YOU WERE ALREADY GUILTY OF TRES-PASSING.
STALKER!
IF SHE HEARS ABOUT THIS, YOU'RE THROUGH.
YOU'LL NEVER WIN HER OVER WITH STUNTS LIKE THAT!
ZING
I THOUGHT YOU WERE WORKING ON BEING MORE BIG-HEARTED.
SIGH
LOSER!
I KNOW...
I'M THE LOWEST OF THE LOW!
DOOM
SO...
HOW'D SHE LOOK?
HUH?
YOU SAW HER, DIDN'T YOU?
BUSTIER THAN YOU THOUGHT, RIGHT?
WHAT?
HOW DO YOU KNOW?!

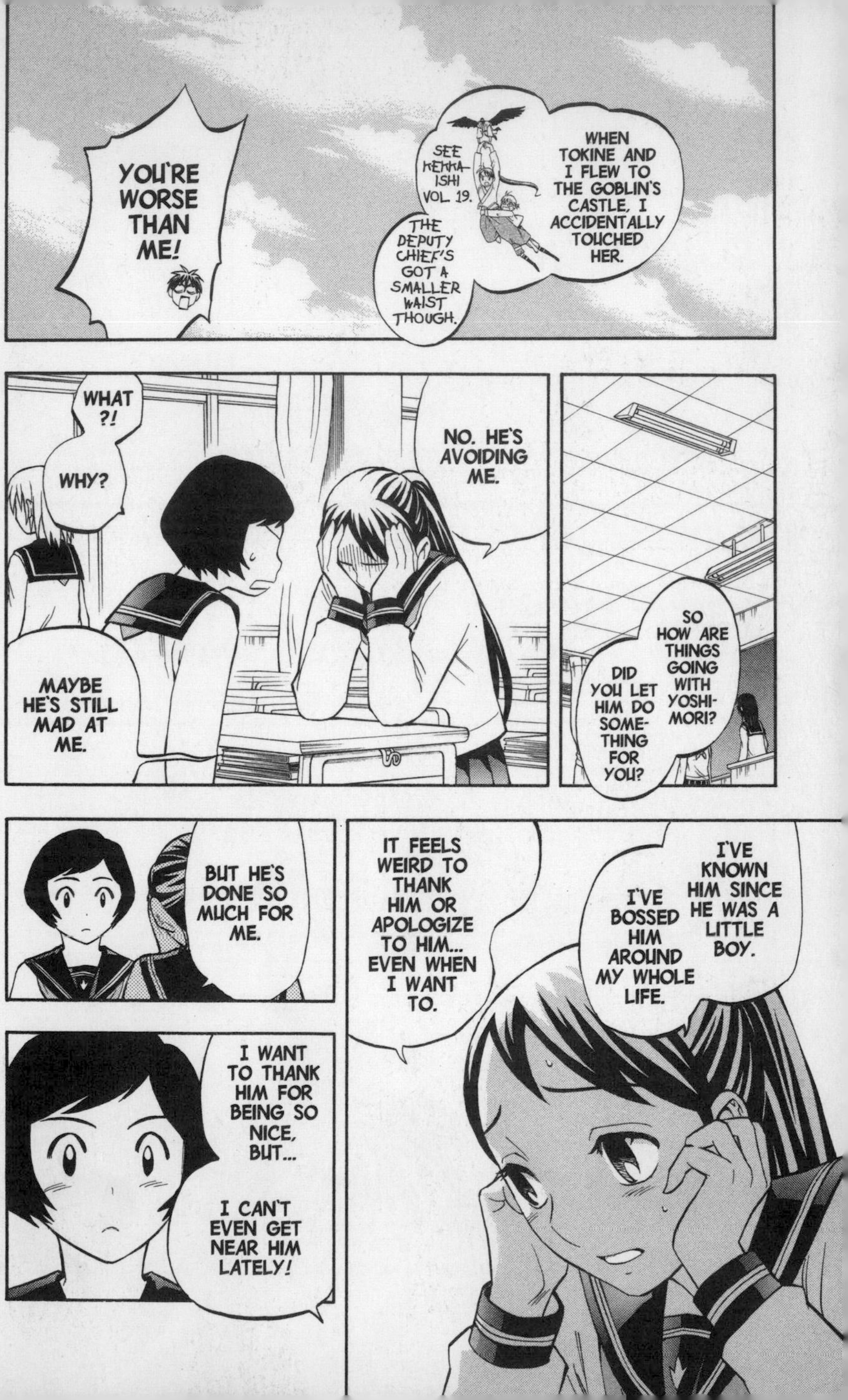
WHEN TOKINE AND I FLEW TO THE GOBLIN'S CASTLE, I ACCIDENTALLY TOUCHED HER.
SEE KEKKAISHI VOL. 19.
THE DEPUTY CHIEF'S GOT A SMALLER WAIST THOUGH.
YOU'RE WORSE THAN ME!
SO HOW ARE THINGS GOING WITH YOSHIMORI?
DID YOU LET HIM DO SOMETHING FOR YOU?
NO. HE'S AVOIDING ME.
WHAT?!
WHY?
MAYBE HE'S STILL MAD AT ME.
I'VE KNOWN HIM SINCE HE WAS A LITTLE BOY.
I'VE BOSSED HIM AROUND MY WHOLE LIFE.
IT FEELS WEIRD TO THANK HIM OR APOLOGIZE TO HIM... EVEN WHEN I WANT TO.
BUT HE'S DONE SO MUCH FOR ME.
I WANT TO THANK HIM FOR BEING SO NICE, BUT...
I CAN'T EVEN GET NEAR HIM LATELY!

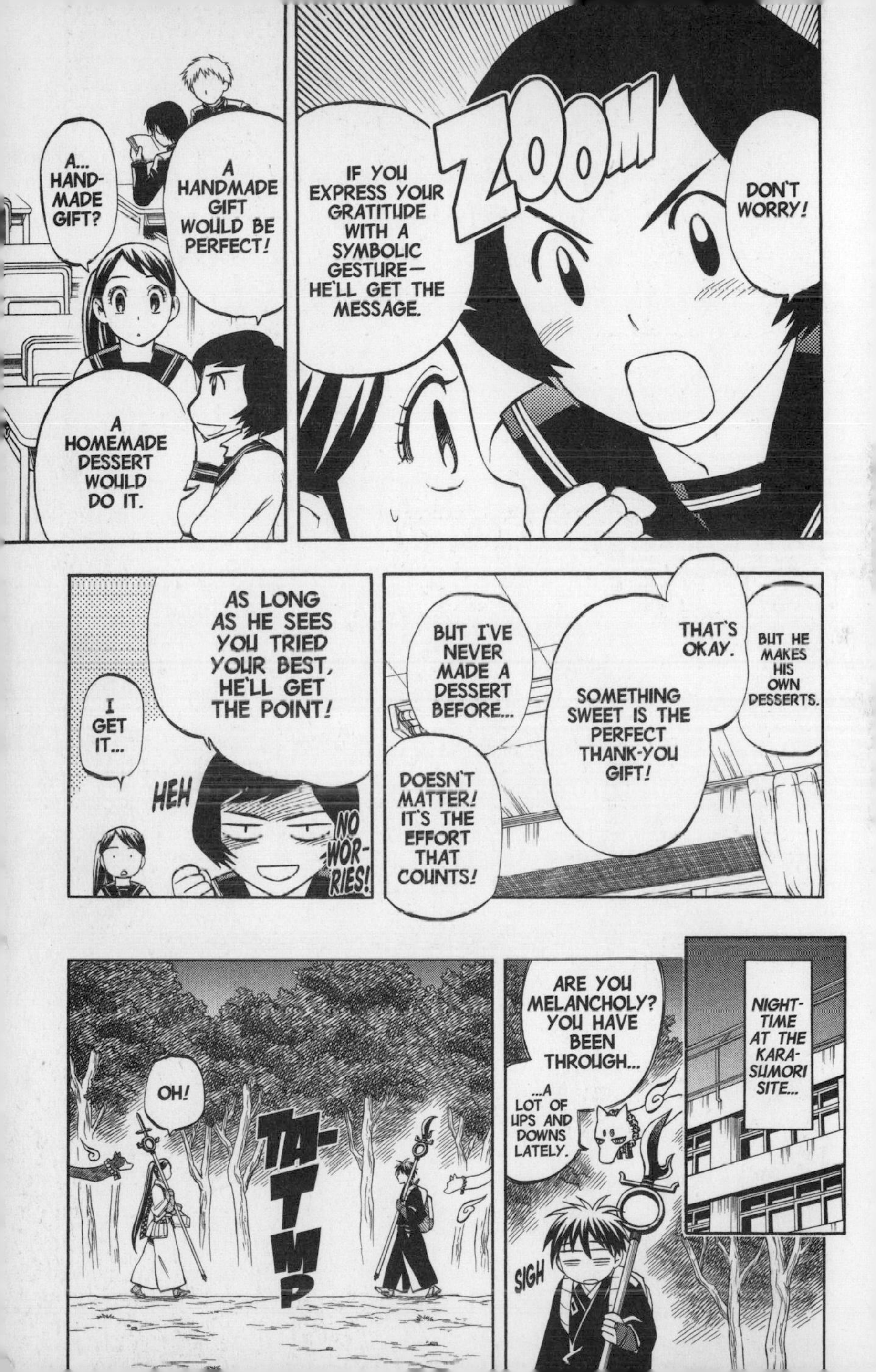
DON'T WORRY!
ZOOM
IF YOU EXPRESS YOUR GRATITUDE WITH A SYMBOLIC GESTURE— HE'LL GET THE MESSAGE.
A HANDMADE GIFT WOULD BE PERFECT!
A... HAND-MADE GIFT?
A HOMEMADE DESSERT WOULD DO IT.
BUT HE MAKES HIS OWN DESSERTS.
THAT'S OKAY.
SOMETHING SWEET IS THE PERFECT THANK-YOU GIFT!
BUT I'VE NEVER MADE A DESSERT BEFORE...
DOESN'T MATTER! IT'S THE EFFORT THAT COUNTS!
AS LONG AS HE SEES YOU TRIED YOUR BEST, HE'LL GET THE POINT!
HEH
NO WOR-RIES!
I GET IT...
NIGHT-TIME AT THE KARA-SUMORI SITE...
ARE YOU MELANCHOLY? YOU HAVE BEEN THROUGH...
...A LOT OF UPS AND DOWNS LATELY.
SIGH
OH!
TA-TMP

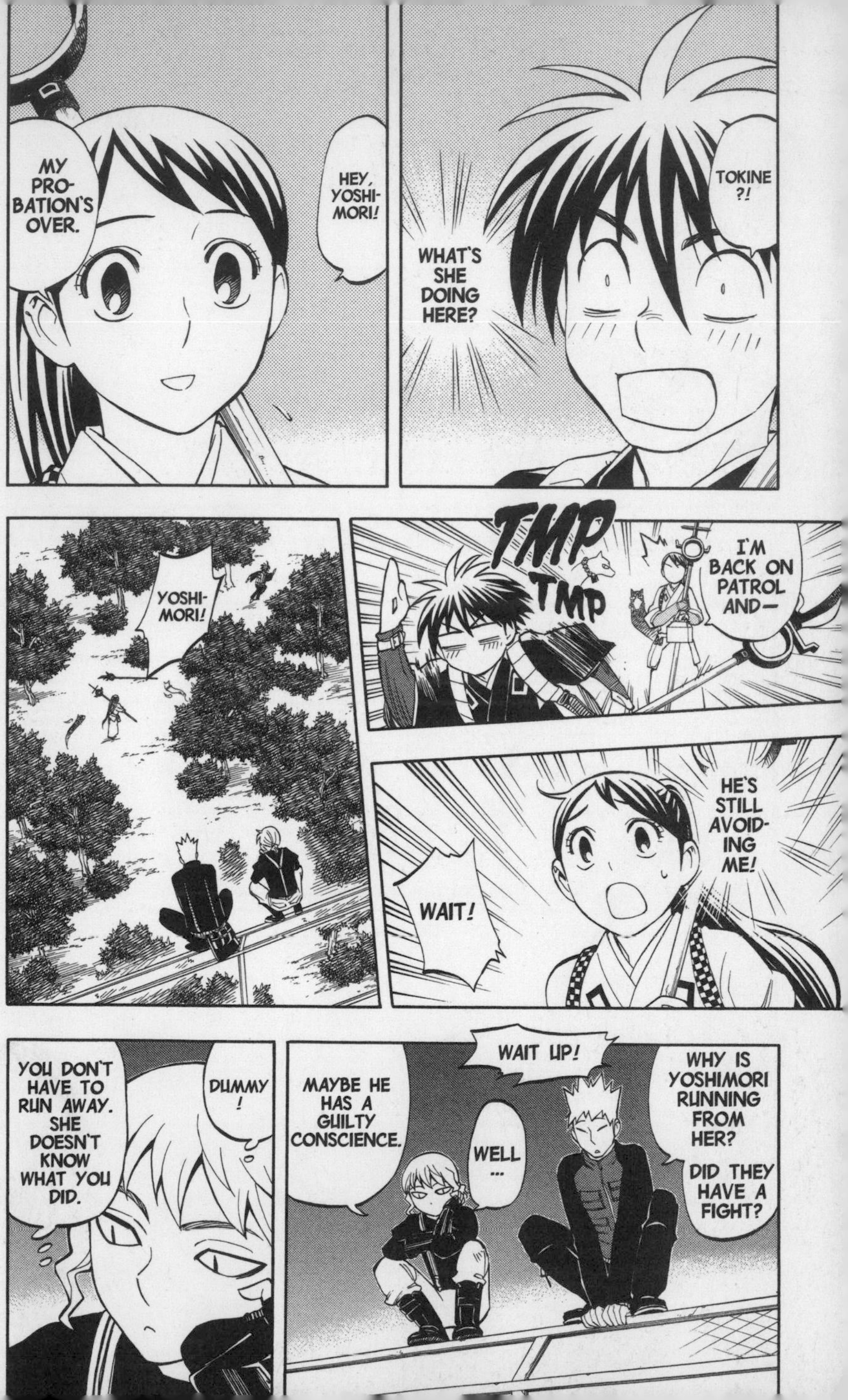
TOKINE?!
WHAT'S SHE DOING HERE?
HEY, YOSHIMORI!
MY PROBATION'S OVER.
TMP
TMP
I'M BACK ON PATROL AND—
HE'S STILL AVOIDING ME!
WAIT!
YOSHIMORI!
WAIT UP!
WHY IS YOSHIMORI RUNNING FROM HER?
DID THEY HAVE A FIGHT?
WELL...
MAYBE HE HAS A GUILTY CONSCIENCE.
DUMMY!
YOU DON'T HAVE TO RUN AWAY. SHE DOESN'T KNOW WHAT YOU DID.

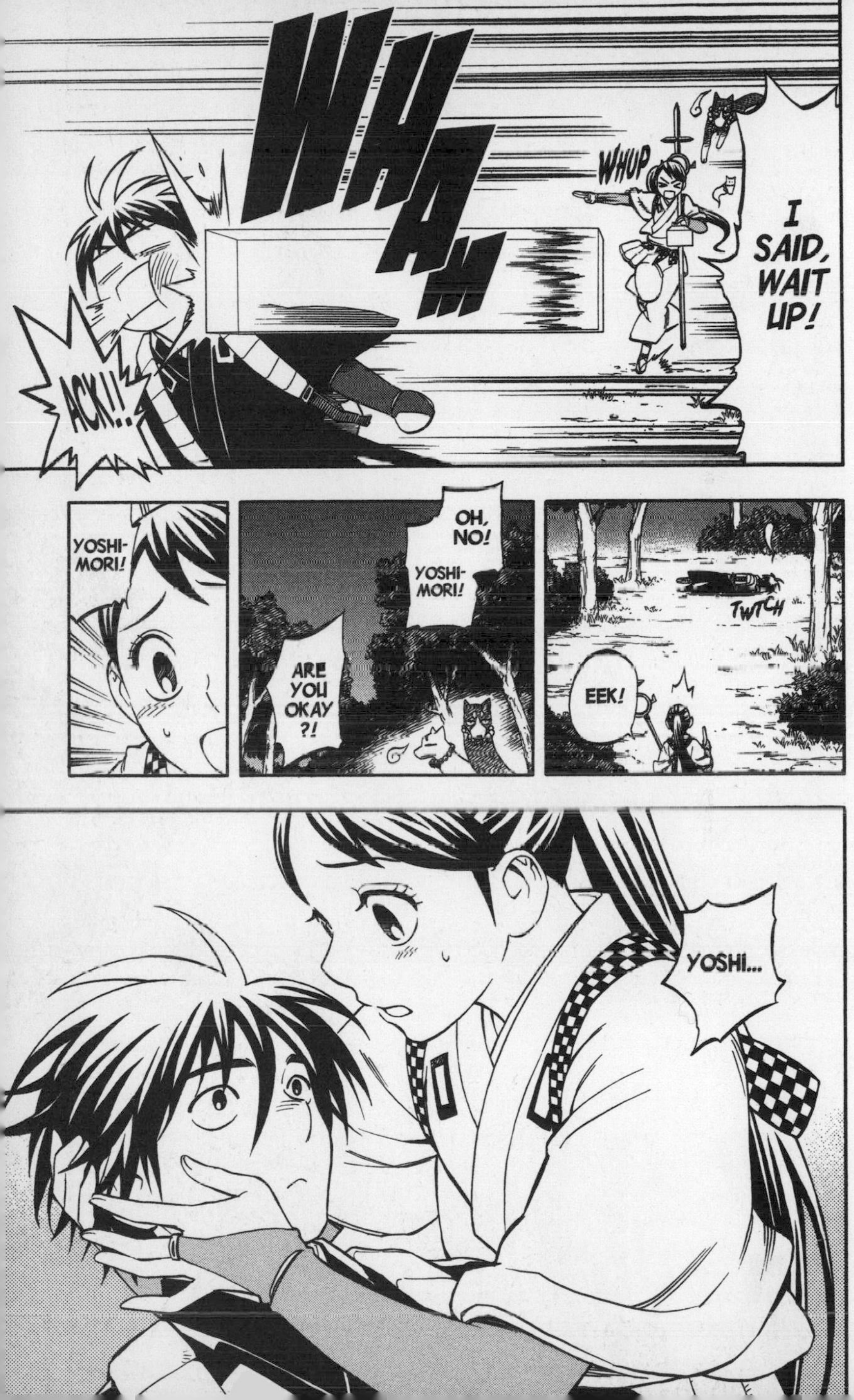
I SAID, WAIT UP!
WHUP
WHAM
ACK!!
TWTCH
EEK!
OH, NO!
YOSHI-MORI!
ARE YOU OKAY?!
YOSHI-MORI!
YOSHI...

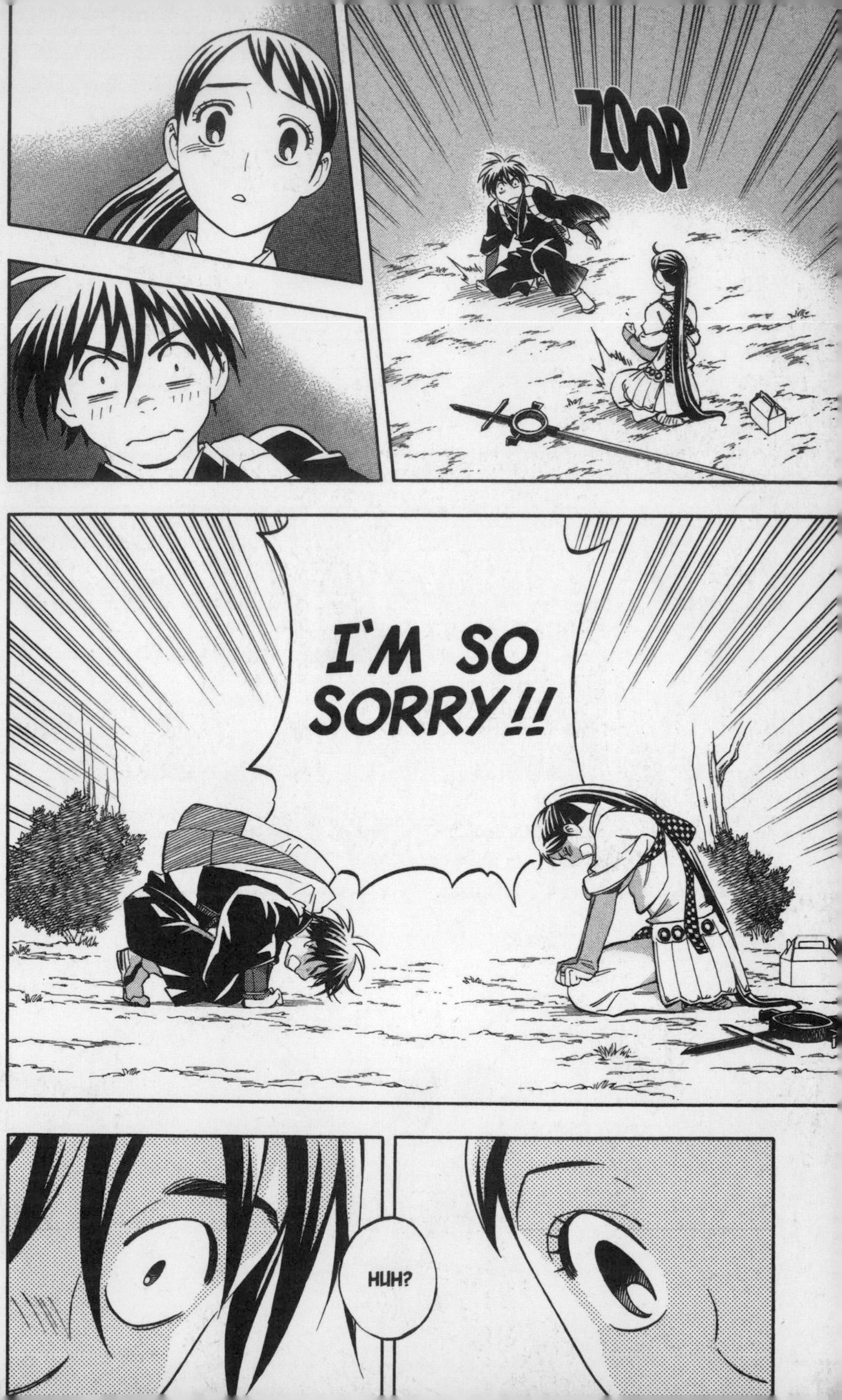
ZOOP
I'M SO SORRY!!
HUH?

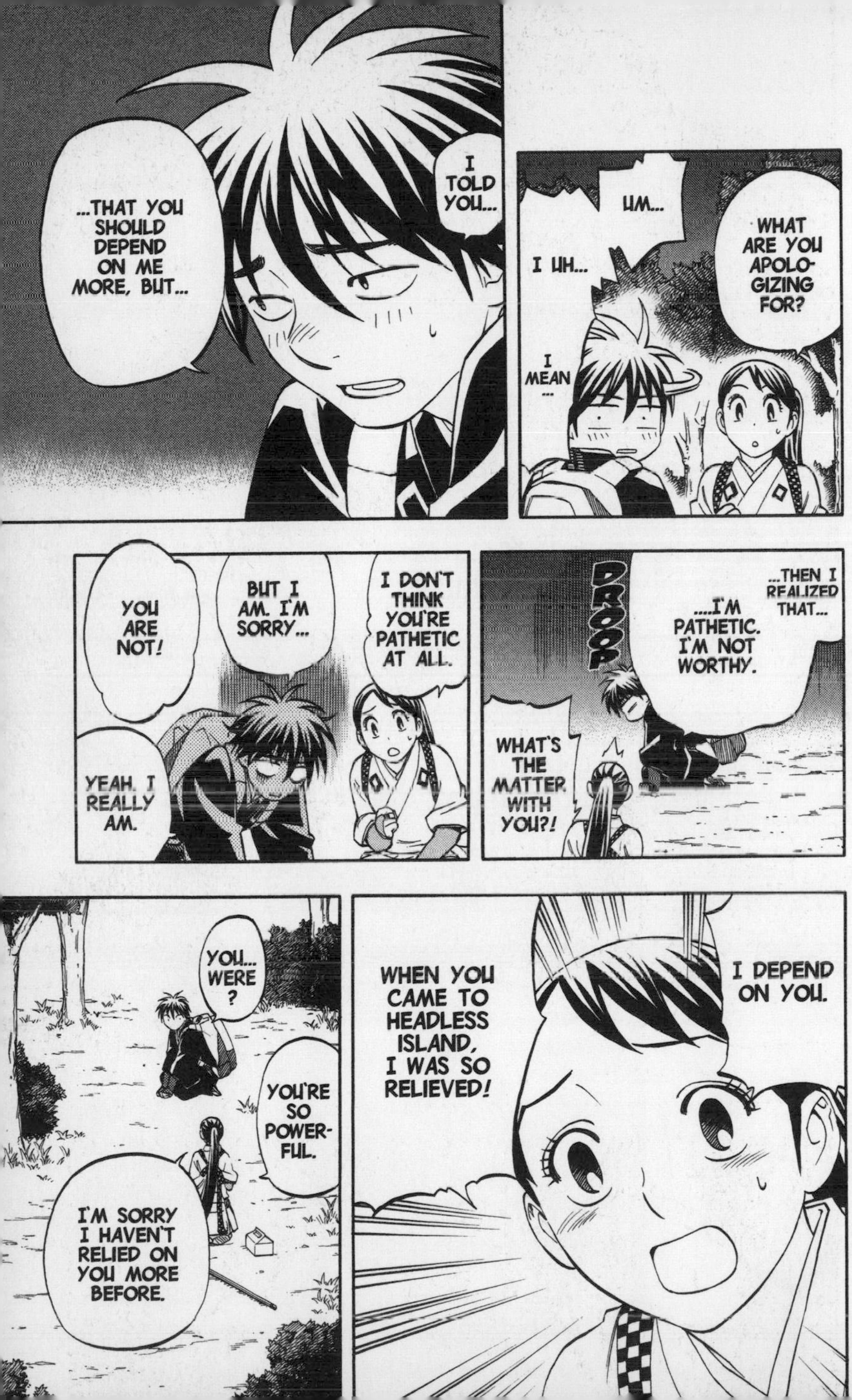
WHAT ARE YOU APOLOGIZING FOR?
UM...
I UH...
I MEAN ...
I TOLD YOU...
...THAT YOU SHOULD DEPEND ON ME MORE, BUT...
...THEN I REALIZED THAT...
....I'M PATHETIC. I'M NOT WORTHY.
DROOP
WHAT'S THE MATTER WITH YOU?!
I DON'T THINK YOU'RE PATHETIC AT ALL.
BUT I AM. I'M SORRY...
YOU ARE NOT!
YEAH. I REALLY AM.
I DEPEND ON YOU.
WHEN YOU CAME TO HEADLESS ISLAND, I WAS SO RELIEVED!
YOU... WERE?
YOU'RE SO POWER-FUL.
I'M SORRY I HAVEN'T RELIED ON YOU MORE BEFORE.

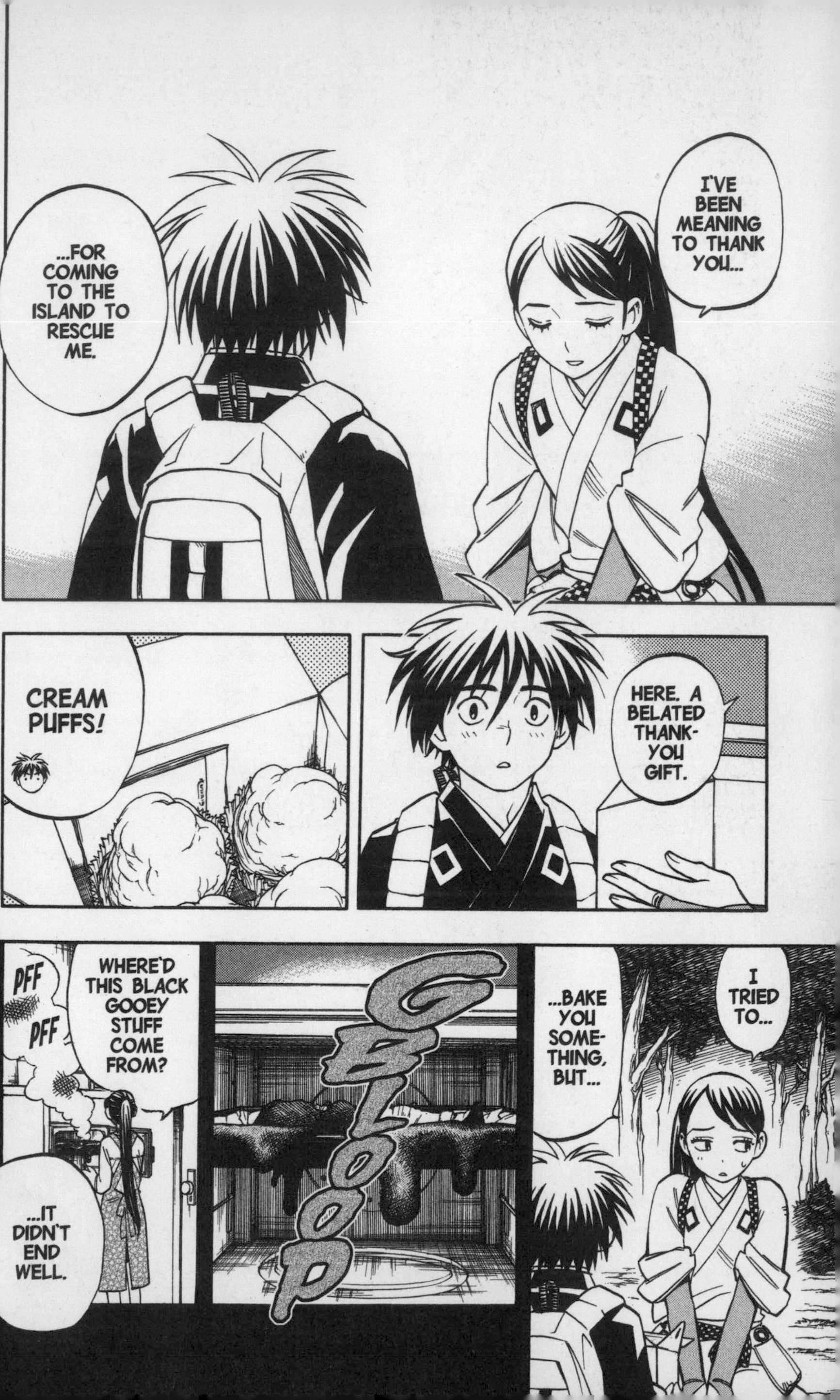
I'VE BEEN MEANING TO THANK YOU...
...FOR COMING TO THE ISLAND TO RESCUE ME.
HERE. A BELATED THANK-YOU GIFT.
CREAM PUFFS!
I TRIED TO...
...BAKE YOU SOMETHING, BUT...
GBLOOP
WHERE'D THIS BLACK GOOEY STUFF COME FROM?
PFF
PFF
...IT DIDN'T END WELL.

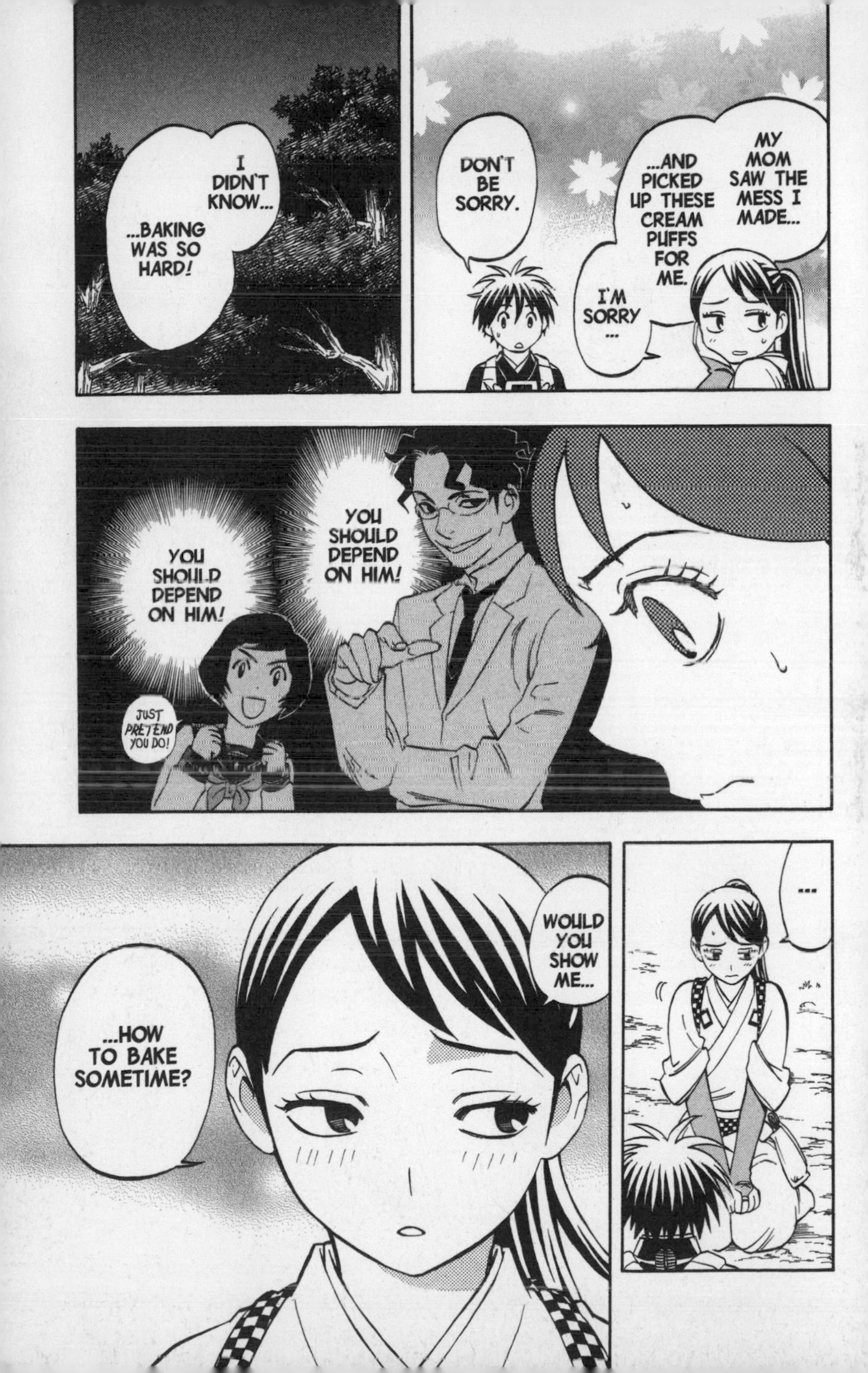
MY MOM SAW THE MESS I MADE...
...AND PICKED UP THESE CREAM PUFFS FOR ME.
I'M SORRY ...
DON'T BE SORRY.
I DIDN'T KNOW...
...BAKING WAS SO HARD!
YOU SHOULD DEPEND ON HIM!
YOU SHOULD DEPEND ON HIM!
JUST PRETEND YOU DO!
...
WOULD YOU SHOW ME...
...HOW TO BAKE SOMETIME?

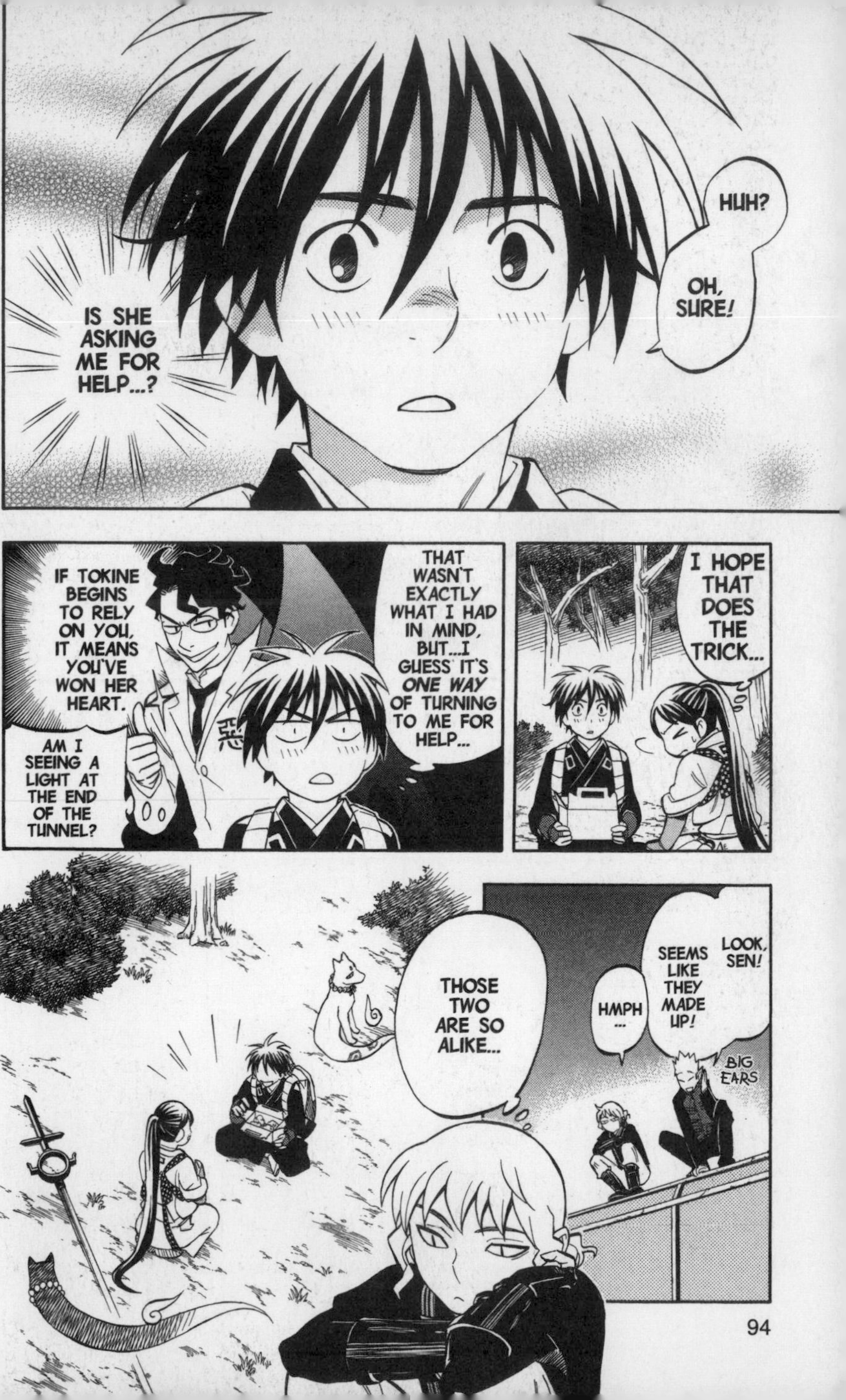
HUH?
OH, SURE!
IS SHE ASKING ME FOR HELP...?
I HOPE THAT DOES THE TRICK...
THAT WASN'T EXACTLY WHAT I HAD IN MIND, BUT...I GUESS IT'S *ONE WAY* OF TURNING TO ME FOR HELP...
IF TOKINE BEGINS TO RELY ON YOU, IT MEANS YOU'VE WON HER HEART.
AM I SEEING A LIGHT AT THE END OF THE TUNNEL?
LOOK, SEN!
SEEMS LIKE THEY MADE UP!
BIG EARS
HMPH...
THOSE TWO ARE SO ALIKE...

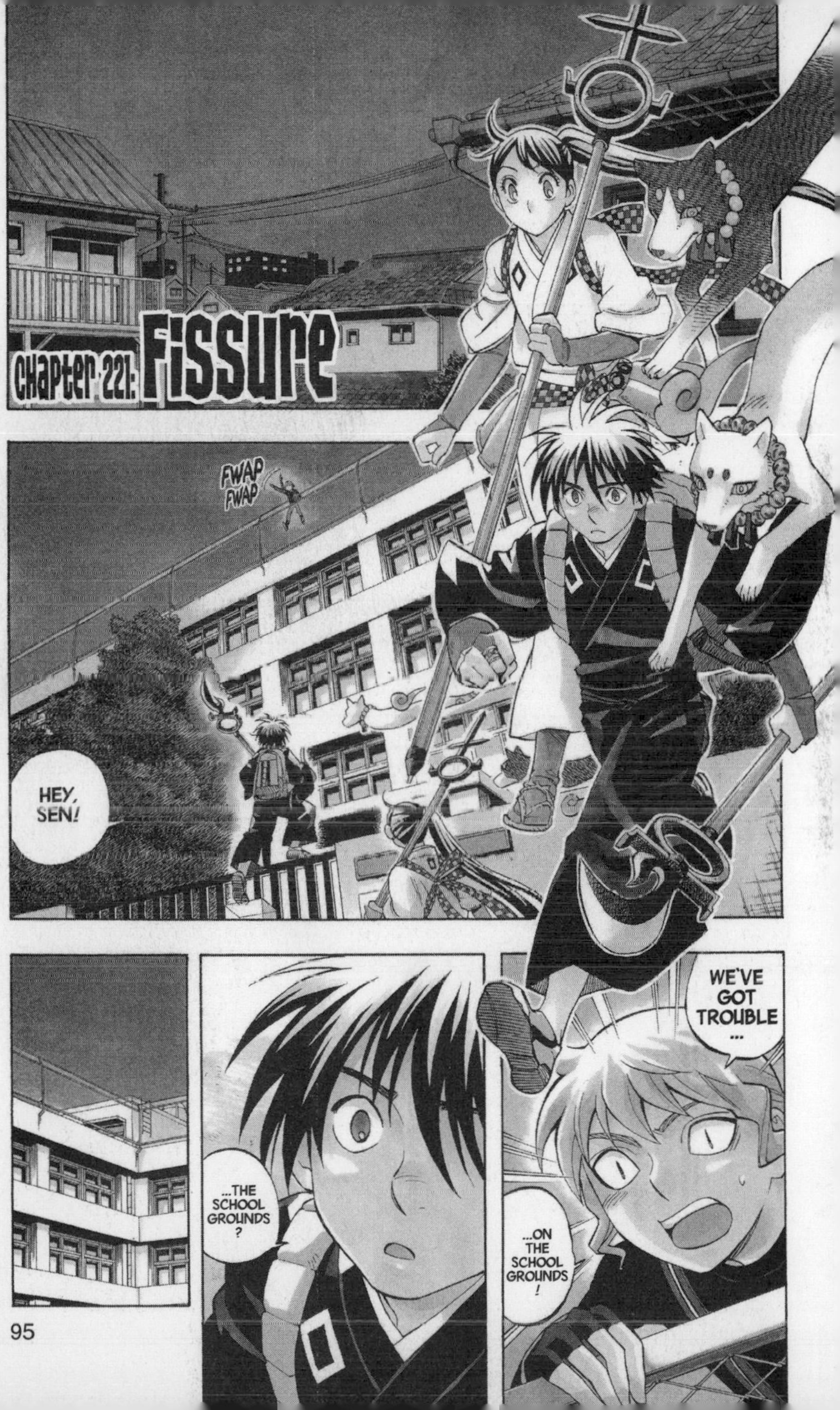
Chapter 221: Fissure
FWAP FWAP
HEY, SEN!
WE'VE GOT TROUBLE ...
...ON THE SCHOOL GROUNDS!
...THE SCHOOL GROUNDS?

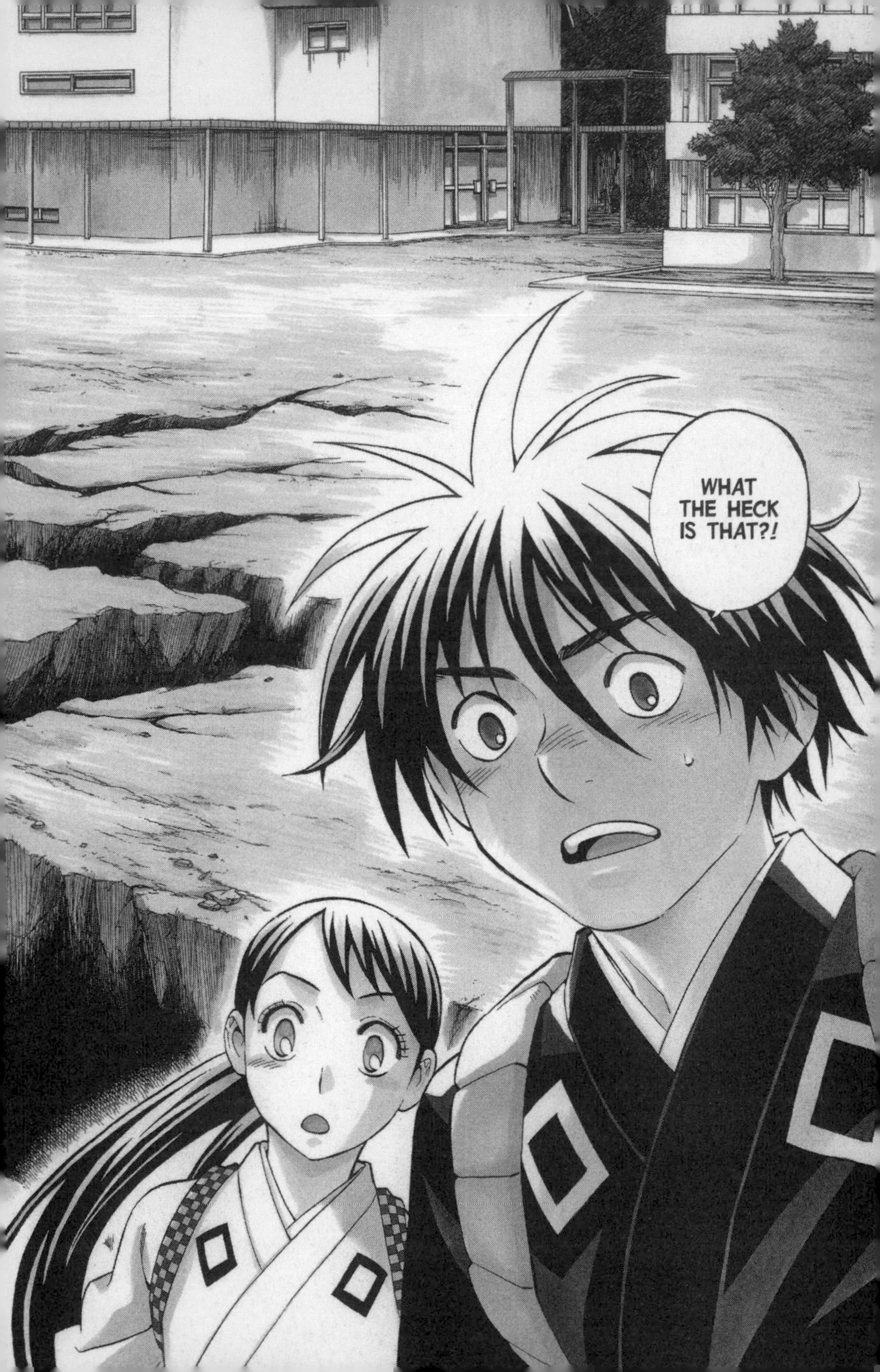
WHAT THE HECK IS THAT?!

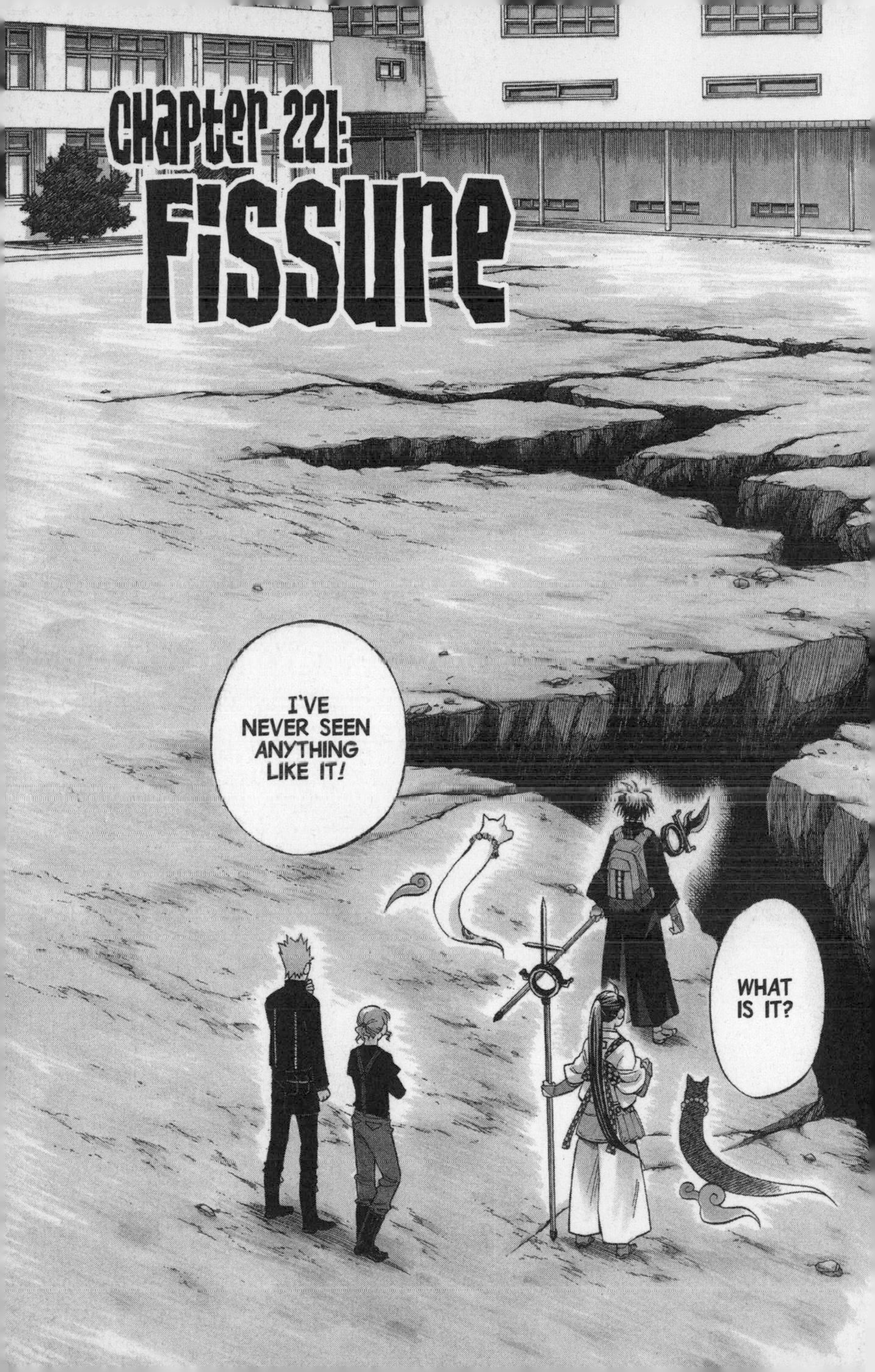
CHAPTER 221:
FISSURE
I'VE NEVER SEEN ANYTHING LIKE IT!
WHAT IS IT?

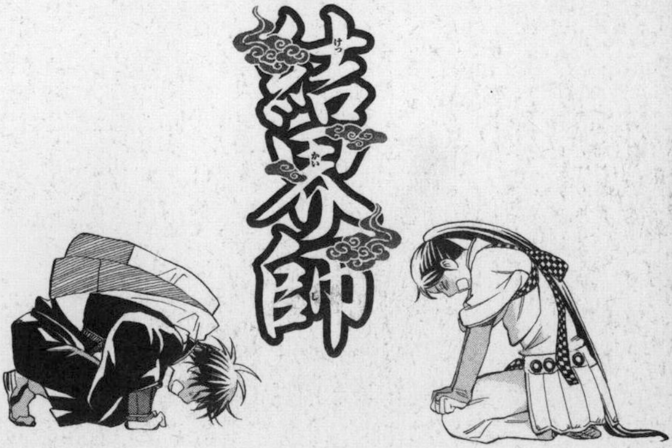
結界師

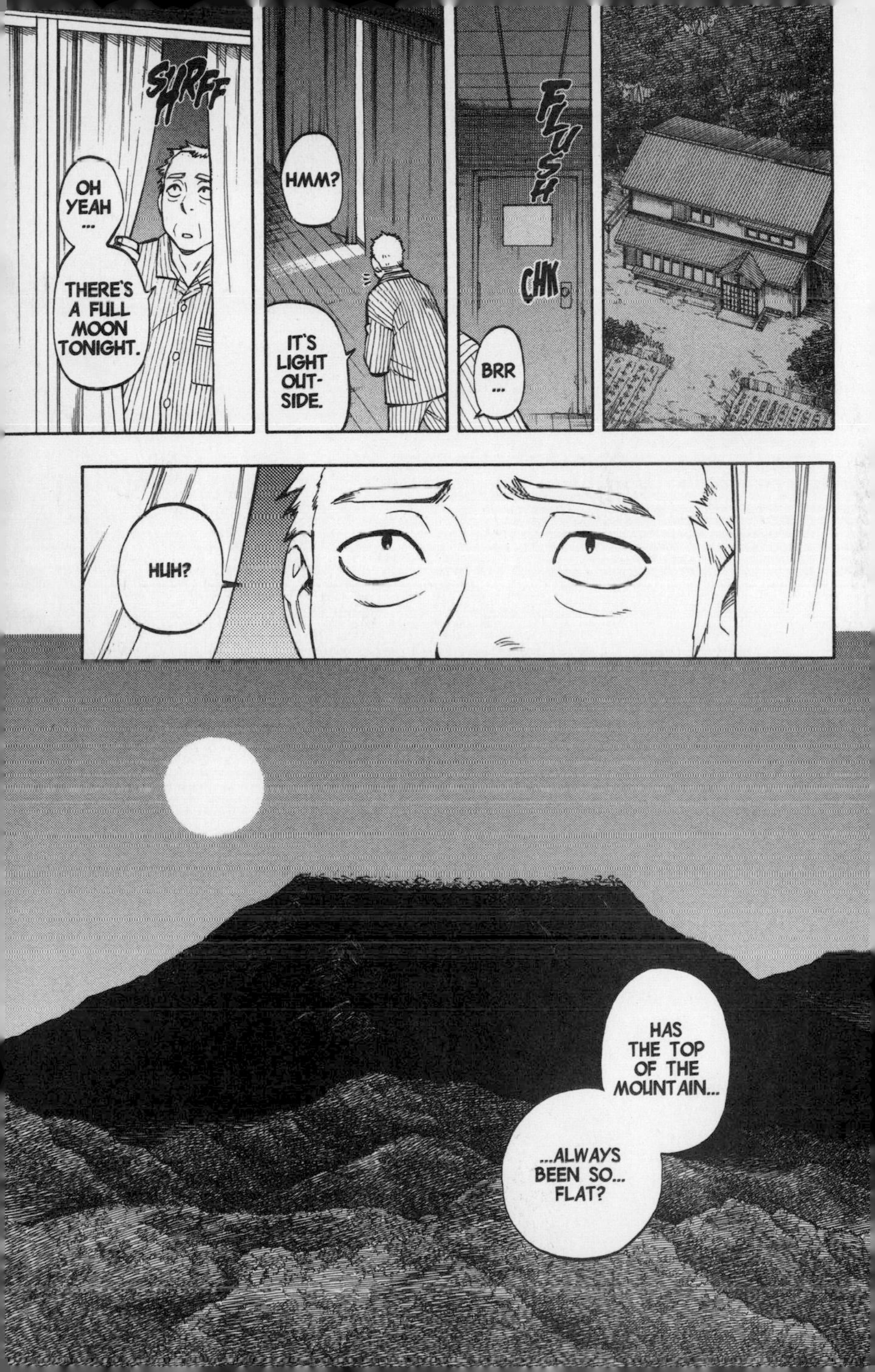
FLUSH
CHK
BRR ...
HMM?
IT'S LIGHT OUT-SIDE.
SHRFF
OH YEAH ...
THERE'S A FULL MOON TONIGHT.
HUH?
HAS THE TOP OF THE MOUNTAIN...
...ALWAYS BEEN SO... FLAT?

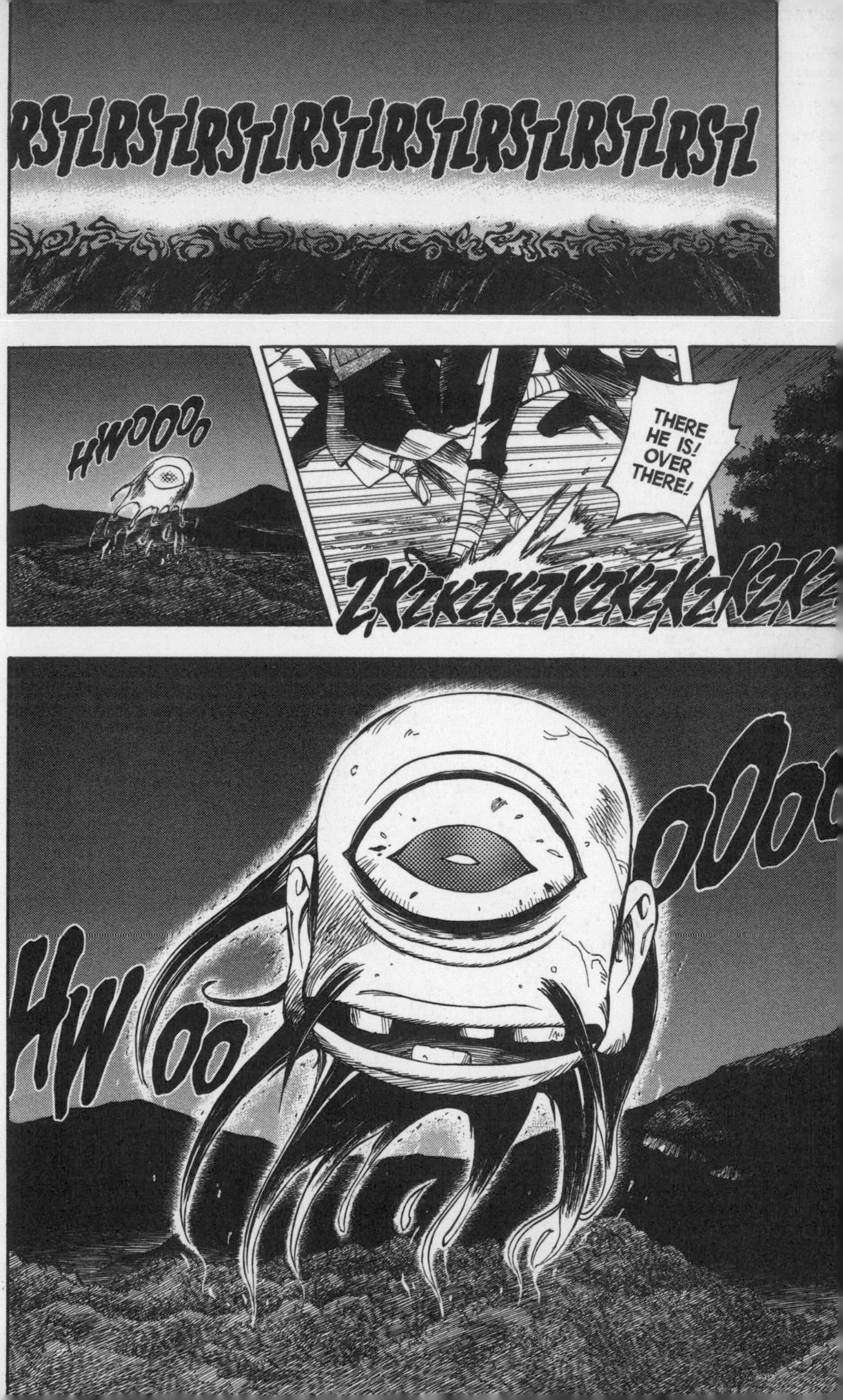
RSTLRSTLRSTLRSTLRSTLRSTLRSTLRSTLRSTL
THERE HE IS! OVER THERE!
ZKZKZKZKZKZKZKZKZK
HWOOOO
HWOOOOOOO

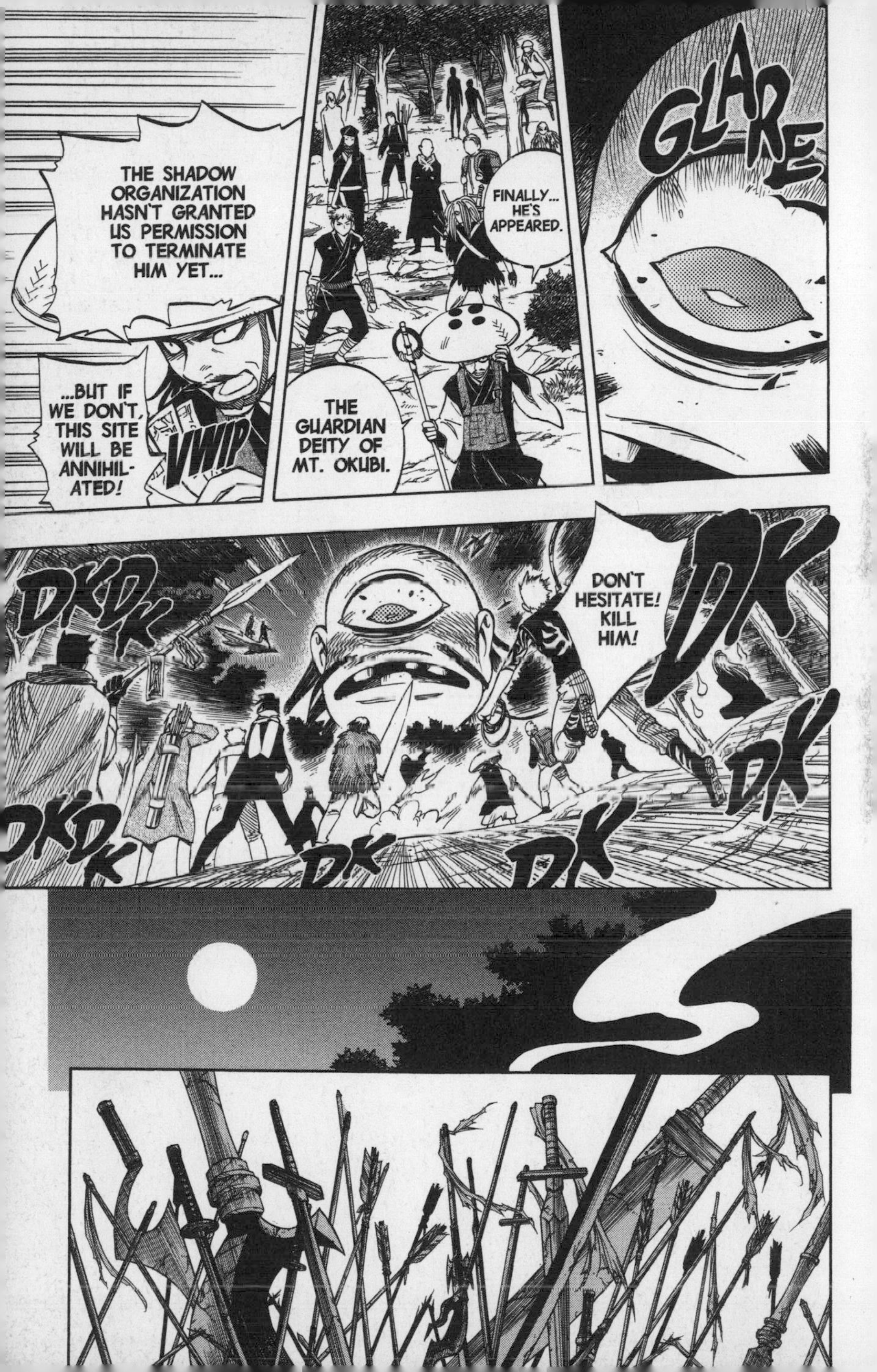
GLARE
FINALLY... HE'S APPEARED.
THE GUARDIAN DEITY OF MT. OKUBI.
THE SHADOW ORGANIZATION HASN'T GRANTED US PERMISSION TO TERMINATE HIM YET...
...BUT IF WE DON'T, THIS SITE WILL BE ANNIHIL-ATED!
VWIP
DON'T HESITATE! KILL HIM!
DK
DK
DK
DK
DKDK
DKDK

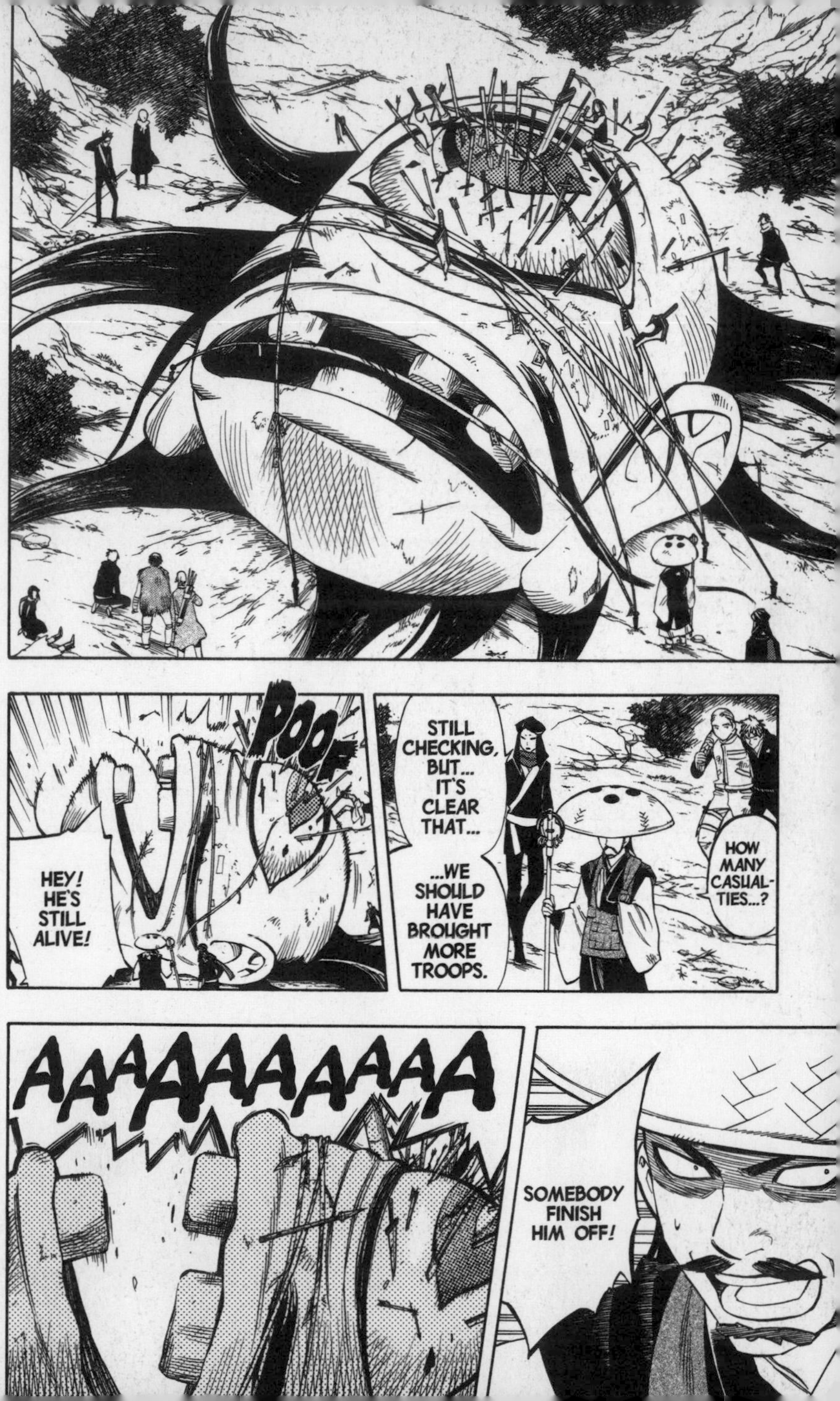
HOW MANY CASUALTIES...?
STILL CHECKING, BUT... IT'S CLEAR THAT...
...WE SHOULD HAVE BROUGHT MORE TROOPS.
POOF
HEY! HE'S STILL ALIVE!
SOMEBODY FINISH HIM OFF!
AAAAAAAAAA

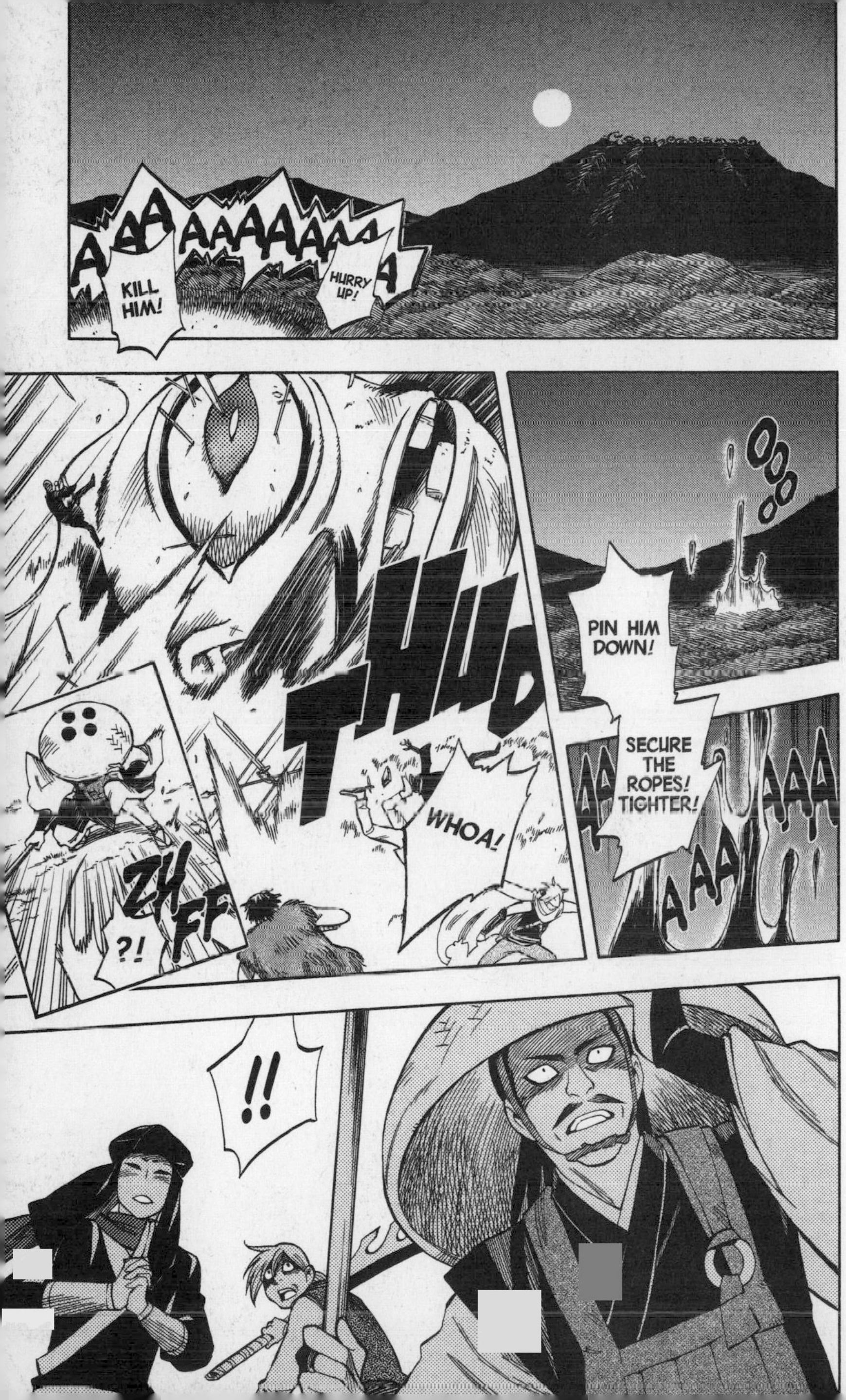
AAAAAAAAAAAA
HURRY UP!
KILL HIM!
OOOO
PIN HIM DOWN!
SECURE THE ROPES! TIGHTER!
AAAAAAA
THUD
WHOA!
ZHFF
?!
!!

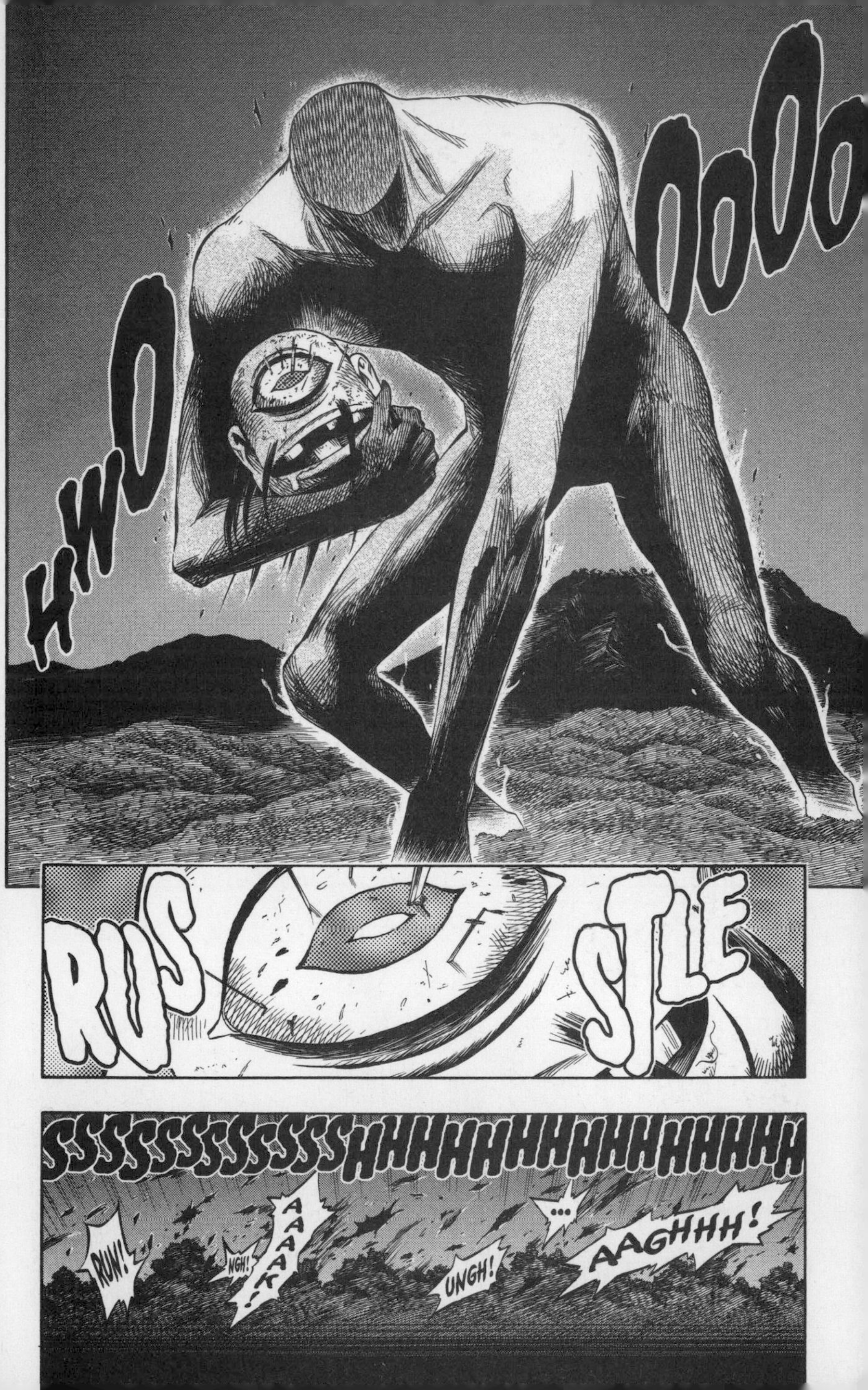
HWOOOOOO
RUS STLE
SSSSSSSSSSSSSHHHHHHHHHHHHHHHHH
AAGHHH!
...
UNGH!
AAAAK!
NGH!
RUN!

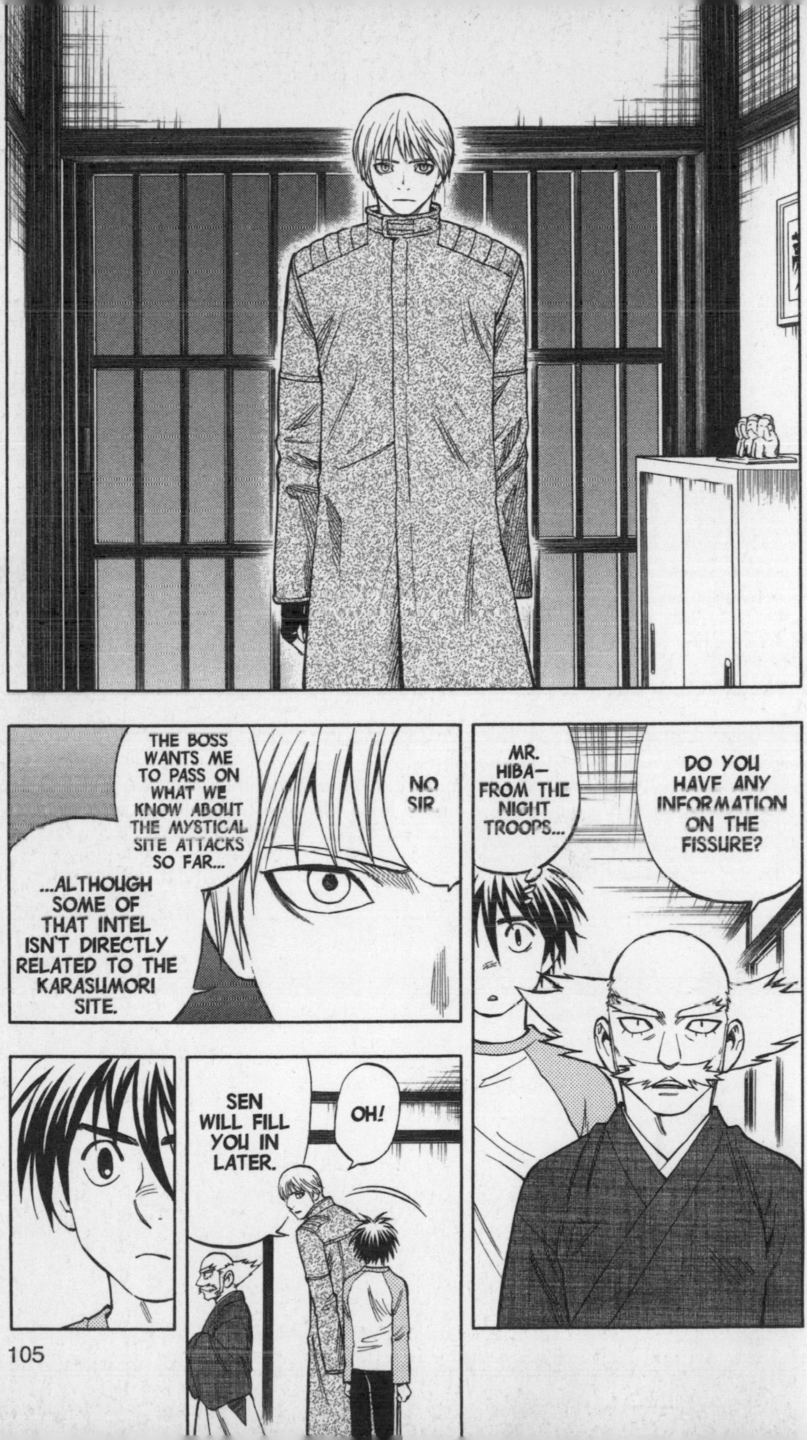
DO YOU HAVE ANY INFORMATION ON THE FISSURE?
MR. HIBA— FROM THE NIGHT TROOPS...
NO SIR.
THE BOSS WANTS ME TO PASS ON WHAT WE KNOW ABOUT THE MYSTICAL SITE ATTACKS SO FAR...
...ALTHOUGH SOME OF THAT INTEL ISN'T DIRECTLY RELATED TO THE KARASUMORI SITE.
OH!
SEN WILL FILL YOU IN LATER.

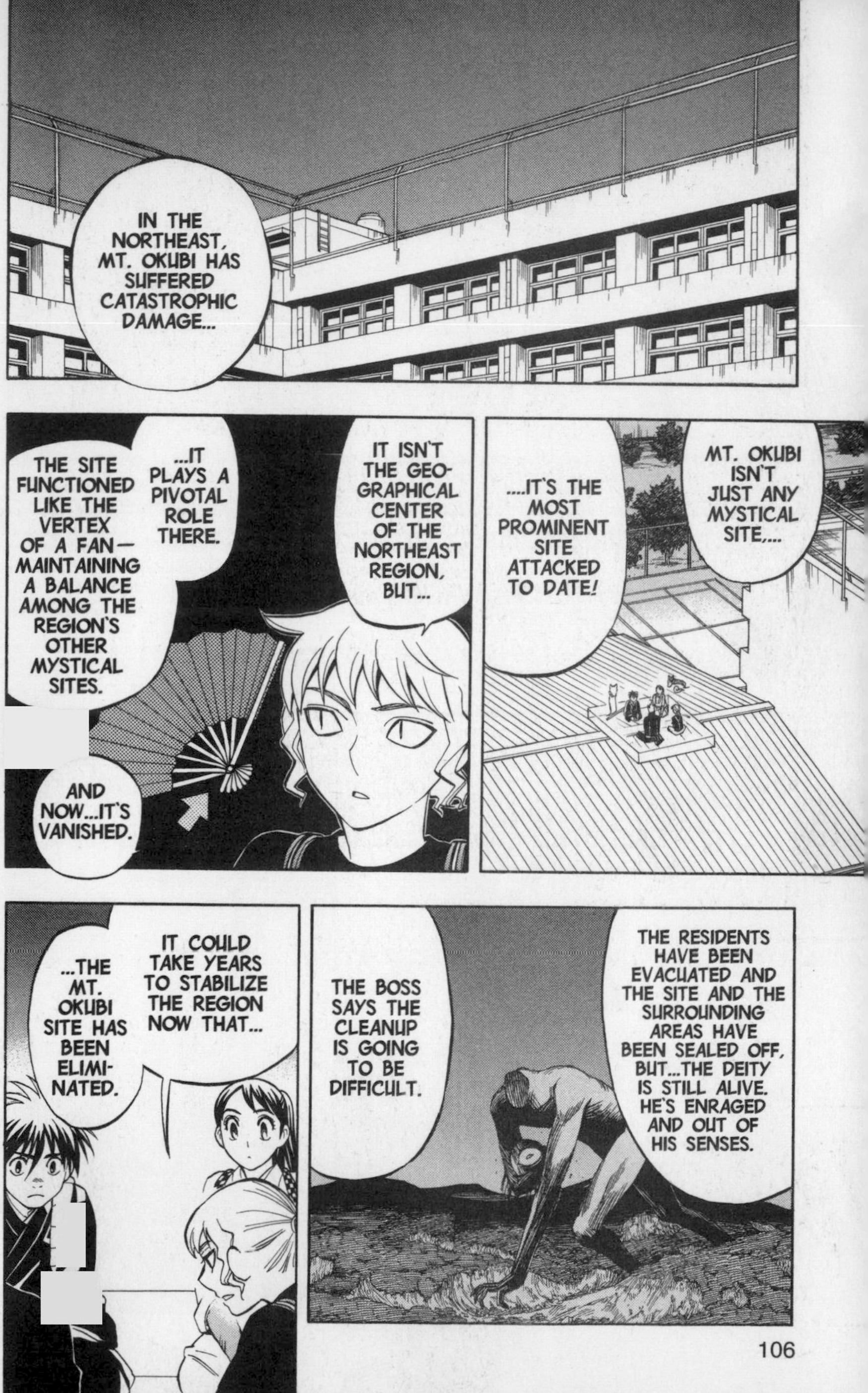
IN THE NORTHEAST, MT. OKUBI HAS SUFFERED CATASTROPHIC DAMAGE...
MT. OKUBI ISN'T JUST ANY MYSTICAL SITE,...
....IT'S THE MOST PROMINENT SITE ATTACKED TO DATE!
IT ISN'T THE GEO-GRAPHICAL CENTER OF THE NORTHEAST REGION, BUT...
...IT PLAYS A PIVOTAL ROLE THERE.
THE SITE FUNCTIONED LIKE THE VERTEX OF A FAN—MAINTAINING A BALANCE AMONG THE REGION'S OTHER MYSTICAL SITES.
AND NOW...IT'S VANISHED.
THE RESIDENTS HAVE BEEN EVACUATED AND THE SITE AND THE SURROUNDING AREAS HAVE BEEN SEALED OFF, BUT...THE DEITY IS STILL ALIVE. HE'S ENRAGED AND OUT OF HIS SENSES.
THE BOSS SAYS THE CLEANUP IS GOING TO BE DIFFICULT.
IT COULD TAKE YEARS TO STABILIZE THE REGION NOW THAT...
...THE MT. OKUBI SITE HAS BEEN ELIMI-NATED.

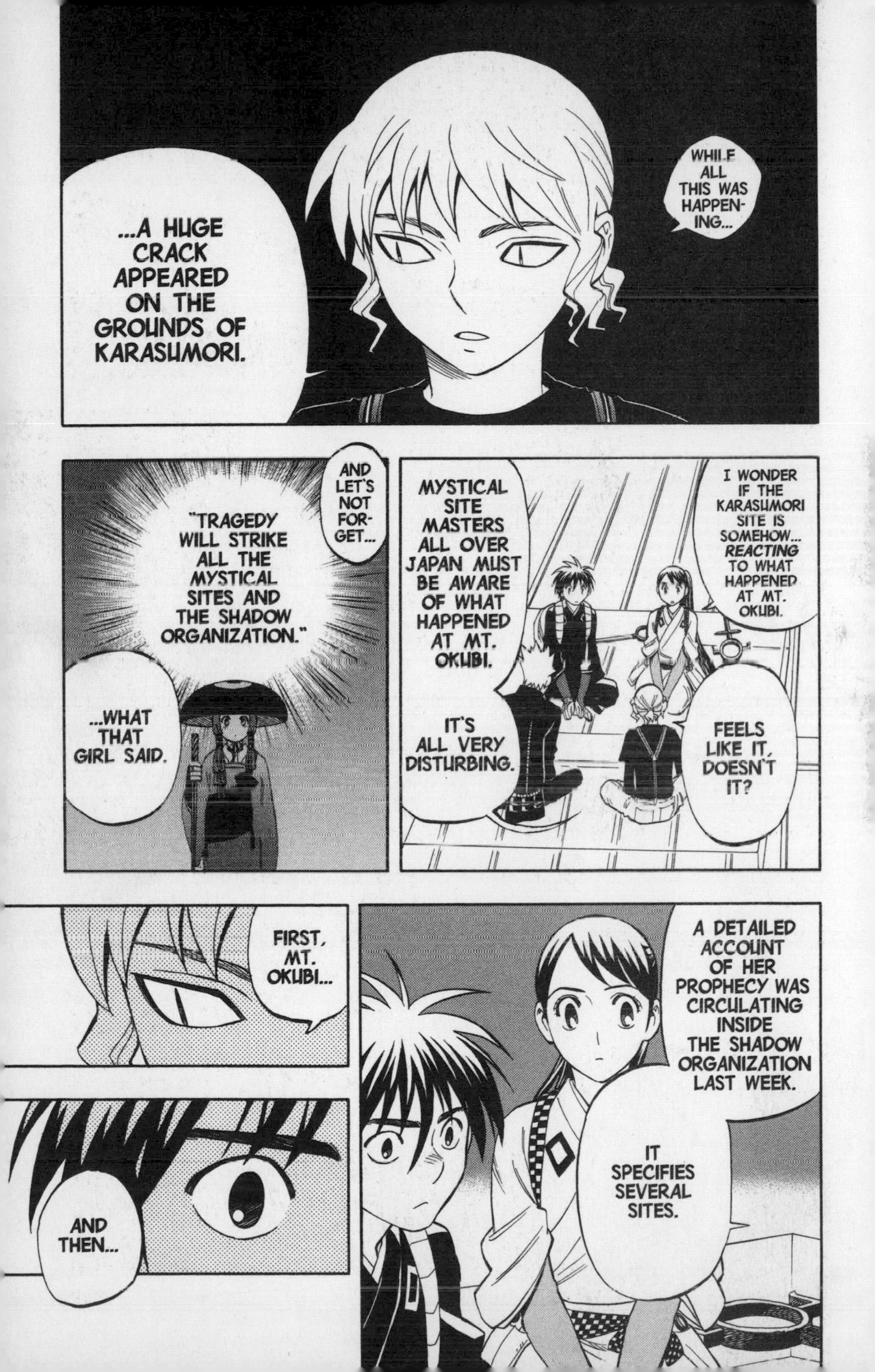
WHILE ALL THIS WAS HAPPEN- ING...
...A HUGE CRACK APPEARED ON THE GROUNDS OF KARASUMORI.
I WONDER IF THE KARASUMORI SITE IS SOMEHOW... *REACTING* TO WHAT HAPPENED AT MT. OKUBI.
FEELS LIKE IT, DOESN'T IT?
MYSTICAL SITE MASTERS ALL OVER JAPAN MUST BE AWARE OF WHAT HAPPENED AT MT. OKUBI.
IT'S ALL VERY DISTURBING.
AND LET'S NOT FOR- GET...
"TRAGEDY WILL STRIKE ALL THE MYSTICAL SITES AND THE SHADOW ORGANIZATION."
...WHAT THAT GIRL SAID.
A DETAILED ACCOUNT OF HER PROPHECY WAS CIRCULATING INSIDE THE SHADOW ORGANIZATION LAST WEEK.
IT SPECIFIES SEVERAL SITES.
FIRST, MT. OKUBI...
AND THEN...

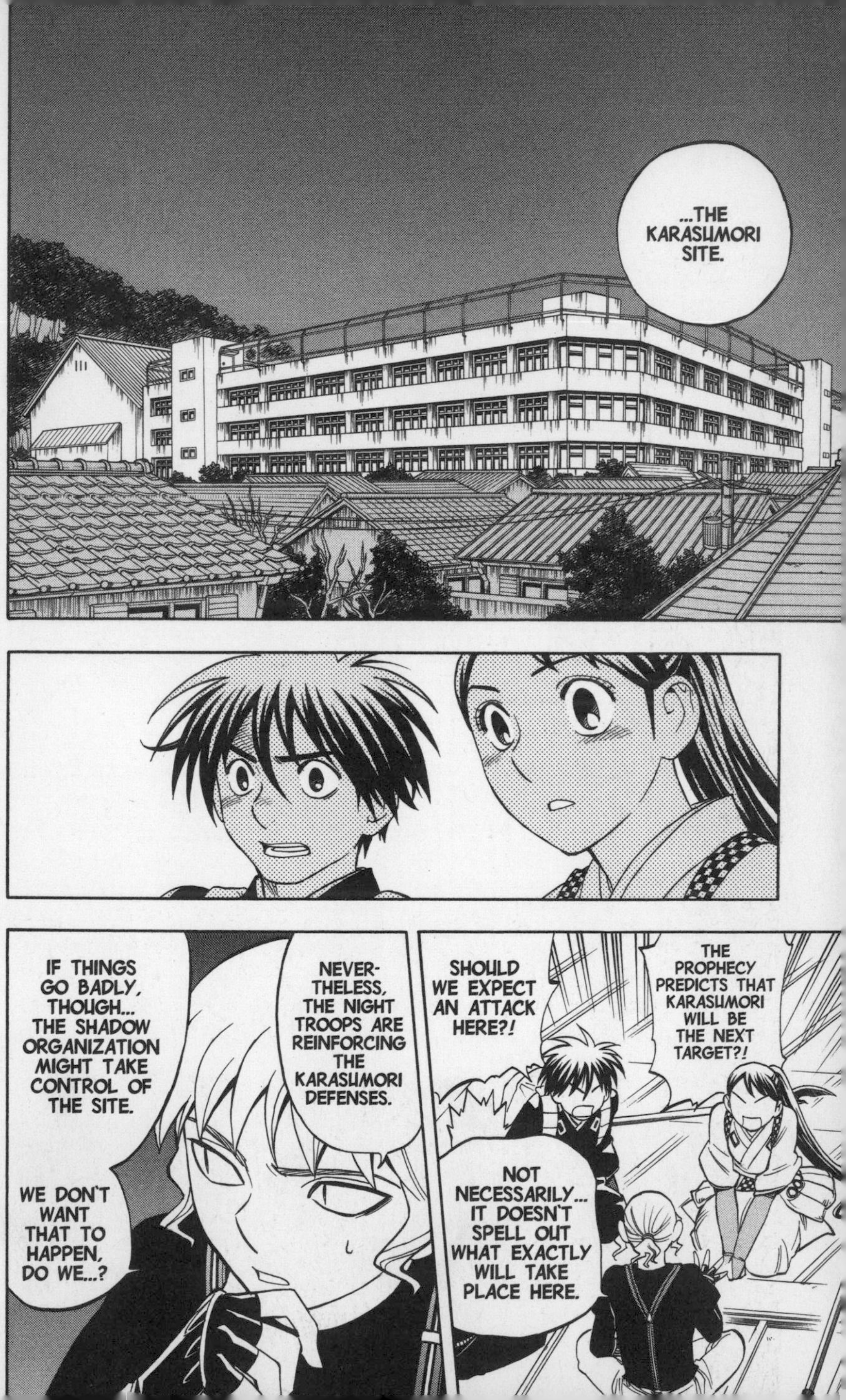
...THE KARASUMORI SITE.
THE PROPHECY PREDICTS THAT KARASUMORI WILL BE THE NEXT TARGET?!
SHOULD WE EXPECT AN ATTACK HERE?!
NOT NECESSARILY... IT DOESN'T SPELL OUT WHAT EXACTLY WILL TAKE PLACE HERE.
NEVER-THELESS, THE NIGHT TROOPS ARE REINFORCING THE KARASUMORI DEFENSES.
IF THINGS GO BADLY, THOUGH... THE SHADOW ORGANIZATION MIGHT TAKE CONTROL OF THE SITE.
WE DON'T WANT THAT TO HAPPEN, DO WE...?

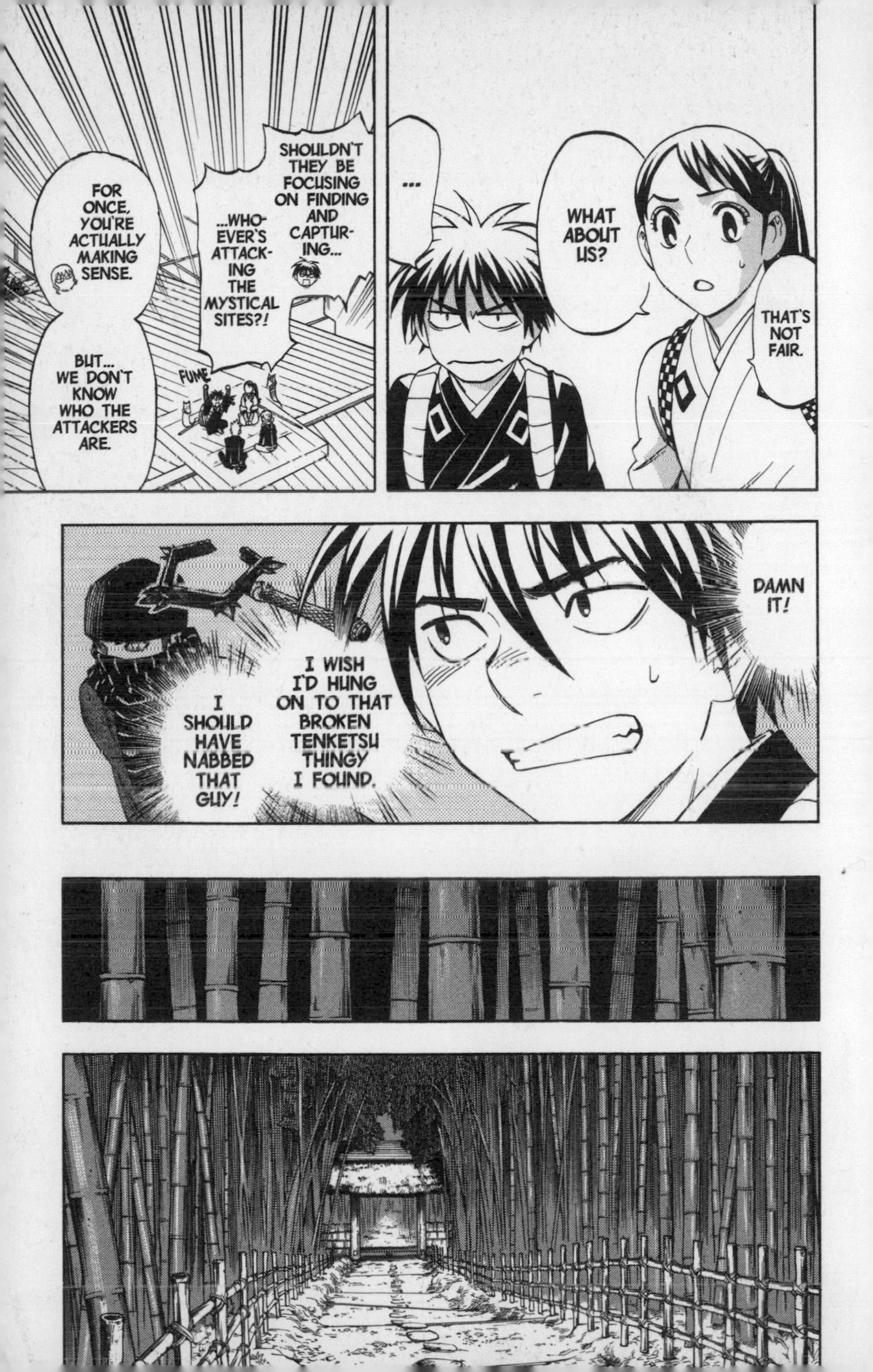
WHAT ABOUT US?
THAT'S NOT FAIR.
...
SHOULDN'T THEY BE FOCUSING ON FINDING AND CAPTURING...
...WHOEVER'S ATTACKING THE MYSTICAL SITES?!
FOR ONCE, YOU'RE ACTUALLY MAKING SENSE.
BUT... WE DON'T KNOW WHO THE ATTACKERS ARE.
FUME
DAMN IT!
I WISH I'D HUNG ON TO THAT BROKEN TENKETSU THINGY I FOUND.
I SHOULD HAVE NABBED THAT GUY!

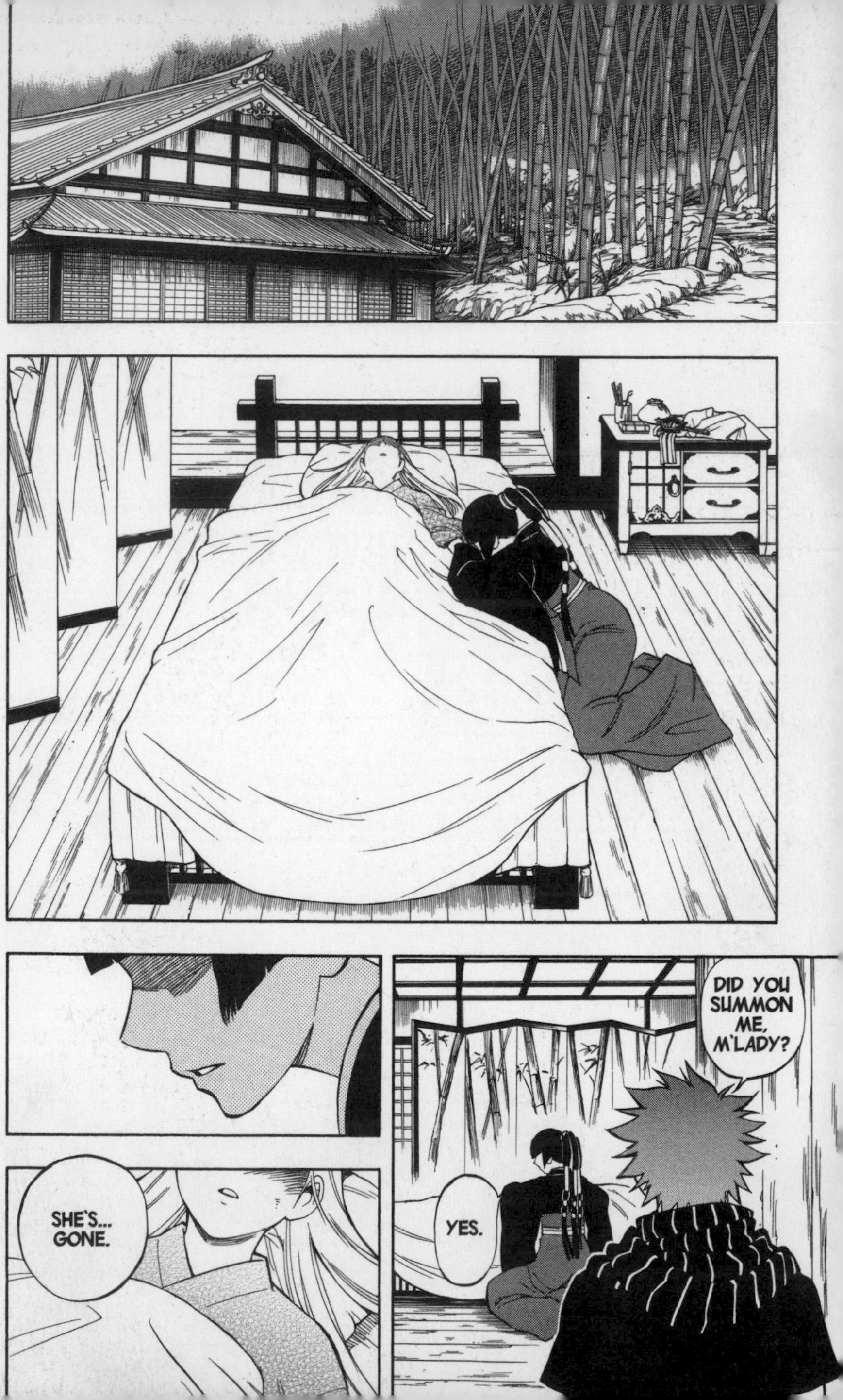
DID YOU SUMMON ME, M'LADY?
YES.
SHE'S... GONE.

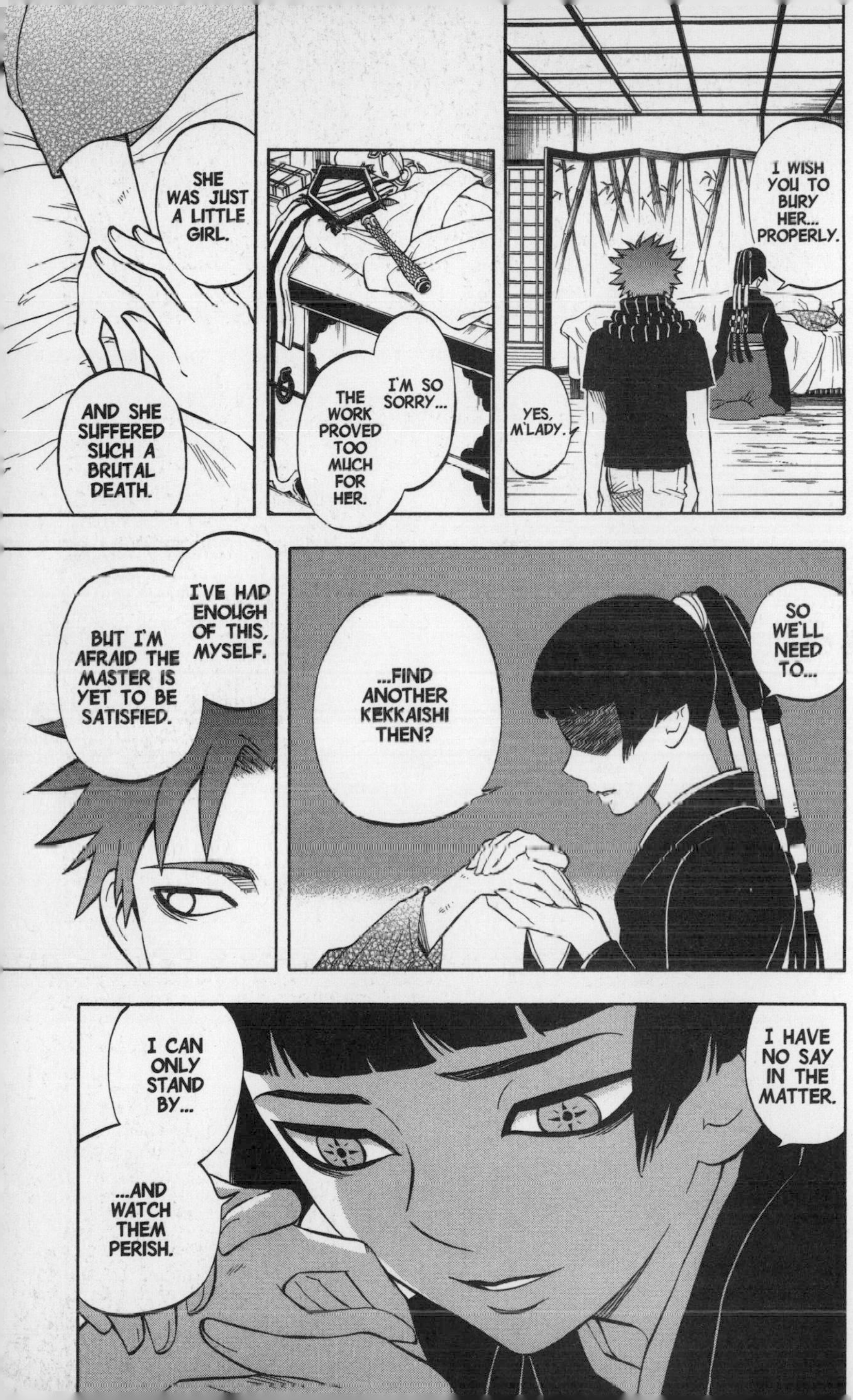
I WISH YOU TO BURY HER... PROPERLY.
YES, M'LADY.
I'M SO SORRY... THE WORK PROVED TOO MUCH FOR HER.
SHE WAS JUST A LITTLE GIRL.
AND SHE SUFFERED SUCH A BRUTAL DEATH.
SO WE'LL NEED TO...
...FIND ANOTHER KEKKAISHI THEN?
I'VE HAD ENOUGH OF THIS, MYSELF.
BUT I'M AFRAID THE MASTER IS YET TO BE SATISFIED.
I HAVE NO SAY IN THE MATTER.
I CAN ONLY STAND BY...
...AND WATCH THEM PERISH.

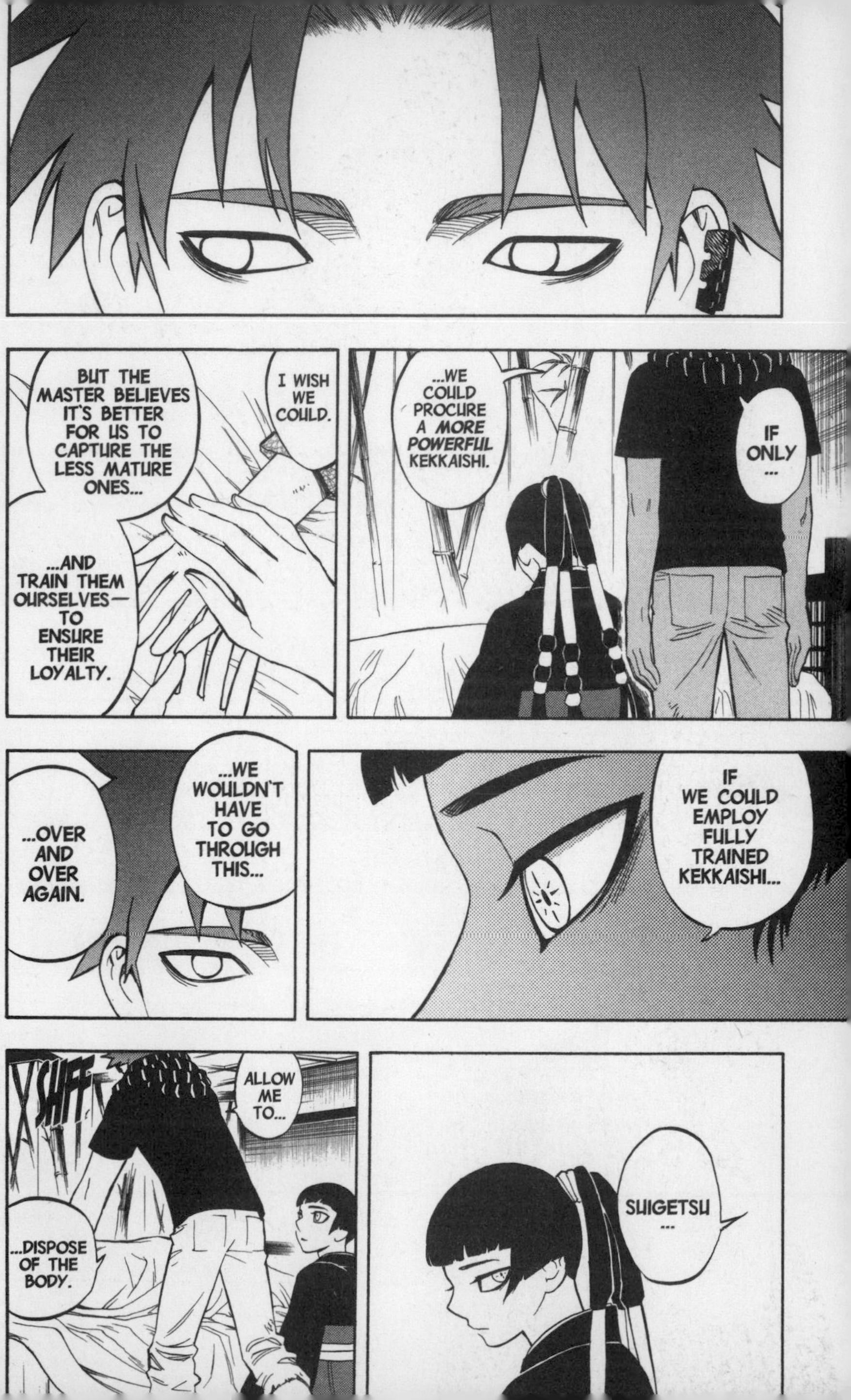
IF ONLY ...
...WE COULD PROCURE A *MORE POWERFUL* KEKKAISHI.
I WISH WE COULD.
BUT THE MASTER BELIEVES IT'S BETTER FOR US TO CAPTURE THE LESS MATURE ONES...
...AND TRAIN THEM OURSELVES—TO ENSURE THEIR LOYALTY.
IF WE COULD EMPLOY FULLY TRAINED KEKKAISHI...
...WE WOULDN'T HAVE TO GO THROUGH THIS...
...OVER AND OVER AGAIN.
SUIGETSU ...
ALLOW ME TO...
SHFF
...DISPOSE OF THE BODY.

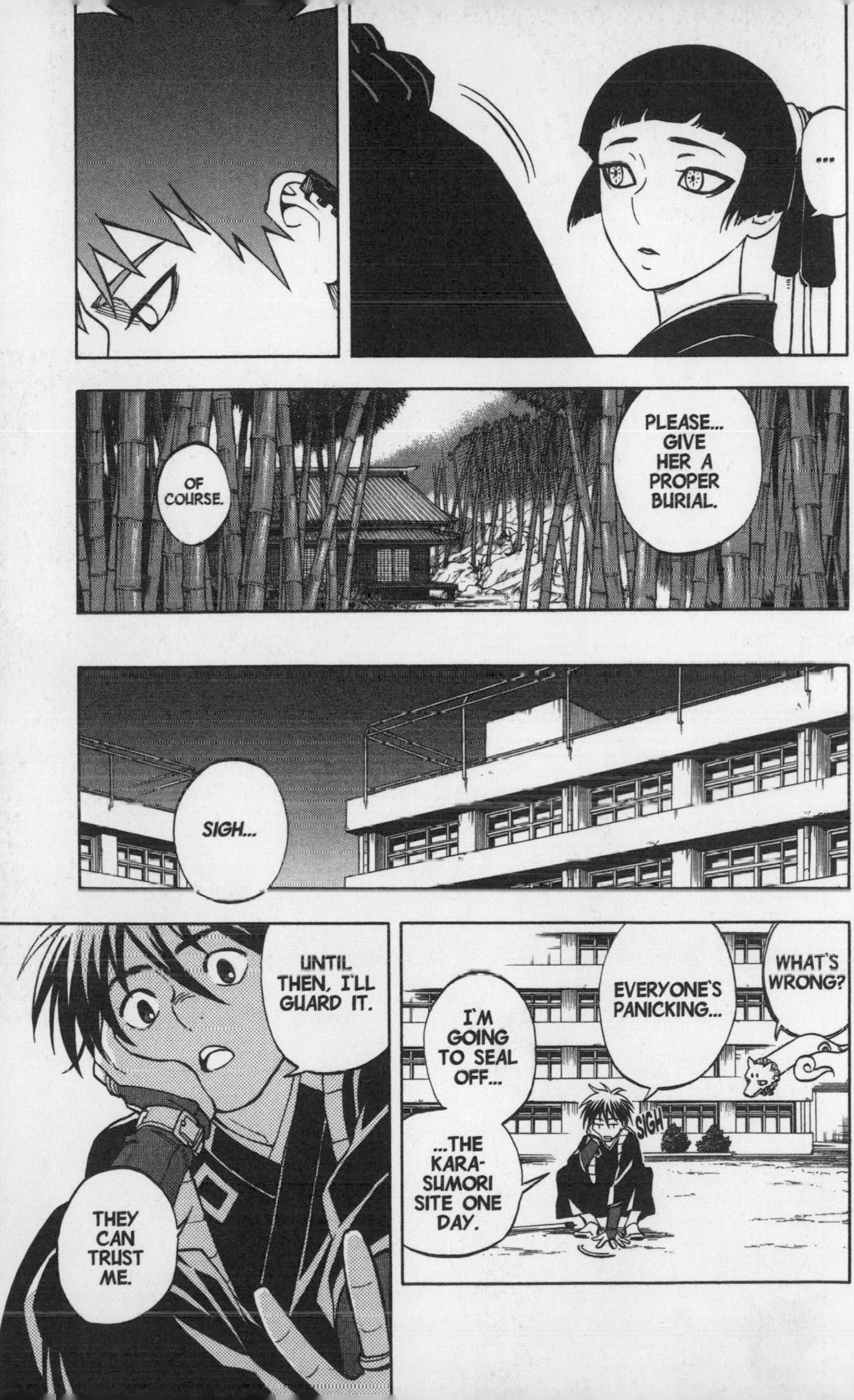
...
PLEASE... GIVE HER A PROPER BURIAL.
OF COURSE.
SIGH...
WHAT'S WRONG?
EVERYONE'S PANICKING...
SIGH
I'M GOING TO SEAL OFF...
...THE KARA-SUMORI SITE ONE DAY.
UNTIL THEN, I'LL GUARD IT.
THEY CAN TRUST ME.

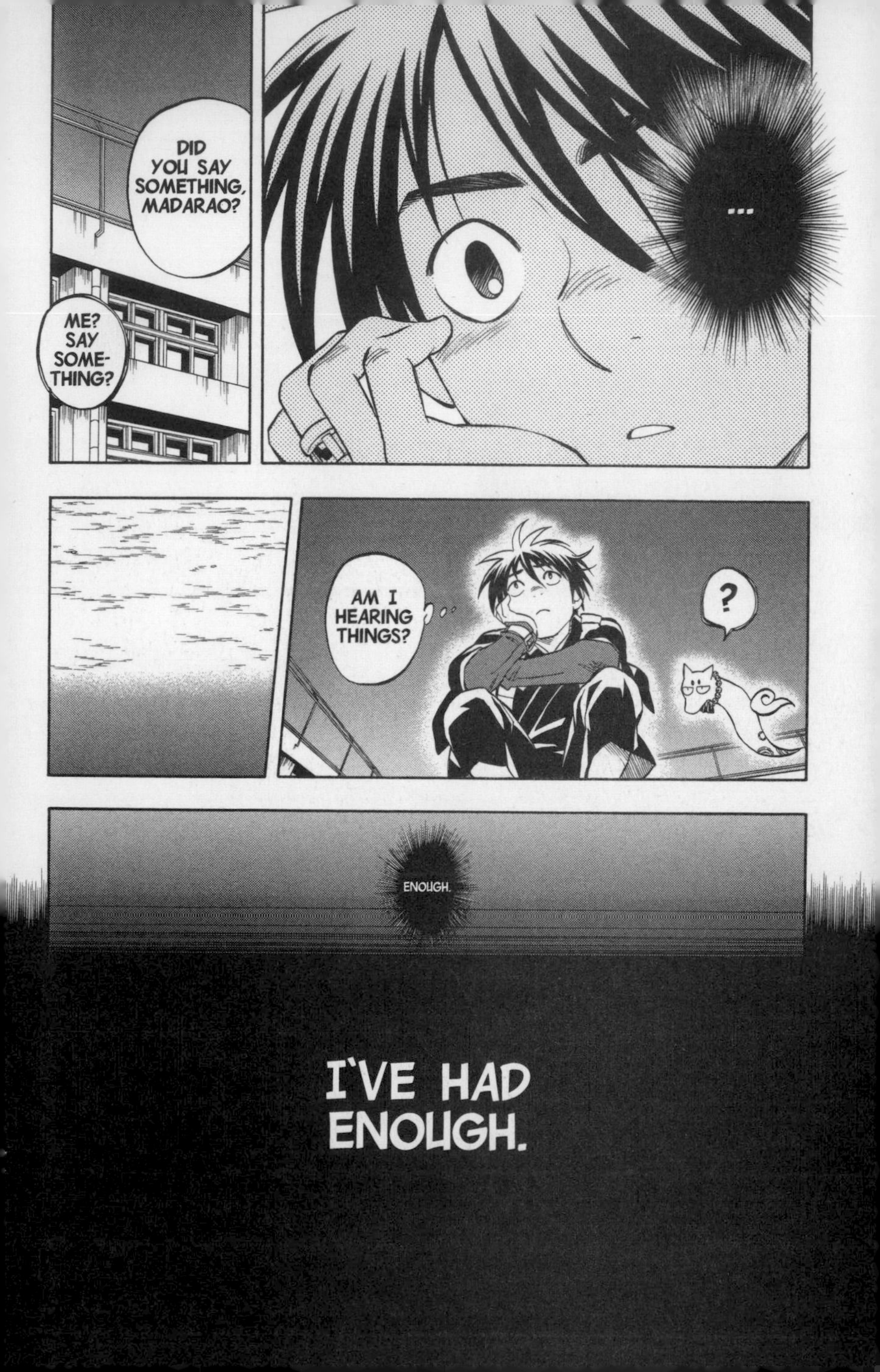
...
DID YOU SAY SOMETHING, MADARAO?
ME? SAY SOME-THING?
?
AM I HEARING THINGS?
ENOUGH.
I'VE HAD ENOUGH.

Chapter 222: Helper

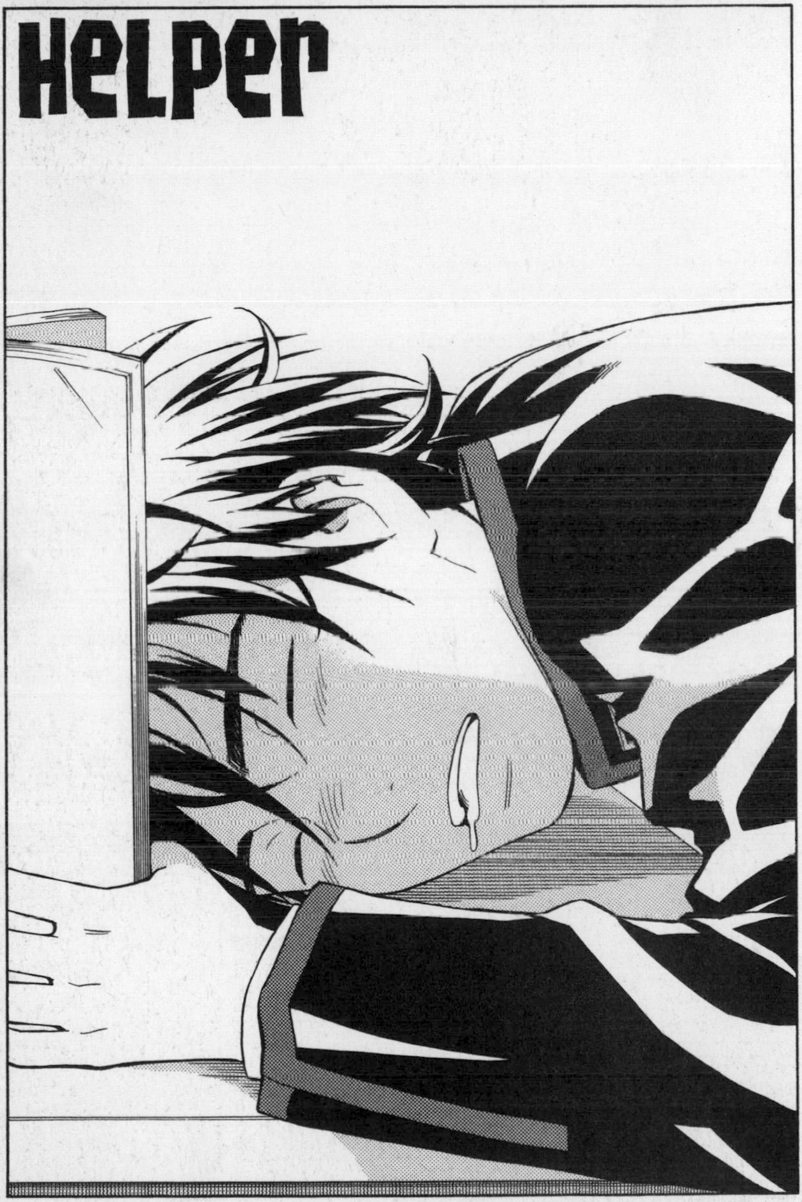

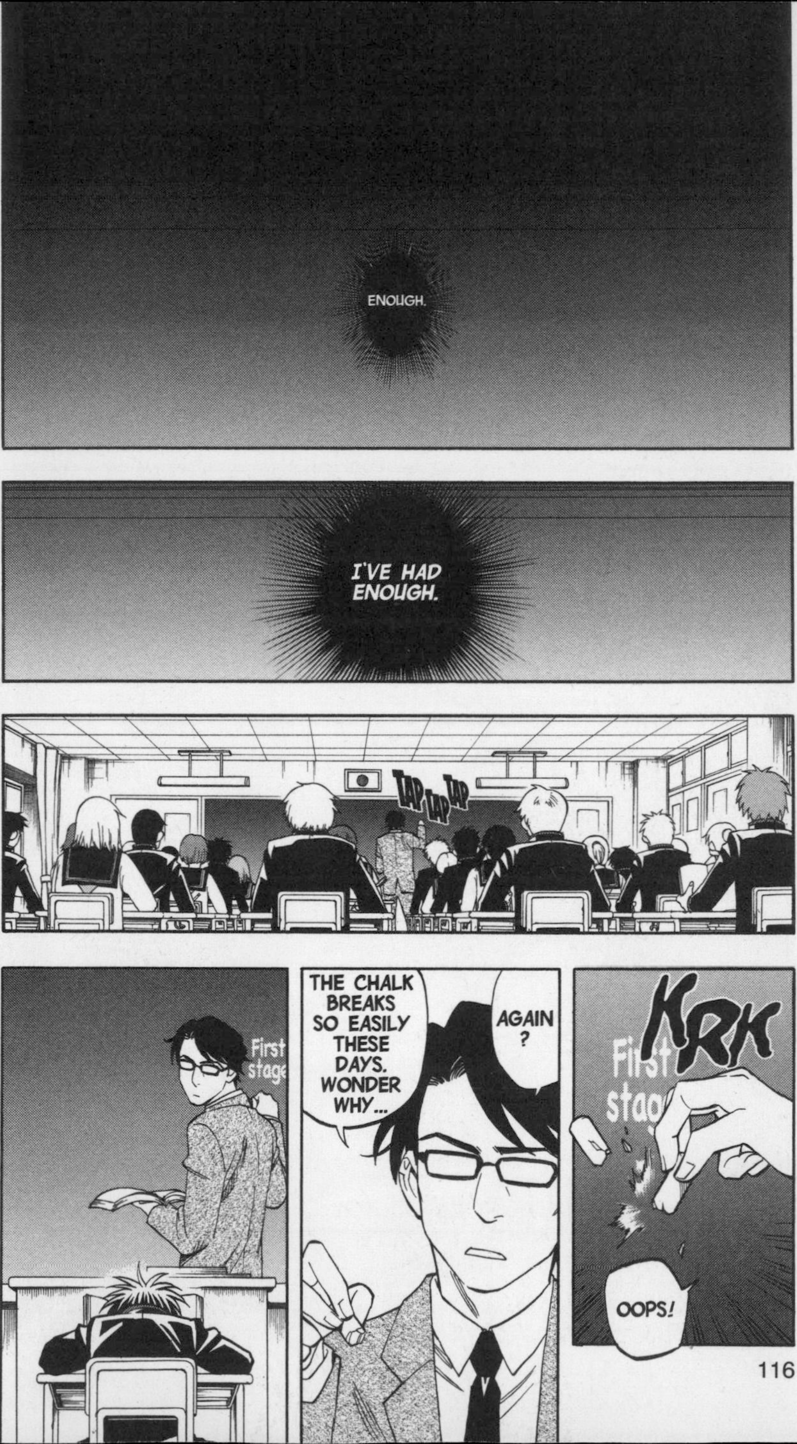
ENOUGH.
I'VE HAD ENOUGH.
TAP TAP TAP
KRK
First stag
OOPS!
AGAIN ?
THE CHALK BREAKS SO EASILY THESE DAYS. WONDER WHY...
First stage

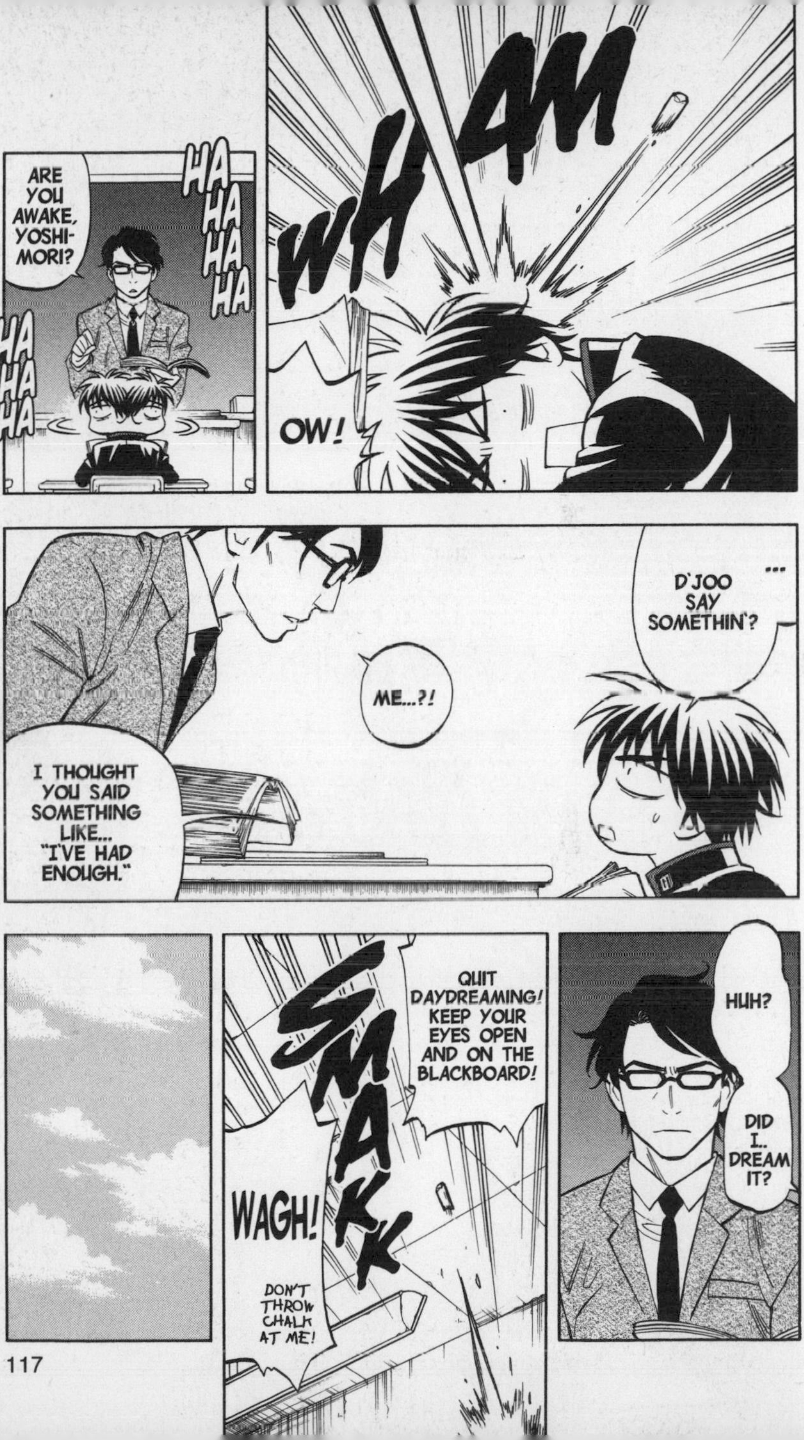
WHAM
OW!
ARE YOU AWAKE, YOSHIMORI?
HA HA HA HA HA
HA HA HA HA
...D'JOO SAY SOMETHIN'?
ME...?!
I THOUGHT YOU SAID SOMETHING LIKE... "I'VE HAD ENOUGH."
HUH?
DID I.. DREAM IT?
QUIT DAYDREAMING! KEEP YOUR EYES OPEN AND ON THE BLACKBOARD!
SMAKK
WAGH!
DON'T THROW CHALK AT ME!

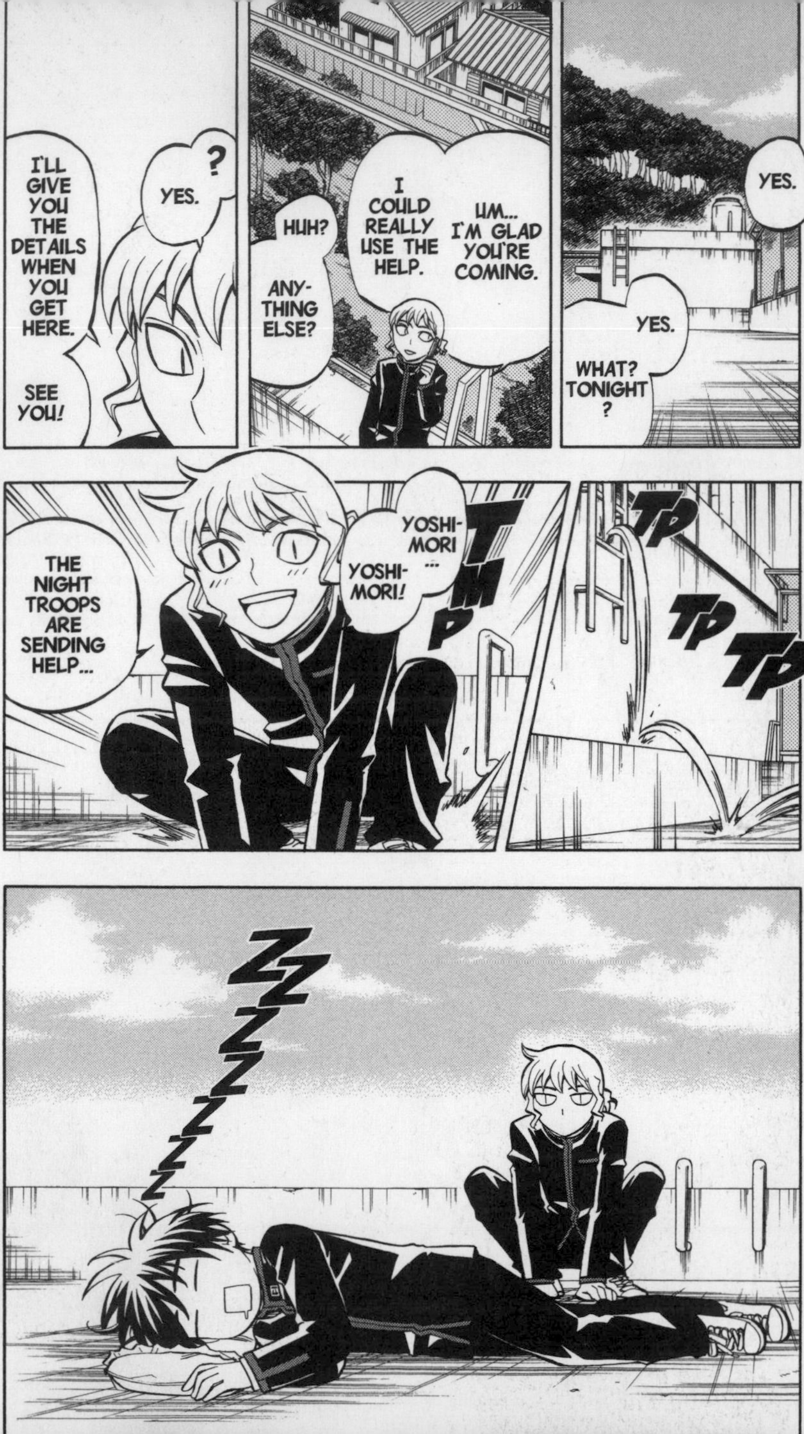
YES.
YES.
WHAT? TONIGHT ?
UM... I'M GLAD YOU'RE COMING.
I COULD REALLY USE THE HELP.
HUH?
ANY-THING ELSE?
?
YES.
I'LL GIVE YOU THE DETAILS WHEN YOU GET HERE.
SEE YOU!
TP
TP
TP
TMP
YOSHI-MORI ...
YOSHI-MORI!
THE NIGHT TROOPS ARE SENDING HELP...
ZZZZZZZZ

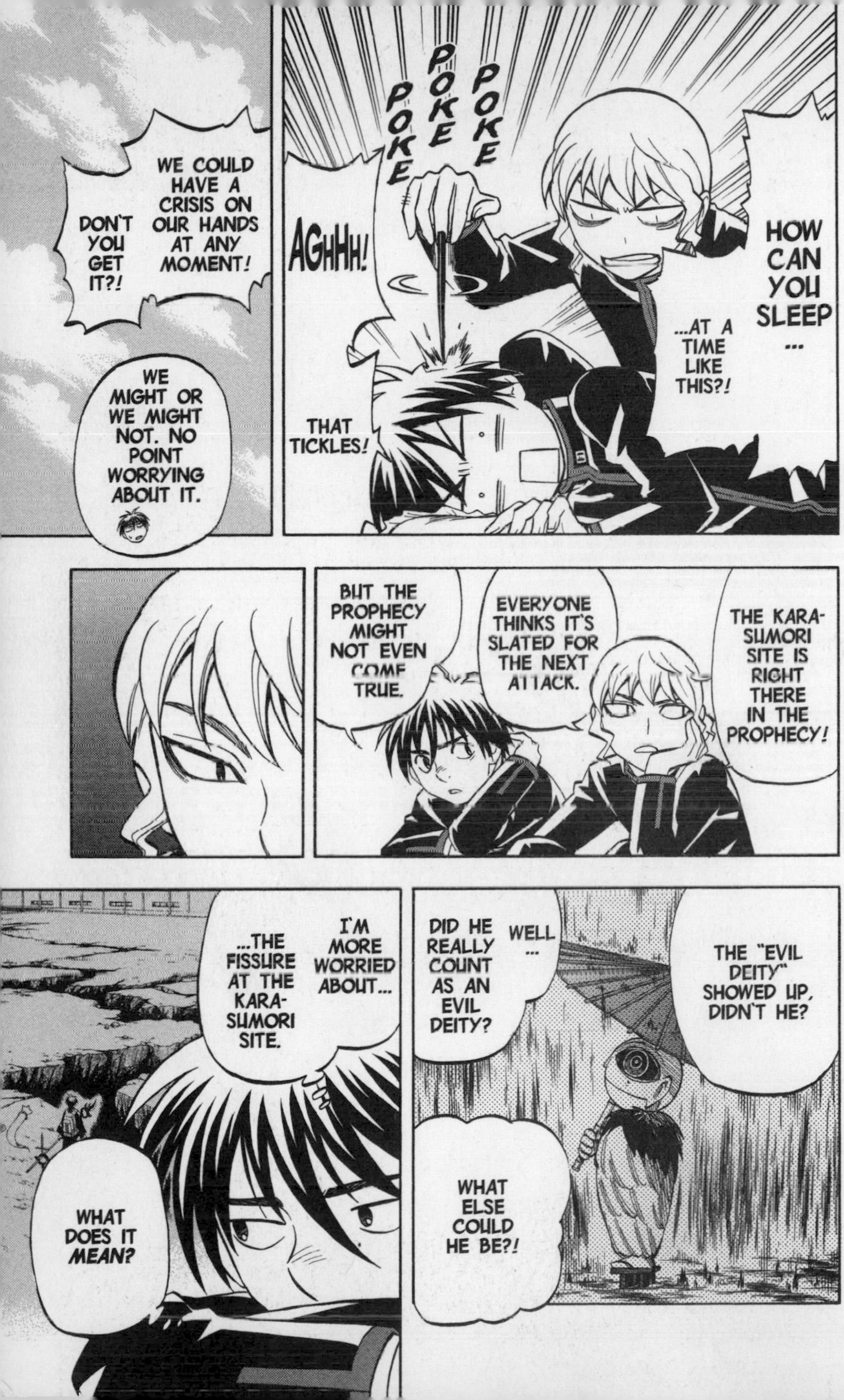
HOW CAN YOU SLEEP...
...AT A TIME LIKE THIS?!
POKE POKE POKE
AGHHH!
THAT TICKLES!
WE COULD HAVE A CRISIS ON OUR HANDS AT ANY MOMENT!
DON'T YOU GET IT?!
WE MIGHT OR WE MIGHT NOT. NO POINT WORRYING ABOUT IT.
THE KARA-SUMORI SITE IS RIGHT THERE IN THE PROPHECY!
EVERYONE THINKS IT'S SLATED FOR THE NEXT ATTACK.
BUT THE PROPHECY MIGHT NOT EVEN COME TRUE.
THE "EVIL DEITY" SHOWED UP, DIDN'T HE?
WELL...
DID HE REALLY COUNT AS AN EVIL DEITY?
WHAT ELSE COULD HE BE?!
I'M MORE WORRIED ABOUT...
...THE FISSURE AT THE KARA-SUMORI SITE.
WHAT DOES IT MEAN?

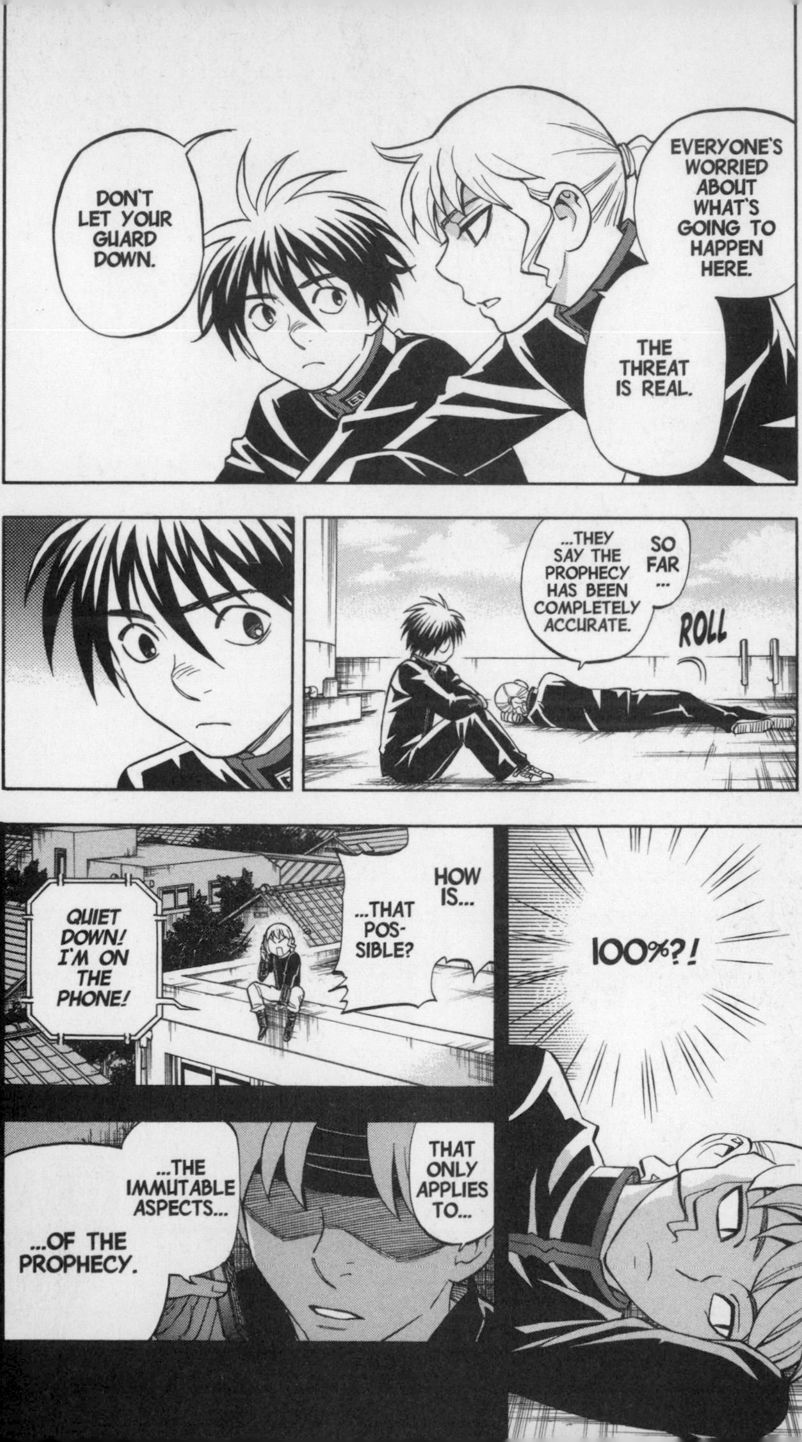
EVERYONE'S WORRIED ABOUT WHAT'S GOING TO HAPPEN HERE.
THE THREAT IS REAL.
DON'T LET YOUR GUARD DOWN.
SO FAR...
...THEY SAY THE PROPHECY HAS BEEN COMPLETELY ACCURATE.
ROLL
100%?!
HOW IS...
...THAT POS-SIBLE?
QUIET DOWN! I'M ON THE PHONE!
THAT ONLY APPLIES TO...
...THE IMMUTABLE ASPECTS...
...OF THE PROPHECY.

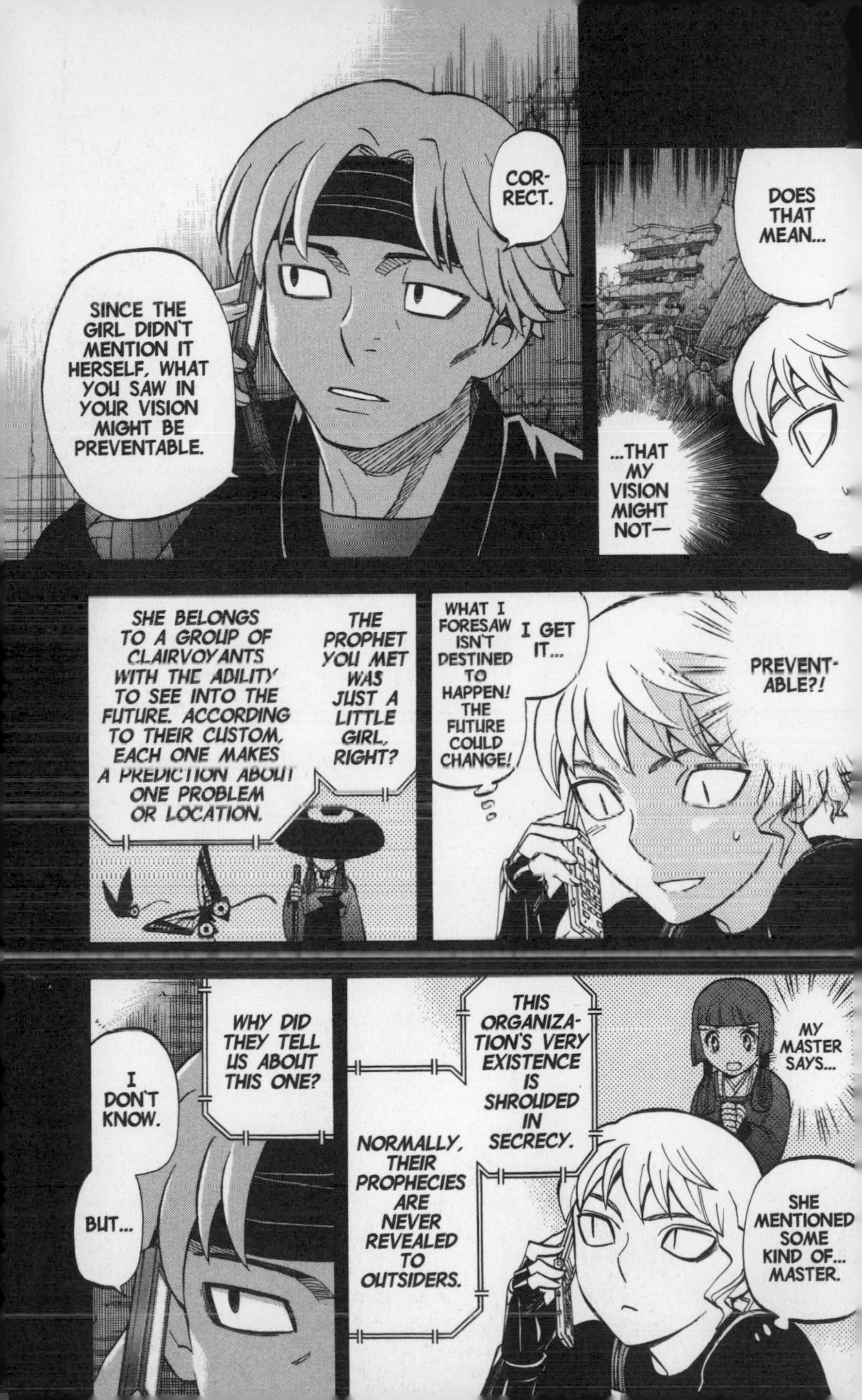
DOES THAT MEAN...
...THAT MY VISION MIGHT NOT—
COR-RECT.
SINCE THE GIRL DIDN'T MENTION IT HERSELF, WHAT YOU SAW IN YOUR VISION MIGHT BE PREVENTABLE.
PREVENT-ABLE?!
I GET IT...
WHAT I FORESAW ISN'T DESTINED TO HAPPEN! THE FUTURE COULD CHANGE!
THE PROPHET YOU MET WAS JUST A LITTLE GIRL, RIGHT?
SHE BELONGS TO A GROUP OF CLAIRVOYANTS WITH THE ABILITY TO SEE INTO THE FUTURE. ACCORDING TO THEIR CUSTOM, EACH ONE MAKES A PREDICTION ABOUT ONE PROBLEM OR LOCATION.
MY MASTER SAYS...
SHE MENTIONED SOME KIND OF... MASTER.
THIS ORGANIZATION'S VERY EXISTENCE IS SHROUDED IN SECRECY.
NORMALLY, THEIR PROPHECIES ARE NEVER REVEALED TO OUTSIDERS.
WHY DID THEY TELL US ABOUT THIS ONE?
I DON'T KNOW.
BUT...

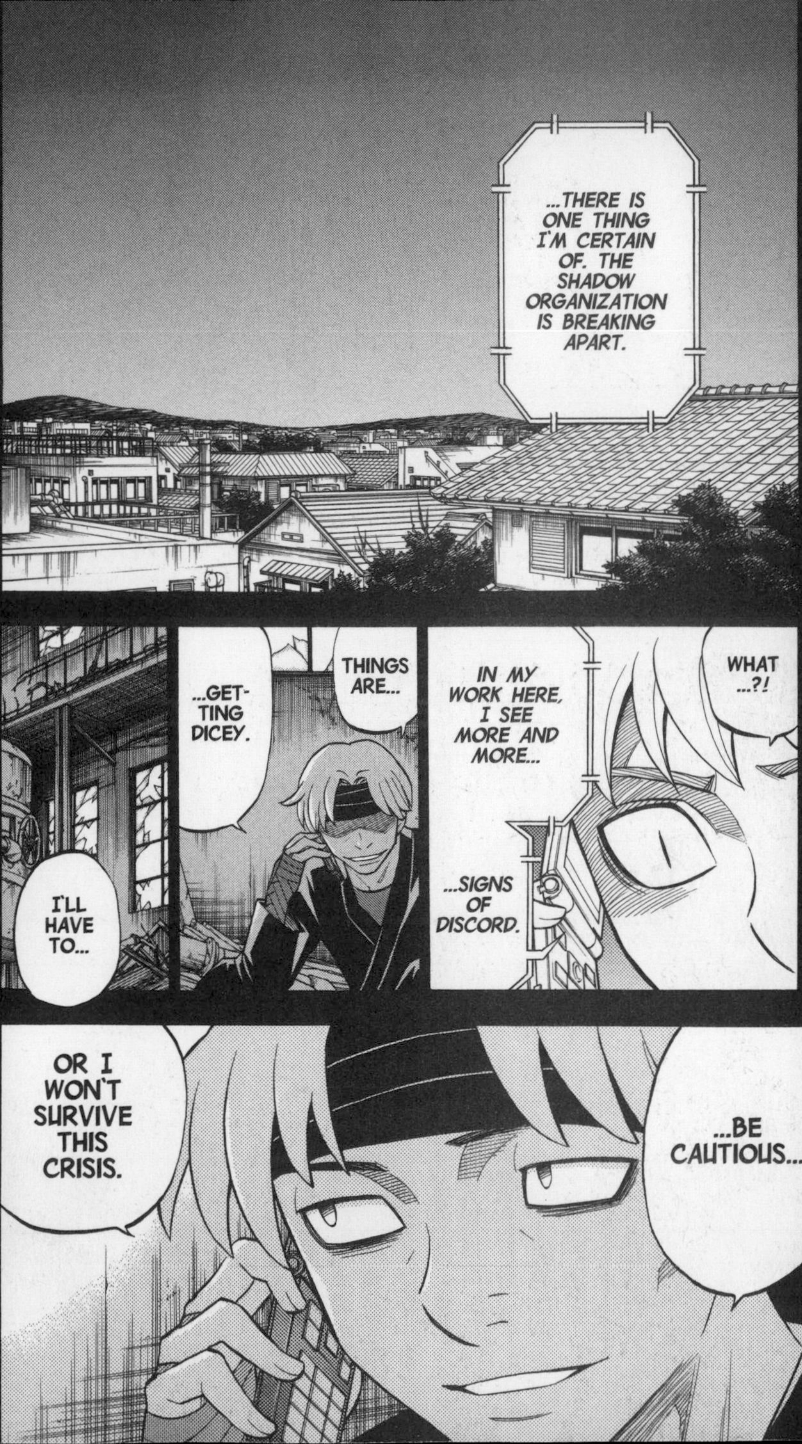
...THERE IS ONE THING I'M CERTAIN OF. THE SHADOW ORGANIZATION IS BREAKING APART.
WHAT ...?!
IN MY WORK HERE, I SEE MORE AND MORE...
...SIGNS OF DISCORD.
THINGS ARE...
...GET-TING DICEY.
I'LL HAVE TO...
...BE CAUTIOUS...
OR I WON'T SURVIVE THIS CRISIS.

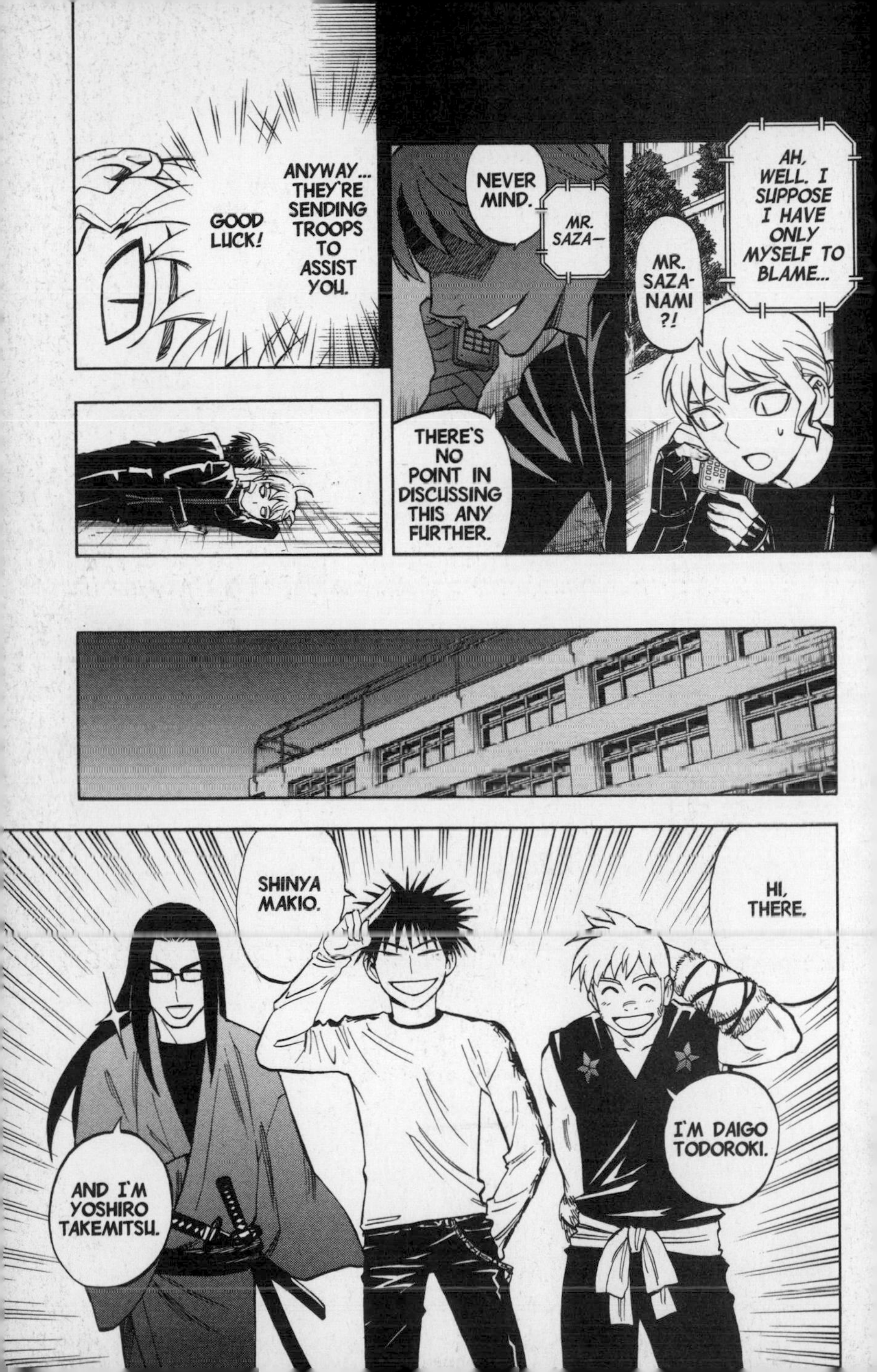
AH, WELL. I SUPPOSE I HAVE ONLY MYSELF TO BLAME...
MR. SAZA-NAMI?!
NEVER MIND.
MR. SAZA—
THERE'S NO POINT IN DISCUSSING THIS ANY FURTHER.
ANYWAY... THEY'RE SENDING TROOPS TO ASSIST YOU.
GOOD LUCK!
HI, THERE.
I'M DAIGO TODOROKI.
SHINYA MAKIO.
AND I'M YOSHIRO TAKEMITSU.

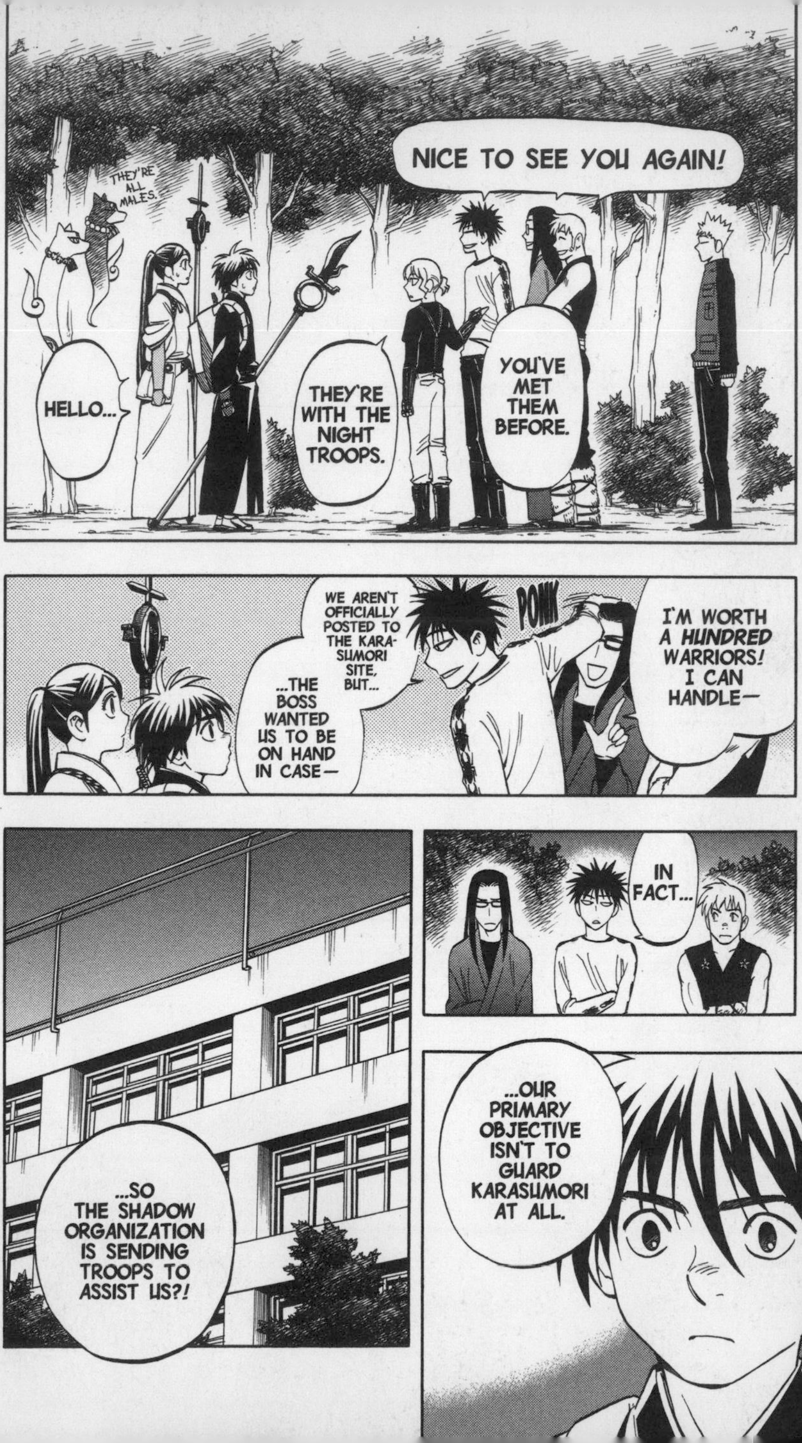
NICE TO SEE YOU AGAIN!
YOU'VE MET THEM BEFORE.
THEY'RE WITH THE NIGHT TROOPS.
HELLO...
THEY'RE ALL MALES.
I'M WORTH A HUNDRED WARRIORS! I CAN HANDLE—
POMK
WE AREN'T OFFICIALLY POSTED TO THE KARA-SUMORI SITE, BUT...
...THE BOSS WANTED US TO BE ON HAND IN CASE—
IN FACT...
...OUR PRIMARY OBJECTIVE ISN'T TO GUARD KARASUMORI AT ALL.
...SO THE SHADOW ORGANIZATION IS SENDING TROOPS TO ASSIST US?!

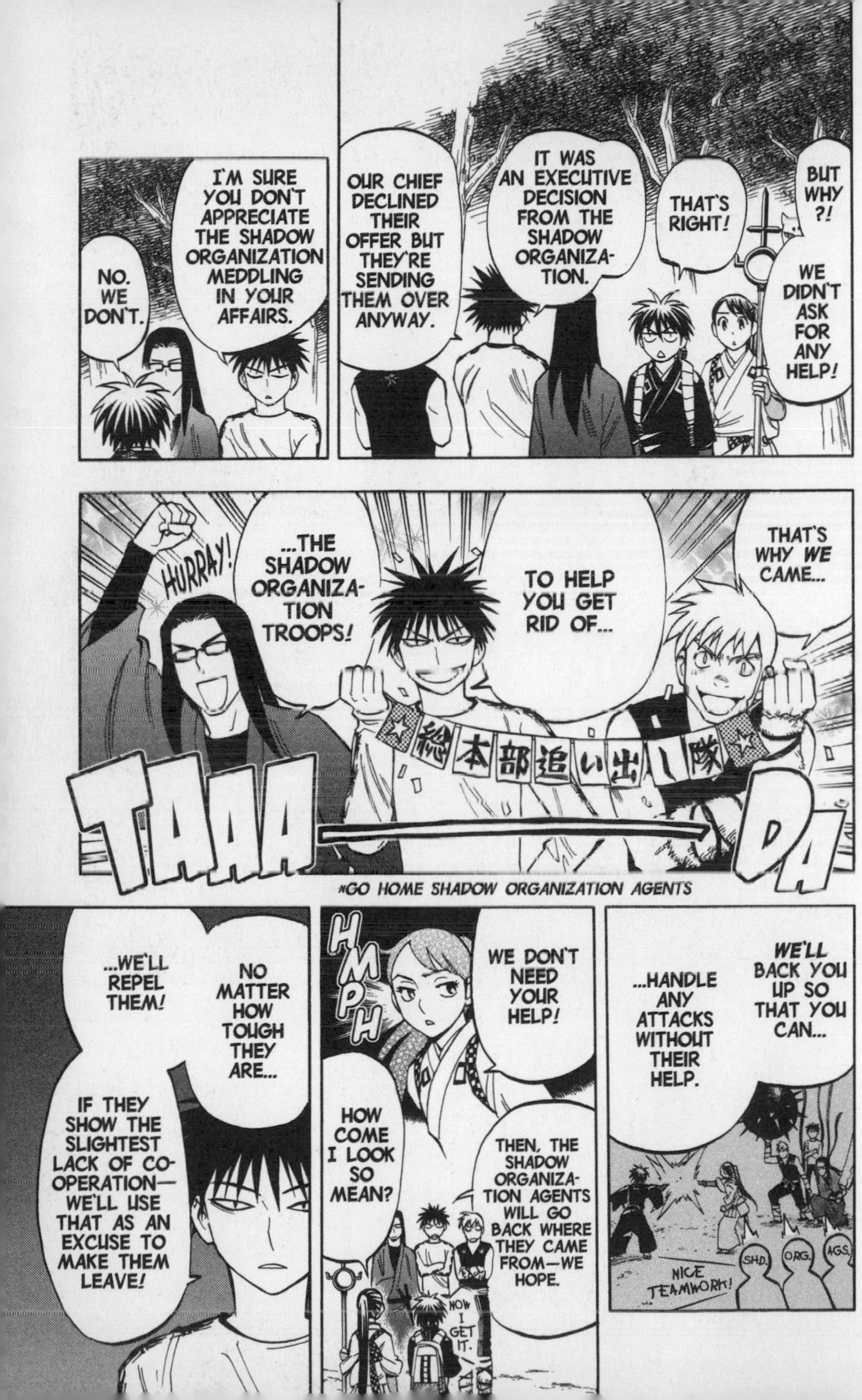
BUT WHY?!
WE DIDN'T ASK FOR ANY HELP!
THAT'S RIGHT!
IT WAS AN EXECUTIVE DECISION FROM THE SHADOW ORGANIZATION.
OUR CHIEF DECLINED THEIR OFFER BUT THEY'RE SENDING THEM OVER ANYWAY.
I'M SURE YOU DON'T APPRECIATE THE SHADOW ORGANIZATION MEDDLING IN YOUR AFFAIRS.
NO. WE DON'T.
THAT'S WHY WE CAME...
TO HELP YOU GET RID OF...
...THE SHADOW ORGANIZATION TROOPS!
HURRAY!
☆総本部追い出し隊☆
TAAA—DA
*GO HOME SHADOW ORGANIZATION AGENTS
WE'LL BACK YOU UP SO THAT YOU CAN...
...HANDLE ANY ATTACKS WITHOUT THEIR HELP.
NICE TEAMWORK!
SHD.
ORG.
AGS.
HMPH
WE DON'T NEED YOUR HELP!
THEN, THE SHADOW ORGANIZATION AGENTS WILL GO BACK WHERE THEY CAME FROM—WE HOPE.
HOW COME I LOOK SO MEAN?
NOW I GET IT.
NO MATTER HOW TOUGH THEY ARE...
...WE'LL REPEL THEM!
IF THEY SHOW THE SLIGHTEST LACK OF CO-OPERATION—WE'LL USE THAT AS AN EXCUSE TO MAKE THEM LEAVE!

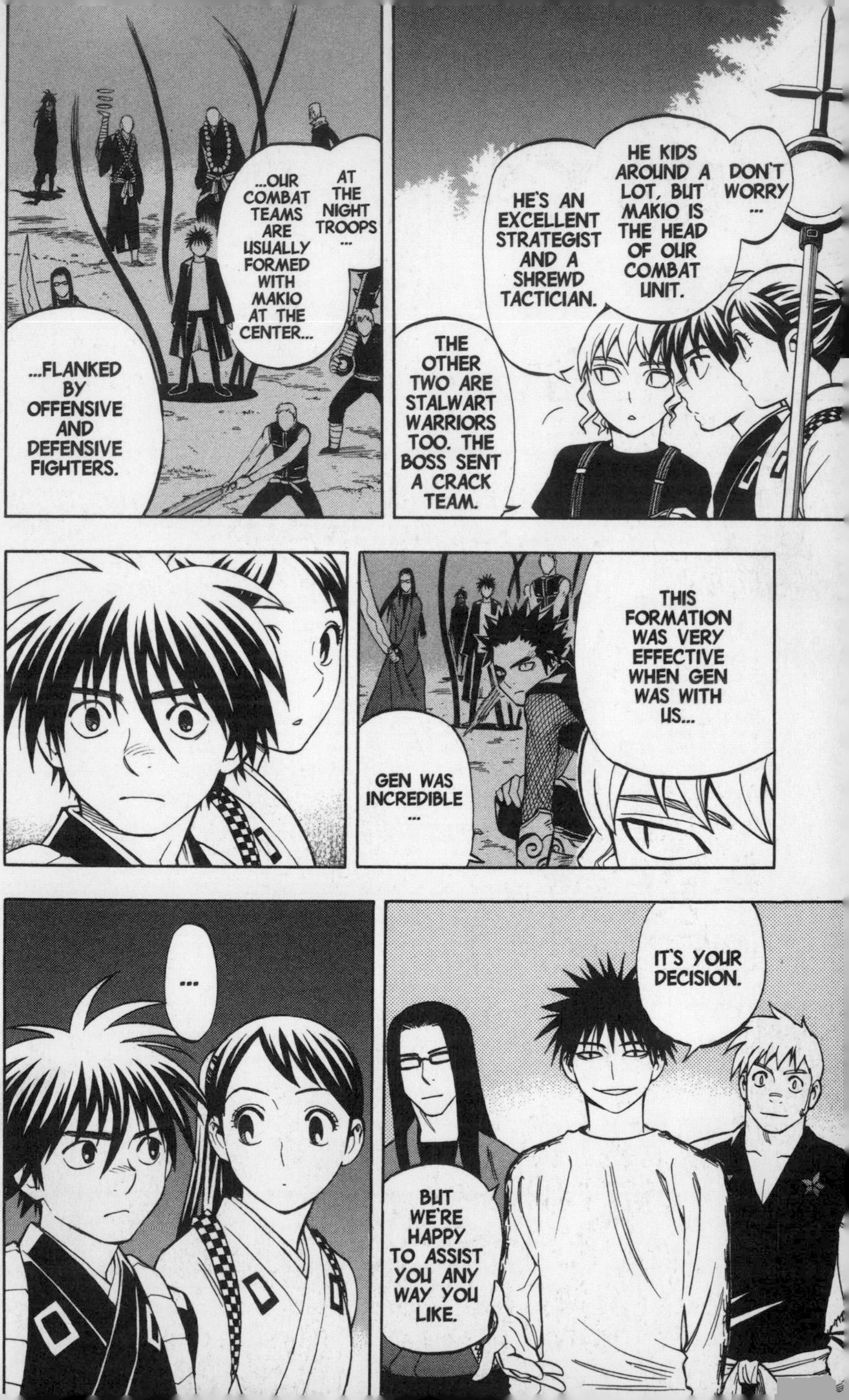
DON'T WORRY ...
HE KIDS AROUND A LOT, BUT MAKIO IS THE HEAD OF OUR COMBAT UNIT.
HE'S AN EXCELLENT STRATEGIST AND A SHREWD TACTICIAN.
THE OTHER TWO ARE STALWART WARRIORS TOO. THE BOSS SENT A CRACK TEAM.
AT THE NIGHT TROOPS ...
...OUR COMBAT TEAMS ARE USUALLY FORMED WITH MAKIO AT THE CENTER...
...FLANKED BY OFFENSIVE AND DEFENSIVE FIGHTERS.
THIS FORMATION WAS VERY EFFECTIVE WHEN GEN WAS WITH US...
GEN WAS INCREDIBLE ...
IT'S YOUR DECISION.
BUT WE'RE HAPPY TO ASSIST YOU ANY WAY YOU LIKE.
...

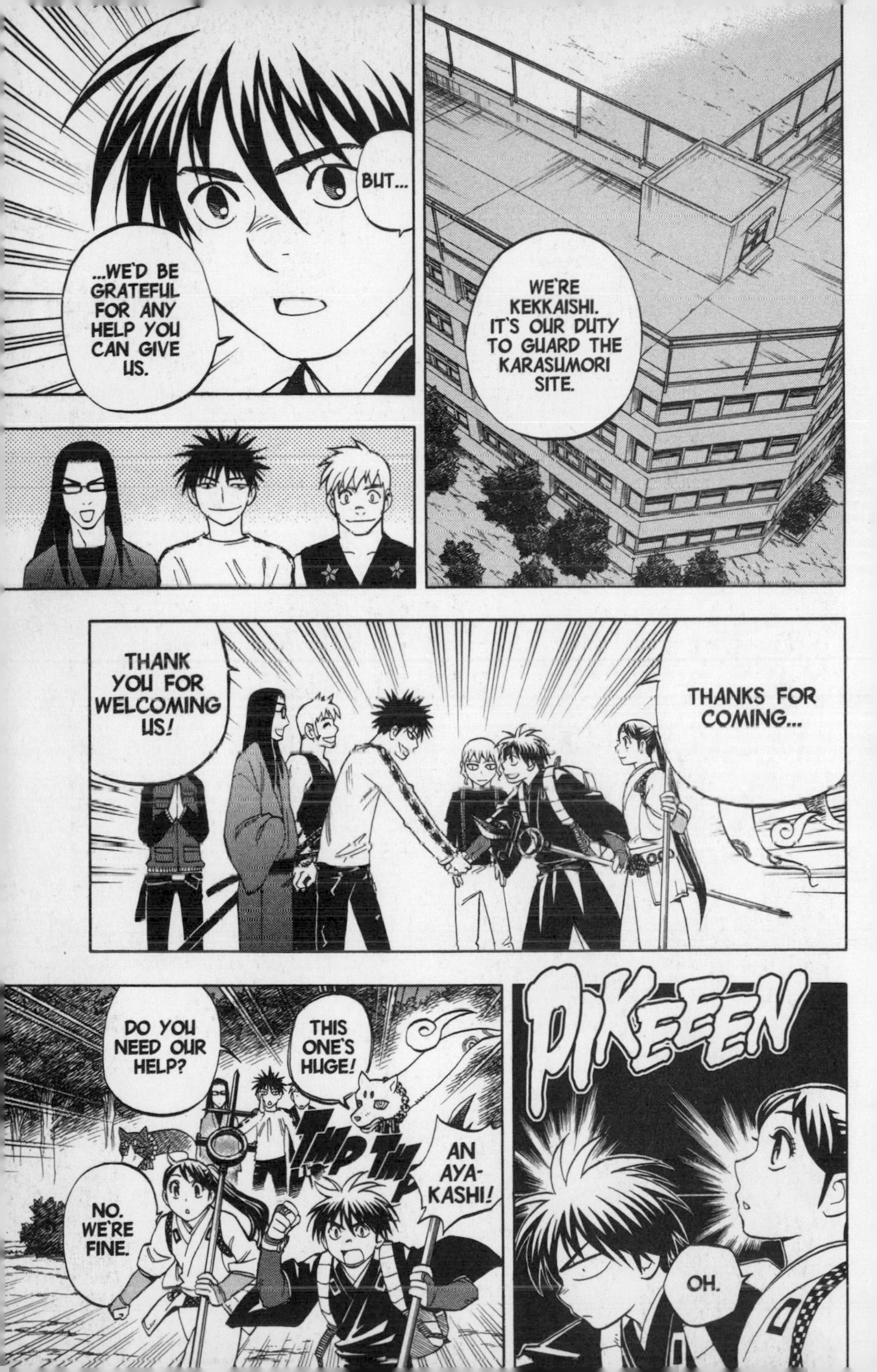
WE'RE KEKKAISHI. IT'S OUR DUTY TO GUARD THE KARASUMORI SITE.
BUT...
...WE'D BE GRATEFUL FOR ANY HELP YOU CAN GIVE US.
THANKS FOR COMING...
THANK YOU FOR WELCOMING US!
PIKEEEN
OH.
AN AYA-KASHI!
THIS ONE'S HUGE!
DO YOU NEED OUR HELP?
NO. WE'RE FINE.

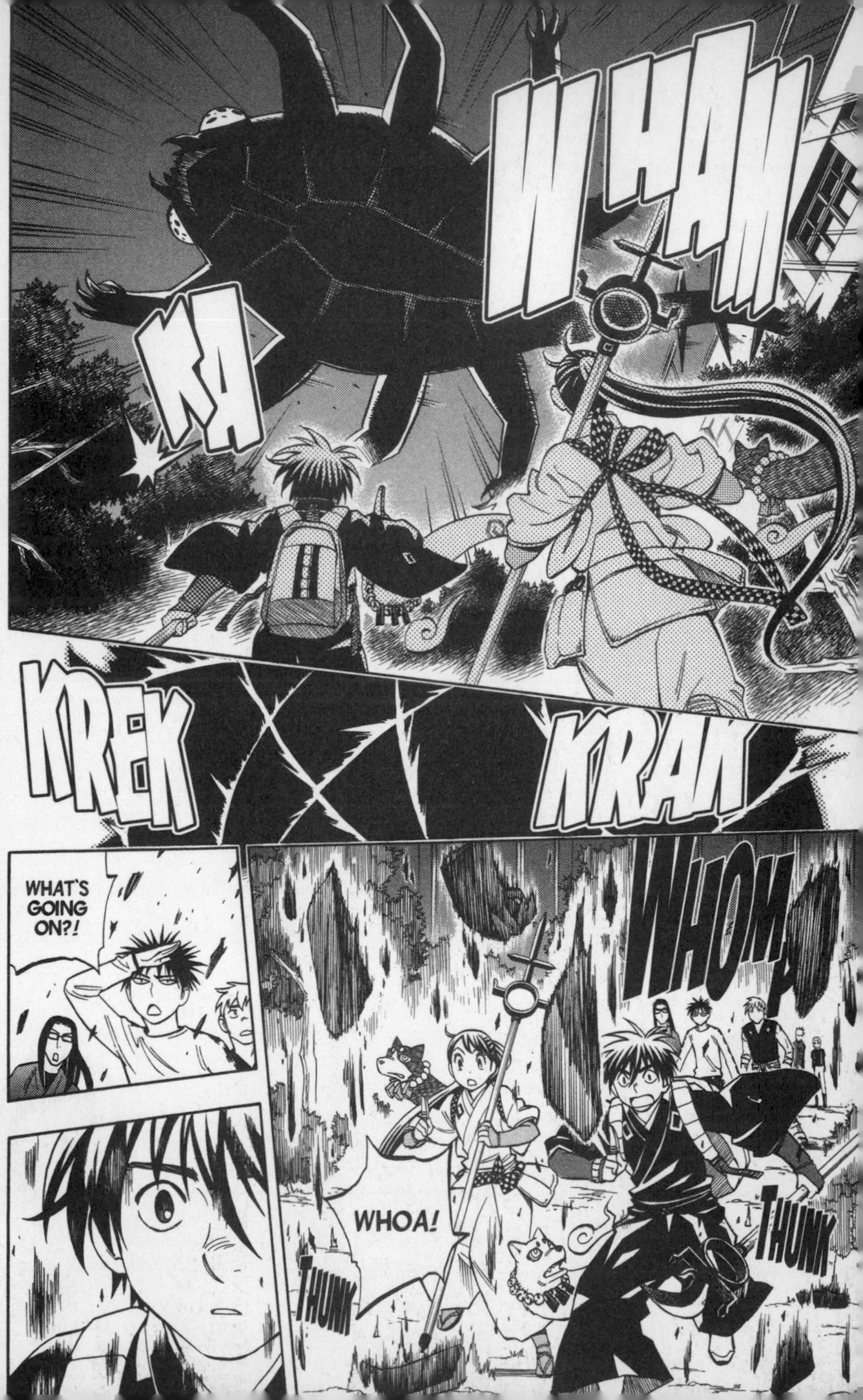
WHAM
KA
KRAK
KREK
THUNK
WHOA!
THUNK
WHAT'S GOING ON?!

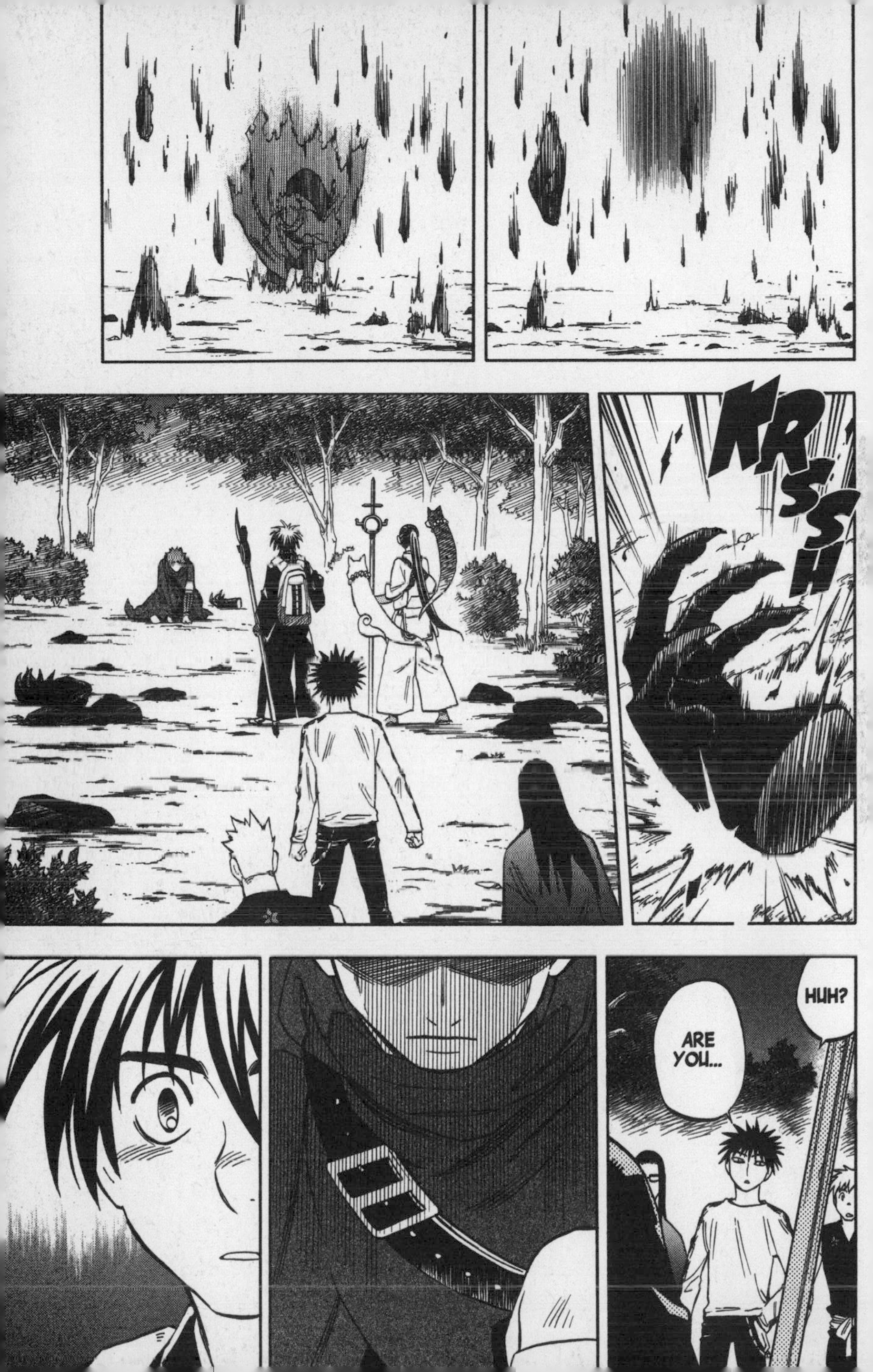
KRSSH
HUH?
ARE YOU...

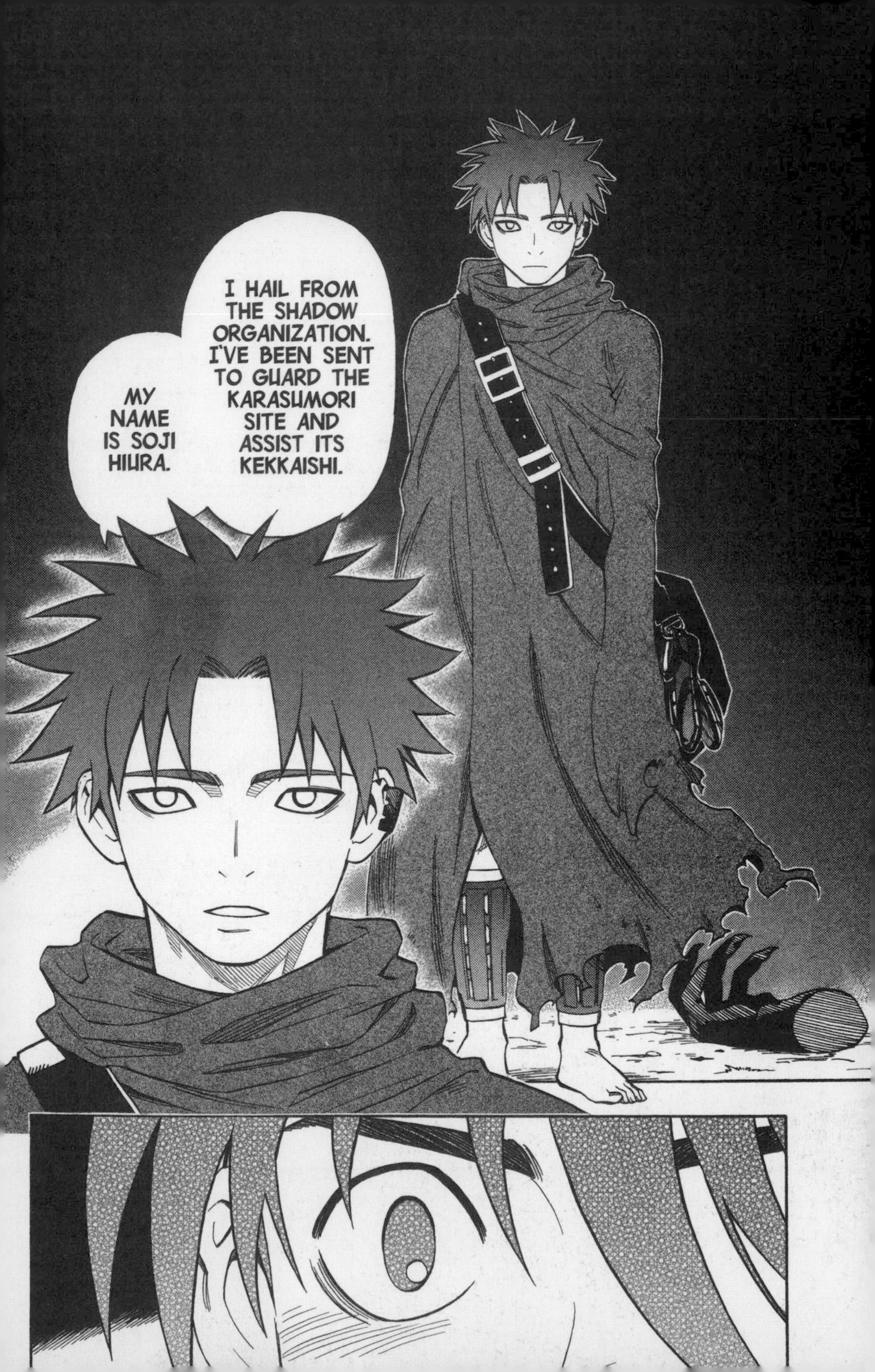
I HAIL FROM THE SHADOW ORGANIZATION. I'VE BEEN SENT TO GUARD THE KARASUMORI SITE AND ASSIST ITS KEKKAISHI.
MY NAME IS SOJI HIURA.

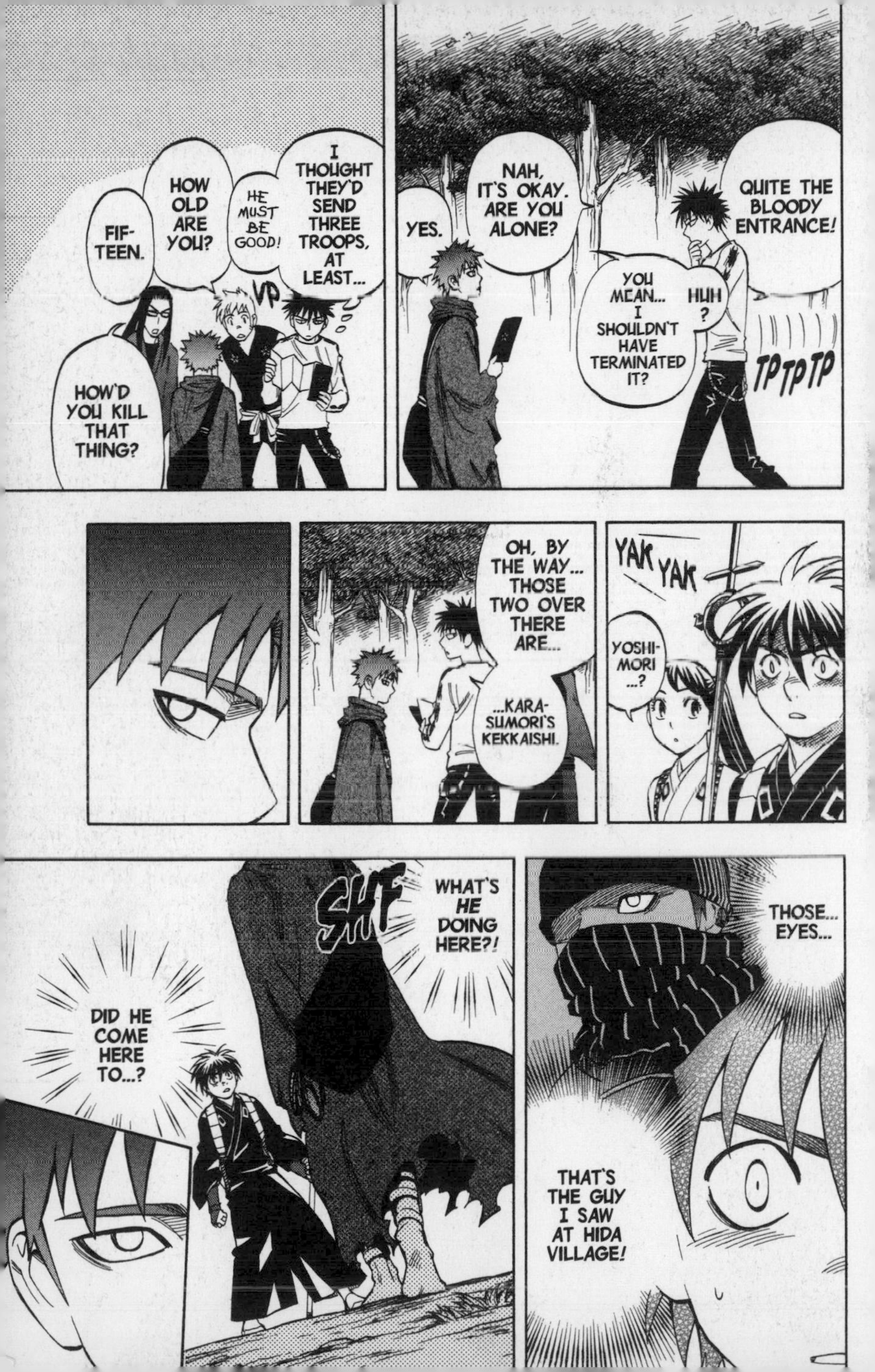
QUITE THE BLOODY ENTRANCE!
TP TP TP
HUH?
YOU MEAN... I SHOULDN'T HAVE TERMINATED IT?
NAH, IT'S OKAY. ARE YOU ALONE?
YES.
I THOUGHT THEY'D SEND THREE TROOPS, AT LEAST...
HE MUST BE GOOD!
VP
HOW OLD ARE YOU?
FIF-TEEN.
HOW'D YOU KILL THAT THING?
YAK YAK
YOSHIMORI...?
OH, BY THE WAY... THOSE TWO OVER THERE ARE...
...KARASUMORI'S KEKKAISHI.
THOSE... EYES...
THAT'S THE GUY I SAW AT HIDA VILLAGE!
SHF
WHAT'S HE DOING HERE?!
DID HE COME HERE TO...?

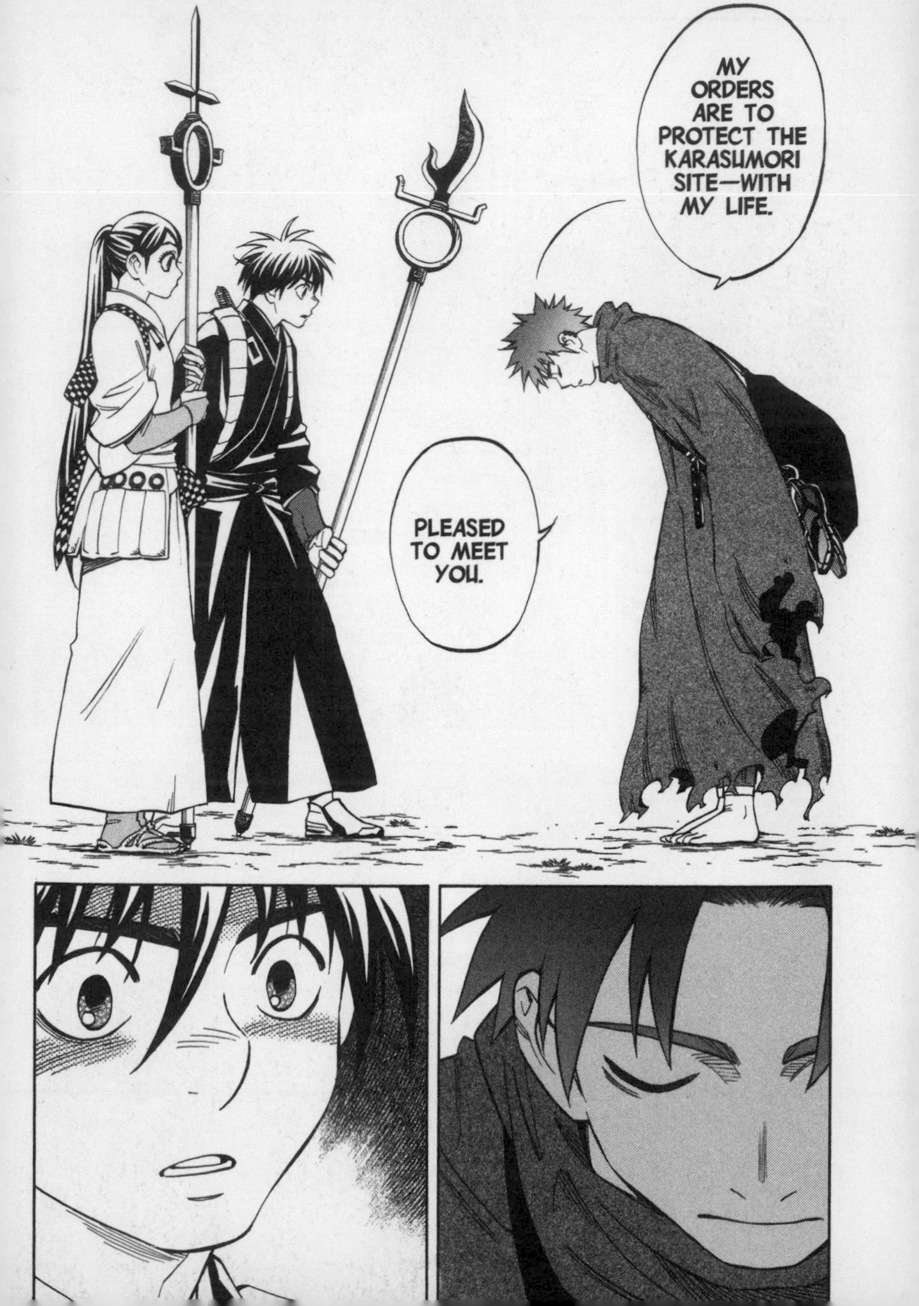
MY ORDERS ARE TO PROTECT THE KARASUMORI SITE—WITH MY LIFE.
PLEASED TO MEET YOU.

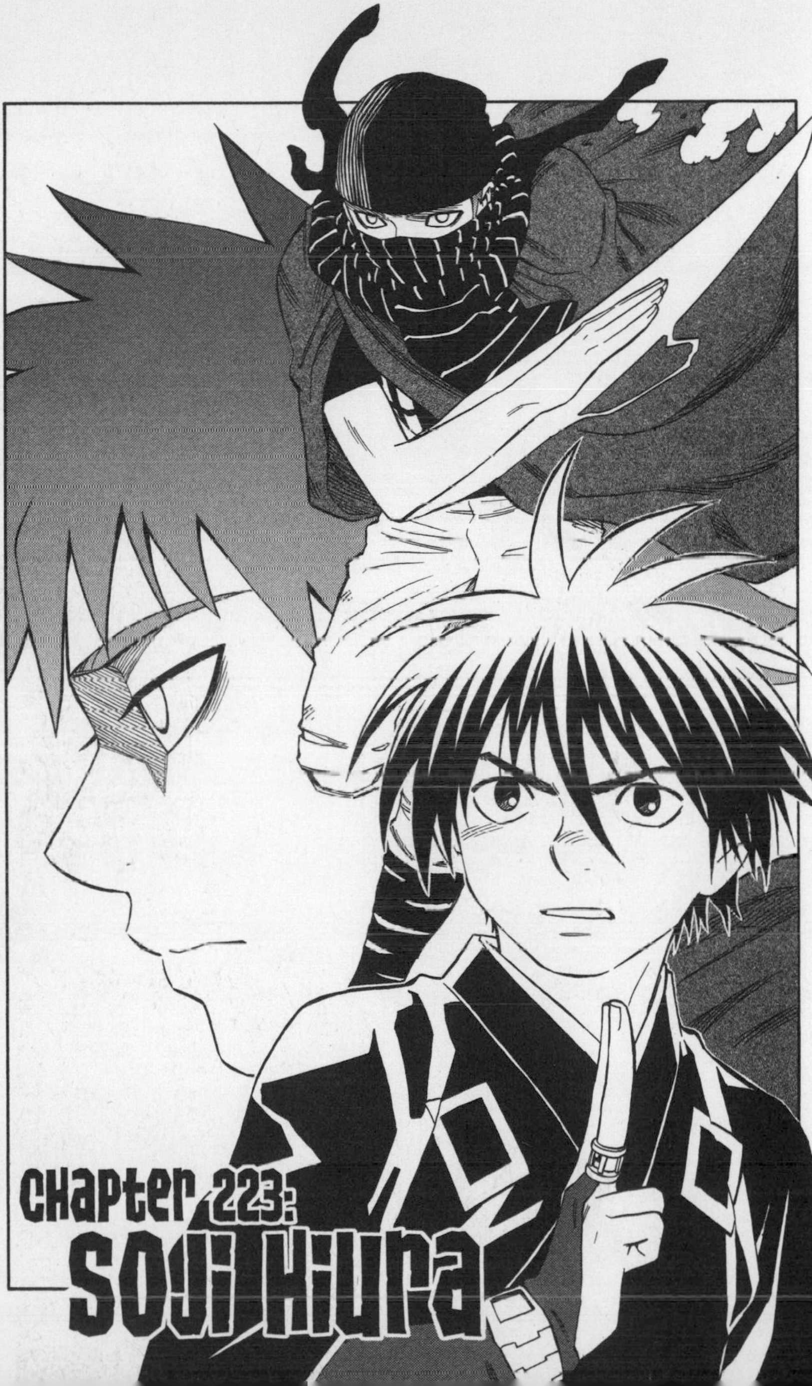
Chapter 223:
Soji Hiura

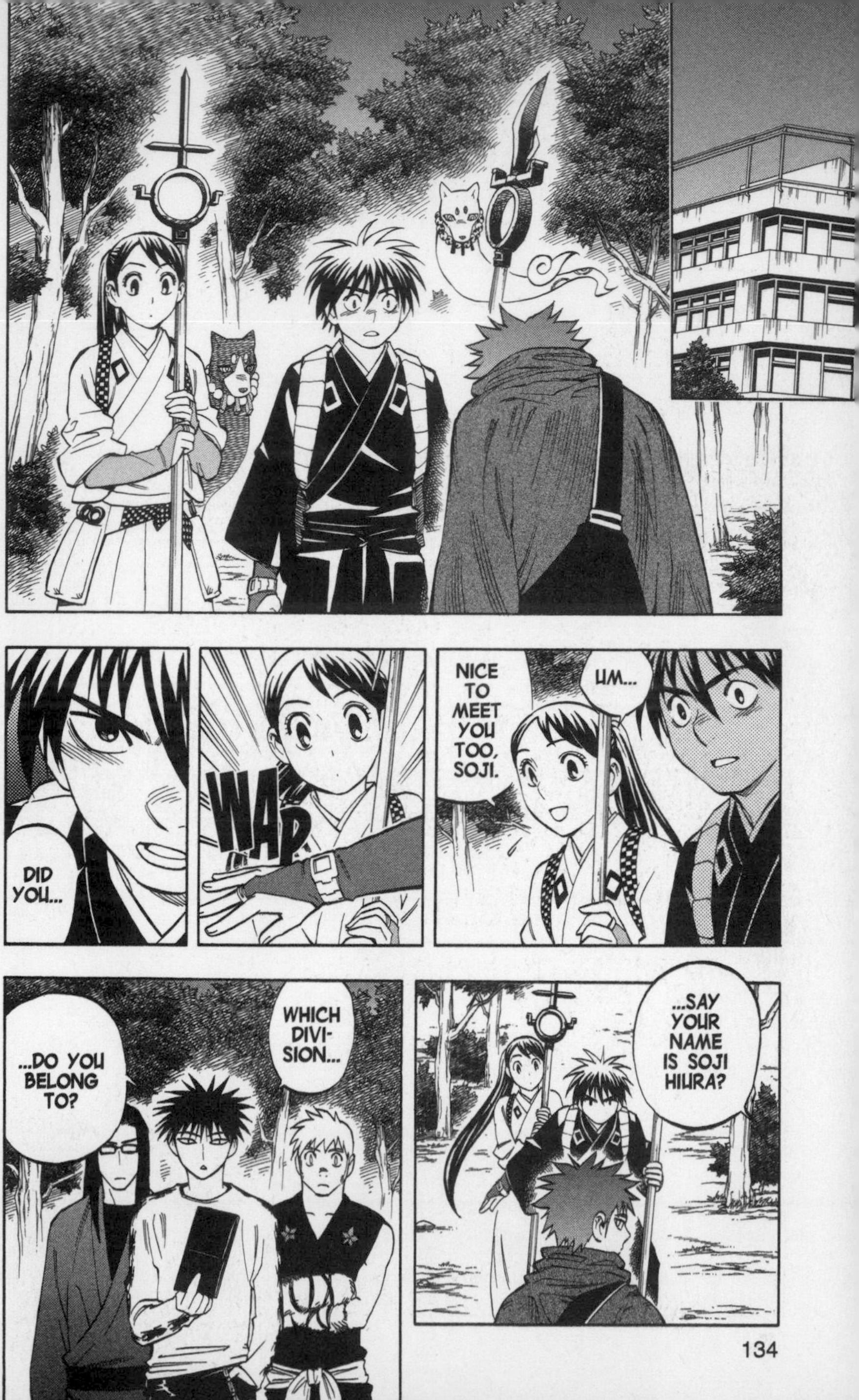
UM...
NICE TO MEET YOU TOO, SOJI.
WAP
DID YOU...
...SAY YOUR NAME IS SOJI HIURA?
WHICH DIVI-SION...
...DO YOU BELONG TO?

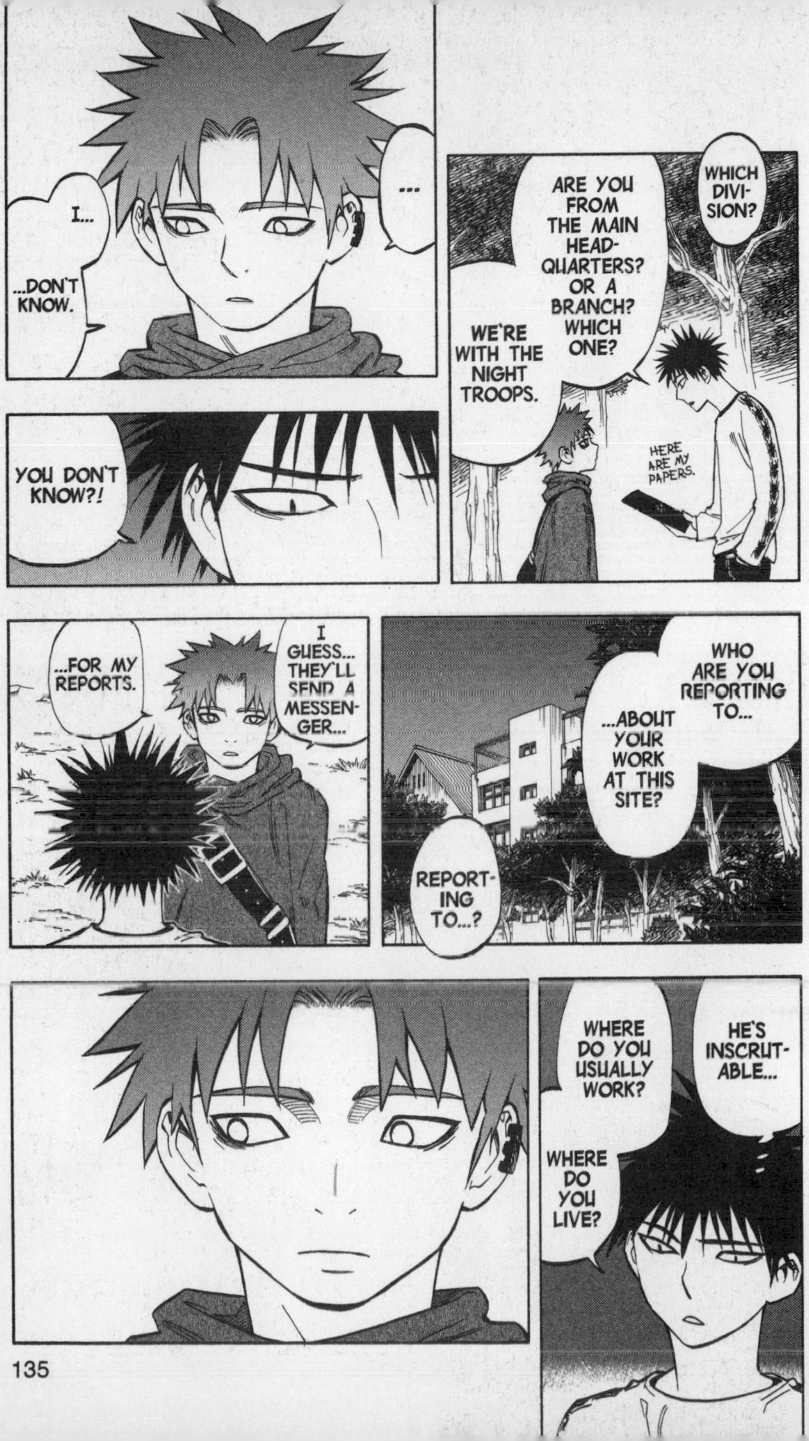
WHICH DIVISION?
ARE YOU FROM THE MAIN HEADQUARTERS? OR A BRANCH? WHICH ONE?
WE'RE WITH THE NIGHT TROOPS.
HERE ARE MY PAPERS.
...
I...
...DON'T KNOW.
YOU DON'T KNOW?!
WHO ARE YOU REPORTING TO...
...ABOUT YOUR WORK AT THIS SITE?
REPORTING TO...?
I GUESS... THEY'LL SEND A MESSENGER...
...FOR MY REPORTS.
HE'S INSCRUTABLE...
WHERE DO YOU USUALLY WORK?
WHERE DO YOU LIVE?

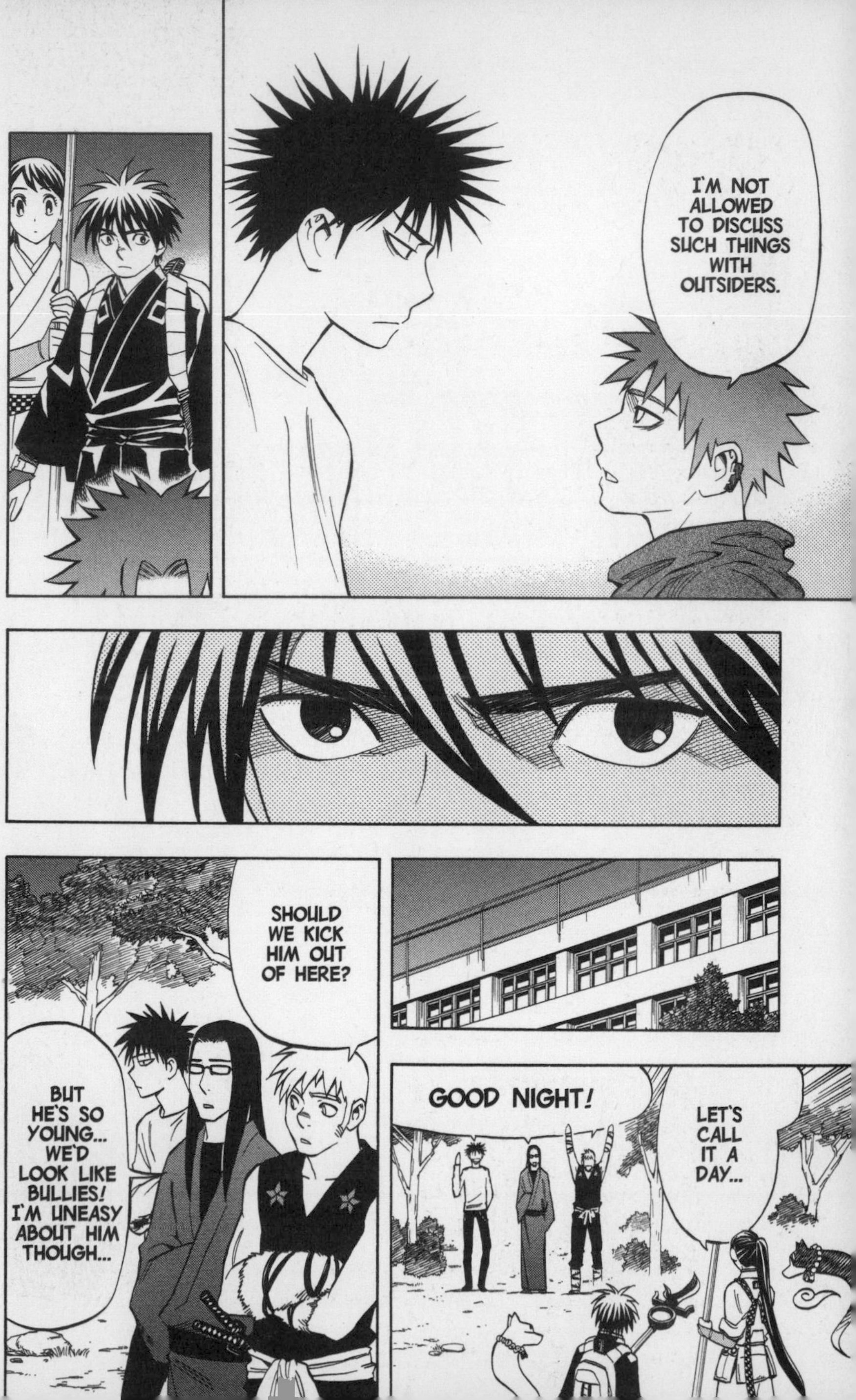
I'M NOT ALLOWED TO DISCUSS SUCH THINGS WITH OUTSIDERS.
LET'S CALL IT A DAY...
GOOD NIGHT!
SHOULD WE KICK HIM OUT OF HERE?
BUT HE'S SO YOUNG... WE'D LOOK LIKE BULLIES! I'M UNEASY ABOUT HIM THOUGH...

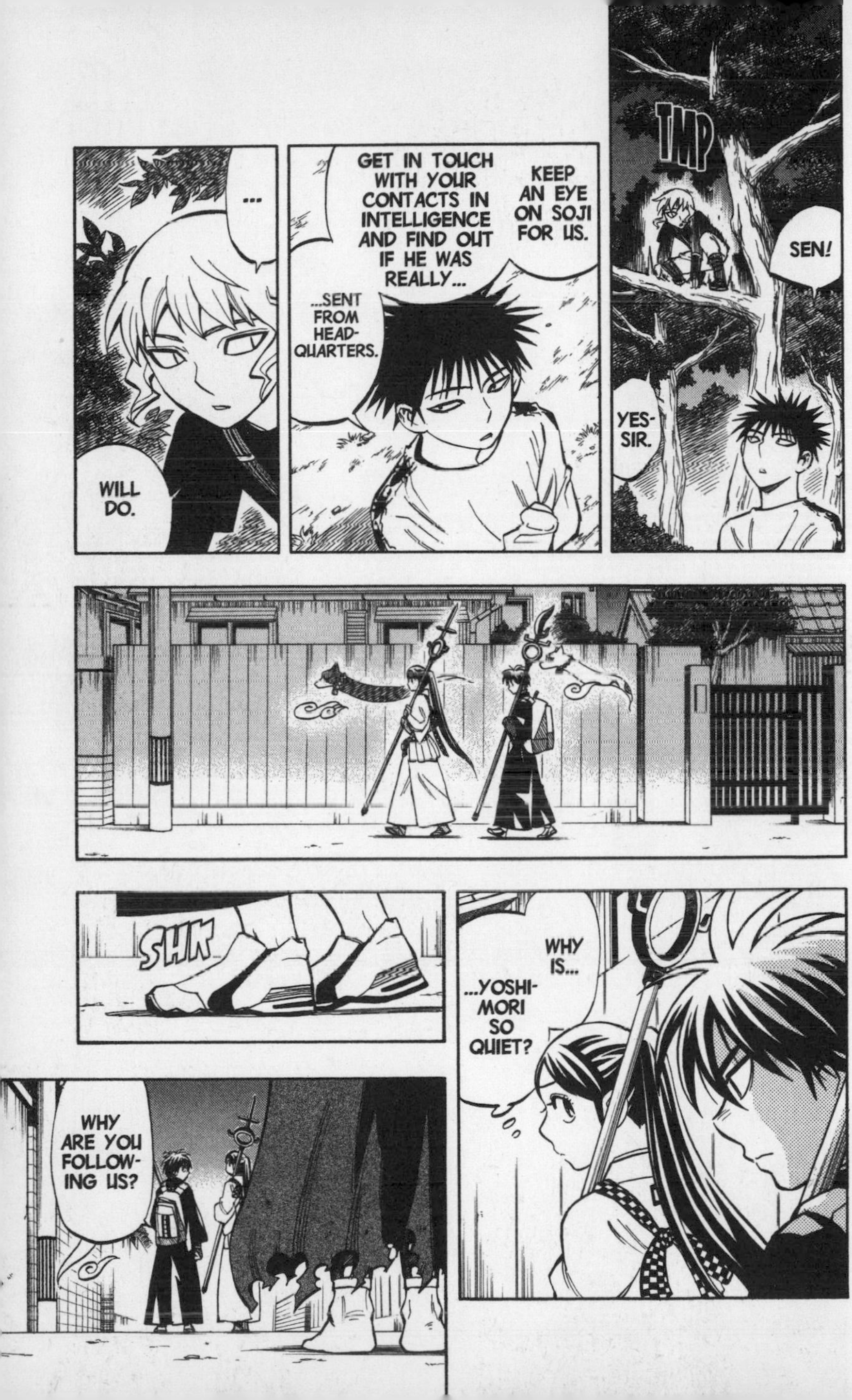
TMP
SEN!
YES-SIR.
KEEP AN EYE ON SOJI FOR US.
GET IN TOUCH WITH YOUR CONTACTS IN INTELLIGENCE AND FIND OUT IF HE WAS REALLY...
...SENT FROM HEAD-QUARTERS.
...
WILL DO.
WHY IS...
...YOSHI-MORI SO QUIET?
SHK
WHY ARE YOU FOLLOW-ING US?

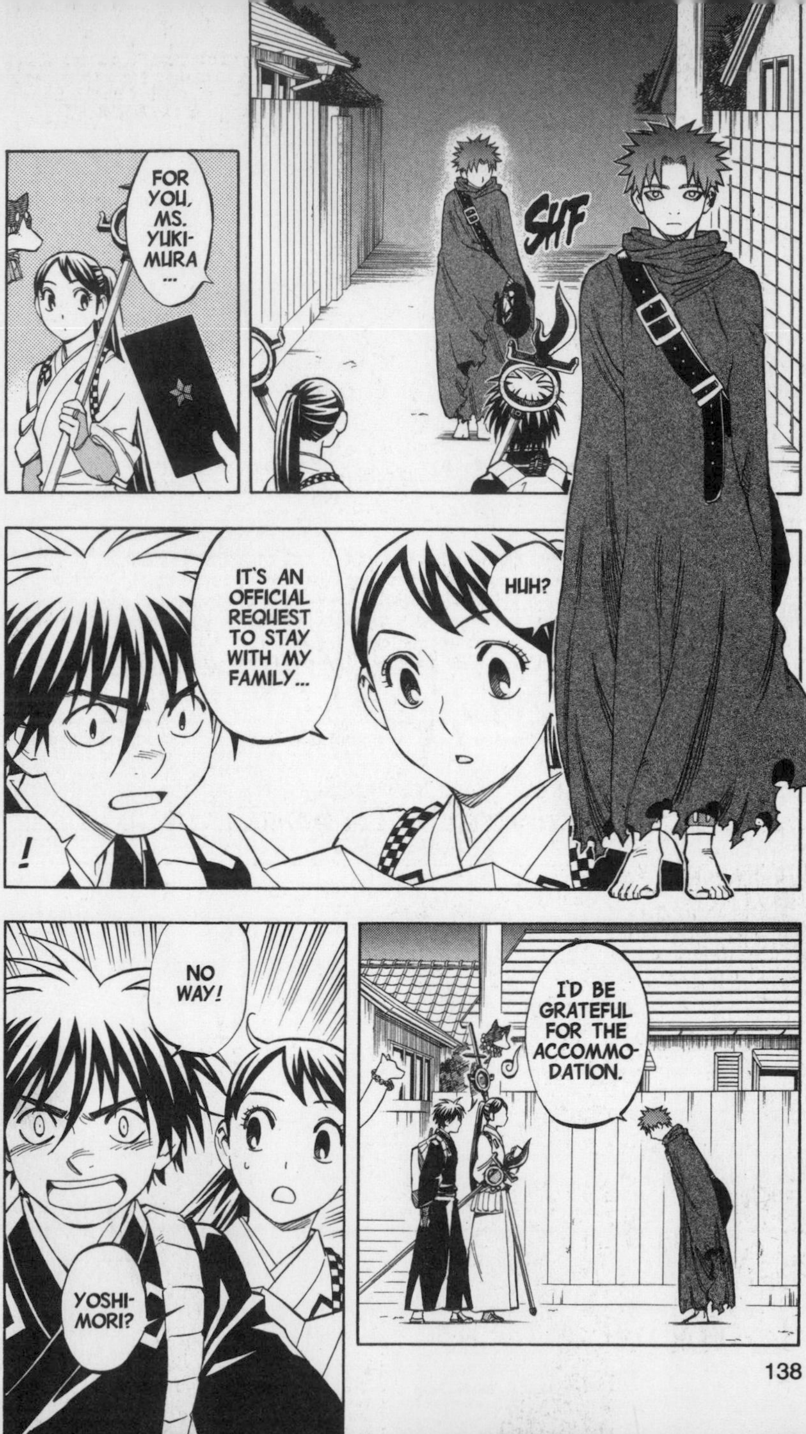
SHF
FOR YOU, MS. YUKIMURA...
HUH?
IT'S AN OFFICIAL REQUEST TO STAY WITH MY FAMILY...
!
I'D BE GRATEFUL FOR THE ACCOMMODATION.
NO WAY!
YOSHIMORI?

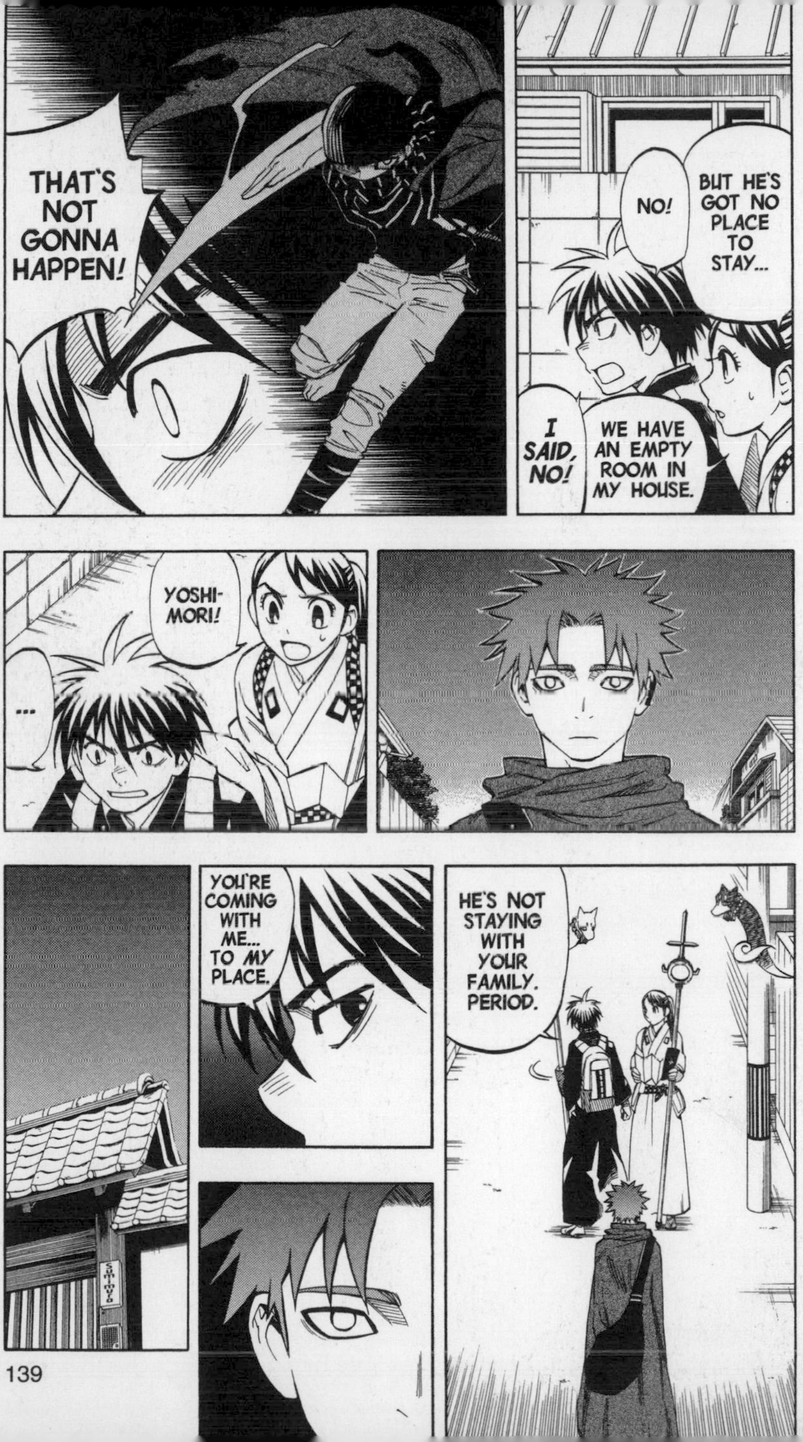
BUT HE'S GOT NO PLACE TO STAY...
NO!
WE HAVE AN EMPTY ROOM IN MY HOUSE.
I SAID, NO!
THAT'S NOT GONNA HAPPEN!
YOSHIMORI!
...
HE'S NOT STAYING WITH YOUR FAMILY. PERIOD.
YOU'RE COMING WITH ME... TO MY PLACE.

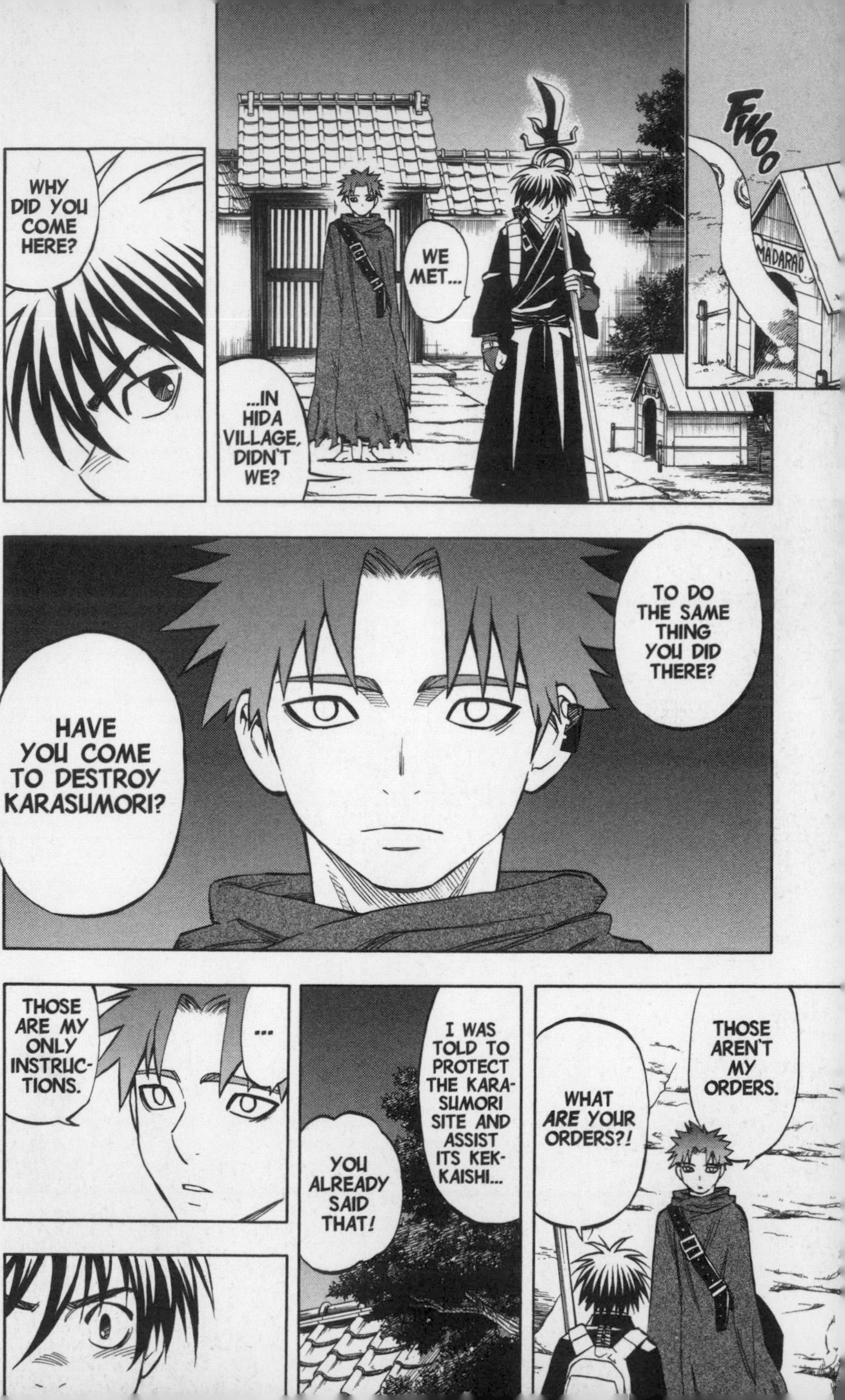
FWOO
MADARAO
WE MET...
...IN HIDA VILLAGE, DIDN'T WE?
WHY DID YOU COME HERE?
TO DO THE SAME THING YOU DID THERE?
HAVE YOU COME TO DESTROY KARASUMORI?
THOSE AREN'T MY ORDERS.
WHAT *ARE* YOUR ORDERS?!
I WAS TOLD TO PROTECT THE KARA-SUMORI SITE AND ASSIST ITS KEK-KAISHI...
YOU ALREADY SAID THAT!
...
THOSE ARE MY ONLY INSTRUC-TIONS.

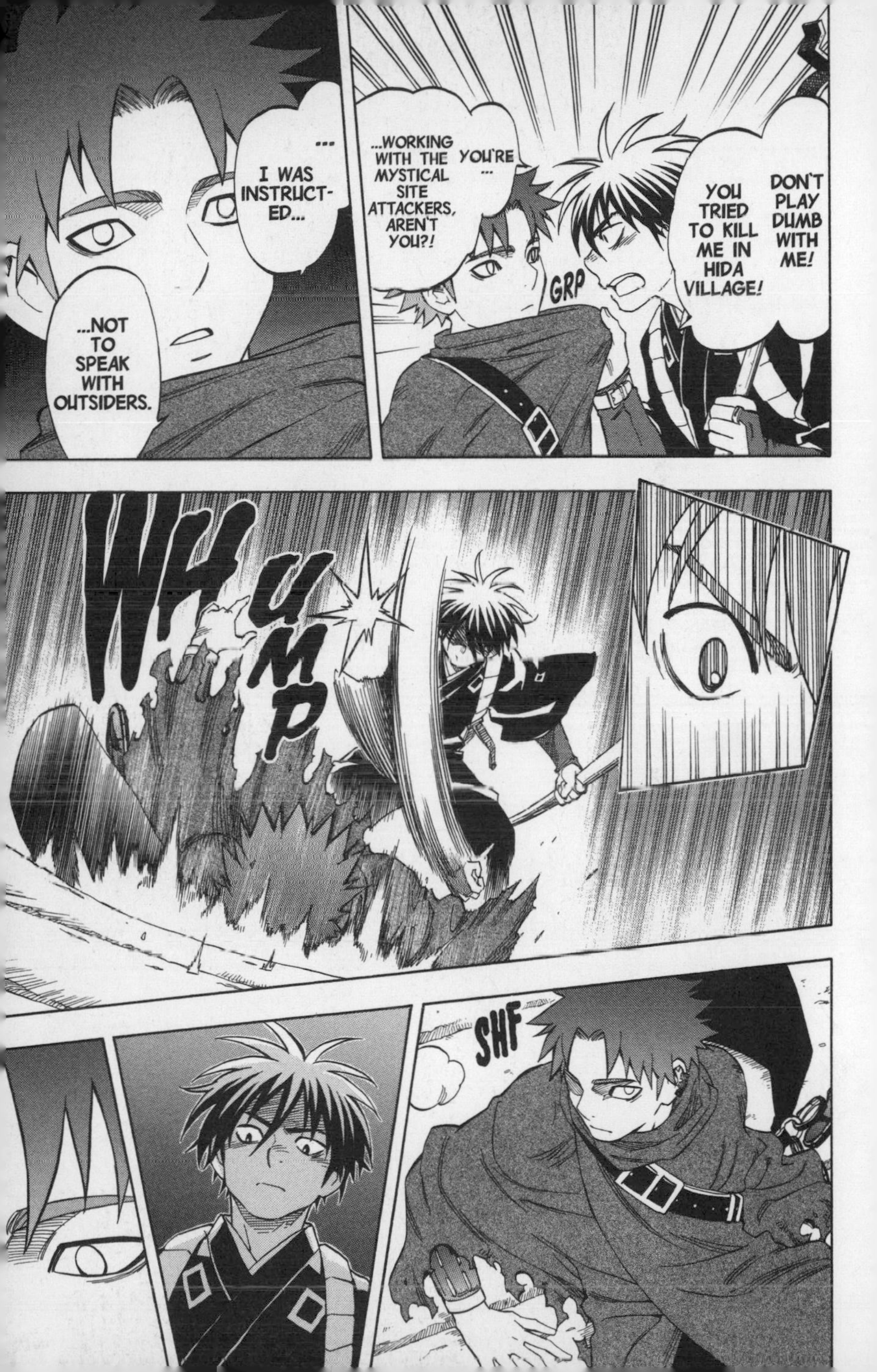
DON'T PLAY DUMB WITH ME!
YOU TRIED TO KILL ME IN HIDA VILLAGE!
GRP
YOU'RE ...
...WORKING WITH THE MYSTICAL SITE ATTACKERS, AREN'T YOU?!
...
I WAS INSTRUCT-ED...
...NOT TO SPEAK WITH OUTSIDERS.
WHUMP
SHF

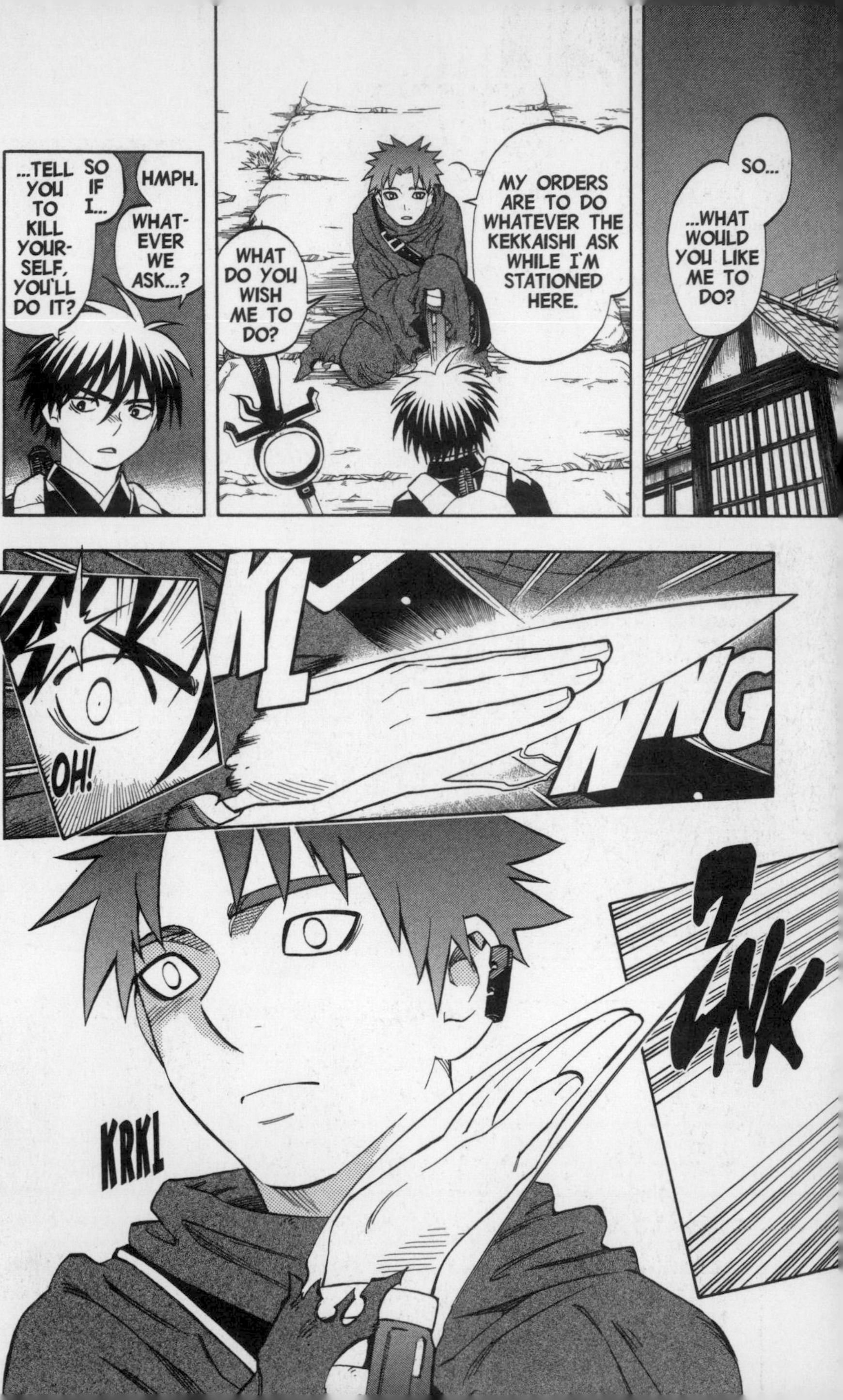
SO...
...WHAT WOULD YOU LIKE ME TO DO?
MY ORDERS ARE TO DO WHATEVER THE KEKKAISHI ASK WHILE I'M STATIONED HERE.
WHAT DO YOU WISH ME TO DO?
HMPH.
WHAT-EVER WE ASK...?
SO IF I...
...TELL YOU TO KILL YOUR-SELF, YOU'LL DO IT?
KL
NNG
OH!
KRKL

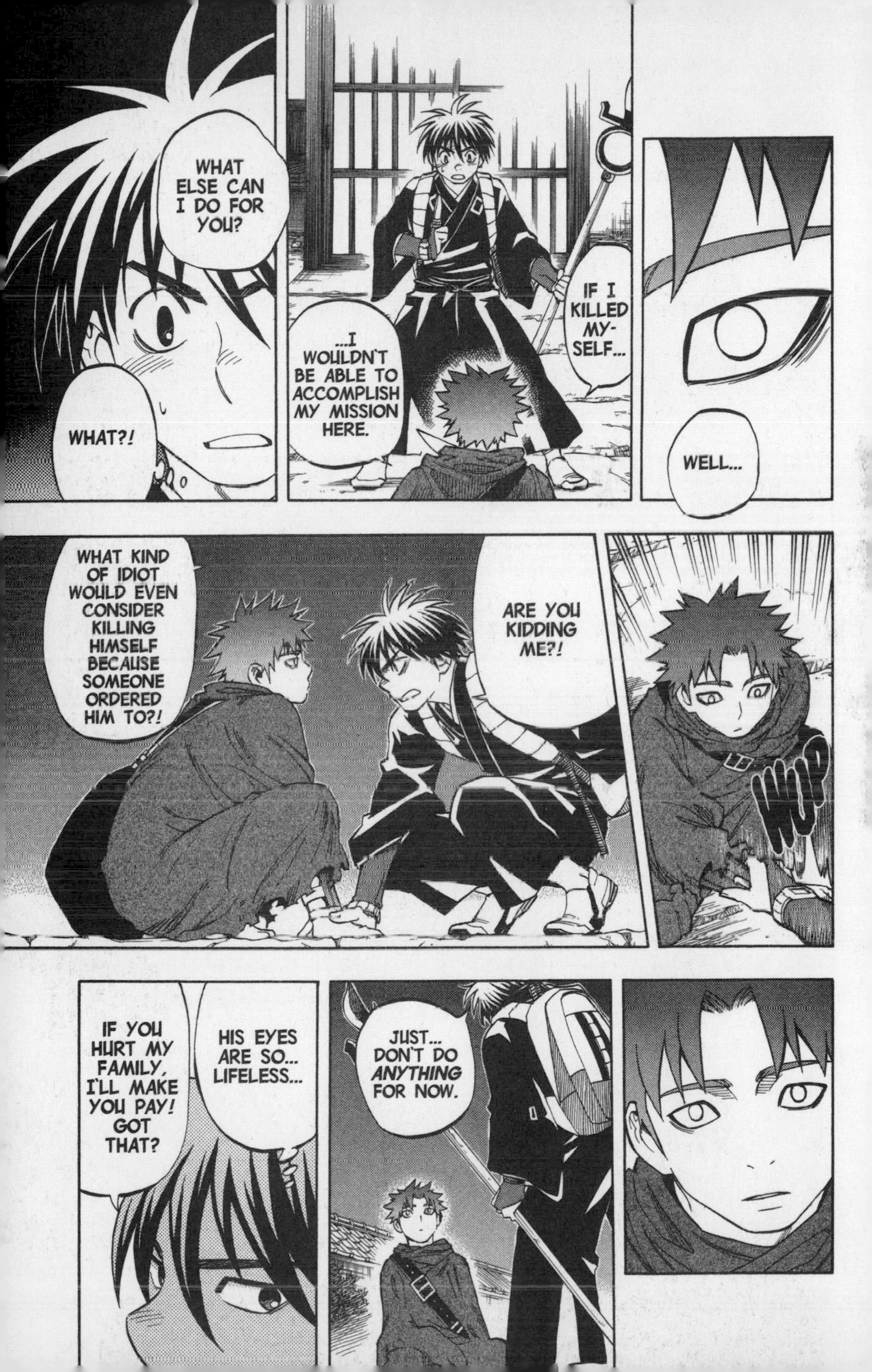
WELL...
IF I KILLED MY-SELF...
...I WOULDN'T BE ABLE TO ACCOMPLISH MY MISSION HERE.
WHAT ELSE CAN I DO FOR YOU?
WHAT?!
WHUP
ARE YOU KIDDING ME?!
WHAT KIND OF IDIOT WOULD EVEN CONSIDER KILLING HIMSELF BECAUSE SOMEONE ORDERED HIM TO?!
JUST... DON'T DO *ANYTHING* FOR NOW.
HIS EYES ARE SO... LIFELESS...
IF YOU HURT MY FAMILY, I'LL MAKE YOU PAY! GOT THAT?

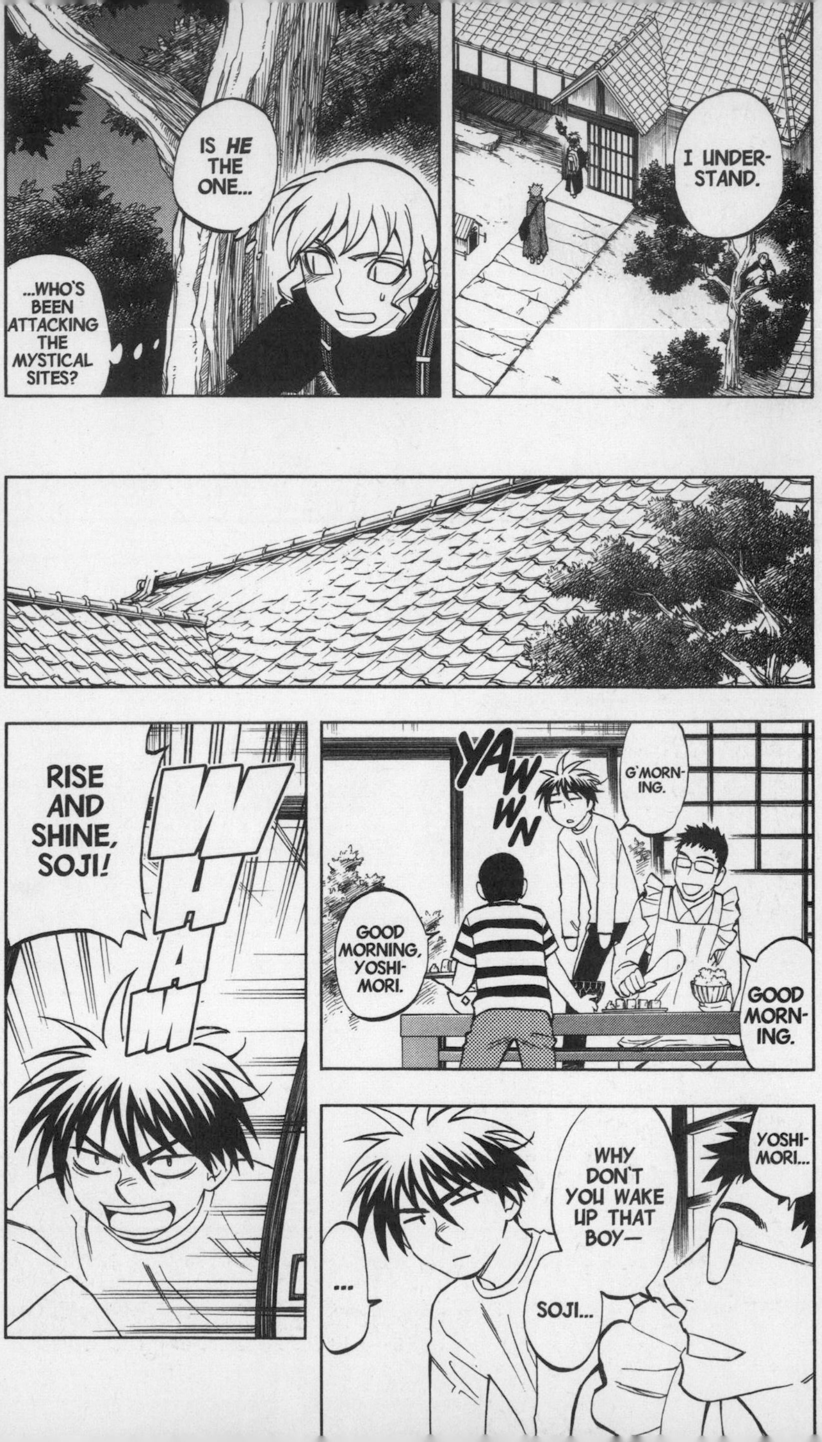
I UNDER-STAND.
IS HE THE ONE...
...WHO'S BEEN ATTACKING THE MYSTICAL SITES?
G'MORN-ING.
YAWWWN
GOOD MORN-ING.
GOOD MORNING, YOSHI-MORI.
YOSHI-MORI...
WHY DON'T YOU WAKE UP THAT BOY—
SOJI...
...
RISE AND SHINE, SOJI!
WHAM

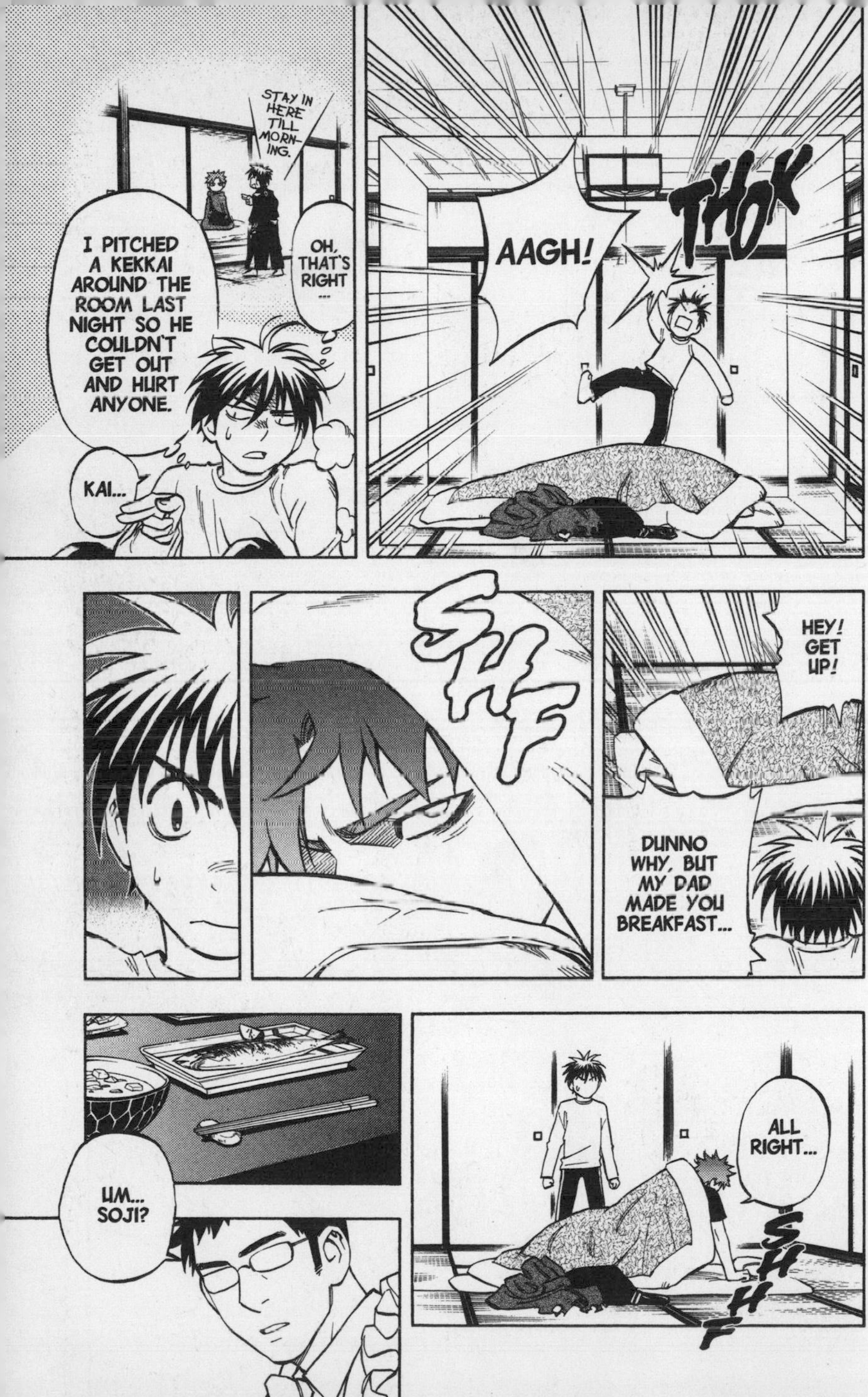
AAGH!
THOK
STAY IN HERE TILL MORNING.
OH, THAT'S RIGHT...
I PITCHED A KEKKAI AROUND THE ROOM LAST NIGHT SO HE COULDN'T GET OUT AND HURT ANYONE.
KAI...
HEY! GET UP!
DUNNO WHY, BUT MY DAD MADE YOU BREAKFAST...
SHF
ALL RIGHT...
SHHF
UM... SOJI?

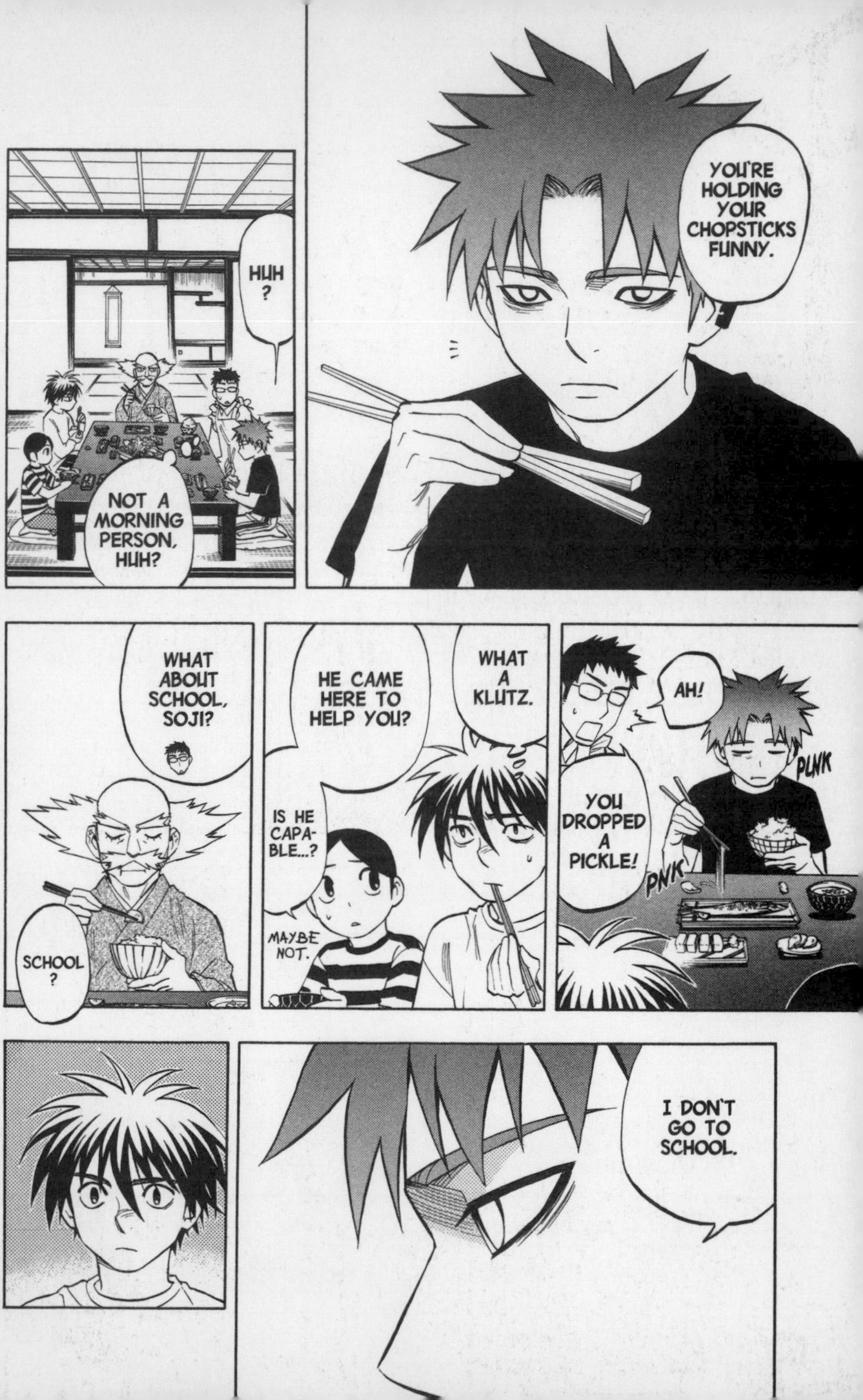
YOU'RE HOLDING YOUR CHOPSTICKS FUNNY.
HUH?
NOT A MORNING PERSON, HUH?
AH!
PLNK
YOU DROPPED A PICKLE!
PNK
WHAT A KLUTZ.
HE CAME HERE TO HELP YOU?
IS HE CAPABLE...?
MAYBE NOT.
WHAT ABOUT SCHOOL, SOJI?
SCHOOL?
I DON'T GO TO SCHOOL.

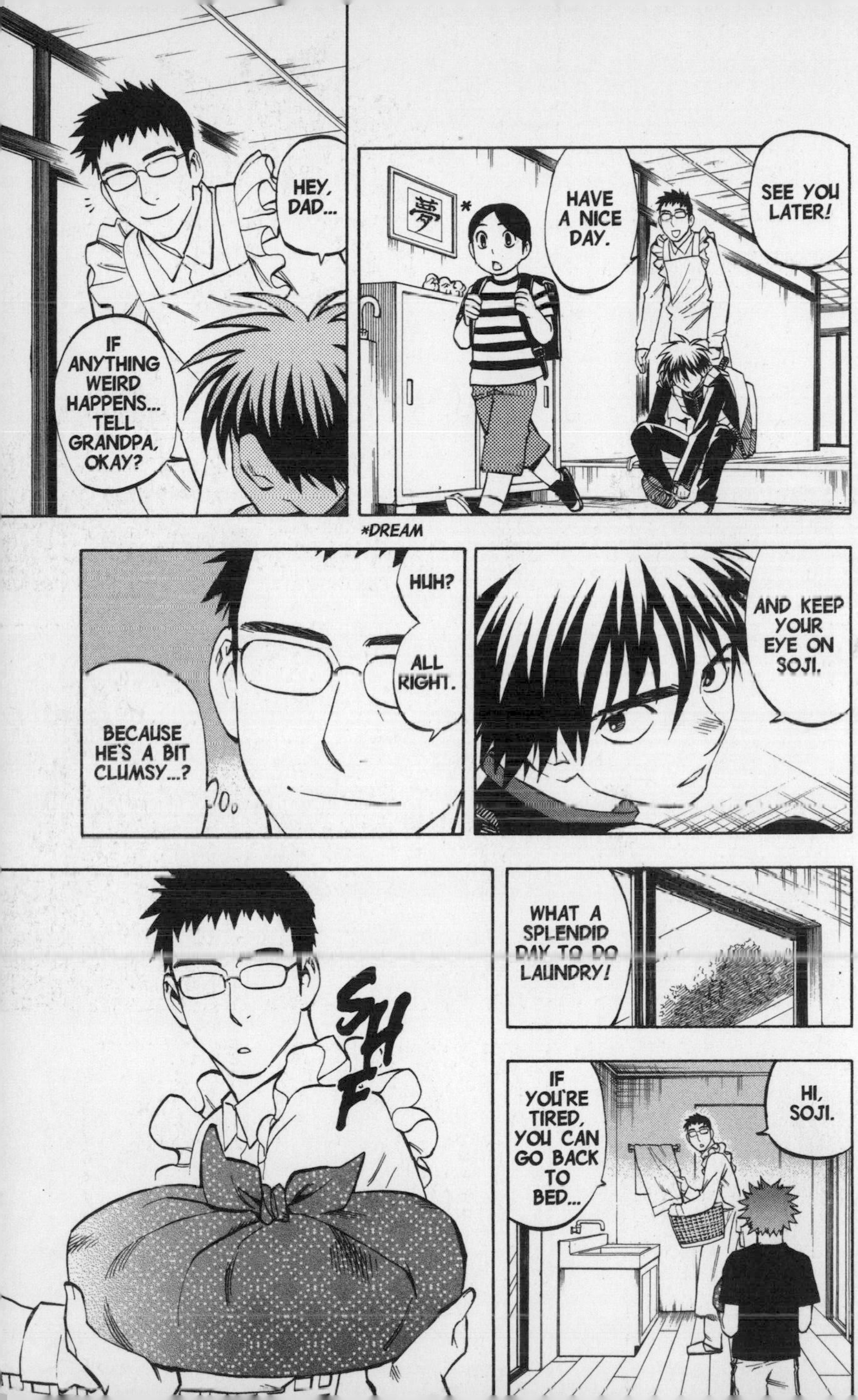
SEE YOU LATER!
HAVE A NICE DAY.
夢 *
HEY, DAD...
IF ANYTHING WEIRD HAPPENS... TELL GRANDPA, OKAY?
*DREAM
AND KEEP YOUR EYE ON SOJI.
HUH?
ALL RIGHT.
BECAUSE HE'S A BIT CLUMSY...?
WHAT A SPLENDID DAY TO DO LAUNDRY!
HI, SOJI.
IF YOU'RE TIRED, YOU CAN GO BACK TO BED...
SHF

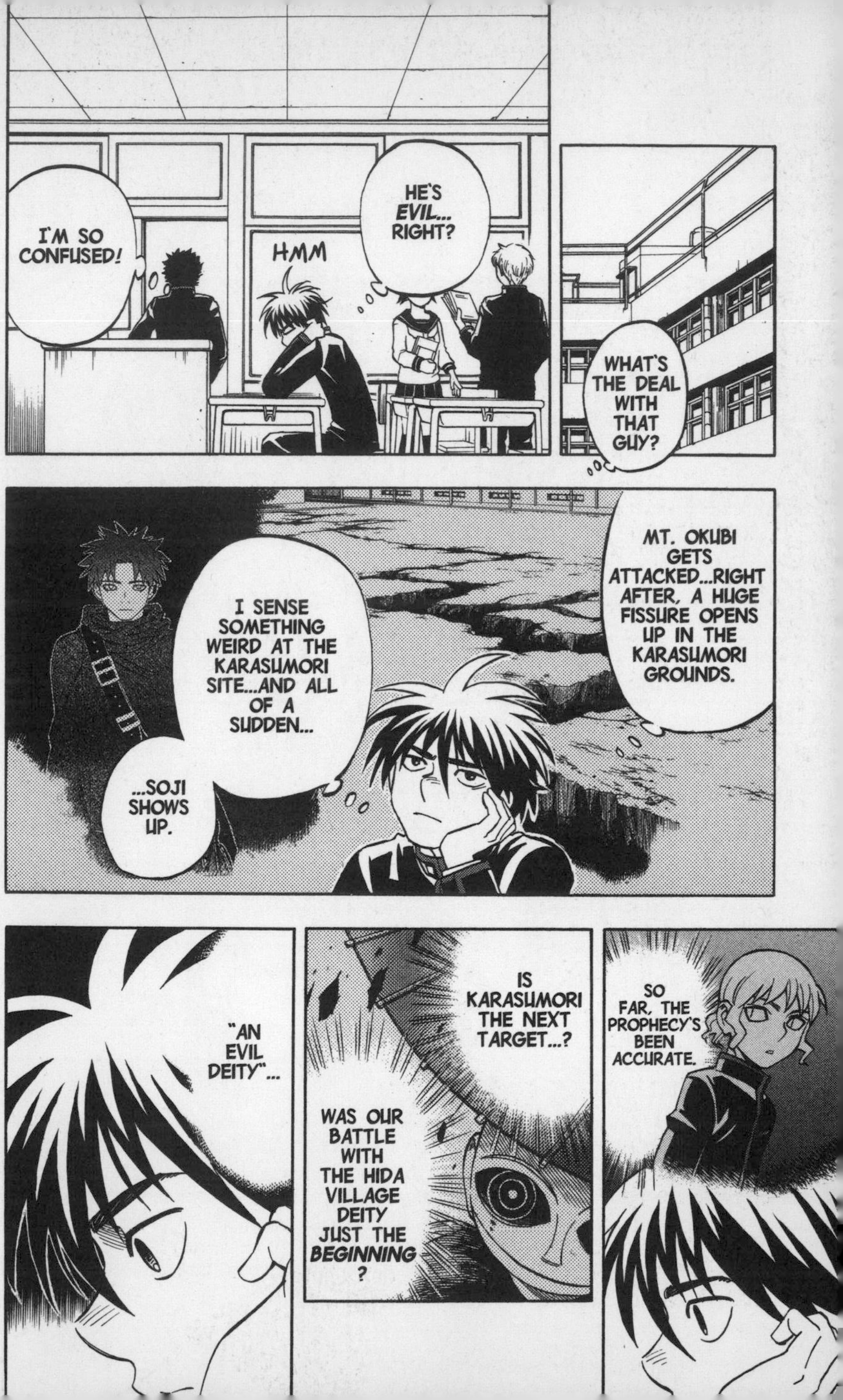
WHAT'S THE DEAL WITH THAT GUY?
HE'S *EVIL*... RIGHT?
HMM
I'M SO CONFUSED!
MT. OKUBI GETS ATTACKED...RIGHT AFTER, A HUGE FISSURE OPENS UP IN THE KARASUMORI GROUNDS.
I SENSE SOMETHING WEIRD AT THE KARASUMORI SITE...AND ALL OF A SUDDEN...
...SOJI SHOWS UP.
SO FAR, THE PROPHECY'S BEEN ACCURATE.
IS KARASUMORI THE NEXT TARGET...?
WAS OUR BATTLE WITH THE HIDA VILLAGE DEITY JUST THE *BEGINNING*?
"AN EVIL DEITY"...

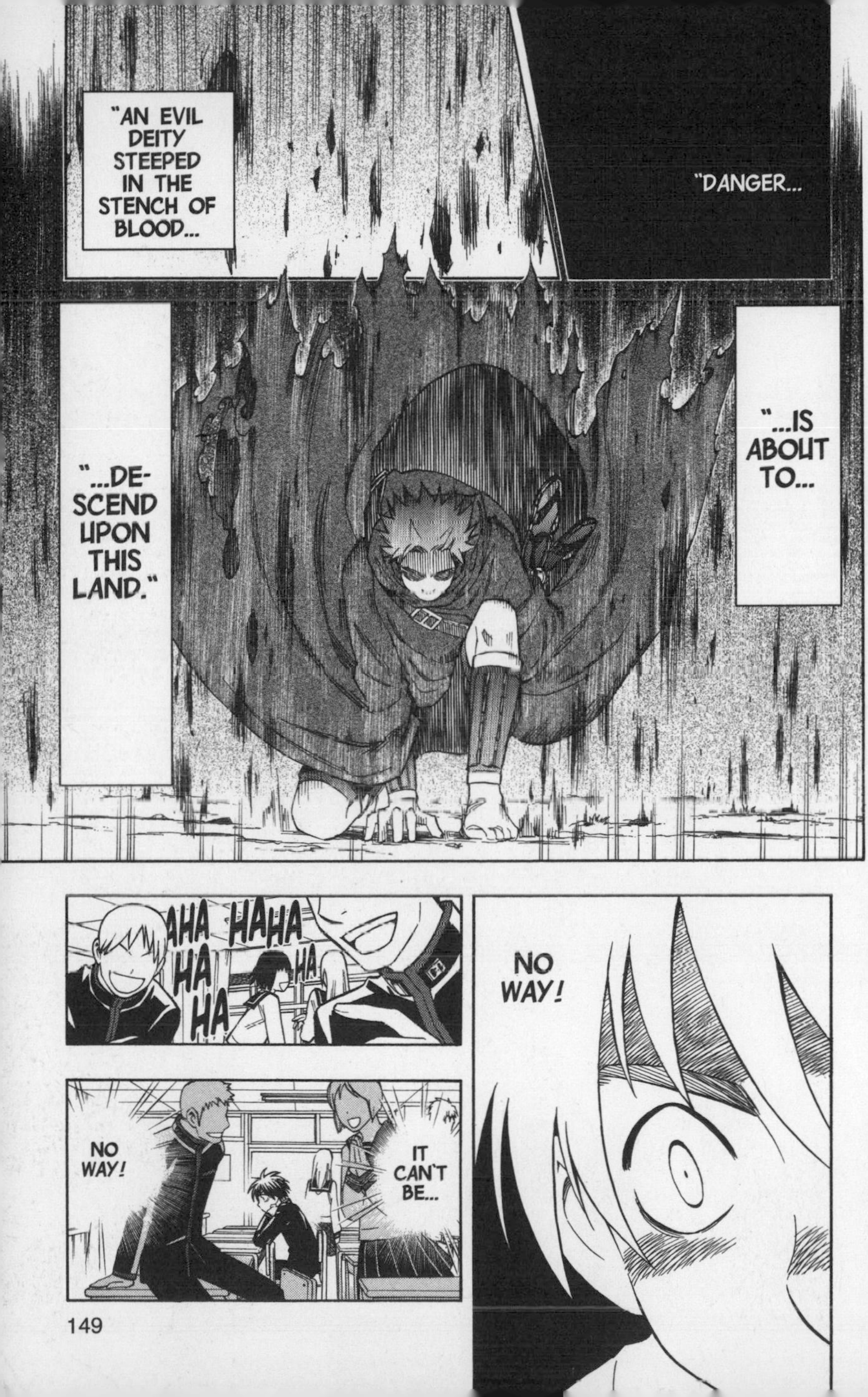
"DANGER...
"AN EVIL DEITY STEEPED IN THE STENCH OF BLOOD...
"...IS ABOUT TO...
"...DE-SCEND UPON THIS LAND."
NO WAY!
HAHA HAHA HA HA HA HA
IT CAN'T BE...
NO WAY!

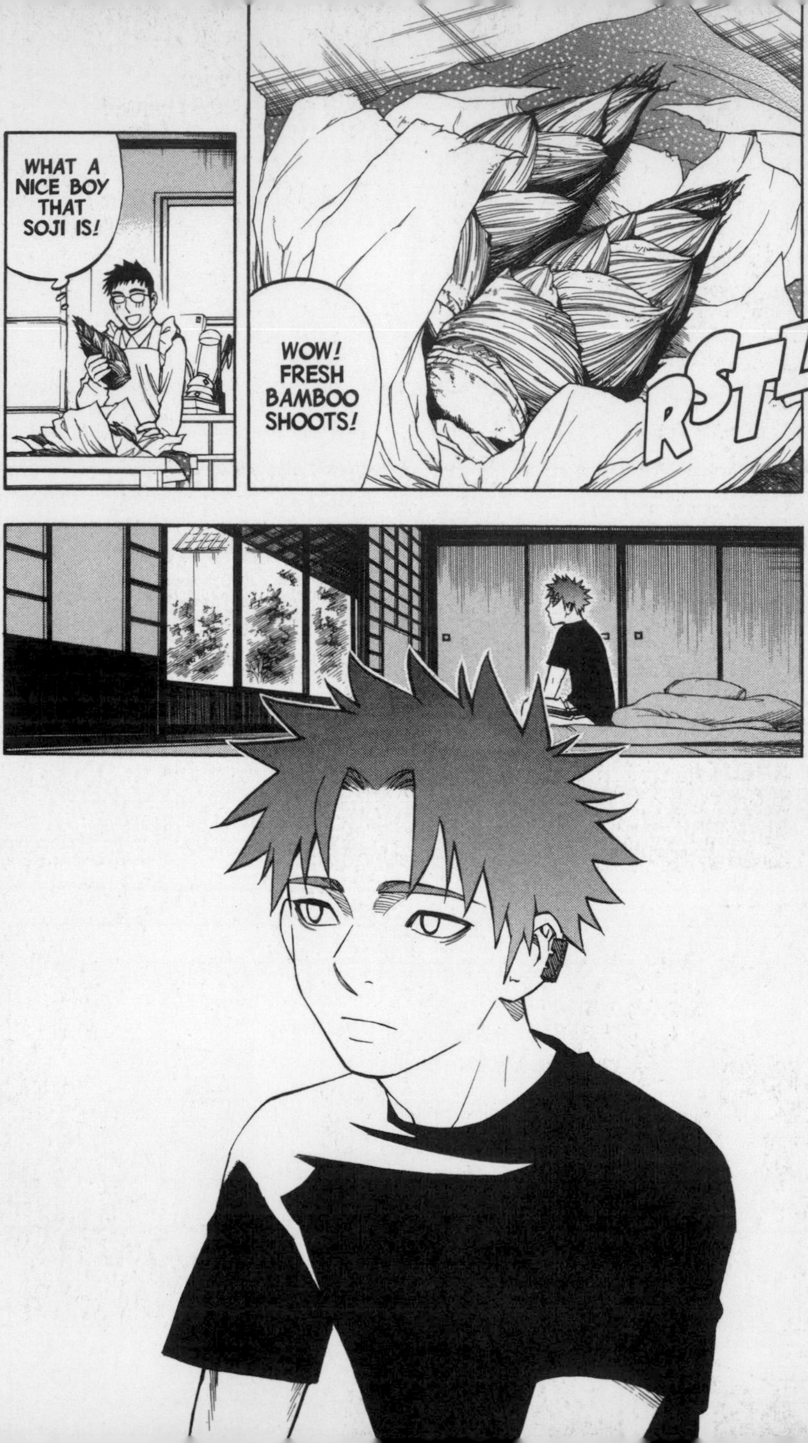
WOW! FRESH BAMBOO SHOOTS!
RSTL
WHAT A NICE BOY THAT SOJI IS!

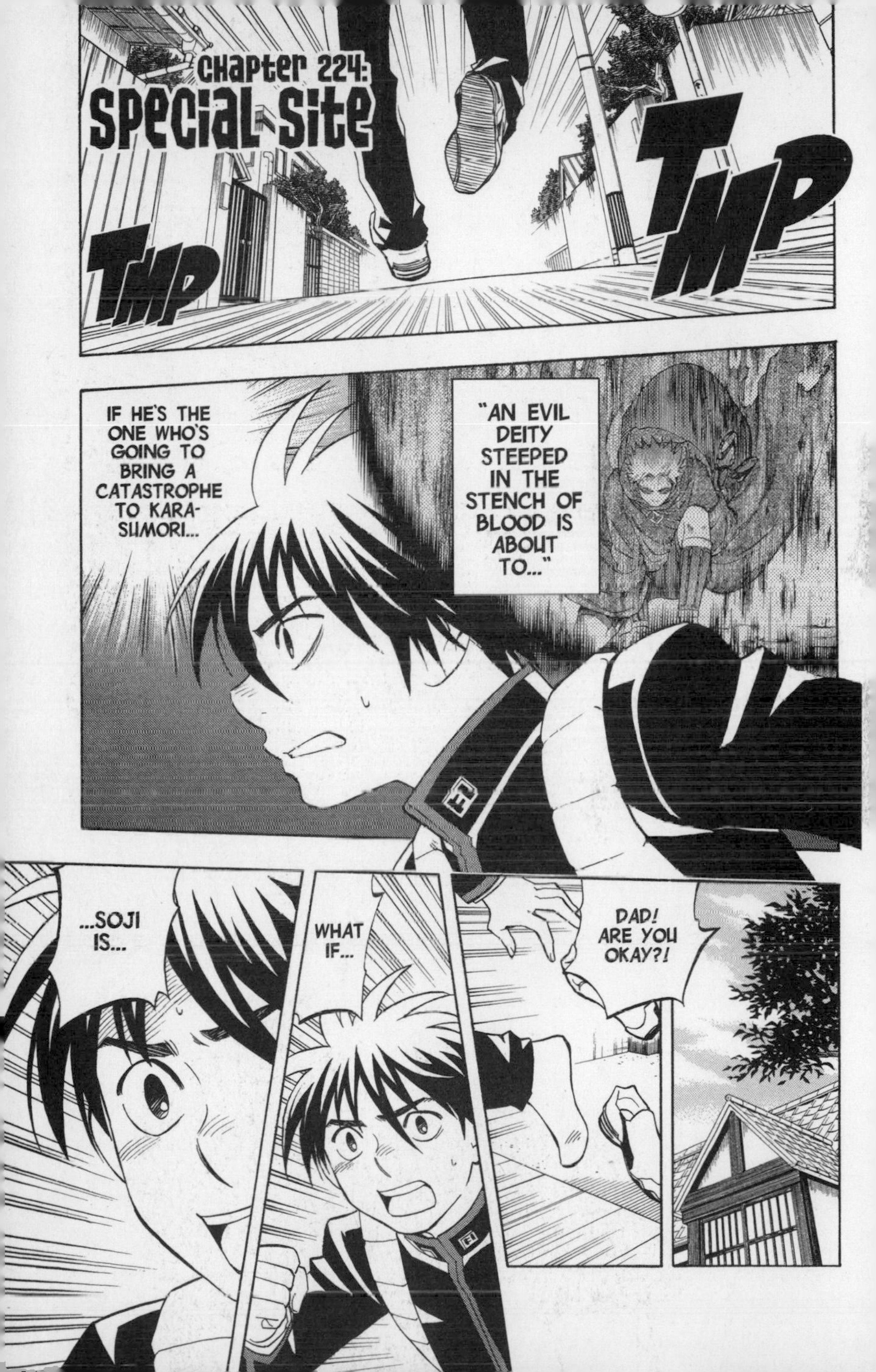

Chapter 224:
Special Site
TMP
TMP
"AN EVIL DEITY STEEPED IN THE STENCH OF BLOOD IS ABOUT TO..."
IF HE'S THE ONE WHO'S GOING TO BRING A CATASTROPHE TO KARA-SUMORI...
DAD! ARE YOU OKAY?!
WHAT IF...
...SOJI IS...

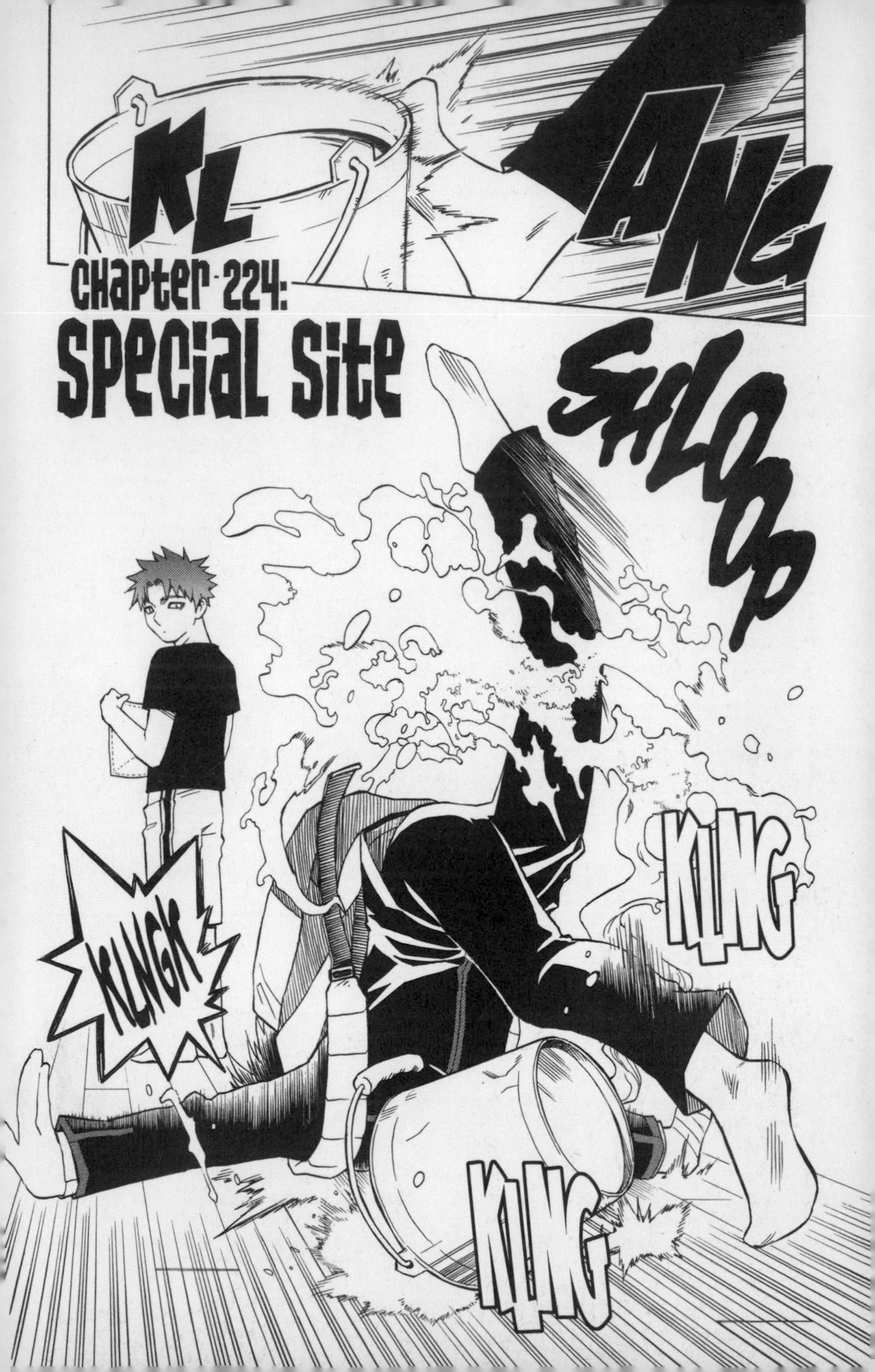
KL
ANG
Chapter 224:
Special Site
SHLOOOP
KLING
KLNGK
KLING

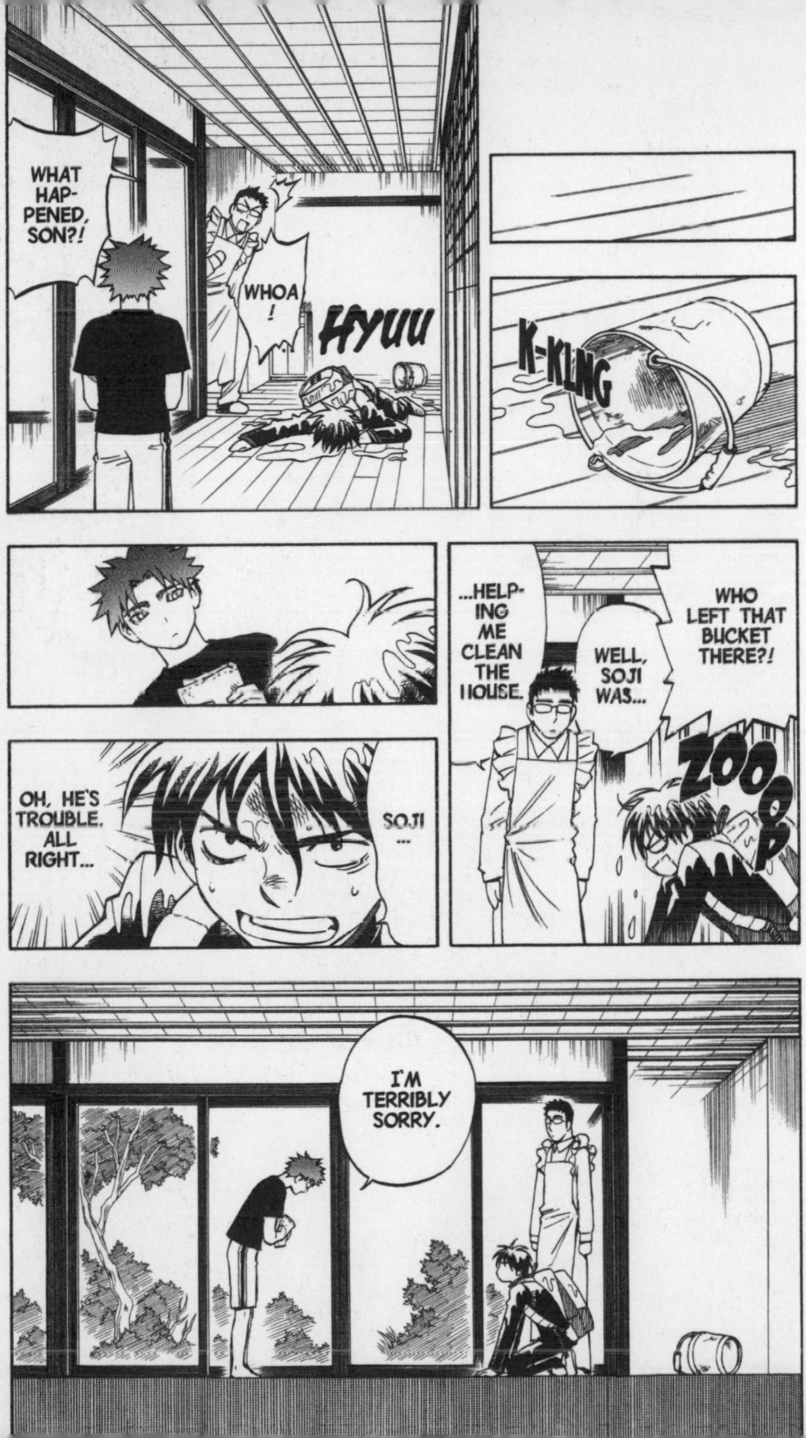
K-KLNG
HYUU
WHOA!
WHAT HAPPENED, SON?!
WHO LEFT THAT BUCKET THERE?!
ZOOOP
WELL, SOJI WAS...
...HELPING ME CLEAN THE HOUSE.
SOJI...
OH, HE'S TROUBLE. ALL RIGHT...
I'M TERRIBLY SORRY.

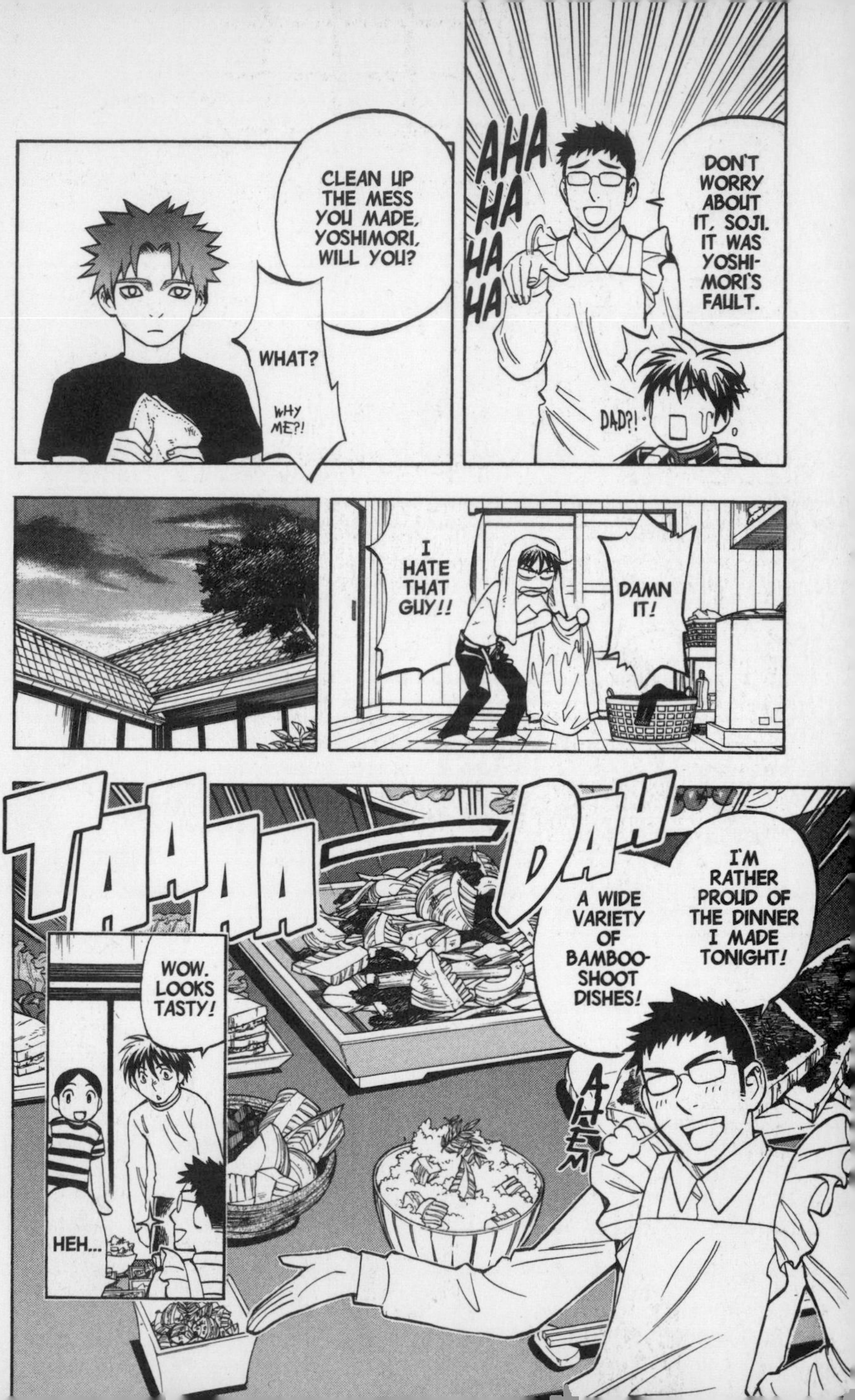
AHA HA HA HA
DON'T WORRY ABOUT IT, SOJI. IT WAS YOSHIMORI'S FAULT.
DAD?!
CLEAN UP THE MESS YOU MADE, YOSHIMORI, WILL YOU?
WHAT?
WHY ME?!
DAMN IT!
I HATE THAT GUY!!
TAAAA DAH
I'M RATHER PROUD OF THE DINNER I MADE TONIGHT!
A WIDE VARIETY OF BAMBOO-SHOOT DISHES!
AHEM
WOW. LOOKS TASTY!
HEH...

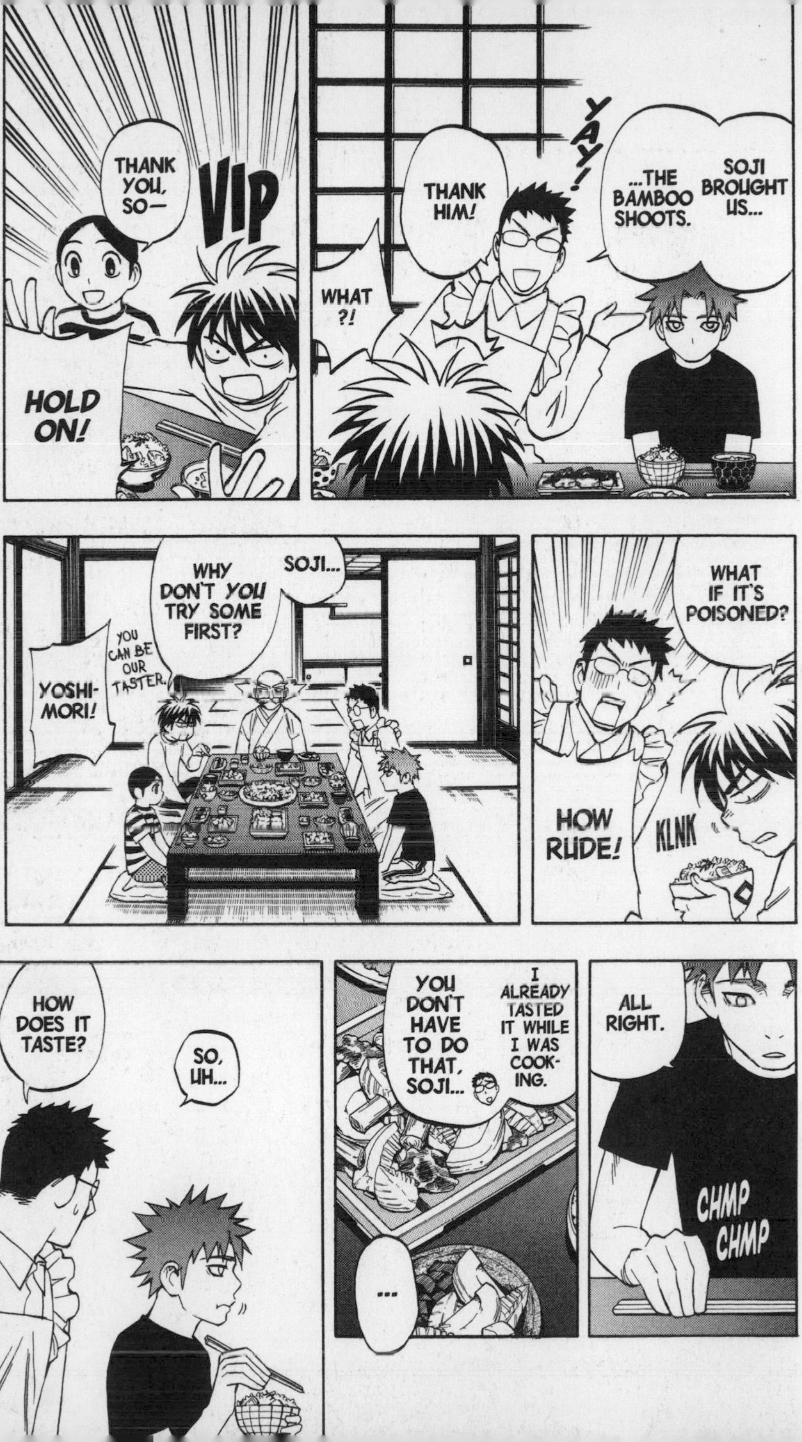
SOJI BROUGHT US...
...THE BAMBOO SHOOTS.
YAY!
THANK HIM!
WHAT ?!
THANK YOU, SO—
VIP
HOLD ON!
WHAT IF IT'S POISONED?
HOW RUDE!
KLNK
SOJI...
WHY DON'T YOU TRY SOME FIRST?
YOU CAN BE OUR TASTER.
YOSHIMORI!
ALL RIGHT.
CHMP CHMP
I ALREADY TASTED IT WHILE I WAS COOKING.
YOU DON'T HAVE TO DO THAT, SOJI...
...
HOW DOES IT TASTE?
SO, UH...

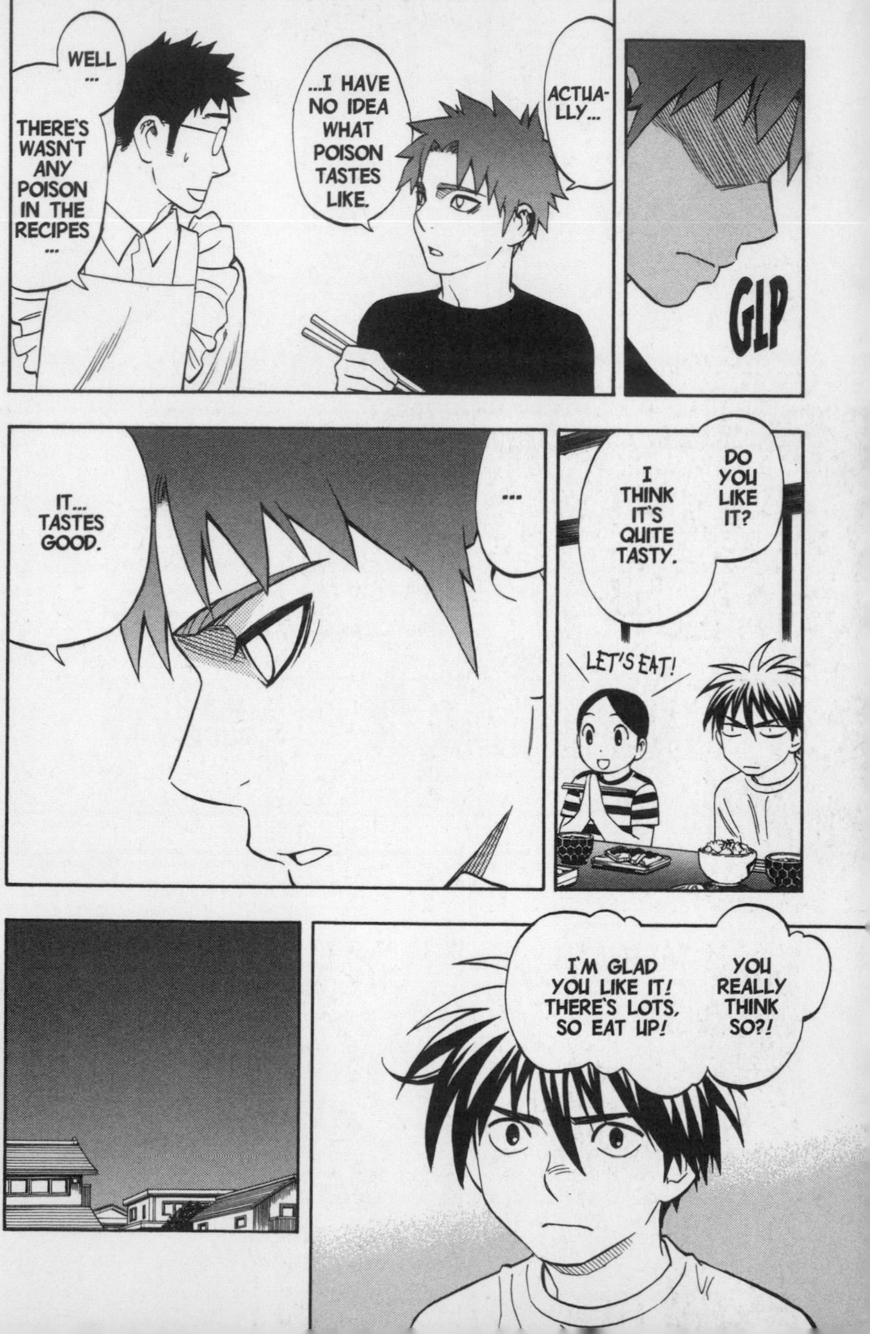
GLP
ACTUA-LLY...
...I HAVE NO IDEA WHAT POISON TASTES LIKE.
WELL...
THERE'S WASN'T ANY POISON IN THE RECIPES...
DO YOU LIKE IT?
I THINK IT'S QUITE TASTY.
LET'S EAT!
...
IT... TASTES GOOD.
YOU REALLY THINK SO?!
I'M GLAD YOU LIKE IT! THERE'S LOTS, SO EAT UP!

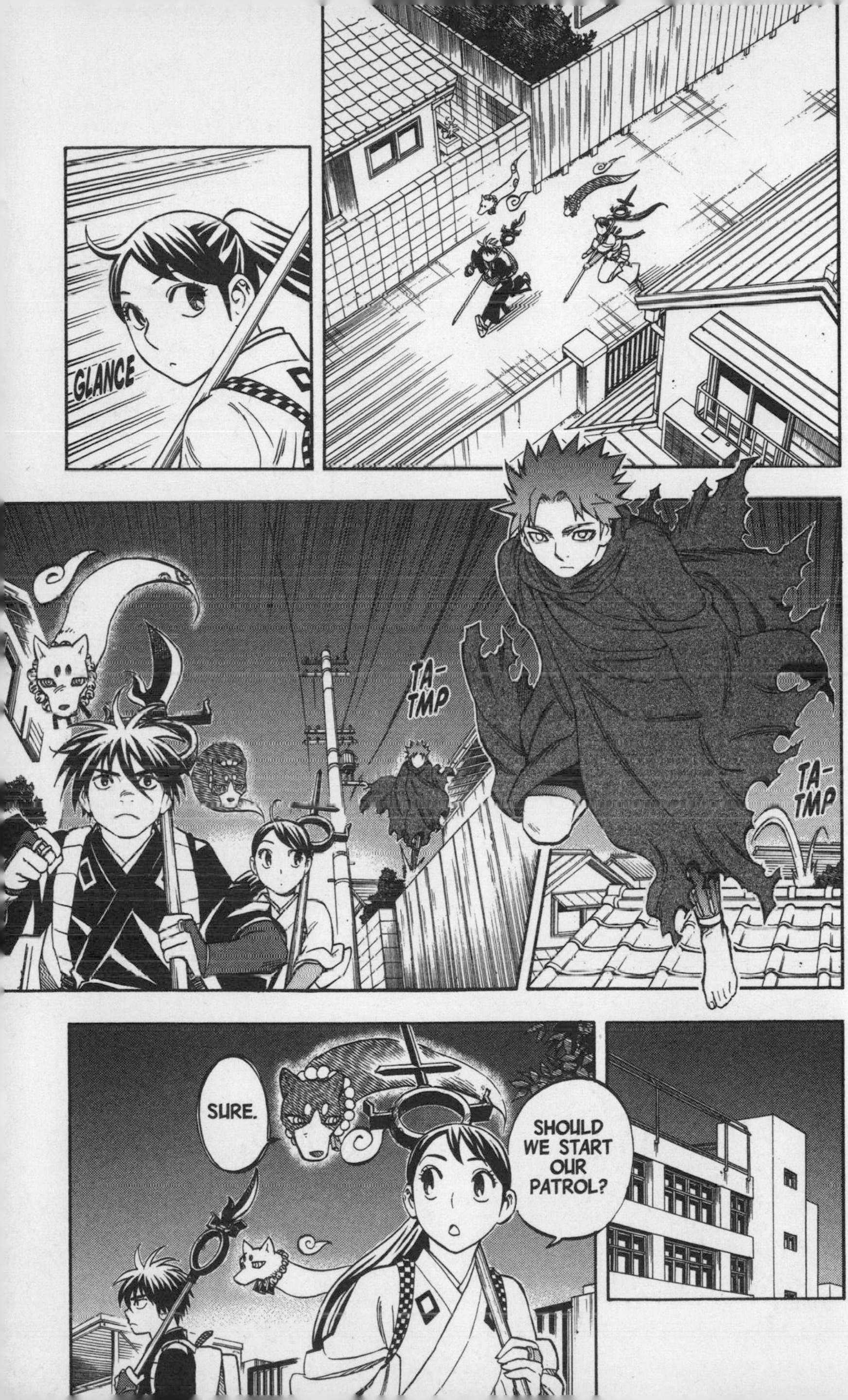
GLANCE
TA-TMP
TA-TMP
SHOULD WE START OUR PATROL?
SURE.

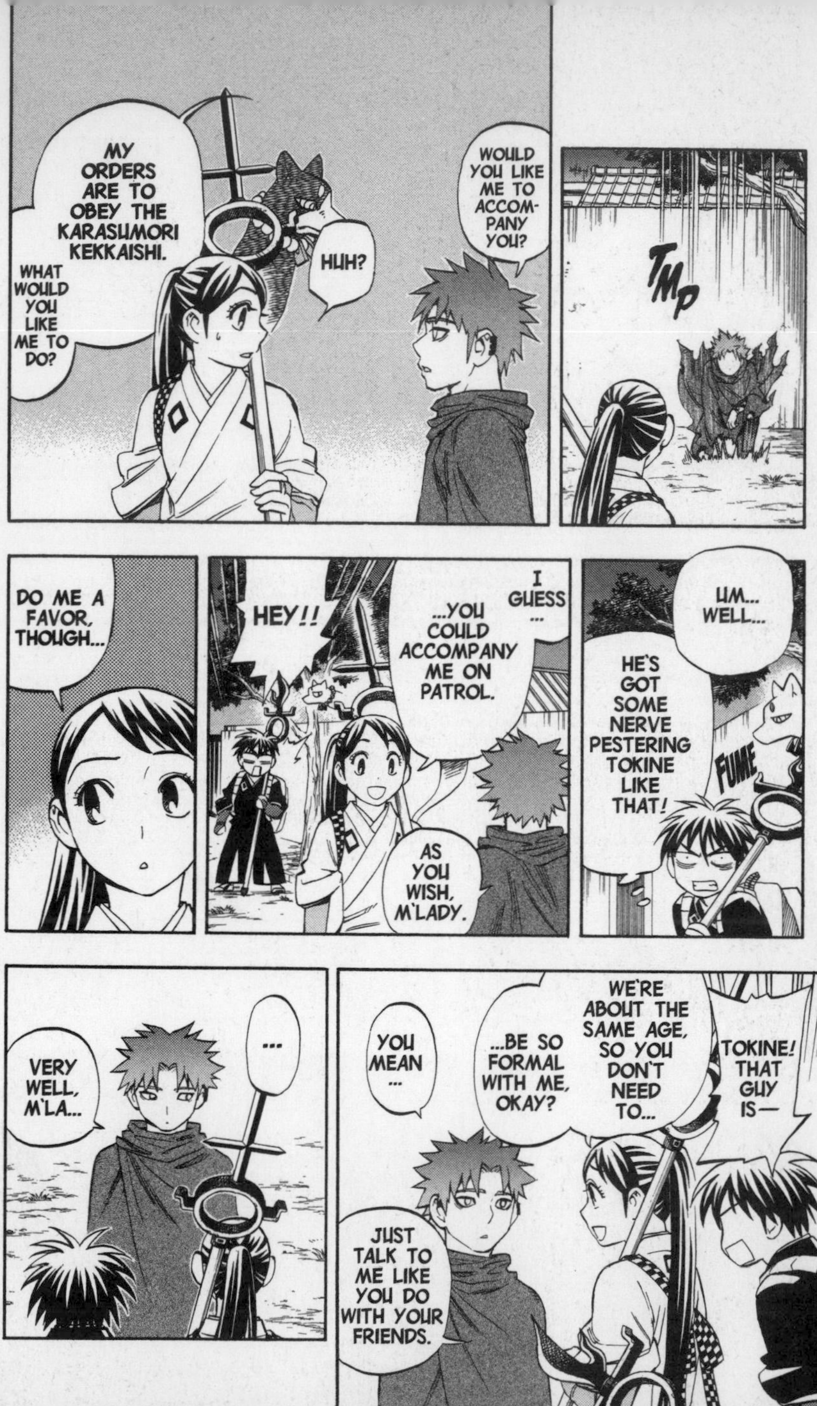
TMP
WOULD YOU LIKE ME TO ACCOMPANY YOU?
HUH?
MY ORDERS ARE TO OBEY THE KARASUMORI KEKKAISHI.
WHAT WOULD YOU LIKE ME TO DO?
UM... WELL...
HE'S GOT SOME NERVE PESTERING TOKINE LIKE THAT!
FUME
I GUESS ...
...YOU COULD ACCOMPANY ME ON PATROL.
HEY!!
AS YOU WISH, M'LADY.
DO ME A FAVOR, THOUGH...
TOKINE! THAT GUY IS—
WE'RE ABOUT THE SAME AGE, SO YOU DON'T NEED TO...
...BE SO FORMAL WITH ME, OKAY?
YOU MEAN ...
JUST TALK TO ME LIKE YOU DO WITH YOUR FRIENDS.
...
VERY WELL, M'LA...

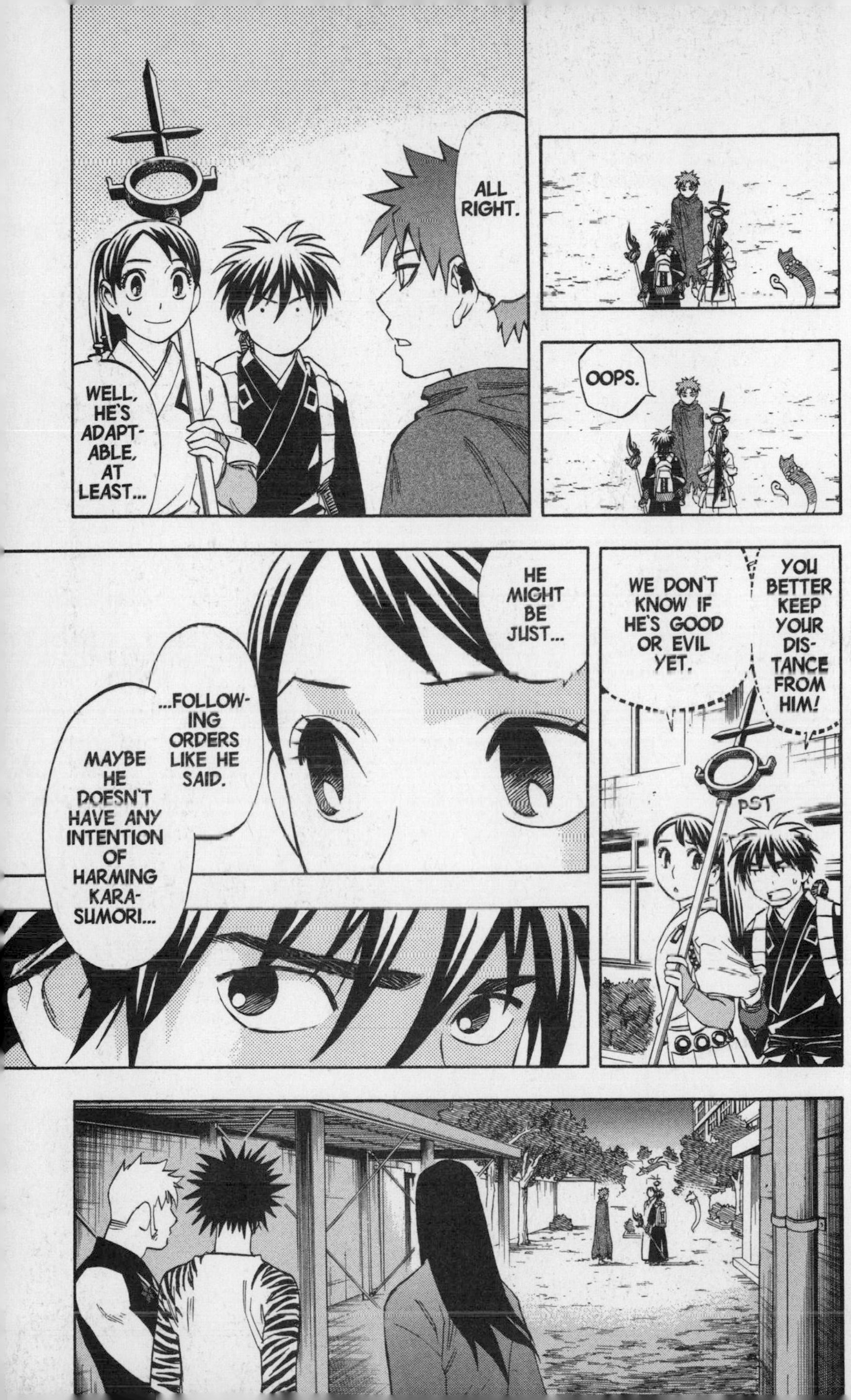
OOPS.
ALL RIGHT.
WELL, HE'S ADAPTABLE, AT LEAST...
YOU BETTER KEEP YOUR DISTANCE FROM HIM!
WE DON'T KNOW IF HE'S GOOD OR EVIL YET.
PST
HE MIGHT BE JUST...
...FOLLOWING ORDERS LIKE HE SAID.
MAYBE HE DOESN'T HAVE ANY INTENTION OF HARMING KARASUMORI...

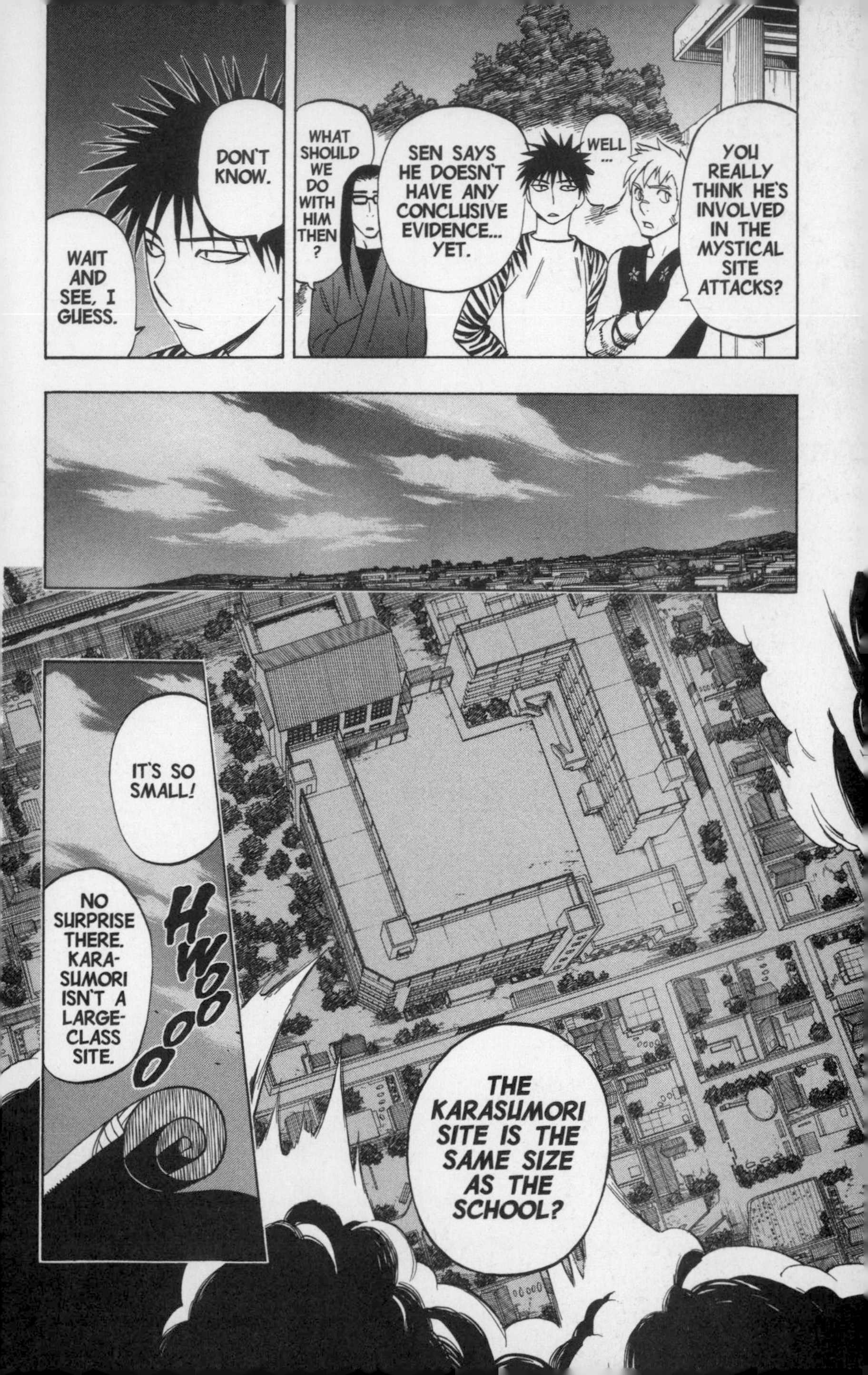
YOU REALLY THINK HE'S INVOLVED IN THE MYSTICAL SITE ATTACKS?
WELL...
SEN SAYS HE DOESN'T HAVE ANY CONCLUSIVE EVIDENCE... YET.
WHAT SHOULD WE DO WITH HIM THEN?
DON'T KNOW.
WAIT AND SEE, I GUESS.
THE KARASUMORI SITE IS THE SAME SIZE AS THE SCHOOL?
IT'S SO SMALL!
NO SURPRISE THERE. KARASUMORI ISN'T A LARGE-CLASS SITE.
HWOOOOO

THIS INFORMATION IS CLASSIFIED, BUT I CAN TELL YOU THAT BOTH SITES SHARE AN "S"—OR "SPECIAL"—DESIGNATION.

ACTUALLY THEY DO HAVE SOMETHING IN COMMON.

...MT. OKUBI WAS A MASSIVE SITE. IT'S NOTHING LIKE KARASUMORI.

BUT...

WELL...

HW OOO

THAT MAKES...

...OUR JOB EASIER.

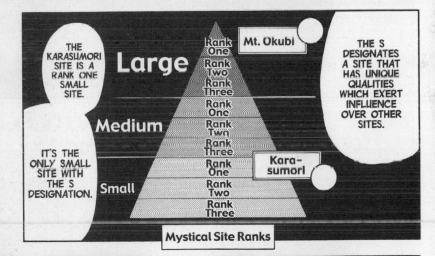

THE KARASUMORI SITE IS A RANK ONE SMALL SITE.

IT'S THE ONLY SMALL SITE WITH THE S DESIGNATION.

Large	Rank One	Mt. Okubi
	Rank Two	
	Rank Three	
Medium	Rank One	
	Rank Two	
	Rank Three	
Small	Rank One	Kara-sumori
	Rank Two	
	Rank Three	

Mystical Site Ranks

THE S DESIGNATES A SITE THAT HAS UNIQUE QUALITIES WHICH EXERT INFLUENCE OVER OTHER SITES.

I SEE.

...SMALL, BUT IT'S ENORMOUSLY POWERFUL.

KARASUMORI MIGHT BE...

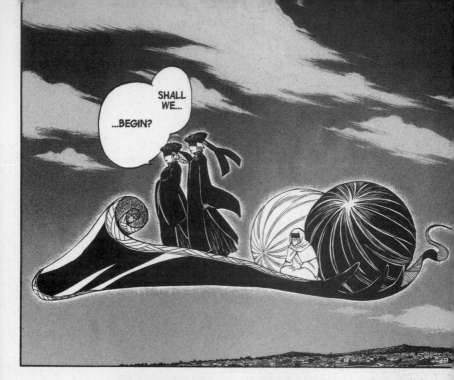

SHALL WE...

...BEGIN?

...YOU DON'T GET IN THE WAY OF OUR ATTACK.

MAKE SURE...

ARE YOU READY?

YES, I AM.

TWITCH

THEY'RE VERY WELL TRAINED.

DON'T WORRY...

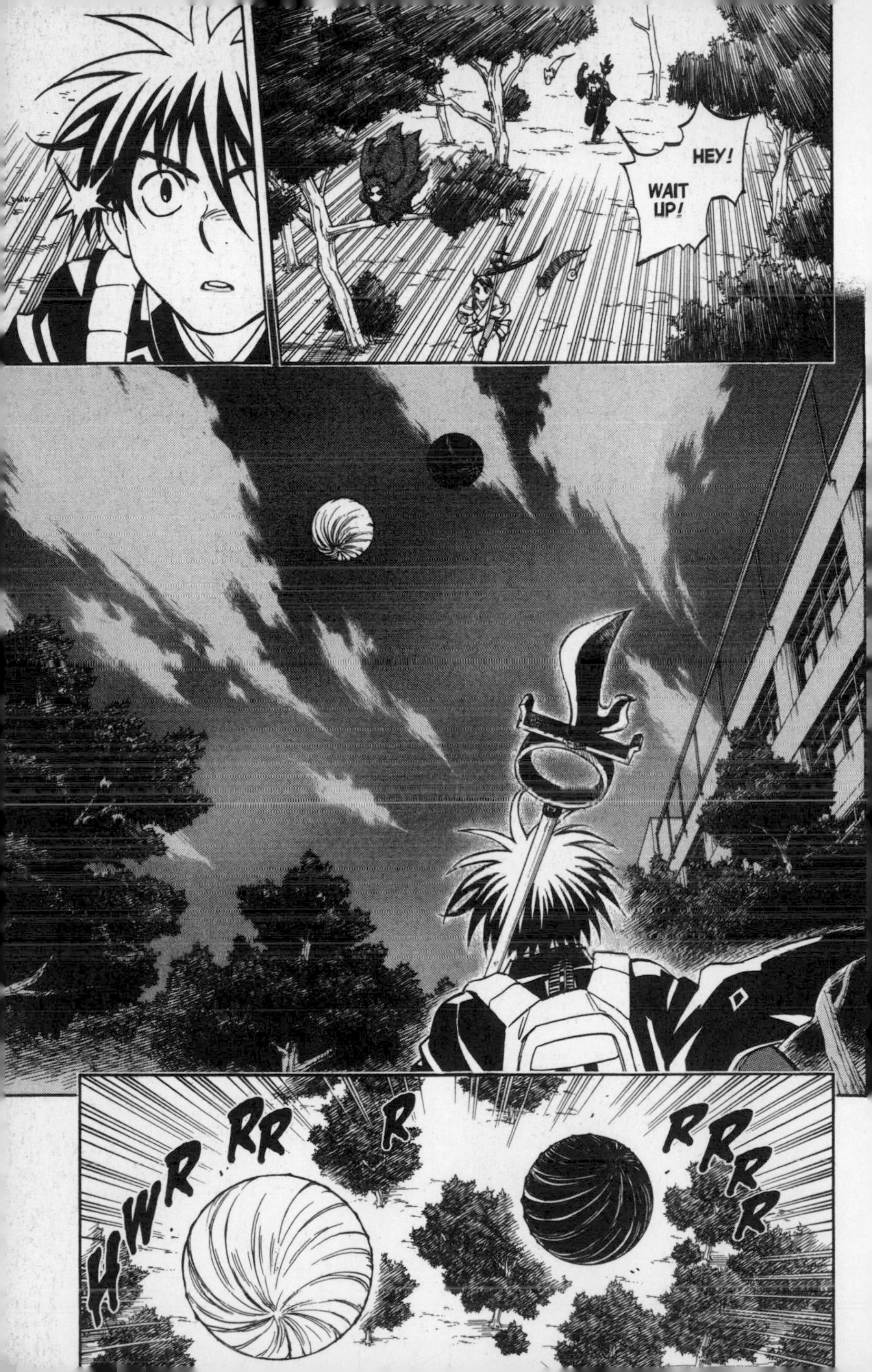
HEY!
WAIT UP!
HWRRR
R
RRRRR

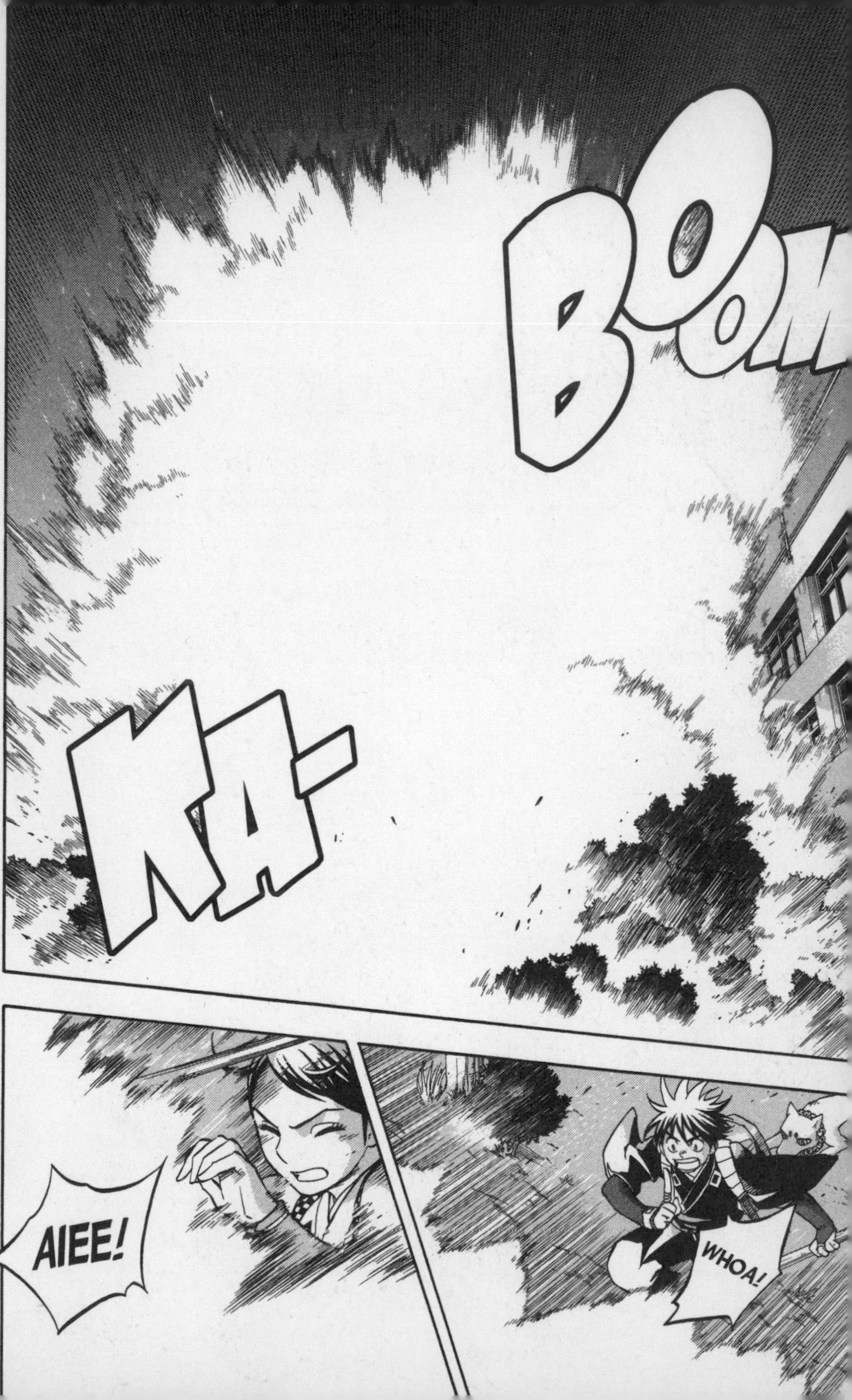
BOOM
KA-
WHOA!
AIEE!

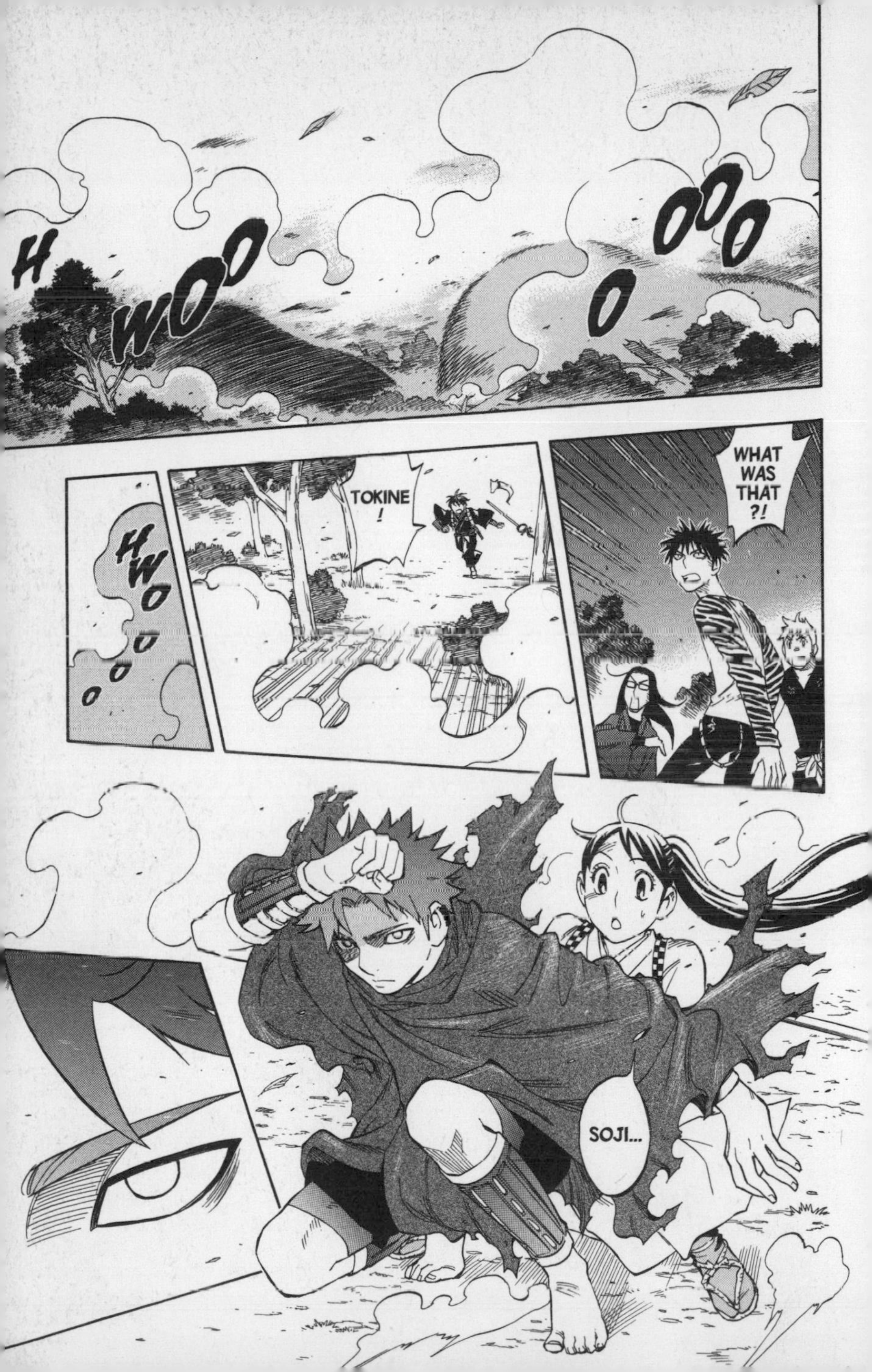
HWOOOOOOO
WHAT WAS THAT ?!
TOKINE !
HWOOOOO
SOJI...

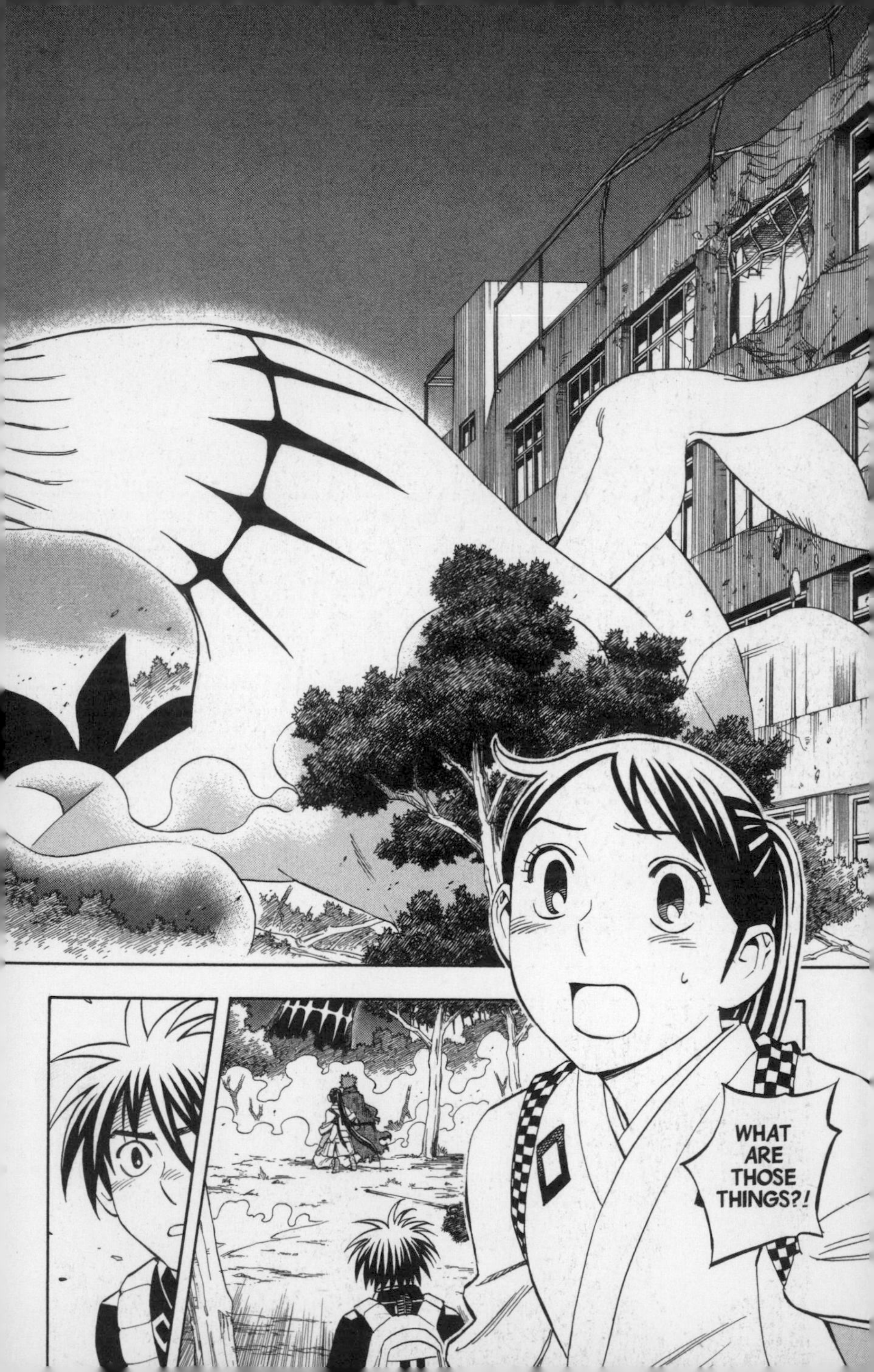
WHAT ARE THOSE THINGS?!

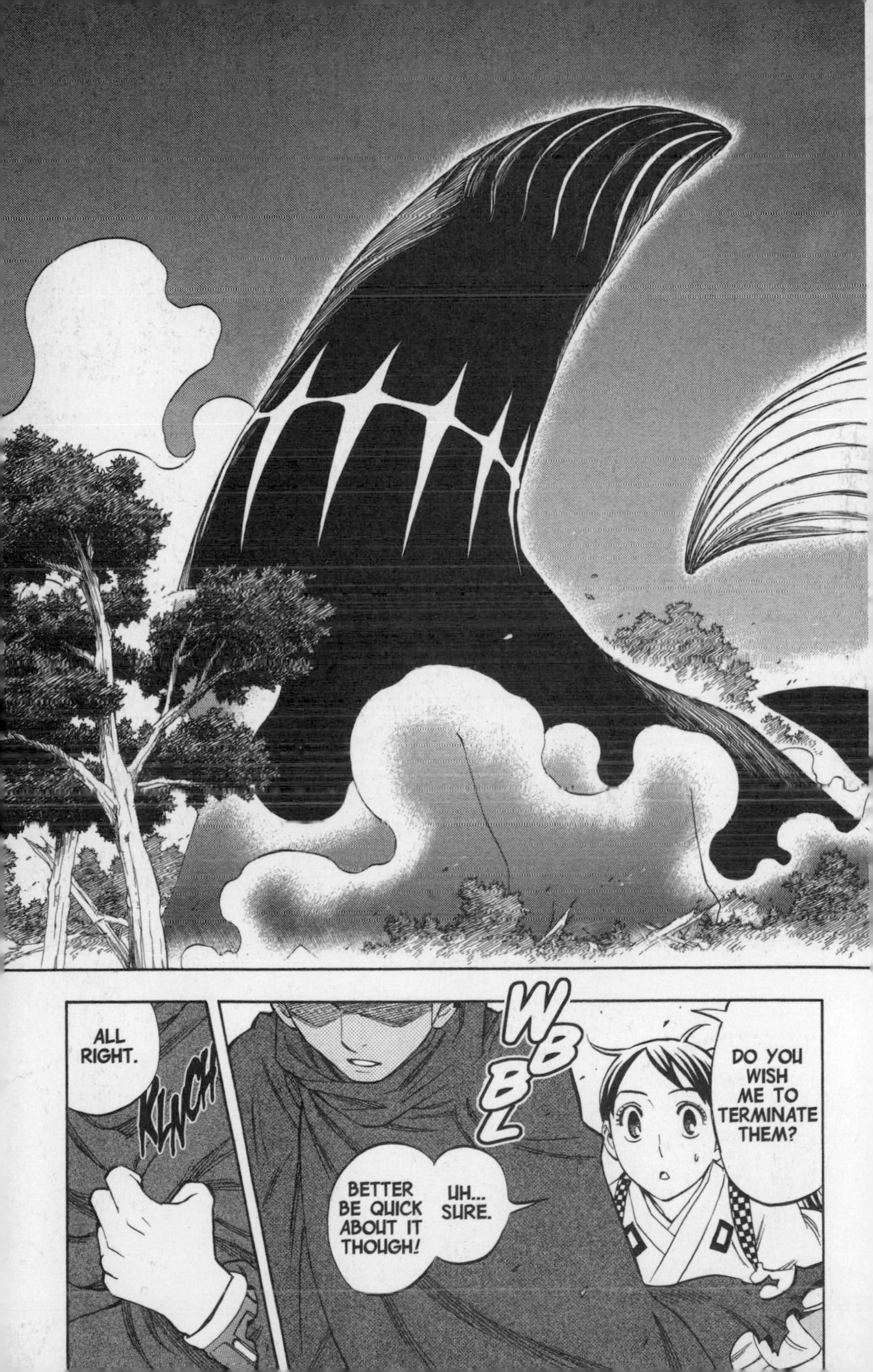
DO YOU WISH ME TO TERMINATE THEM?
WBBL
UH... SURE.
BETTER BE QUICK ABOUT IT THOUGH!
ALL RIGHT.
KLNCH

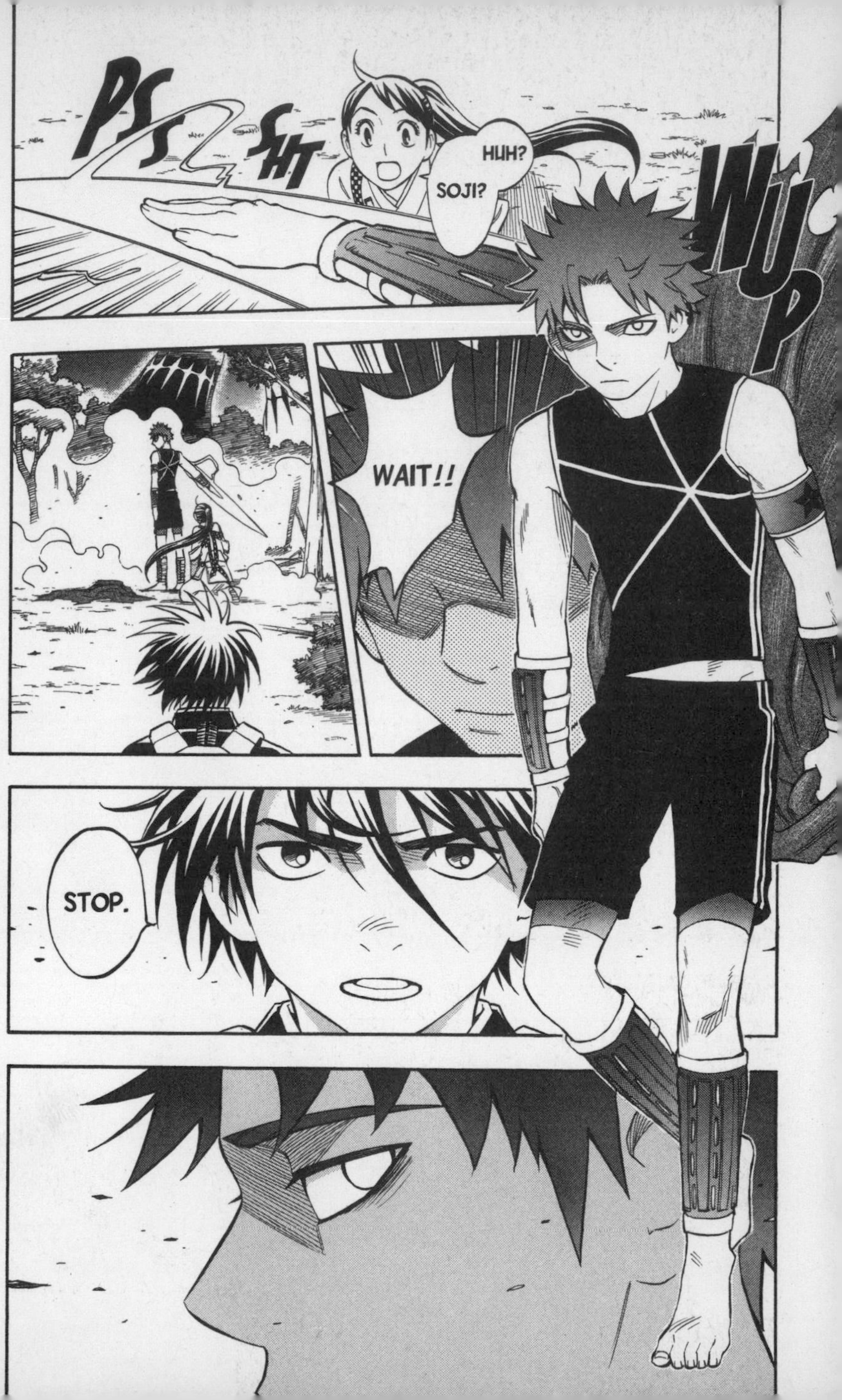
WUP
HUH?
SOJI?
PSSHT
WAIT!!
STOP.

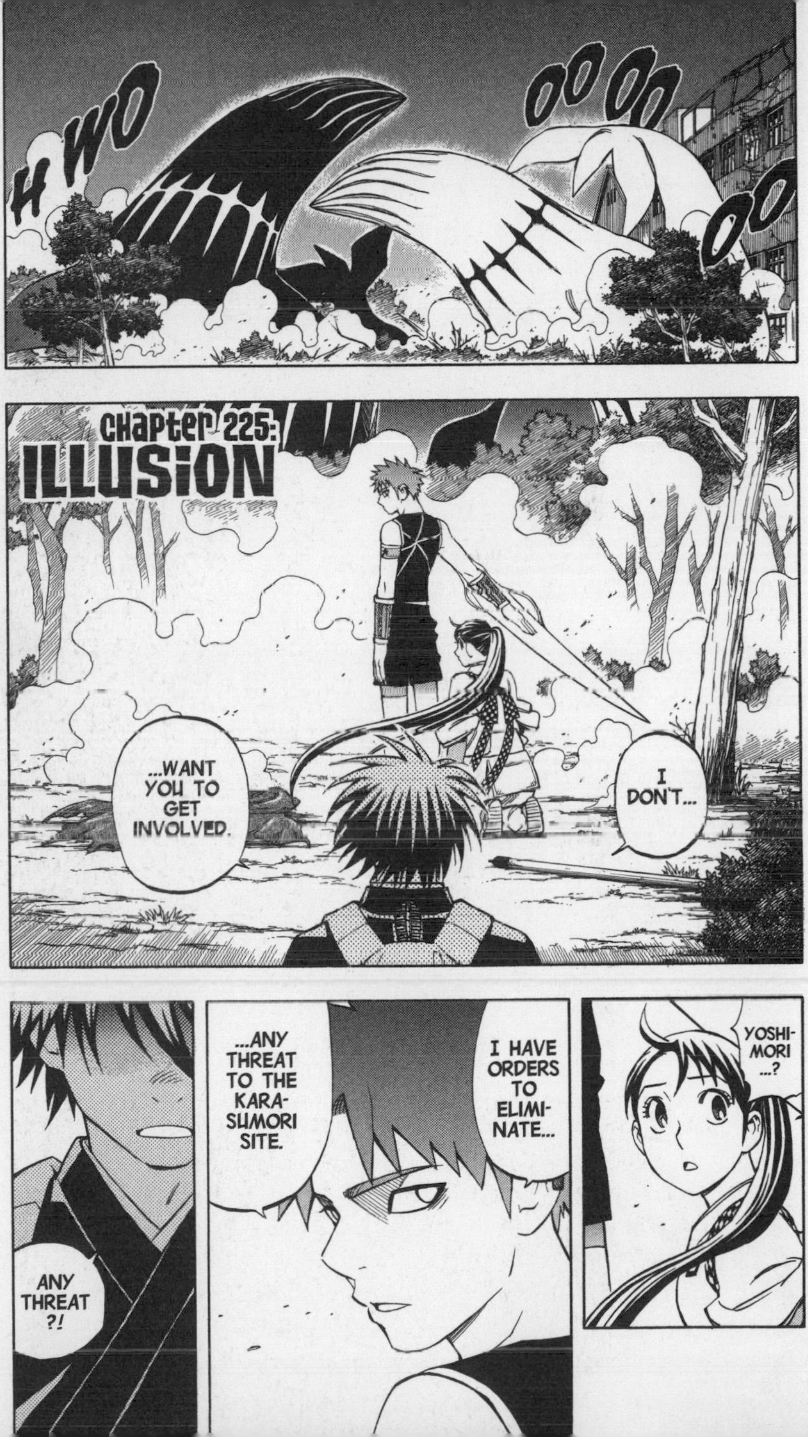
H WO OO OO OO
Chapter 225: ILLUSION
I DON'T...
...WANT YOU TO GET INVOLVED.
YOSHIMORI...?
I HAVE ORDERS TO ELIMINATE...
...ANY THREAT TO THE KARASUMORI SITE.
ANY THREAT?!

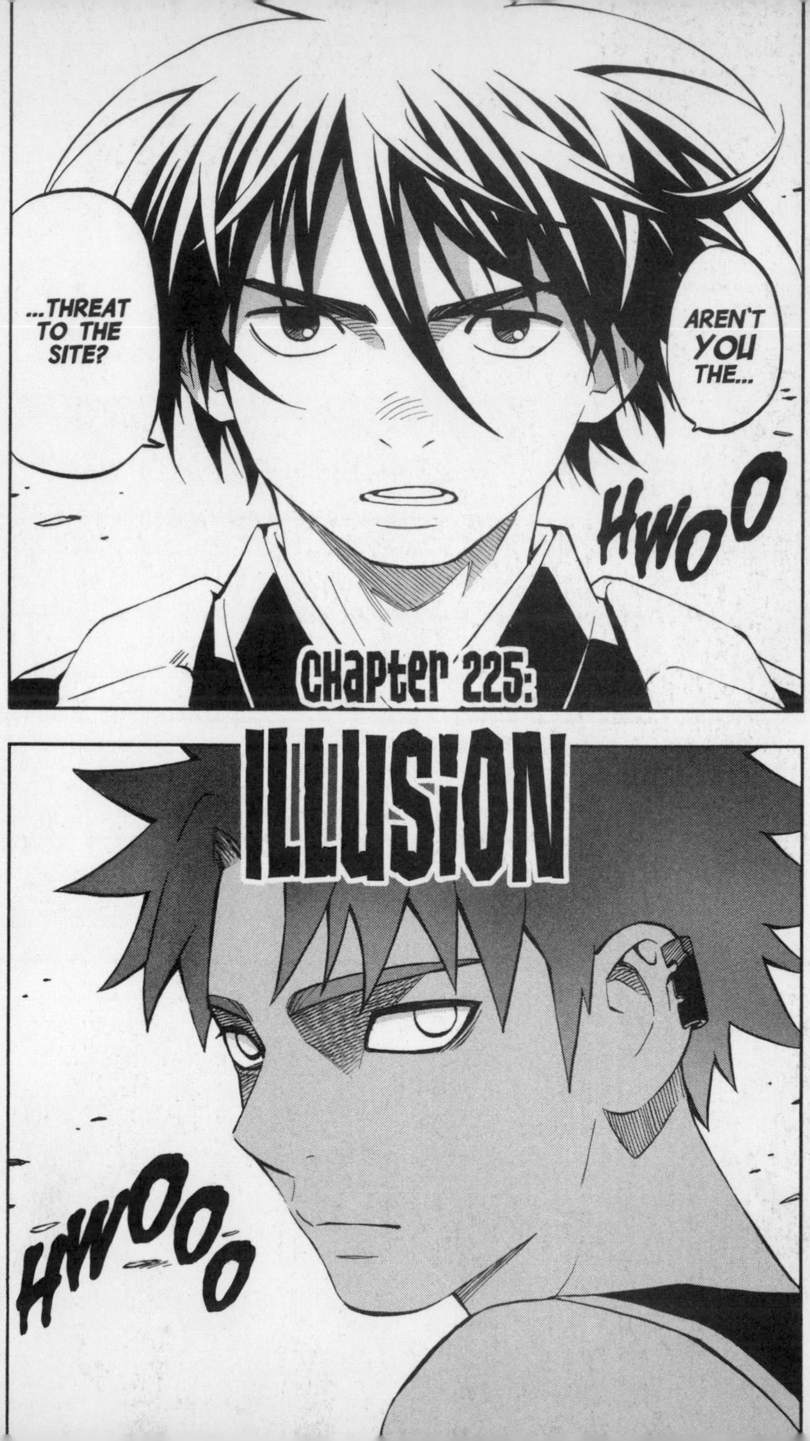
AREN'T YOU THE...
...THREAT TO THE SITE?
HWOO
CHAPTER 225:
ILLUSION
HWOOO

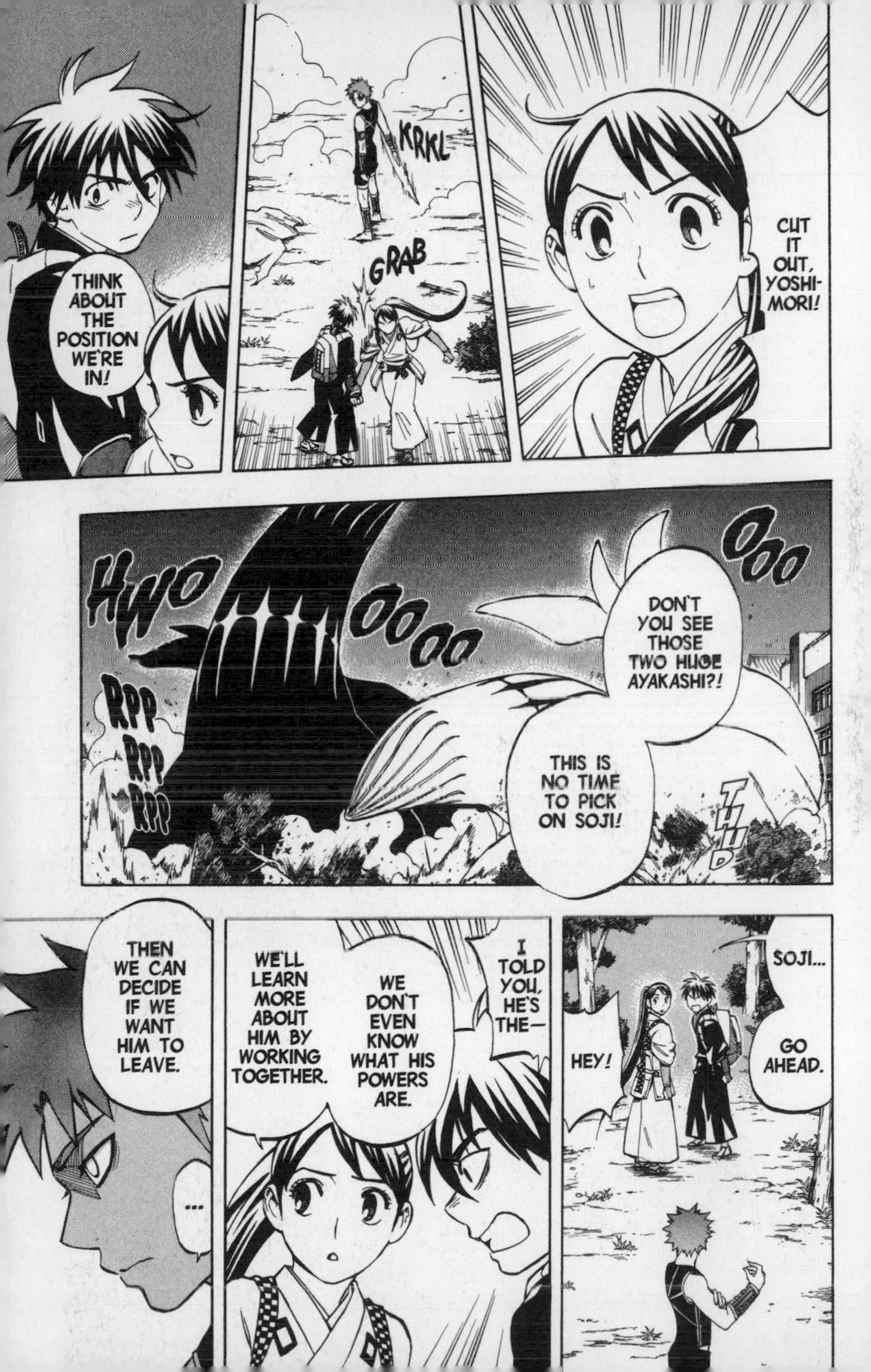
CUT IT OUT, YOSHIMORI!
KRKL
GRAB
THINK ABOUT THE POSITION WE'RE IN!
OOO
DON'T YOU SEE THOSE TWO HUGE AYAKASHI?!
THIS IS NO TIME TO PICK ON SOJI!
THUD
HWOOOOO
RPP RPP RPP
SOJI...
GO AHEAD.
HEY!
I TOLD YOU, HE'S THE—
WE DON'T EVEN KNOW WHAT HIS POWERS ARE.
WE'LL LEARN MORE ABOUT HIM BY WORKING TOGETHER.
THEN WE CAN DECIDE IF WE WANT HIM TO LEAVE.
...

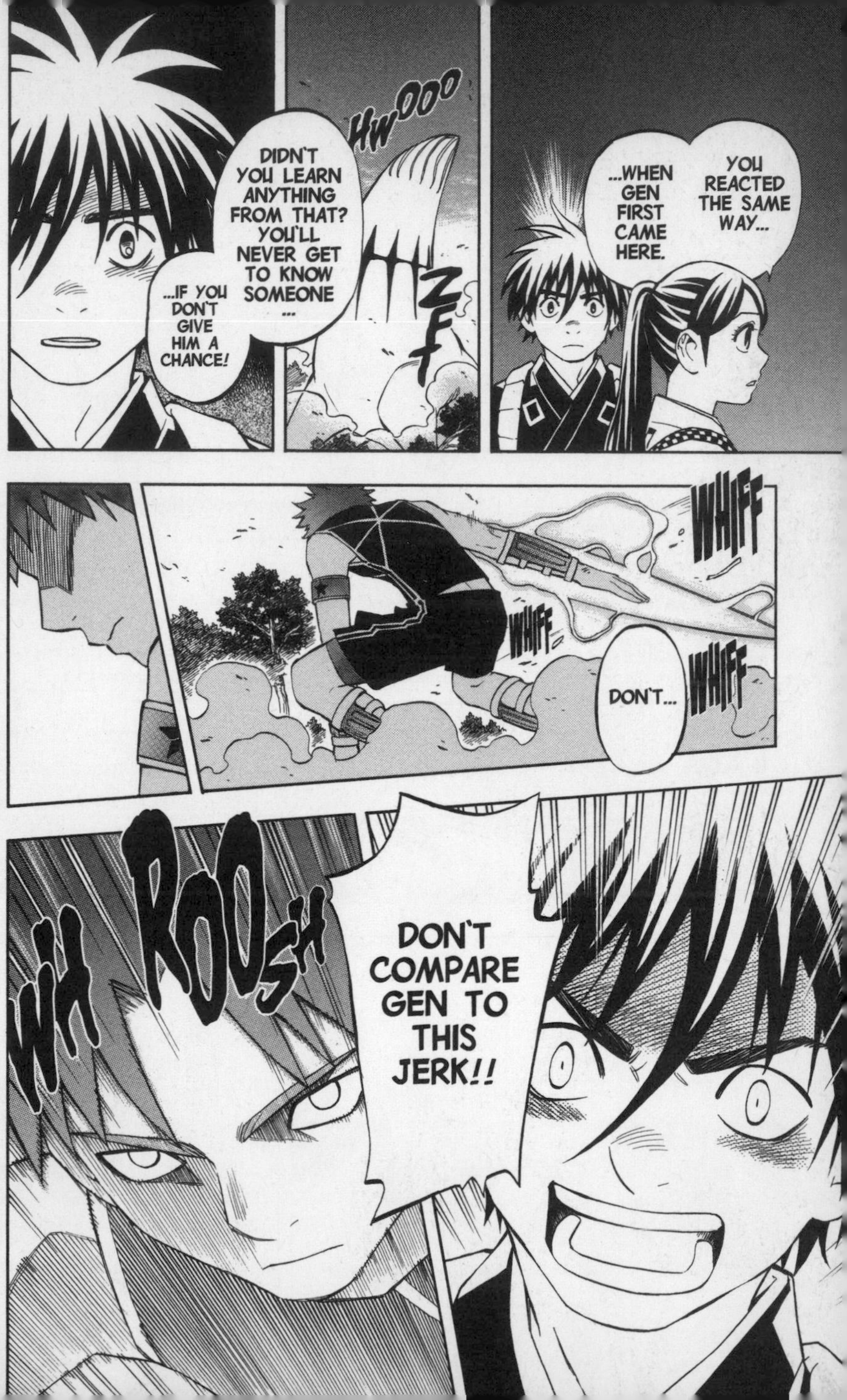
YOU REACTED THE SAME WAY...
...WHEN GEN FIRST CAME HERE.
HWOOO
DIDN'T YOU LEARN ANYTHING FROM THAT? YOU'LL NEVER GET TO KNOW SOMEONE ...
ZFF
...IF YOU DON'T GIVE HIM A CHANCE!
WHIFF
WHIFF
DON'T...
WHIFF
DON'T COMPARE GEN TO THIS JERK!!
WHROOSH

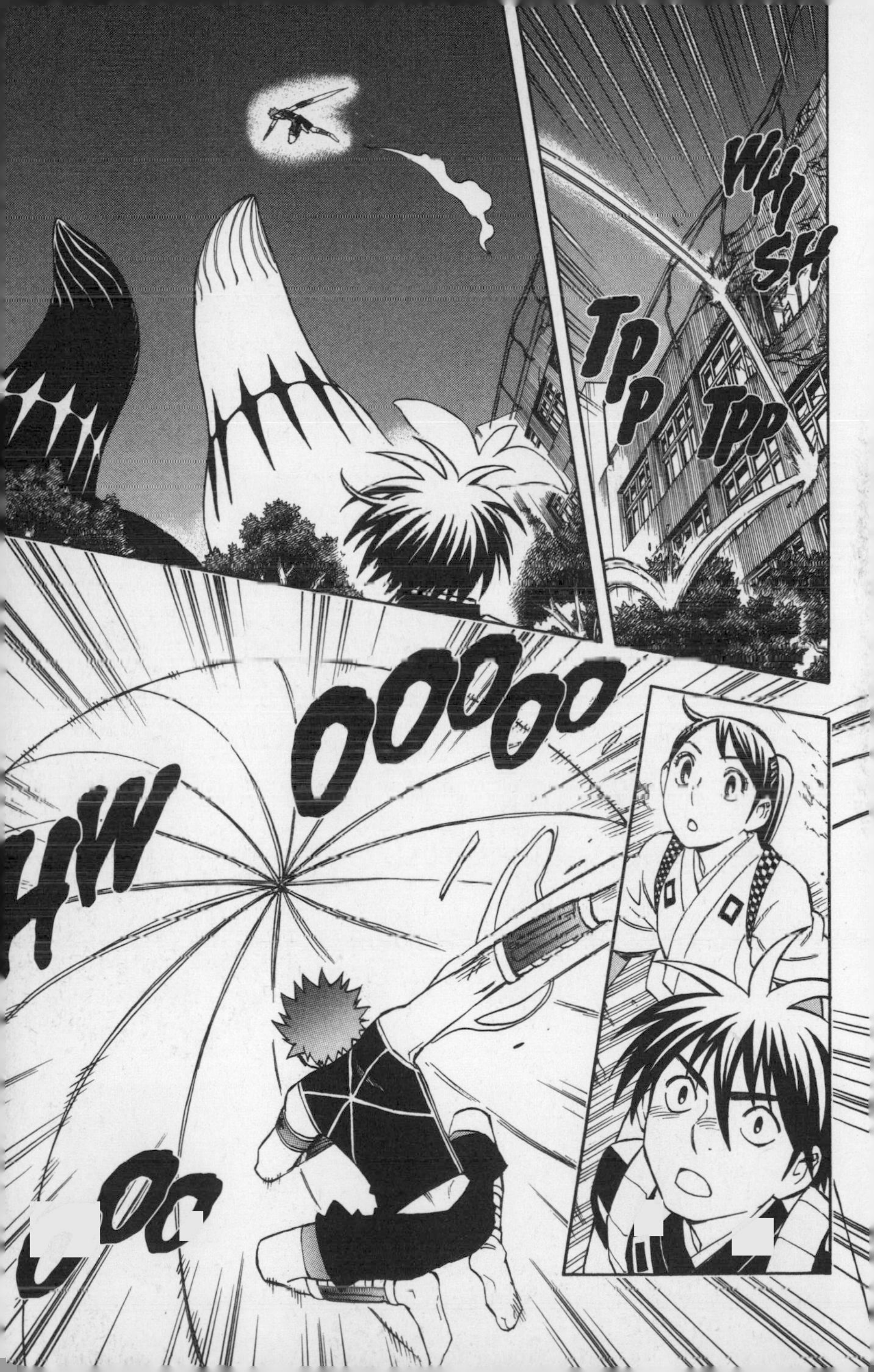
WHISH
TPP
TPP
HW
OOOOOO
OOC

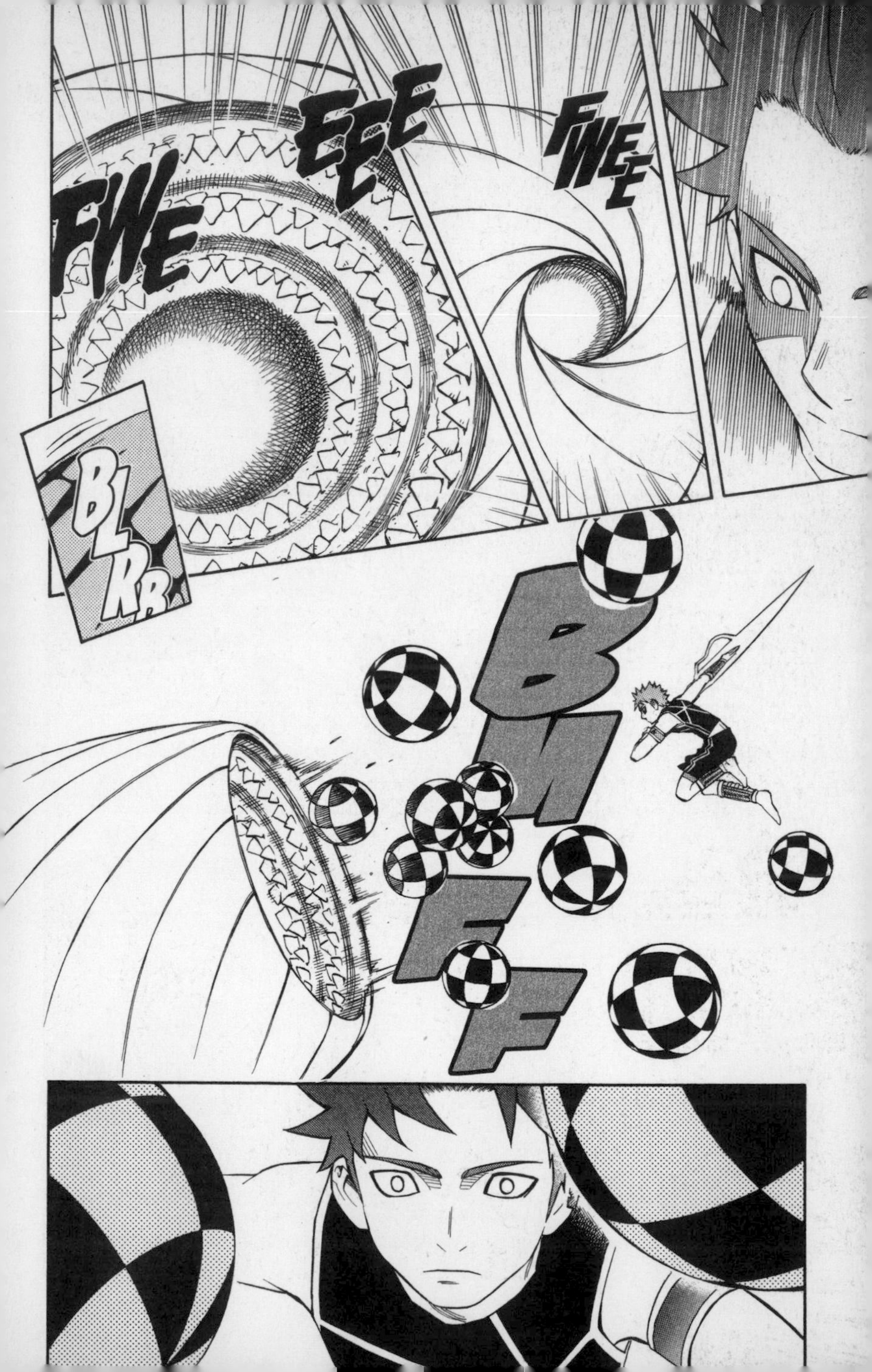
FWEE
FWEEEE
BLRB
BWFF

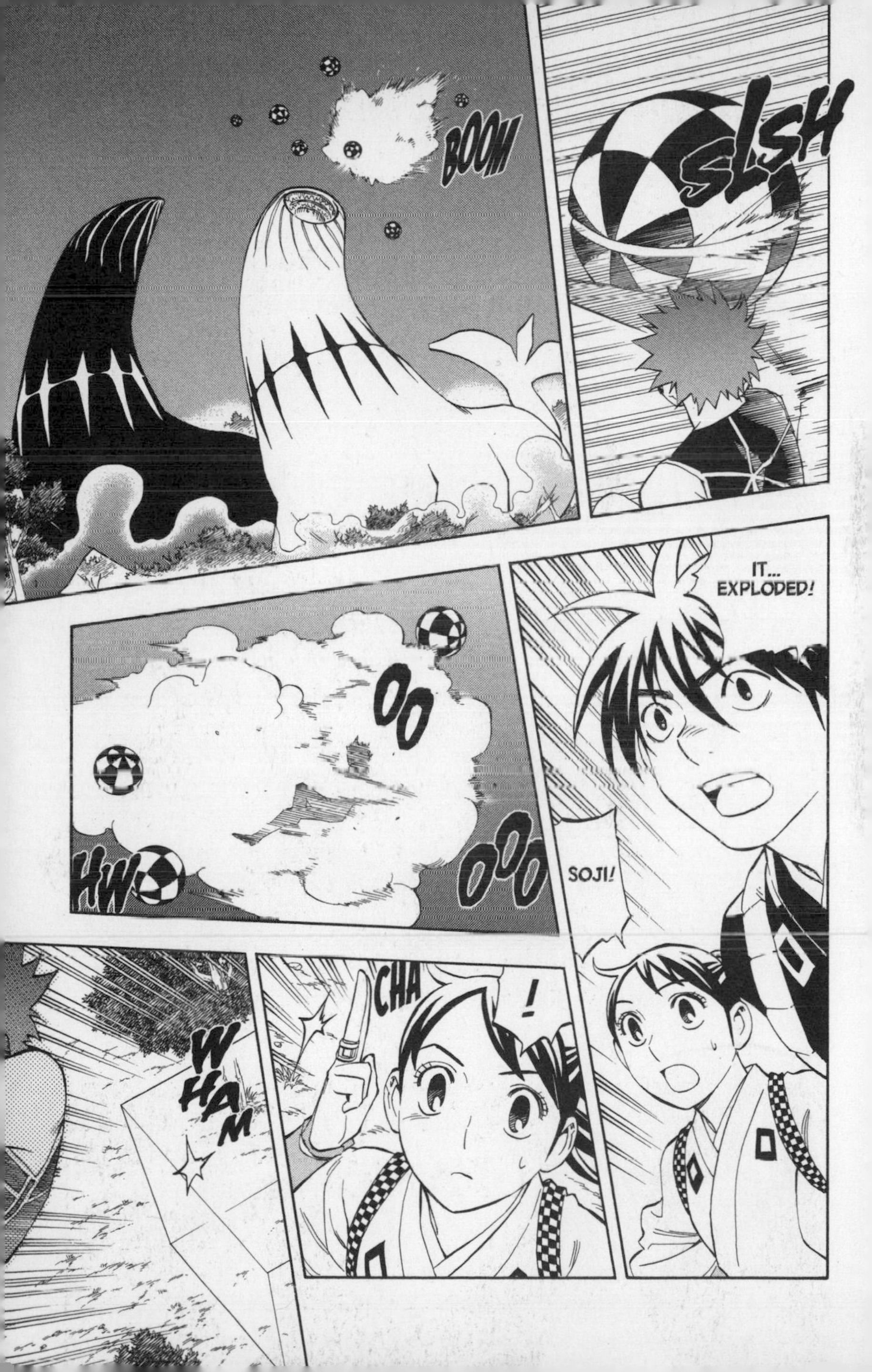
SLSH
BOOM
IT... EXPLODED!
SOJI!
OO
OOO
HW
CHA
!
WHAM

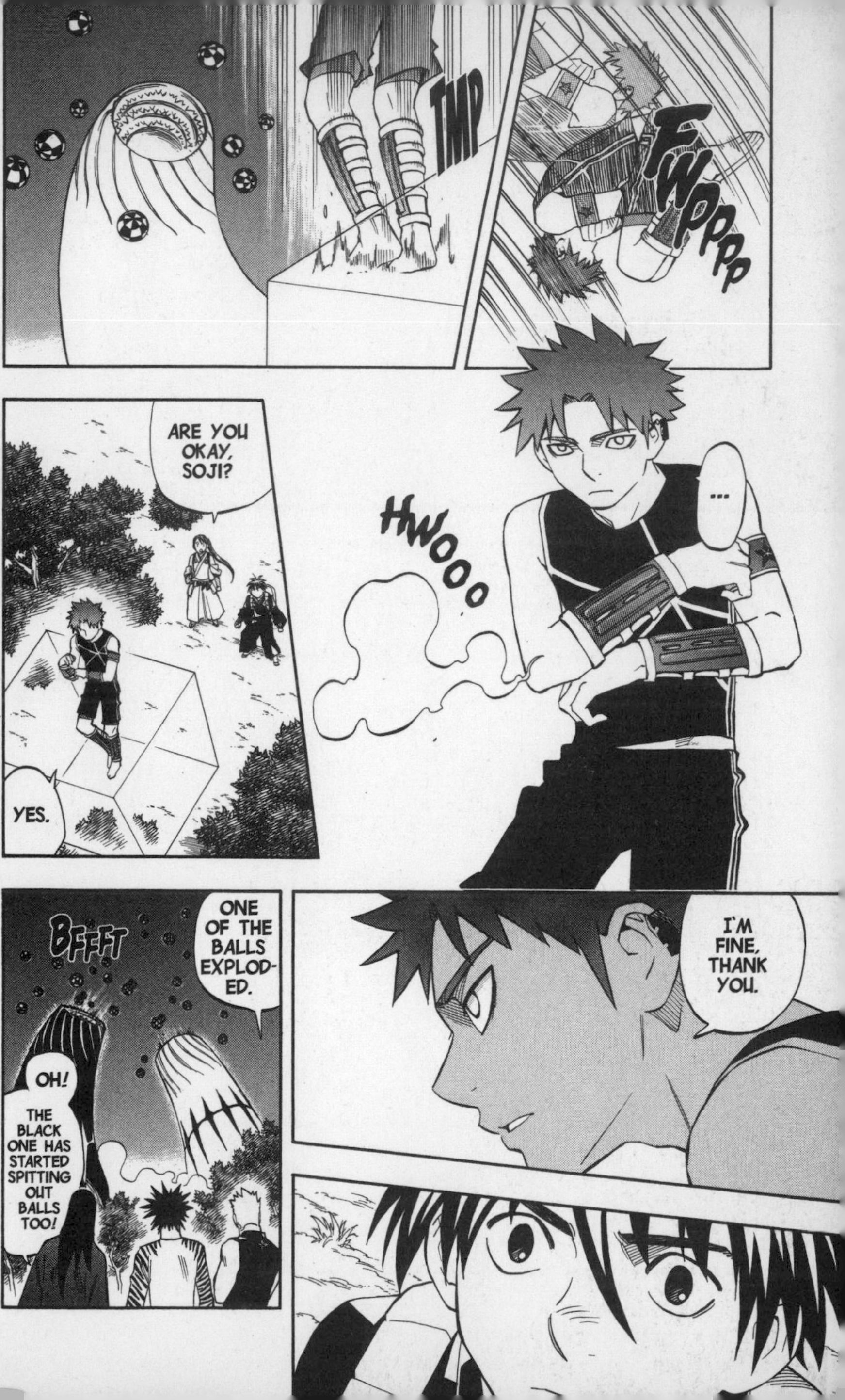
FWPPPP
TMP
...
HWOOO
ARE YOU OKAY, SOJI?
YES.
I'M FINE, THANK YOU.
ONE OF THE BALLS EXPLODED.
BFFFT
OH!
THE BLACK ONE HAS STARTED SPITTING OUT BALLS TOO!

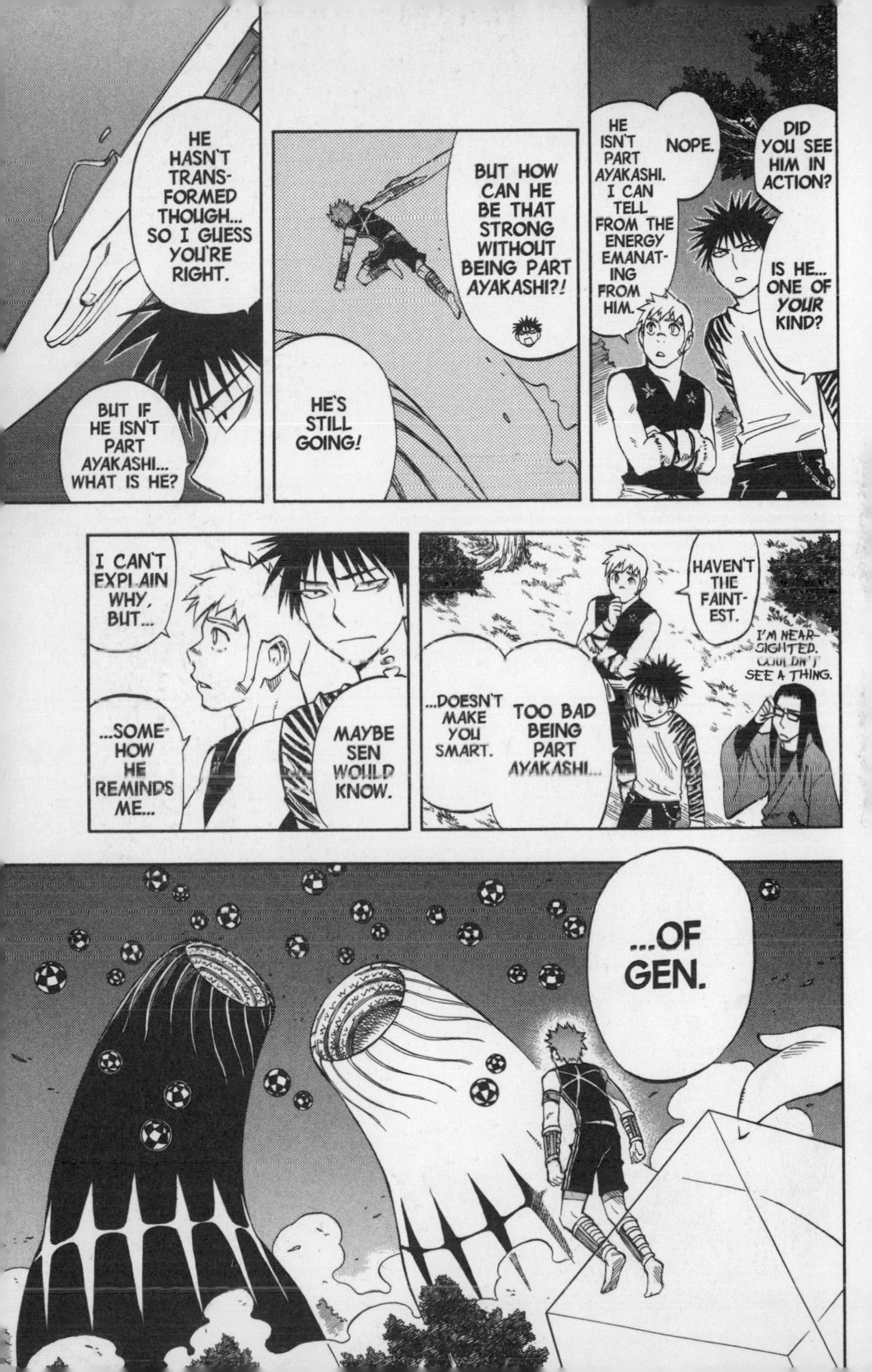
DID YOU SEE HIM IN ACTION?
IS HE... ONE OF YOUR KIND?
NOPE.
HE ISN'T PART AYAKASHI. I CAN TELL FROM THE ENERGY EMANATING FROM HIM.
BUT HOW CAN HE BE THAT STRONG WITHOUT BEING PART AYAKASHI?!
HE'S STILL GOING!
HE HASN'T TRANSFORMED THOUGH... SO I GUESS YOU'RE RIGHT.
BUT IF HE ISN'T PART AYAKASHI... WHAT IS HE?
HAVEN'T THE FAINTEST.
I'M NEAR-SIGHTED. COULDN'T SEE A THING.
TOO BAD BEING PART AYAKASHI...
...DOESN'T MAKE YOU SMART.
MAYBE SEN WOULD KNOW.
I CAN'T EXPLAIN WHY, BUT...
...SOMEHOW HE REMINDS ME...
...OF GEN.

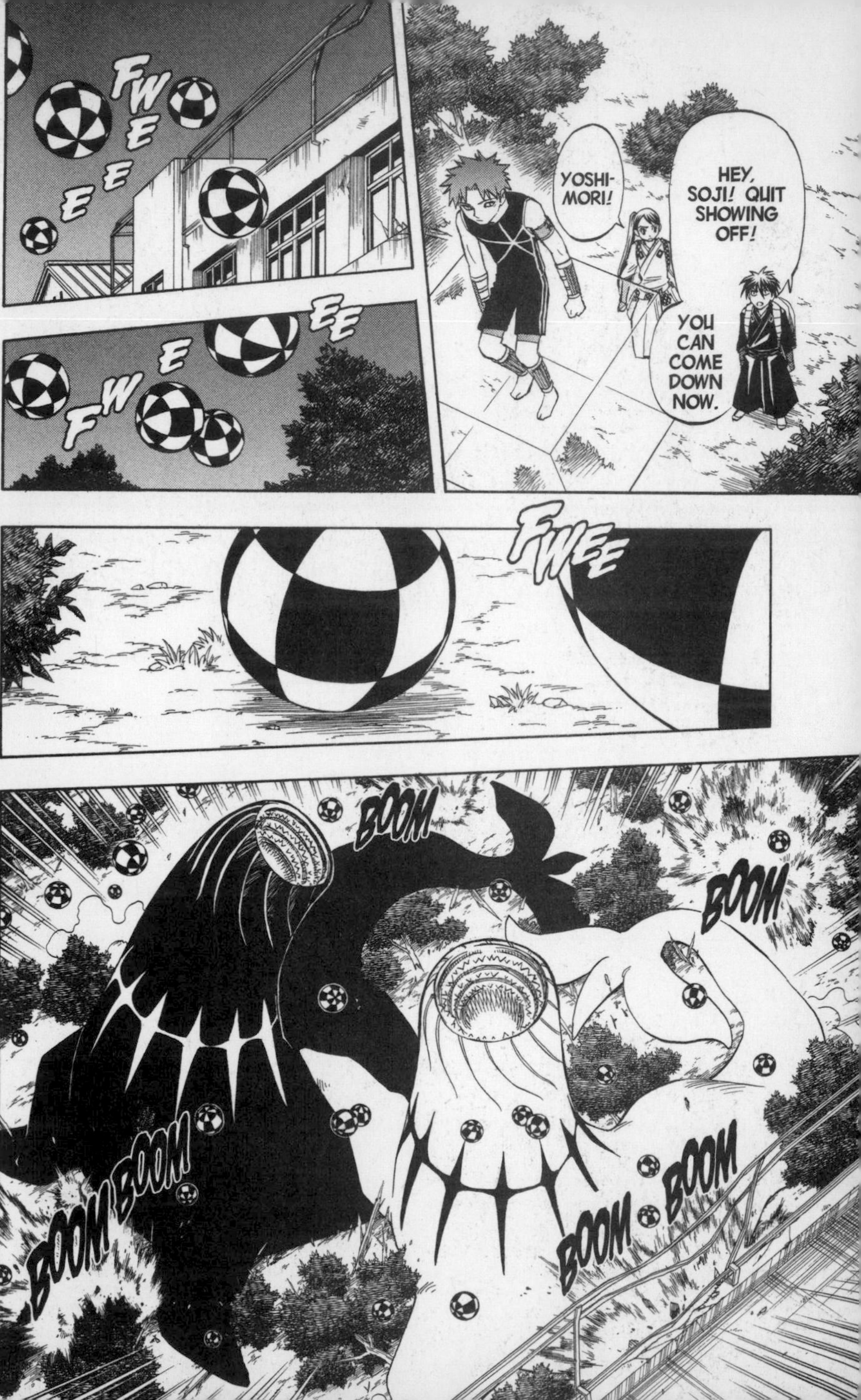
HEY, SOJI! QUIT SHOWING OFF!
YOSHI-MORI!
YOU CAN COME DOWN NOW.
FWEEEE
FWEEE
FWEE
BOOM
BOOM
BOOM BOOM
BOOM BOOM

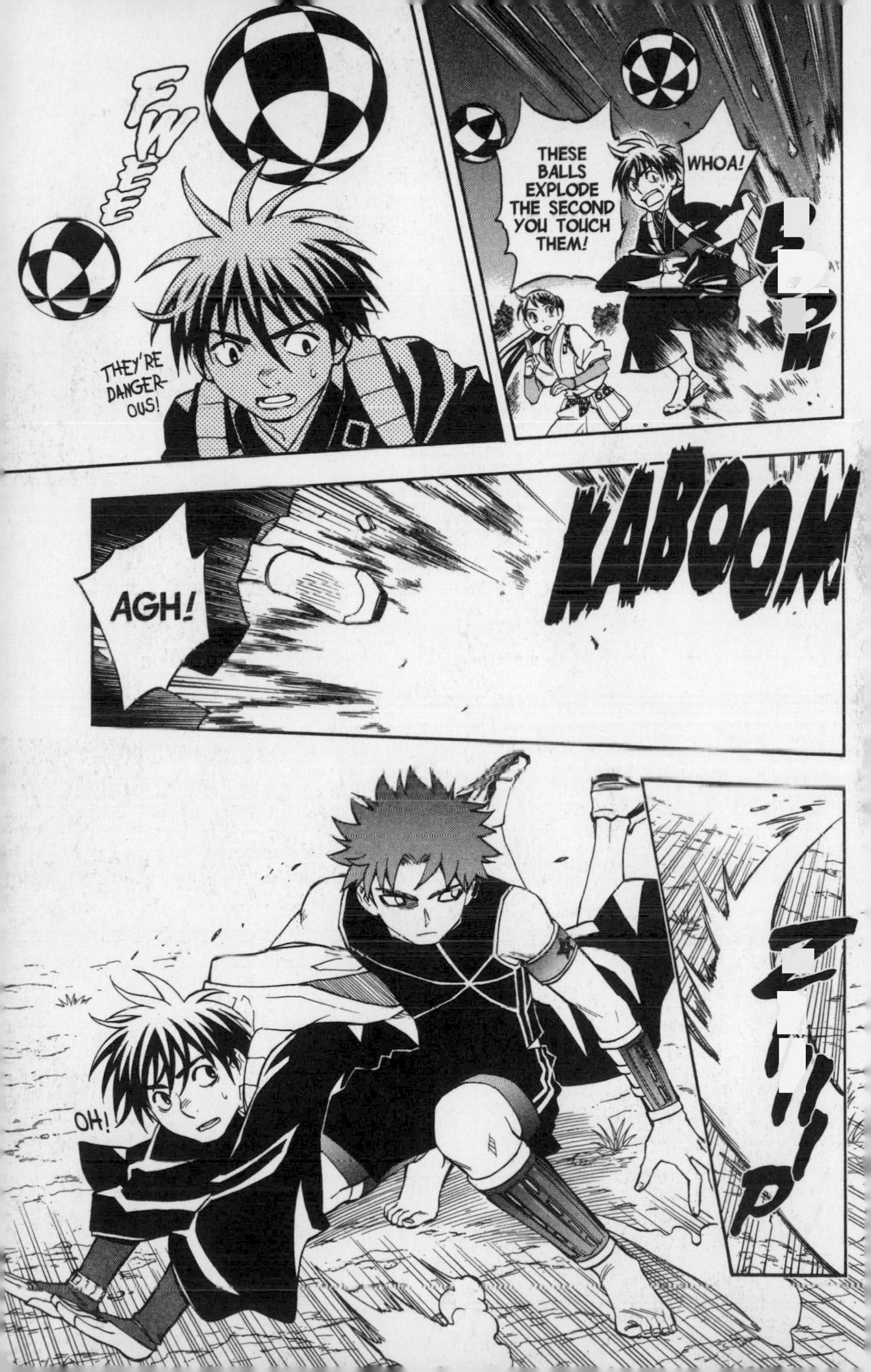
WHOA!
THESE BALLS EXPLODE THE SECOND YOU TOUCH THEM!
FWEEE
THEY'RE DANGER-OUS!
KABOOM
AGH!
OH!

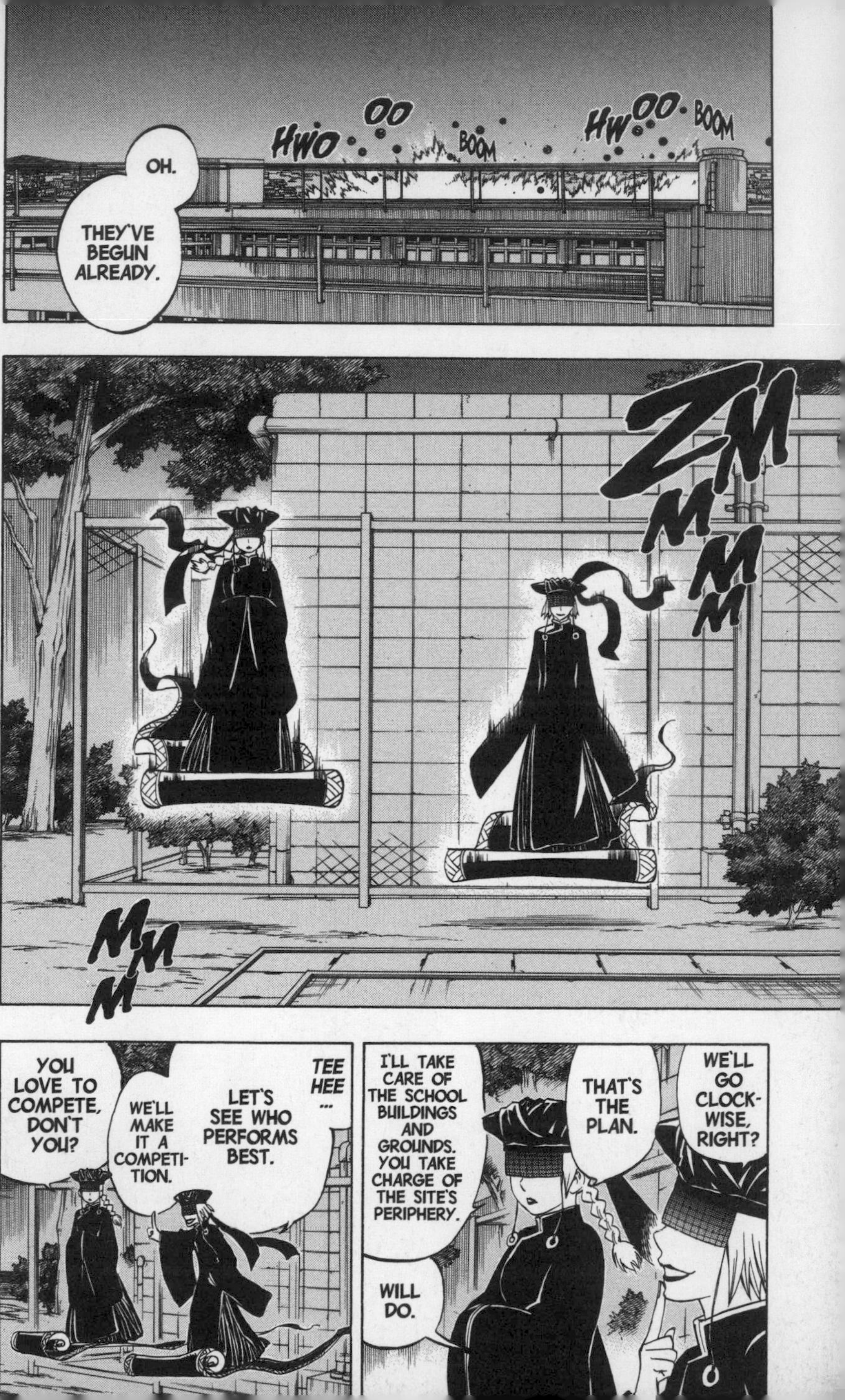
HWOO BOOM
HWOO BOOM
OH.
THEY'VE BEGUN ALREADY.
ZMMMM
MMM
WE'LL GO CLOCKWISE, RIGHT?
THAT'S THE PLAN.
I'LL TAKE CARE OF THE SCHOOL BUILDINGS AND GROUNDS. YOU TAKE CHARGE OF THE SITE'S PERIPHERY.
WILL DO.
TEE HEE ...
LET'S SEE WHO PERFORMS BEST.
WE'LL MAKE IT A COMPETITION.
YOU LOVE TO COMPETE, DON'T YOU?

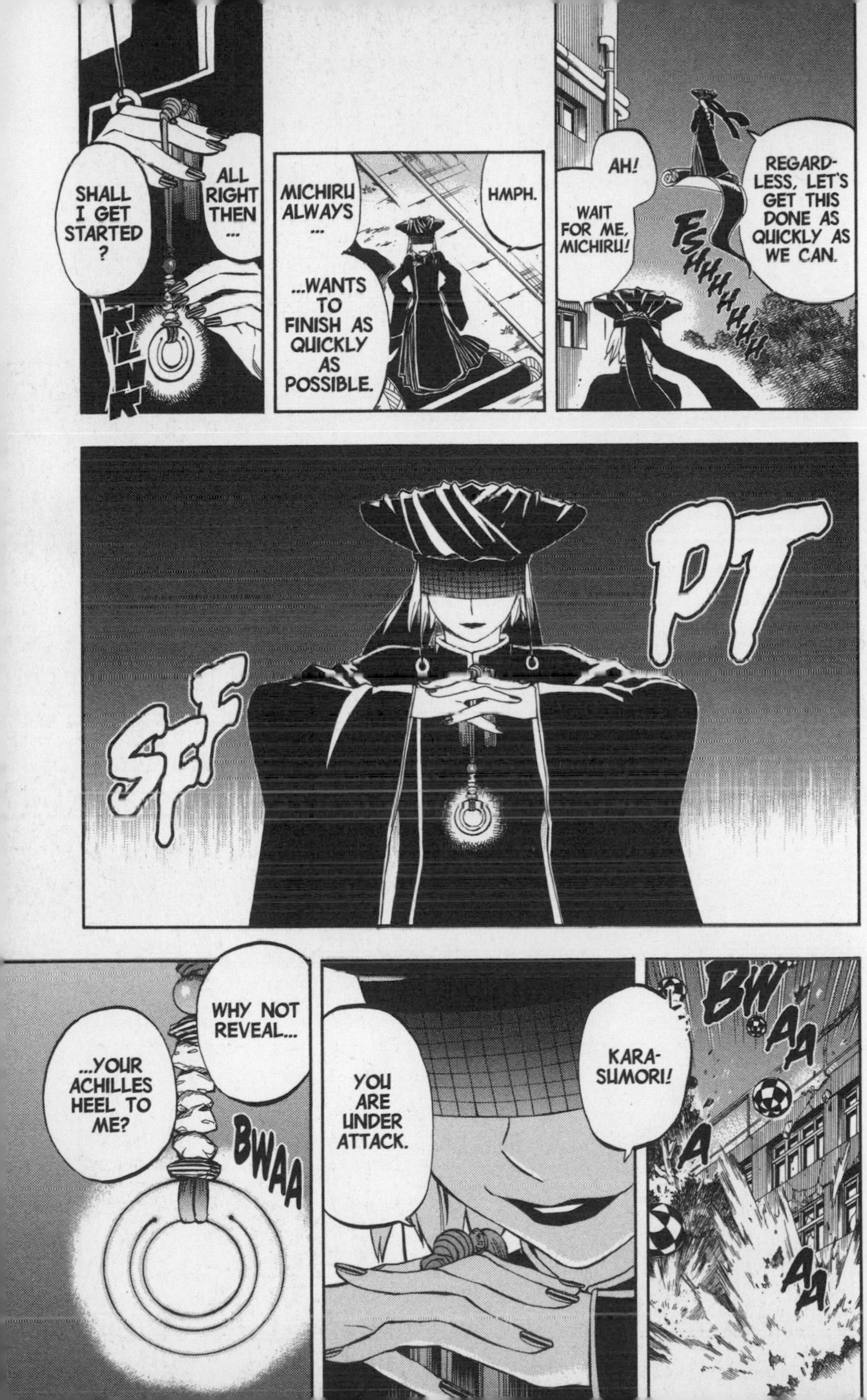
REGARD-LESS, LET'S GET THIS DONE AS QUICKLY AS WE CAN.
AH!
WAIT FOR ME, MICHIRU!
FSHHHHHHH
HMPH.
MICHIRU ALWAYS...
...WANTS TO FINISH AS QUICKLY AS POSSIBLE.
ALL RIGHT THEN...
SHALL I GET STARTED?
KLNK
PT
SFF
BWAAAAA
KARA-SUMORI!
YOU ARE UNDER ATTACK.
WHY NOT REVEAL...
...YOUR ACHILLES HEEL TO ME?
BWAA

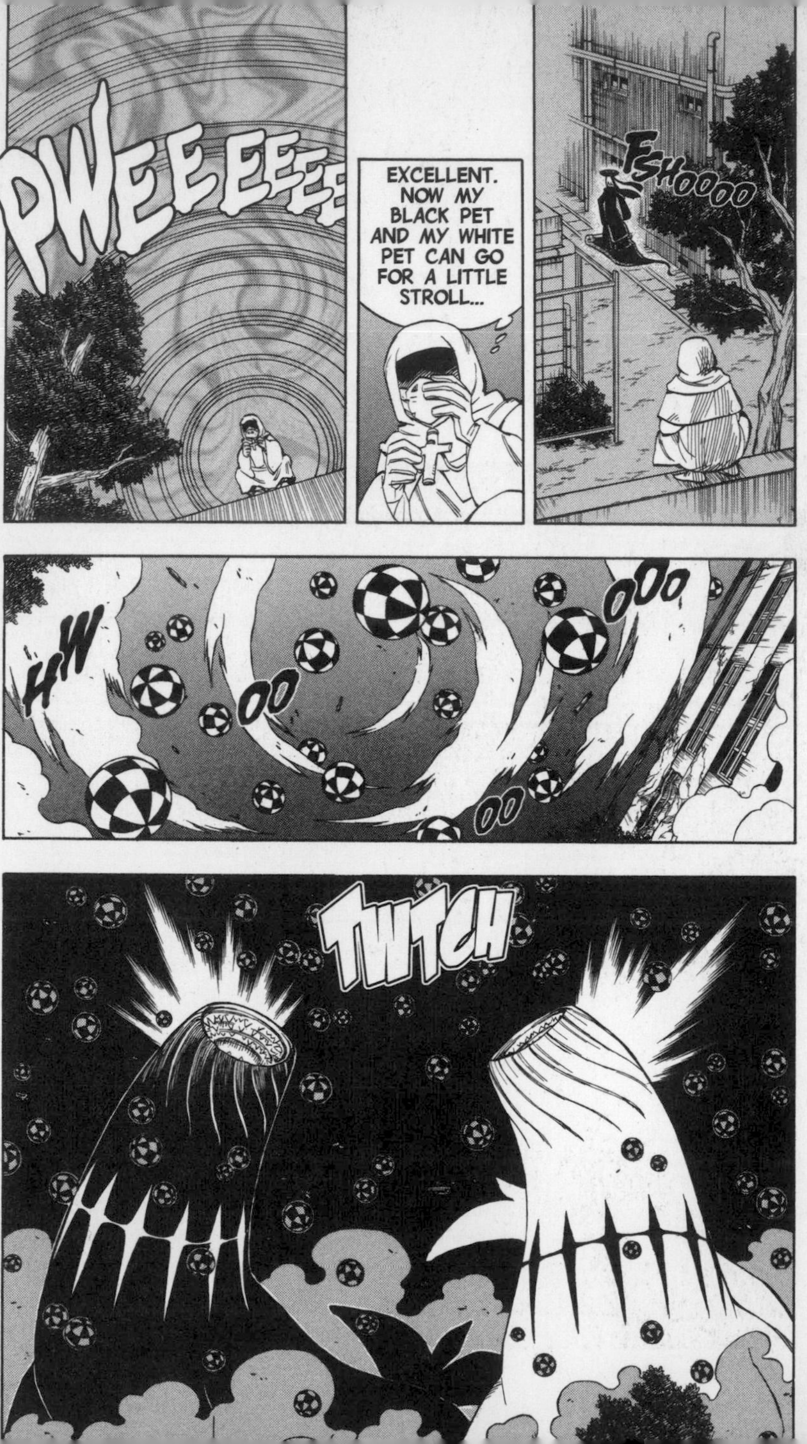
FSHOOOOO
EXCELLENT. NOW MY BLACK PET AND MY WHITE PET CAN GO FOR A LITTLE STROLL...
PWEEEEEE
OOO
HW
OO
OO
TWITCH

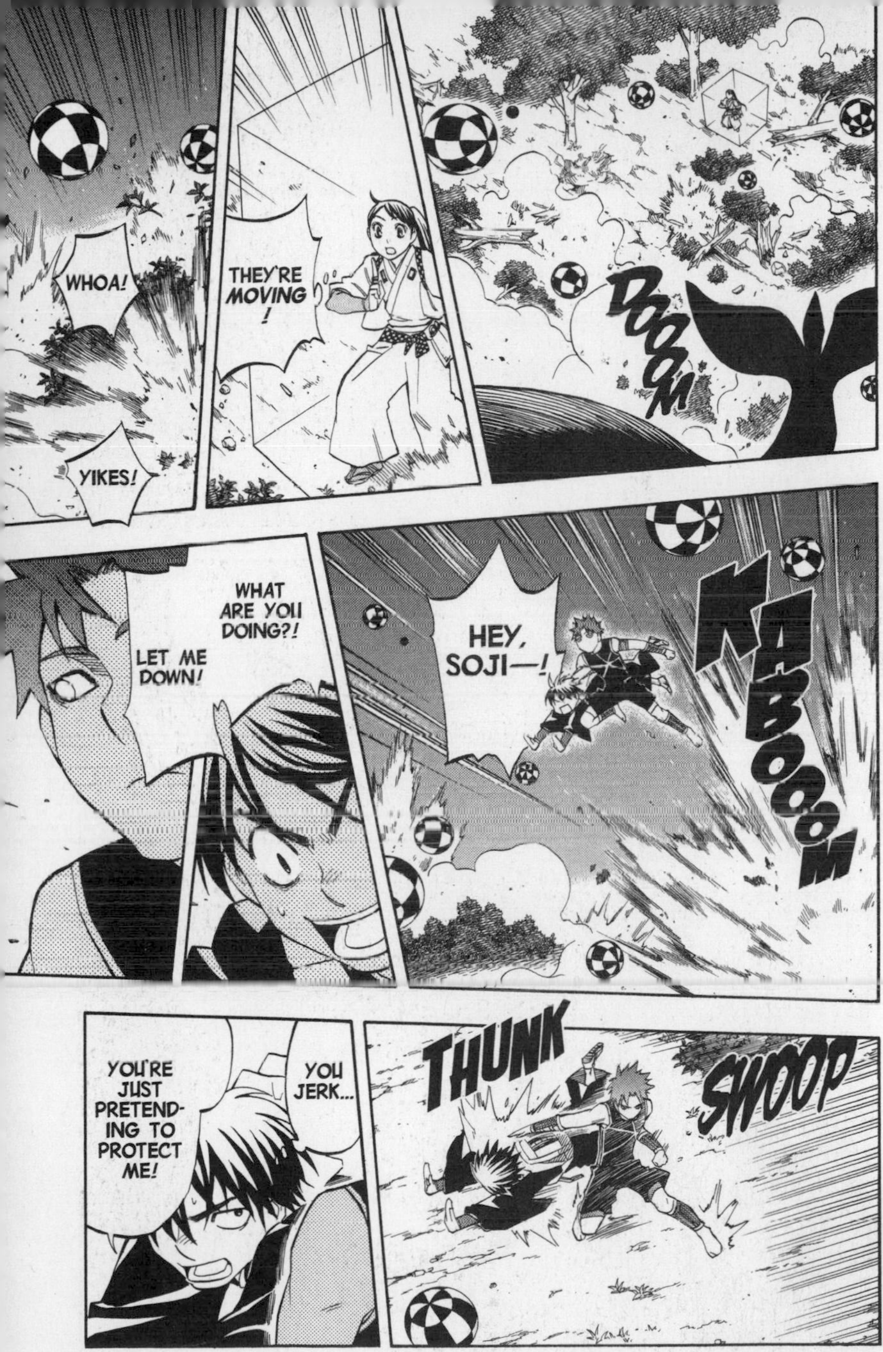
DOOOOM
THEY'RE MOVING!
WHOA!
YIKES!
KABOOOM
HEY, SOJI—!
WHAT ARE YOU DOING?!
LET ME DOWN!
SWOOP
THUNK
YOU JERK...
YOU'RE JUST PRETENDING TO PROTECT ME!

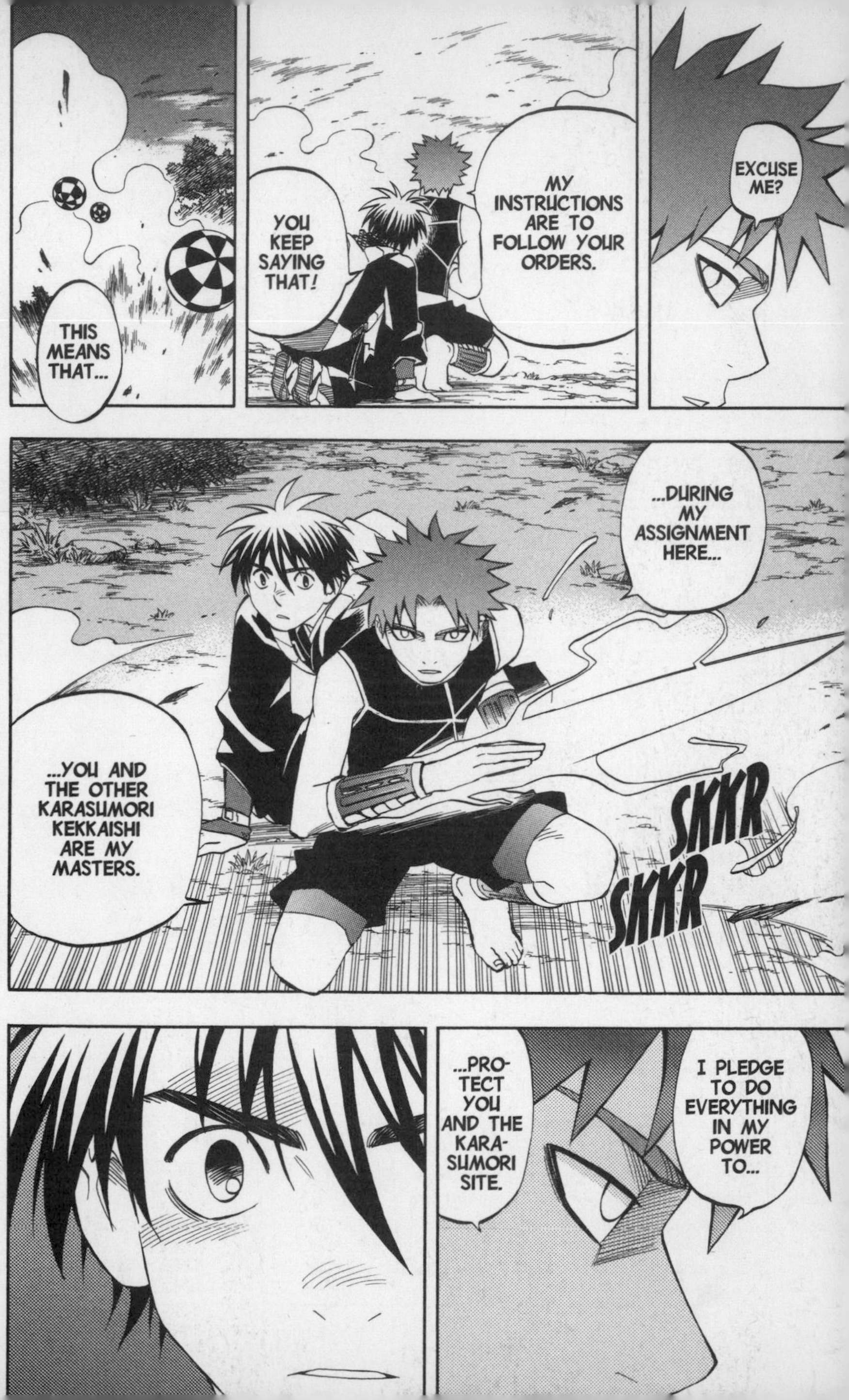
EXCUSE ME?
MY INSTRUCTIONS ARE TO FOLLOW YOUR ORDERS.
YOU KEEP SAYING THAT!
!
THIS MEANS THAT...
...DURING MY ASSIGNMENT HERE...
...YOU AND THE OTHER KARASUMORI KEKKAISHI ARE MY MASTERS.
SKKR SKKR
I PLEDGE TO DO EVERYTHING IN MY POWER TO...
...PRO-TECT YOU AND THE KARA-SUMORI SITE.

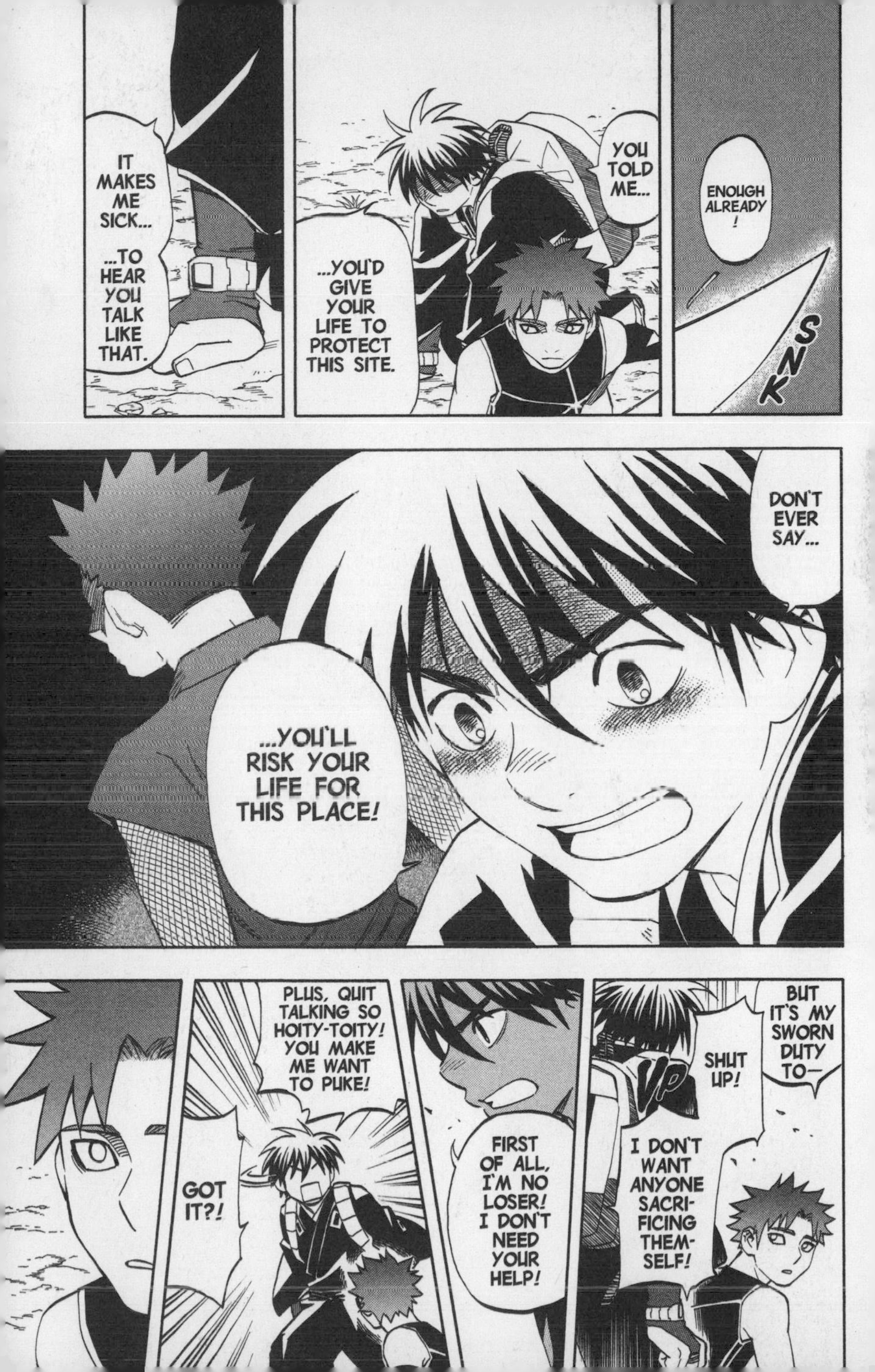
ENOUGH ALREADY!
SNK
YOU TOLD ME...
...YOU'D GIVE YOUR LIFE TO PROTECT THIS SITE.
IT MAKES ME SICK...
...TO HEAR YOU TALK LIKE THAT.
DON'T EVER SAY...
...YOU'LL RISK YOUR LIFE FOR THIS PLACE!
BUT IT'S MY SWORN DUTY TO—
SHUT UP!
VP
I DON'T WANT ANYONE SACRIFICING THEMSELF!
FIRST OF ALL, I'M NO LOSER! I DON'T NEED YOUR HELP!
PLUS, QUIT TALKING SO HOITY-TOITY! YOU MAKE ME WANT TO PUKE!
GOT IT?!

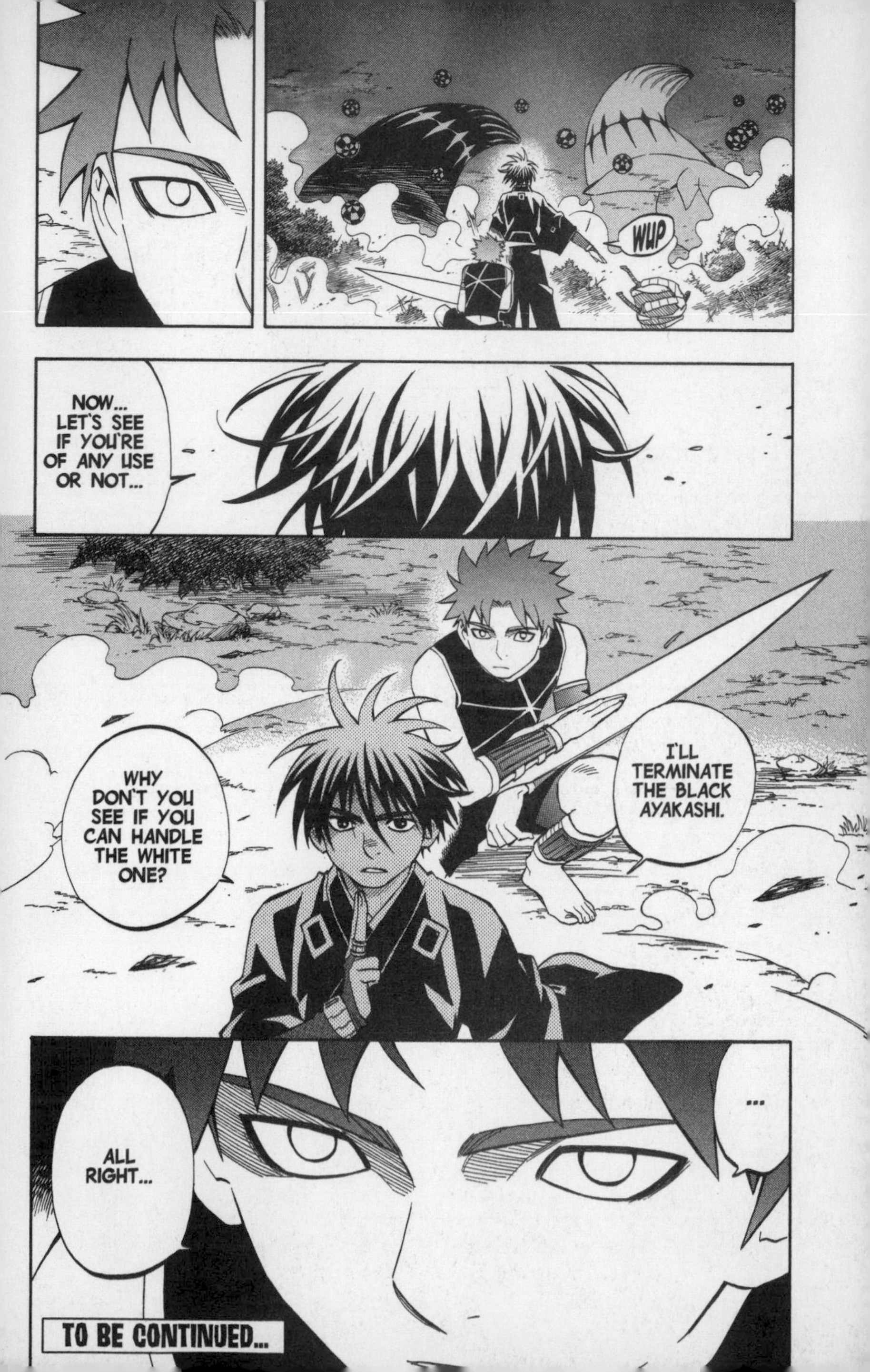
WUP
NOW... LET'S SEE IF YOU'RE OF ANY USE OR NOT...
I'LL TERMINATE THE BLACK AYAKASHI.
WHY DON'T YOU SEE IF YOU CAN HANDLE THE WHITE ONE?
...
ALL RIGHT...
TO BE CONTINUED...

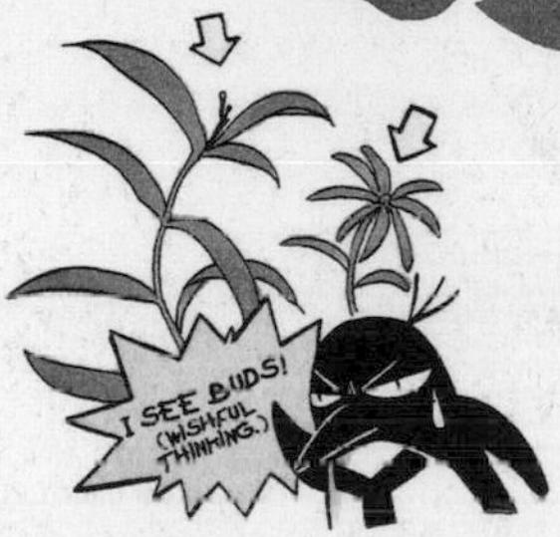
I SEE BUDS!
(WISHFUL THINKING.)

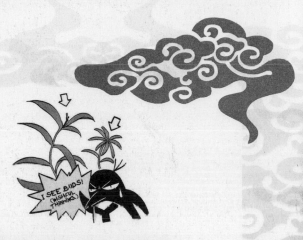

MESSAGE FROM YELLOW TANABE

Update on my gardening kit: Looks like buds have finally appeared! Will they bloom into flowers? Will they?!

Winter is just around the corner, but I'm not going to worry.

KEKKAISHI

VOLUME 23
SHONEN SUNDAY EDITION

STORY AND ART BY YELLOW TANABE

© 2004 Yellow TANABE/Shogakukan
All rights reserved.
Original Japanese edition "KEKKAISHI" published by SHOGAKUKAN Inc.

Translation/Yuko Sawada
Touch-up Art & Lettering/Stephen Dutro
Cover Design & Graphic Layout/Julie Behn
Editor/Annette Roman

Printed in the U.S.A.

Published by VIZ Media, LLC
P.O. Box 77010
San Francisco, CA 94107

10 9 8 7 6 5 4 3 2 1
First printing, October 2010

PARENTAL ADVISORY
KEKKAISHI is rated T for Teen
and is recommended for ages
13 and up. It contains fantasy
violence.
ratings.viz.com

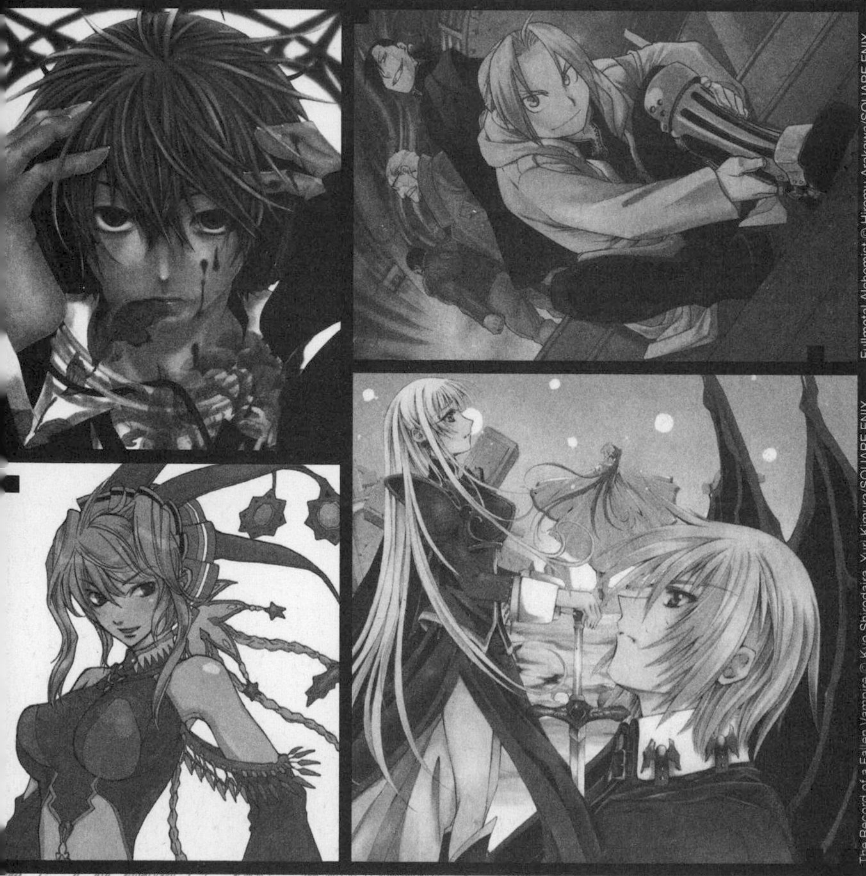